بسم الله الرحمن الرحيم

In the Name of Allāh, the Most Generous, the Most Merciful

Islamic Theology

He is Allāh, there is no Deity other than Him, the Knower of the seen and the unseen. He is the Beneficent, the Most Merciful.

He is Allāh, there is no Deity other than Him, the King (Sovereign), the Holy, the Giver of Peace, the Bestower of Faith, the Overall Controller, the Eminent (Almighty), the Compeller, the Splendid. Allāh is far above anything that they associate with Him.

He is Allāh, the Creator, the Originator, the Fashioner, His are All the Most Beautiful Names. All things that are in the heavens and the earth glorify Him. He is the Eminent, the Wise.

Qur'ān 59:22-24

Islamic Theology

Ayatollah Sayyid Fadhel Hosseini Milani

Recorded and edited by Amar Hegedüs

ISLAM IN ENGLISH PRESS

ISLAM IN ENGLISH PRESS
First published in 2016 by Islam in English Press

A CIP catalogue record for this book can be found in The British Library

ISBN 978-0-9541585-5-2

Islam in English Press
42 Donnington Road, London, NW10 3QU

Printed and bound in Great Britain by CPI Antony Rowe

ISLAM IN ENGLISH PRESS
for accessible guidance to Islamic knowledge

Contents

Acknowledgements

Islam in English Press would like to thank Iskander Khaleeli, a past student of the Islamic College who kindly offered his assistance in the translation of parts of Ayatollah Milani's Arabic lectures delivered over the last quarter of a century at the International Colleges for Islamic Studies.

Editor's Note

The variety of presentations of Islām disseminated in both Muslim and non-Muslim countries has triggered such confusion and dissension that some groups of people, who refer to themselves as Muslims, stridently claim the 'right' to brand those who disagree with their version infidels (*kāfirs*) and then vehemently attempt to extirpate them.

Problems of interpretation and misinterpretation of original texts have caused chaos in what is believed to be Islām or not Islām.

In spite of the fact that Allāh provided guidelines via His final Messenger ﷺ to ensure a safe and sound future for the Muslim nation – 'for as long as there is one individual left on this earth' – deception and chicanery employed by those intent on grasping power and political ascendancy have established discord, division and strife.

While Islāmic theology is the subject of many Arabic and Persian-language works, poor translations have resulted in a dearth of comprehensible information on it in the English language. Furthermore, English-language texts that focus on the result of abstruse academic research are not readily understood by non-specialist readers.

With every statement supported by the Holy Qur'ān and authentic *aḥādīth*, and the variety of opinions within each subject patiently examined and presented without bias, this first comprehensive English-language coverage of Islāmic theology is a long-awaited and much-needed text.

In its publication, Islam in English Press is privileged to have had access to the consummate scholarship of the renowned Muslim theologian and jurist, Ayatollah Sayyid Fadhel Milani.

Amar Hegedüs

Foreword

For an in-depth exploration of Islām, three subjects, Creed, Law and Ethics, need to be carefully considered. While Islāmic Law, the very bedrock of its structure, is manifest in the parameters of what Muslims do and do not do, ethical considerations are based upon the condition (*fiṭrah*) that is innate in all human beings. Creed and faith are matters of personal commitment, with no one being expected to accept or follow anything that they do not find convincing.

Muslim jurists recognize this and recommend that in the field of Islāmic law, those without expertise should consult scholars who are able to deduce rulings from the sources of the Qur'ān, Sunnah, Consensus and Intellectual Reasoning. In contrast, reliance on experts is not considered to be acceptable practice vis-à-vis matters of faith and belief – these are the prerogative of all individuals to decide for themselves.

Monotheism, prophethood and resurrection are the pillars of the creed of Islām. Denial of any of them puts one outside the faith. Details of divine attributes, issues that relate to the final divine message and discussion about life after death and the 'Day of Judgement', are all integral components of subjects that relate to monotheism, prophethood and resurrection. The most crucial aspects are the succession to the Prophet Muḥammad ﷺ and those granted authority to guide the Muslim nation after him. These aspects have preoccupied Muslim scholars throughout the centuries and thousands of books have been written about them.

Three main schools of theology came into being as the result of academic investigations directed by political motivation. While some of these investigations were conducted within peaceful logical debates, others had fatal consequences for those who rejected the opinions put forward by their opponents.

This work presents the textual and rational methodologies employed by Muslim scholars to prove the existence of God. Some of these benefit from a combination of philosophical arguments employed by Greek philosophers and those from within Islāmic scholarship which have come to be known as Islāmic theology or *ʿIlm al-Kalām*.

While all divine religions, the Abrahamic ones in particular, share the three principles of religion outlined above, large differences occur in the detail put forward by scholars of each religion and sect. Concepts such as monotheism as opposed to trinity, free will as opposed to predestination, divine attributes being necessary constituents of divine essence as opposed to existing external to it, the succession to the Prophet Muḥammad ﷺ being a Divine Covenant as opposed to being the result of politically manipulated election – all these in addition to many other subjects are analysed and objectively presented in this work.

I am confident that those interested in researching the true Islāmic creed will find this work a useful tool in their academic endeavours.

We beseech Allāh Almighty to enlighten our hearts and minds and to guide us to the Right Path.

Sayyid Fadhel

فاضل الحسيني الميلاني

Hosseini Milani

Conventions

- صلى الله عليه وآله وسلم *Sallalahu Alayhi wa alihi wa Salaam* – May Allāh's greetings and blessings be upon him and his progeny (used immediately after referring to the Prophet Muḥammad)
- عليها السلام *Alayha al-Salaam* – Peace be upon her (used immediately after referring to Khadījah, Faṭimah, Zaynab and Maryam)
- عليه السلام *Alayhi al-Salaam* – May Allāh bless him (used immediately after referring to a single Imām or Prophet)
- عليهما السلام *Alayhima al-Salaam* – May Allāh bless them (used immediately after referring to two Imāms or two Prophets)
- عليهم السلام *Alayhum al-Salaam* – May Allāh bless them (used immediately after referring to three or more Imāms or Prophets)
- رحمه الله *Rahimahu Allāh* – May Allāh grant him mercy (used immediately after referring to a single deceased and respected person)
- رحمهم الله *Rahimahum Allāh* – May Allāh grant them mercy (used immediately after referring to deceased and respected people)
- قدس سره *Quddisa Sirroh* – May his soul be blessed (used immediately after referring to a single deceased and respected scholar)
- قدس سرهما *Quddisa Sirrohuma* – May their souls be blessed (used immediately after referring to deceased and respected scholars)
- رضي الله عنه *Radi Allahu anhu* – May Allāh be pleased with him (used after referring to a respected companion of the Prophet or the Imāms)

PART ONE

Arguments Regarding the Existence of God

Through the ages philosophers and lay people have sought answers to important questions. Is it possible to know Allāh? If so, how? What methodologies may be used? There are many ways in which people have tried to answer these questions. The following arguments for the existence of God will be discussed:

1. The Ontological Argument
2. The Cosmological Argument
3. The Teleological Argument
4. The methodology of the error-free Imāms عليهم السلام

1 The Ontological Argument

If I were to drop a few globules of oil on a piece of glass, sprinkle flour over it to absorb it, wipe the glass clean with a tissue that I then use to wipe my hands, anyone who shook hands with me would feel an oily hand. If I told them it came from a tissue, they might wonder why the tissue was oily. If I then said that the oil came from flour, most would think I was telling a joke that demanded they ask why the flour was oily. But if I then say that its oiliness came from a piece of glass, they would continue their questioning in anticipation of a 'punch line' being delivered at any moment. However, once they learned that I had deliberately poured oil on to the glass, they would stop asking about the source of the oil on my hands.

Why is this so?

Every rational person distinguishes between those things that have an **inherent** quality and those that **acquire** a quality. In our example glass, flour, tissue and hands acquired oiliness. It is only the oil itself that has the inherent quality of oiliness because this is a characteristic of oil. One cannot imagine oil being otherwise.

So, does everything that exists around us, mountains, seas, valleys, trees, land, fruit, animals, humans etc. each have an inherent quality of existence, or does each acquire qualities from some other source?

The Ontological Argument for the existence of God is not based on observation of the world nor on any form of external evidence; it rests simply on the definition of the word God. It may be summarized thus: 'If you understand what God is, you understand that He must exist.'

The **source of existence** must be the One who does not need anyone for His existence, but is needed by all others for their existence. Although not a being, He is the source of all being, which is the reason behind the Muslim belief that 'the world of being' is the creation of a single Creator.

It is important to distinguish between **logical** necessity and **factual** necessity.

If the statement, 'God exists', is a '*logical* necessity' (i.e. if it is an analytic statement), then the statement, 'God does not exist', is self-contradictory. However, if 'God exists' is a '*factual* necessity', it confirms that it is impossible for things to be as they are if God did not exist, and it follows that it is actually not possible for there to be no God.

The nature of this kind of understanding is so strong within the human psyche that it even existed among polytheists. The Holy Qur'ān records that polytheists, the idol worshippers who lived in Makkah during the time of the Prophet Muḥammad ﷺ, said that they did not believe their idols were creators, but merely a means for drawing near to the one God. They said, 'We do not serve them except in that they may bring us nearer to Allāh.'[1]

So it becomes clear that in its initial stages, the inclination to religion and belief in God draws upon our **instinctive** motives and **innate** perceptions. This later develops and evolves with the help of rational deduction and reflection.

One of those to reflect was Archbishop of Canterbury St Anselm (1033–1109).[2] Indeed, Western philosophers such as St Thomas Aquinas, Descartes, Spinoza, Leibniz and Kant all made major contributions to the literature regarding the Ontological Argument. In the opening chapters of his book *Proslogion*, St Anselm proposed an argument for the existence of God based on **reason**. This is the Ontological Argument that attempts to prove – from an examination of the concept of God – that a being to whom the concept would apply must in fact exist: 'And so, Lord, do thou, who dost give understanding to faith, give me so far as thou knowest it to be profitable, to understand that thou art as we believe; and that thou art that which we believe.'[3]

In *Meditation*, Descartes argues that 'there is not any less repugnance to our conceiving a God (that is to say a being supremely perfect) to whom existence is lacking, than to conceive of a mountain without a valley. Existence is inseparable from Him and hence He really exists.'[4] An elaboration on the above argument may be made as follows:

1. The concept of a supremely perfect being is the concept of a being that has all those properties that no other jointly possesses, for example, wisdom, power, knowledge and perfection.
2. The concept of existence is the concept of such a property.

Thus

3. It is a conceptual truth that a supremely perfect being is one that possesses the property of existence.

By admitting that the world around us is not imaginary, as Plato posited in his cave (see below), we logically conclude that, as existence is an acquired characteristic of what actually does exist, the universe must acquire its existence from existence's inherent quality.

'Imagine that you have lived your whole life imprisoned in a dark cave. Your hands and feet shackled, your head restrained so that you may only look at the wall immediately in front of you. Behind you, a blazing fire casts shadows on to this wall.' In this way, Plato supposed that earthly knowledge is nothing other than a shadow. Such a view indirectly denies us access to reality – that can be seen from this statement to be incorrect.

The monk Gaunilo, who lived at the time of Anselm, challenged him by positing the idea of a perfect island. He claimed that for Anselm's argument to be true, the most perfect island would also have to exist. Anselm's response was that an island is a specific and limited thing, and one can always imagine better and better islands. But **'that than which no greater can be thought'** is unique.

Some disputed St Anselm's proposition, others supported it, and a variety of examples were employed to express the argument differently.

Descartes, for example, maintained that it was impossible to have a triangle without it having three sides and angles. It is a logical necessity for the triangle to have three sides. In the same way, he claimed, it is impossible to have God without recognizing that He must exist.

Anselm's argument is based on the understanding that God is 'that than which no greater can be thought'. This does not refer to something that just happens to be greater than anything else – he did not line up a whole range of things and happen to decide that God is the greatest of them. Rather, the phrase 'that than which no greater can be thought' expresses his idea of 'perfection', 'the absolute', 'the most real thing'.

The Islāmic views that respond to Anselm's concept of greatness lie in *Al-ʿAliyy* and *Al-ʿAẓīm* – two of Allāh's most beautiful attributes:

1. **Al-ʿAliyy**: The Most High

He is the Most High . . . [5]

ʿAla is 'on' or 'upon', *ʿUluw* is 'height', *ʿĀli*, 'high' and *Al-ʿAliyy*, 'The Most High'.

Al-ʿAliyy, being Most High, does not refer to difference in spatial height but rather to a difference of rank. Such rational gradings are perceptions. One is above another in that it is the cause; the other being below, in that it is the result of the former. Thus it is that the cause of all existence holds the highest position in the diversity of grades. All are in more lowly, inferior positions to *Allāh al-ʿAliyy* – the Most High.

Humankind cannot share in this aspect other than in relation to other humans. An individual's physical height, or their being located on the top floor of a skyscraper or on the peak of a mountain, plays no part in their position in life, for this is determined solely by the rank they hold. The rank that is 'most high' for humankind – that none can surpass – is that held by Allāh's final Prophet Muḥammad ﷺ.

Another aspect of being Most High is that of being above and beyond comprehension and imagination. For no matter how hard we may try to be precise in identifying Him, He is still beyond that which we describe. The following *āyah* confirms this:

> 'He is above what they attribute to Him'.[6]

2. ***Al-ʿAẓīm:*** The Tremendous (The Supremely Glorious)

> The most Tremendous in Glory.[7]

ʿAẓamah means 'greatness' or 'mightiness'. *ʿAẓim*, derived from *ʿAẓamah*, means 'the great' or 'the mighty'. *Al-ʿAẓīm*, associated with Allāh, is translated as 'tremendous' in its sense of immensity. In terms of visual perception 'tremendous' has two connotations: the first of capturing attention and filling one's sight, the second of there being no possibility of seeing something in its entirety. Similarly, differences apply to intellectual perceptions. We may comprehend the essential reality of some objects but not of others. While a few intellects may comprehend the essential reality of these latter, most intellects will not. Essential realities of still other objects remain in principle inconceivable for humankind to comprehend. The essence of *al-ʿAẓīm* is tremendous, in precisely the sense that it is beyond the limit of human intellectual comprehension.

Those who are tremendous among humankind are Allāh's Prophets and Imāms عليهم السلام – ordered by Him to bring new laws and to teach people obedience. They are considered in this light because they had to be, and remain, free of error in order to discharge their duties accurately. Whilst they are undoubtedly tremendous in comparison to us, it is *al-ʿAẓīm* alone who is absolutely tremendous.

Interestingly, Descartes, whose language is very precise, also had a view of perfection. In its modern usage, the word perfection tends to imply something such as 'the best ever' or 'the best possible'. This is partially misleading as the Latin root of the word *perfectum* means complete. When we refer to something as being perfect in the proper sense of the word, we mean that it is complete in the sense that it is fully and truly itself. From this, two things follow:

a. Perfection is synonymous with reality, in so far as the perfection of a being is its completion, so that it becomes wholly and really itself.

b. In its pure sense, the term perfection is properly applicable to God alone (for all creatures are relatively imperfect and unreal).

1 Necessity and Possibility

All propositions, be they simple or complex, incorporate two fundamentals: a subject and a predicate. For example, in the axiomatic statement, 'The sun shines', the concept established for the sun is shining – with the 'sun' being the subject and 'is shining' being the predicate. A predicate for a subject can have no more than three states: it could be impossible, as in 'the number three is greater than the number four'; or it could be necessary, as in 'the number two is half of four', or it could be neither impossible nor necessary, for instance, 'the sun is above our heads'.

In the terminology of logic, the first proposition has the state of impossibility (*imtināʿ*), the second proposition is given the attribute of necessity (*wujūb*), and the third state is considered as being possible (*imkān*).

In our analysis of existence, things that are not capable of being or occurring can never exist in the external world (*al-wujūd al-khāriji*). For this reason, existence is logically perceived to be either necessary or possible.

Necessary Existence is exemplified by an existent that exists in itself and is not dependent upon any other existent. It follows that such existence can have no beginning and no end, because the non-existence of something at a particular time indicates that its existence is not from itself. This is because, in order to come into existence, it would need another existent to be the cause or condition for its realization. The absence of such condition or cause would be the reason for its annihilation.

A possible existent (*mumkin al-wujūd*) is known as an existent that does not exist in itself, but depends upon another existent for its realization.

Divisions structured through intellectual perception essentially disregard impossible existence and do not indicate if a particular existent is a possible or necessary existent. The principles of this point of view may be conceptualized in three essential forms:

1. Every existent is a necessary existent.
2. Every existent is a possible existent.
3. Some existents are necessary existents and some are possible existents.

On the basis of the first and third assumptions, the existence of a necessary existent is established and, therefore, the assumption that should be reviewed is whether or not all existents are possible existents.

However, in disproving the assumption 'that every existent is a possible existent', existence of the Necessary Existent is definitely and conclusively proven, leaving the establishment of unity and other attributes to be proven via other arguments.

In order to disprove the second assumption additional arguments need to be utilized – one of which is that it is impossible for all existents to be possible existents.

As this argument is not self-evident, it is explained as follows: Every possible existent needs a cause – but as it is not possible for there to be an endless chain of causes, the chain must terminate at an existent that is not in need of a cause, i.e. the Necessary Existent.

Impossibility of infinite regression

Infinite 'regress' (*tasalsul*) is logically impossible, and its impossibility is self-evident. That is to say, considering that the existence of an effect requires a cause, and is conditional upon that cause, if we assume this state of being caused (*maʿlūliyyah*) and this conditionality is universal, then no existents would be realized anywhere. The assumption that the total of all existents are dependent, without an existent upon which they depend, is not logical.

Let us assume that a group of runners are waiting to begin a race. They have all decided that they will not start running until the others have started. Should this decision prevail, then none of them would start to run.

In the same manner, if the existence of every existent were to be conditional upon the realization of another existent, then no existent would come into being. The occurrence of external existents indicates that there has to be an existent that is needless and unconditional.

2 Ibn Sīnā's Demonstration of the Necessary Existent

This demonstration is formulated upon three premises:

a. The existents of this cosmos are contingent, and the existence of a contingent existent lacks necessity to exist. For, if one of them were the Necessary Existent, the argument would end.

b. To become existent every contingent existence requires a cause to bring it about. This premise is another way of stating that every effect is in need of an efficient cause. It is illogical to claim that chance or accident has brought into being the whole universe and everything in it as they now appear.

c. It is impossible for there to be a circle, or regress of causes.

Given these premises, the demonstration may be formulated as follows. Every existent in this world, that is assumed to be a contingent existent, needs an efficient cause. It is impossible for the chain of causes to proceed infinitely, or for there to be a circular relation among them. Hence, the chain of causes unavoidably leads to an ultimate cause at its beginning that is itself without need of a cause, and is thus the Necessary Existent.

This demonstration formulated by Ibn Sīnā (980–1037)[8] was presented in his *Ishārāt*: 'An existent is either the Necessary Existent or a contingent existent. If it is the Necessary Existent the point is proven – and if it is a contingent existent, it must ultimately lead to the Necessary Existent in order to avoid a circle or regression'.[9]

The significance of this version is that it does not require recourse to the attributes of creatures, or a demonstration that they have temporal origin, motion or other attributes.

Thus: this demonstration turns upon nothing other than the acceptance of 'entified existence' that is self-evident and undeniable. Only those who deny the most self-evident and most intuitive things – including presentational knowledge of themselves – never accept the existence of anything, even their own existence, thoughts, words and principles!

3 Mulla Ṣadrā's Demonstration of the Necessary Existent

This demonstration was formulated by Mulla Ṣadrā Shirāzi (1571–1640)[10] on the basis of the transcendent theosophy that he himself propounded. He considered it to be the firmest demonstration and the one most deserving of the name 'Demonstration of the Sincere'. It has been formulated in a number of different versions, the strongest one being based upon the following premises:

a. The principle of the realization of anything is [existence] while quiddity [the inherent nature or essence of a person or thing] is merely posited. In other words, existence is real while quiddity is a subjective point of view.

b. There are several levels of existence due to graduations between cause and effect, i.e. the existence of the effect is not independent of the existence of its existence-granting cause.

c. The criterion for 'the need of the effect of the cause' – being relative and dependent for its existence on the cause; in other words, the weakness of a level of existence is necessarily an effect of its need of a higher existent from which it has no independence.

Given these premises, the Demonstration of the Sincere can be formulated in accordance with Mulla Ṣadrā in the following manner:

> The levels of existence – other than for its highest level that possesses infinite perfection, absolute needlessness and independence – relate to dependence. If the highest level did not exist, neither would the other levels. This is because it is implied in the assumption of the occurrence of other levels – without the occurrence of the highest level of existence – that the mentioned levels would be independent and without need of it. However, their existential aspect is the relation itself with its concomitant poverty and need.

This demonstration excels that of Ibn Sīnā in the following aspects: Firstly, Mulla Ṣadrā's demonstration focuses upon the concept of existence, and neither 'quiddity' nor 'characteristic contingencies' is mentioned. It is clear that such a demonstration is more suitable to the doctrine of 'existence being fundamentally real'.

Secondly, it does not require a falsification of the circle or infinite regress, but is itself a demonstration of the incorrectness of the assumption of an infinite regress of efficient causes.

Thirdly, with the help of this demonstration, not only Unity but also other attributes of Allāh Almighty's perfection will be established.

4 Allamah Ḥilli's Presentation

Allamah Ḥilli (648–726 AH) was the auther of many books on Imāmi theological doctrine, the first in 680 AH being *Manāhij al-Yaqīn fi Uṣūl al-Din*. In 684 AH he wrote a commentary on Nawbakhti's book *al-Yāqūt* that he titled *Anwār al-Malakūt fi Sharḥ al-Yāqūt*.

In 699 AH, in response to a request from his son, he wrote *Nahj al-Mustarshidīn*.

Minhāj al-Karāmah fi al-Imāmah followed his lengthy and detailed debates with ibn Taymiyah and later, in refutation of the Muʿtazilite doctrine regarding free will, *Istiqṣā' al-Naẓar fi al-Qaḍā' wal Qadar*.

Of all of his theological works, the two still used as textbooks in contemporary Shiʿah seminaries (*Ḥawzāt*), are *Al-Babul Ḥadi ʿAshar* (written in 723 AH) with a commentary by Al-Fāḍil al-Miqdād[11] and *Kashf al-Murād fi Sharḥ Tajrīd al-Iʿtiqād* (written in 694 AH).[12]

For further reading on Allamah Ḥilli's theological works, refer to *The Theology of Allamah Ḥilli* by Sabine Schmidtke.

To quote Allamah Ḥilli regarding the existence of God from *Al-Babul Ḥadi ʿAshar*:

> There is no doubt that in the universe there is that which exists of necessity. If this be the necessary in itself, then that was what we are seeking. And if it be the possible, then it would need a bringer-into-existence [*Mūjid*] which would bring it into existence of necessity. Now, if the bringer-into-existence be the necessary in itself, then that was what we are seeking. And, if it be the possible then it would need another bringer-into-existence. If it be the first, then it is a circle, and that is a fallacy of necessity. And if it be another possible, then it is an endless chain, and that also is a fallacy. For all the links in the chain which includes all possible existents [*al-Mumkinā*] are possible of necessity. Hence, they share in the impossibility of existence in themselves. Hence they need some bringer-into-existence necessarily outside of themselves. And that is the Necessary Existent [*Al-Wājib*].[13]

Although the Ontological Argument had already faced and answered the criticism, 'you can either have a triangle or not, but you simply cannot have no God, clarifying that the two situations are not exactly parallel', numerous people continued to challenge it. Kant presented one of the clearest criticisms of the Ontological Argument in his *Critique of Pure Reason*. In response to the version set out by Descartes, Kant's arguments may be summarized thus:

- If you have a triangle
- It must have three angles

- But if you do not have a triangle, you do not either have its three angles or sides.
- It is not factually necessary for there to be a triangle

Kant utilized the Ontological Argument to say that if you accept there is a God, it is logical to accept also that His existence is necessary. However, you do not have to accept that there is a God.[14]

The Islamic response to this sort of argument is that, as this automatically concludes that one does not have to accept there is a God, it cannot serve the purpose of proving that there is one, and is thus irrelevant to that argument.

Arguments in both opposition and defence circulate around the concept of 'greatness', i.e. relative greatness of numbers as opposed to absolute greatness. The first one implies that no matter how great a thing you find may be, there will always be one that is greater. If God's greatness were such, Anselm's argument would be invalid. However, Alvin Plantinga defends Anselm and argues that the greatness of God is a different kind of attribute, one that is non-quantifiable.

2 The Cosmological Argument

The first argument for the existence of God, the Ontological, dealt only with the concept of existence, the idea of God being the Necessary Existent – the source of all existents. We then investigated and discussed its source and implications. Cosmology, on the other hand, deals with the universe as it is, characterized by order and harmony and including great complexity of detail. Thus the Cosmological Argument for the existence of God is based on observations of the world.

The Cosmological Argument that appeared in Plato and Aristotle played a prominent role in Jewish, Christian and Islamic thought. During the medieval and in more modern times, such arguments were presented by Thomas Aquinas, Leibniz and Clarke, yet are also severely criticized by David Hume and Immanuel Kant. Notwithstanding this, the Cosmological Argument is based upon the following:

- Whatever begins to exist has a cause.
- The universe began to exist.
- Therefore, there is a cause behind the existence of the universe.

If there is a unity of all being and we call this unity the Universe, it follows that we must assume the universe itself depends on something for its existence. What it depends on cannot, in turn, depend on something else for its own existence (for it would then be a part of the universe).

In addition to the philosophical argument against the possibility of the world always having existed, we refer to scientific theories that indicate that the world indeed had a beginning. With the development of modern science and technology, scientists have been able to offer new theories for the age of the earth – based upon the radioactive decay of substances such as radium and uranium – and they have stated that:

a. the earth is approximately 4.6 billion years old,

b. the genus *Homo* about 2.8 million years old,

c. *Homo sapiens* nearly 200,000 years ago,

d. the universe was the result of a Big Bang that occurred about 13.75 billion years ago.

Common to all such calculations is that the universe had a beginning and is not eternal. Therefore, it has clearly been originated.

One of the major European figures to discuss the Cosmological Argument was Thomas Aquinas (1224–1274 CE), who set out the Argument in his famous 'Five Ways'. These are five versions of the same argument and are a mixture of his own effort, his study of Aristotle, and most probably, the studies of the Muslim scholars of *Kalām* who preceded him: al-Kindi (801–873 CE), Ibn Sīnā (980–1037 CE) and al-Ghazāli (1058–1111 CE). The five ways in which Aquinas believed the existence of God could be shown are:

1. the argument from an unmoved mover

2. the argument from an uncaused cause

3. the argument from possibility and necessity

4. the argument from degrees of quality

5. the argument from design

In the discussion below we examine the argument from an uncaused cause, from an unmoved mover, and that from design. 'Possibility and necessity', that constitute the elements of the Ontological Argument, have already been discussed. 'Degrees of quality' are aspects of the gradation of existence that are covered in Mulla Ṣadrā's demonstration (see chapter 1). Thus we will here only examine the remaining three.

1 The Argument from an Unmoved Mover

The structure of the argument that Aristotle presented is as follows:

- Everything that moves or changes is moved or changed by something.
- The mover or changer is in turn moved or changed by something else.
- But such a chain of movers or changers cannot infinitely regress – 'the buck' has to stop somewhere.
- Therefore, to cause movement or change in everything, there has to be an unmoved mover or an unchanged changer, that is not itself subject to movement or change.
- This unmoved mover or unchanged changer is what people understand to be 'God'.[15]

Muslim theologians present the above argument in the following manner:

- All motion requires a mover.
- The action of the mover and its effect occur simultaneously, despite the former preceding the latter in ontological sequence.
- Every mover is either in motion or is stationary.
- Every physical being is subject to motion and change.
- An infinite regress of causes and effects is impossible.

In conclusion, the chain of movers and moving objects must start with the 'unmoved mover'.

This can be rephrased as: 'Everything was non-existent and then existed'. 'All things were non-existent before they existed'. This is change. Change is motion and motion requires a mover. As for a mover, it is either itself subject to change or it is not. If it is subject to change it depends on yet another mover, and so on, resulting in either circular or infinite regress (both being logically impossible), or it depends on a mover that is not itself subject to either change or motion, whose existence was not preceded by non-existence but which exists in itself. This is the 'Necessary Being'.

The only possible point of contention is that this argument posits a 'prime mover', not necessarily the Almighty Creator who in Qur'ānic terminology is The Originator (*Al-Bārī*). In other words, whilst the Ontological Argument sets out to support the 'Necessary Existent', it also proves divine attributes as evidence of perfect and absolute existence. However, the argument from the 'unmoved mover' makes no contribution to this concept.

2 The Argument from an Uncaused Cause

The structure of this argument is:

- Everything has a cause.
- Every cause itself has a cause.
- But you cannot have an infinite number of causes (as discussed earlier).
- Therefore, there must be an uncaused cause that causes everything to happen – without itself being caused by anything.
- Such an uncaused cause is what people understand to be God.

This method was clearly explained by Ibn Sīnā in his book *Kitab al-Shifā* (The Book of Healing), the most extensive philosophical encyclopaedia ever to have been written by a single person.[16]

In Aristotelian philosophy, the 'uncaused cause' is called the 'first cause'. This posits that the entire universe was created by a chain of causes, and that these causes do not stand by their own existence but rely upon a cause that is self-sustained without itself ever having needed to be caused.

In Islamic understanding, this concept is summarized in one of the most beautiful names of Allāh – *Al-Qayyūm* – The Self-Subsisting or Eternal Being. *Āyat al-Kursi* [17] mentions all that we can ever know about Allāh:

> Allah! There is no god but He, the Ever-Living, the Self-Subsisting Supporter and Sustainer of all . . .[18]

There are two philosophical objections to the Cosmological Argument: The first is stated by Kant, who argued that the whole notion of cause and effect is a way in which to mentally interpret the world, and that we cannot help but impose causality upon physical experience. If Kant is right, then an uncaused cause is a mental impossibility that is disproved by the very fact that logical discussions concerning this have continued for centuries.

The second objection came from David Hume (1711–1776),[19] who claimed that all knowledge is based on observations of the world. Something is said to be a cause because it is seen to occur just before the thing that is called its effect. The link of cause upon effect therefore depends on the observation of them as two separate things. But in the case of the world as a whole (the universes in the Cosmological Argument), we have a unique effect and therefore cannot observe its cause. To support this statement Hume said: 'We cannot get outside the world to see both the world and its cause and thus establish the relationship between them.' He therefore rejects the Cosmological Argument.

The Islāmic response to Hume is that sensual impressions are not the basis of all knowledge, and that cosmological proof cannot be denied just because the Creator exists via senses that lie outside the known world. Denial of causality leads to a single illogical conclusion – namely that everything in the universe must have randomly come into existence. There have been many attempts to show that this cannot be. Abraham Cressy Morrison (1884–1955) provided an eloquent explanation of the probabilities involved for simple existence to emerge randomly, in his work *Man Does Not Stand Alone*. To present a modified version:

Imagine one hundred numbered pages being removed from a book and then shuffled, prior to being handed to a blind or illiterate person to put into their correct sequential order. That person, not being able to read the content or page numbers, selects one page at random in the hope of it being the first page. The probability of it actually being the first page is precisely 1 in 100. The second randomly picked page has a probability of 1 in 99 of being the correct one. The probability of these pages being in sequence is expressed mathematically as:

$$1/100 \times 1/99 = 1/9900.$$

That is to say, correctly picking the second page has only a likelihood of 1 in 9,900 of being successful. The chance of the third randomly picked page being correct is 1 in 98 and the probability of all three being in correct sequence is:

$$1/100 \times 1/99 \times 1/98 = 1/970200$$

The odds of such a person returning all the shuffled pages to their correct sequential order is stated mathematically as a 1 followed by 200 zeros.

For an illustration of the scale of probability/improbability, imagine sending three billion people (roughly half the world's population) to live each on their own separate planets. Over time, each person has three billion descendants. There would then be 9,000,000,000,000,000,000 people on all these planets. If we further imagine that we repeat the same process, with each person having 9,000,000,000,000,000,000 descendants, we would arrive at a total population of

81,000,000,000,000,000,000,000,000,000,000,000,000.

Now imagine you have a ticket in a lottery, in which just one person in this vast number of people is able to win a fortune. What would be the odds of it being you? They can be mathematically expressed as:

1/81,000,000,000,000,000,000,000,000,000,000,000,000.

If winning appears to be so highly improbable as to be negligible – with a number that has thirty-six zeros – imagine the infinitesimal chance of winning with a number that is followed by 200 zeros, the probability of success calculated for a blind or illiterate person sorting 100 numbered pages into their correct sequence. What if we apply such odds to the creation of humankind, who are infinitely more complex? And are humans the only beings to manifest the great secrets and signs of a powerful Creator?

An objection that might be raised to the claim (that everything randomly and spontaneously comes into existence without reason or plan) is that, if true, why has nothing that has randomly 'popped' into existence been observed and recorded? If the order of the universe were founded on randomness – with no Creator or Being to instil order – it would follow that the law of cause and effect does not exist. And was there only a single instance of randomness in the existence of all beings, and are they still subject to randomness?

The great Islāmic philosopher, Muḥammad Ḥusayn Ṭabāṭabā'ī[20] summarizes the Cosmological Argument (*Kalām*) as follows:

> As careful investigation will show, the different components of the universe have a powerful connection one to another . . . and this connection is not restricted to any one part of the universe; rather, we see it more precisely and thoroughly the more we

scrutinize the furthest and most hidden bodies in space. Even those who adhere to the theory of natural selection, and deny any purpose to existence, cannot deny that connections exist between different parts of the universe. This connection is not imaginary; it reveals a reality that is independent and separate from our own minds. Therefore, the universe, with all its component parts, constitutes an external unity.

This external unity is constantly changing and transforming; that is, it has the property of existence after having not existed, because it is always in motion whether in physical motion or substantial motion (*al-ḥarakah al-jawhariyyah*) and motion is the act of coming into existence from non-existence, or existence mixed with non-existence. The general law of cause and effect requires that every originated being – a being that did not exist and then did (*mawjūd ḥādith*) – has a creative cause. Even if we did not suppose that the universe or some part thereof was subject to change, there is still no way to deny that it has a creative cause, because every contingent being, even if it does not change, requires a cause.

From this we conclude that the universe requires a creative cause that is external to it.'[21]

3 The *Kalām* Argument

Muslim scholars also used another form of the Cosmological Argument known as *ʿIlm al-Kalām*,[22] its main contributors being Ibn Sīnā, Al-Kindi and Al-Ghazāli.

The structure of this argument is as follows:

- Everything that begins to exist has a cause for its existence.
- The cosmos/universe began to exist.
- Therefore the cosmos/universe must have a cause.

- The cause of its existence is GOD.

Al-Ghazāli argued that when two states of affairs are equally possible, the one that comes about must be willed by a personal agent.

- The world began to exist.
- There was a time when one of two states was possible – that there should, or should not, be a universe.

4 The Argument from Design

The structure of this argument is:

- The universe displays intelligent design.
- Whatever displays intelligent design is the product of an intelligent designer.
- Therefore, the universe is the creation of an intelligent designer.

The first premise above is proven via both induction and intuition. For complete and precise order is manifest in both massive bodies such as galaxies and planets, in the way in which they cluster together, as well as in minute bodies such as protons, electrons and neutrons within atoms.

How then to prove that such design is indeed intelligent – and thereby the product of an intelligent designer? Order is the opposite of chaos. Order denotes harmony and arrangement, and these two qualities cannot come about spontaneously (we have already illustrated that order is not established via random acts or chance). Rather, they emerge as the result of will, awareness and power. The degree of order and harmony that exists between particles in the universe evidences it being the product of an absolute and unlimited will. Therefore, whatever displays intelligent design has to be the product of an **intelligent designer**.

We might ask if it is not possible to attribute the existence of order in the universe to nature itself? The answer is that a contemplative look at nature demonstrates that whatever it contains is either matter or some secondary condition of matter. In so far as matter lacks awareness and consciousness, it is subject to non-existence and change, affected by existential poverty and neediness.

On the other hand, if what is meant by nature is some great power that is both conscious and aware, as well as being unaffected by external agents, to whom we wish to attribute the intelligent design that is apparent in the universe – this then affirms the existence of the Creator. However, it does this in a way that shows we are averse to naming Him as Allāh or God, so we refer to Him instead as being Nature.

Examples of intelligent design in the universe

Some examples of evidence that reinforce the contention that 'intelligent design' does exist are listed below.

The properties of water

Water is distinguished by four properties that preserve life in oceans, lakes, rivers and ponds, particularly during severely cold periods.

- Oxygen is vital for the organisms that have aerobic types of respiration and live in water. Oxygen saturation of water is affected by temperature, with minimum values of dissolved oxygen content occurring during summer months. The dissolved oxygen content of water is expressed either as the absolute quantity of oxygen in one unit of water (mg/l; ppm), or as relative oxygen saturation (%).

- Water is at its most dense at four degrees centigrade – a density that is maintained down to zero degrees, when it begins to reduce.

- In freezing temperatures, ice, which has a lower density than water, provides a protective layer to permit life to continue beneath it.

- The freezing of water generates heat that helps preserve life below it.

These characteristics of water were not known to science when Allāh revealed: '. . . and we made every living thing from water . . .'[23]

Essential fluids (sap) that circulate in the vascular system of plants

The stems of all plants contain a variety of hollow tubes. One type conveys materials from the roots, the other material produced in the leaves. These ascending and descending functions are diligently and precisely carried out in delicate plants as well as in gigantic trees – an example of 'intelligent design'.

In order to appreciate the significance of this we need to note that, until the Flemish chemist Jan Baptist van Helmont's (1577–1644) investigations into 'How plants grow' in the seventeenth century, scientists believed that plant sustenance and growth came from eating the soil.[24]

Soil consists largely of aluminium silicates and other compounds that play no role to speak of in metabolism. The function of soil is, for the most part, mechanical – it forms a solid permeable foundation into which the plant can root, and in which water can be conserved. Water, on the other hand, not only makes up a considerable portion of plant tissue (as it does for all living things), it also dissolves small quantities of inorganic substances that plants are only able to absorb 'in solution'.

Allāh tells us in Qur'ān 20:53–54, 'He made the earth a bed for you and made paths for you, and sent down water from the heavens. Thereby We have brought forth a variety of vegetation. Eat and pasture your cattle; truly, in this are signs for those that have the mental faculties to understand.'

The epiglottis

There are two cavities at the back of the mouth: the pharynx, which leads to the oesophagus, a muscular tube through which food and drink pass to the stomach; and the larynx, a hollow cartilaginous and muscular organ that forms the upper part of the trachea or windpipe, through which air passes to and from the lungs.

A thin leaf-shaped flap of cartilage, the epiglottis, situated immediately behind the root of the tongue, covers the entrance to the larynx during swallowing to prevent food from entering the windpipe. This functions with great precision, whether we are awake or asleep. However, there is also a 'fail-safe' device, designed to return us to a safe condition in the event of a failure or malfunction of the epiglottis – muscles around the windpipe are designed to reflexively contract and cough up and expel extraneous material. Allāh tells us: 'Soon We shall show them Our signs in the horizons and their own souls, until it becomes clear to them that He is true.'[25]

The nourishment of the fetus and its development

Through the umbilical cord, the fetus within the womb draws its nourishment from the placenta connected to the maternal circulatory system. Those nutriments, absorbed by the fetal liver, maintain the development and growth of the fetus.

However, a few days prior to the child's emergence from the womb, mammary glands in its mother's bosom begin to secrete colostrum and then, later, breast milk – the nutriment that will from then on maintain the development and growth of the new-born child. In a very short space of time, this new life's source of sustenance is changed from dark blood to white milk.

Allāh tells us in Qur'ān 16:66: 'And in cattle [too] you will find a sign. We give you to drink what is in their bodies, between their excretion and their blood – pure milk that is pleasant and delicious to drink.'

The dromedary

The Arabian camel/dromedary, used for millennia as a riding and pack animal that can carry large loads for up to 25 miles a day, is uniquely equipped for desert conditions.

- Dromedary kidneys are specialized so that not much water is excreted. Even so, they are able to tolerate more than 30 per cent water loss. Dromedaries are able to fluctuate their body temperatures throughout the day 34–41.7°C/93–107°F to avoid sweating as external temperatures rise. At 30–40°C (86–104°F), they only need water every 10 to 15 days, and only in the hottest temperatures do they need water every four to seven days. The body obtains the water it needs primarily from interstitial and intracellular bodily fluids. The oval red blood cells, unique to camels, help them survive for over six months without water. They have the unique capability of being able to drink 100 litres of water in just 10 minutes and can withstand both brackish and salty water.

- The hump stores up to 80 lb (36 kg) of fat, which the dromedary can break down into water and energy when sustenance is not available. If the hump is small the animal may exhibit signs of starvation. The adipose tissues in the external part of the hump have cells to store lipids (adipocytes) that are related to their unique mechanism of food and water storage.

- Their main food source is coarse thorny desert vegetation that they are able to grasp with their thick lips. They chew each bite 40–50 times keeping their mouths open. In cases of starvation, they may even eat fish and bones.

- Dromedaries have bushy eyebrows in addition to two rows of long eyelashes to protect their eyes, plus a unique ability to close their nostrils to block the entry of sand and dust, even during sandstorms.

- Dromedaries have thick footpads and two toes on each foot resembling flat leathery pads, that enable them to cover rough rocky terrain and shifting sand. The pads widen under their weight as they step to help prevent them sinking into the sand.

The above 'intelligent design', that distinguishes the dromedary from all other animals, is referred to in Qur'ān 88:17: 'Do they not observe how the camel [dromedary] has been created?'

The relationship between yucca flower and yucca moth

The *Yucca* species of the Liliaceae family consists of relatively large succulent plants, with stiff perennial leaves and large heads of creamy-white, waxy flowers that depend upon yucca moths, of the Prodoxidae family to transfer pollen from the stamens of one flower to the pistil of another. The moth does this by collecting and holding a ball of pollen in its mouth-parts and then purposefully and carefully placing it into the cup-shaped stigma of another flower. This pollination system is so precise that only yucca moths are able to pollinate these plants.

Having ensured a supply of food for her future larvae, the moth then lays her egg in the flower. The primary food source for yucca moth larvae is yucca plant seeds – and the exclusive pollinator of yucca plants is the yucca moth. This arrangement is so finely tuned that yucca plants will even abort fruit development if too many eggs are laid in one flower.

Such intricate harmony – such intelligent design.

The relationship between figs and wasps

Fig wasps (family Agaonidae) may be any of about 900 species of tiny wasp that are responsible for pollinating the world's 900 species of figs. Each species of wasp pollinates only one species of fig, and each fig species has its own specific wasp species to pollinate it.

Among the Agaonidae, females are normal insects and males mostly wingless. Their life cycle is closely intertwined with the fig trees they inhabit. These wasps may be loosely divided into two groups: those that pollinate and those that do not. While the pollinating group form mutually beneficial symbiotic relationships with the tree, the non-pollinators are parasitic.

The green fig is actually an inverted flower with a thick fruity shell that covers its reproductive organs. Being so protected, neither wind- nor bee-transported pollen can reach the pistils to fertilize the flower – figs depend upon specific fig wasps to enter the unripe fig and deliver pollen from another fig. Most fig inflorescences contain three types of flower: male, short female and long female. Female fig wasp ovipositors are able to reach the ovaries of short female flowers but not long female flowers. Thus short flowers grow wasps and develop into figs while the long flowers develop seeds.

The male wasp has two functions; after going through its pupal stage a mature male must mate with a female within the fig *syconium* and then chew an exit passage for the females to escape the fig interior.

The female function is to mate and collect pollen as she escapes her birth chamber. A mature female pollinator wasp must enter the immature 'fruit' (a stem-like structure known as a *syconium*) at just the right stage of its development, through a small natural opening called the *ostiole* that is covered in male flowers, and then deposit her eggs in the cavity covered in female flowers. Often, in forcing her way through the *ostiole* the female loses her wings and most of her antennae, but to facilitate her passage the underside of her head is covered in short spines that provide purchase on the ostiole walls. In depositing her eggs, the female also deposits the pollen she has picked up from her original host fig. This pollinates some of the female flowers on the inside surface of the fig and allows them to mature. After the female wasp has laid her eggs she dies.

Some of the eggs hatch, and while figs lose flesh that feed the larvae, it is the damage done during the wasp's escape that seems to be the trigger for its fruit to ripen.

The 'intelligently designed' symbiotic relationship between figs and wasps is so specific and profound that neither organism is able to exist without the other. And Allāh tells us in Qur'ān 20:50: '. . . Our Lord is He who created everything and then guided it.'

Butterfly, ant and oregano

As butterflies do not look after their own offspring, a critical choice for them is where and when to lay their eggs. Once Large Blue butterfly eggs hatch into caterpillars they need to browse on a specific plant before being able to feed on the richer nutriment, upon which they develop 98 per cent of the weight they need before they metamorphose into pupae and butterflies.

Large Blue butterflies lay their eggs on wild oregano plants because the caterpillars feed on their flower buds. And, at dusk some two weeks later, while the *Myrmica* species of red ants forage and other ant species do not, they drop to the ground. There, by mimicking the scent and posture of *Myrmica* ant grubs, they appear to be assumed to have strayed and get taken into the nest. Then, once inside, they imitate the sounds made by the queen ant and are able to access and feast, for some 11 months, on the nutrient-rich ant brood.

When *Myrmica* ant colonies tunnel beneath and disturb the roots of an oregano plant it doubles its output of the principal ingredient of its defence system, the toxic antifungal and insecticide carvacrol. As *Myrmica* ants have a higher capability to detoxify this than other ant genera, competition is kept away from their nests below the oregano plant. It is suggested that carvacrol is the chemical cue that directs female Large Blues to the right food for the different stages of their caterpillars' development.

In this symbiotic relationship the oregano sacrifices approximately 17 florets to each Large Blue caterpillar before it is abandoned by it – but this is outweighed by the potential benefit of the caterpillars getting rid of the ants that irritate its roots. The *Myrmica* ants may lose a few colonies to Large Blue caterpillars, but this is outweighed by the benefit of domination of the competitor-free space made available by the oregano's security system. The Large Blue benefits from its choice of host-plant because it provides the initial sustenance for its larvae and co-occurs with the source of their subsequent nourishment.

The design of such intricate and intimate interactions provides yet further evidence of the existence of an intelligent designer.

The amazingly complex life cycle of the Brazil nut tree

The Brazil nut tree (*Bertholletia excelsa*) survives as the result of a number of complex ecological interactions between the tree, its flowers, its seed pods, the life cycle of a bumble bee, a rainforest orchid, the agouti (the most important predator and scatterhoarder disperser of its seeds) that all co-exist within a delicately balanced natural forest ecosystem.

- *Bertholletia excelsa* trees grow to heights of 40 to 60 metres, have straight trunks of 20 metres or more, diameters of between 2 and 4 metres and lifespans of several hundred years. They flourish in non-flooding areas of the moist lowland rainforest within groups or 'stands' of 50 or more similar trees. After 10–30 years of maturation these trees are able each season to produce between 60 and 100 pods that enclose as many as two dozen individual seeds – 'Brazil nuts'.

- *Bertholletia excelsa*, unable to be fertilized by its own pollen, begins to flower during the drier months, peaking between October and December. The type of flowering, classified as 'cornucopia', is characterized by a large number of one-day-long flowers opening each day within a period of three to eight weeks in the majority of the tree population. The 'hood' coverings of these bisexual flowers obstruct wind pollination. The flowers are large and fleshy with stamens arranged in a manner not found in any other plant family on the planet. Stamens ring the summit of the ovary that surrounds the part that receives pollen in impregnation. This ring has a prolongation or 'hood' that has at its apex appendages that turn inward towards the interior of the 'hood'. From the point where they arise a small amount of nectar is produced. This 'hood' covers the top of the ovary and six petals form a cup-shaped overlap that restricts entrance to pollinators without the physical vigour and compatible size to gain entrance to its nectar and reproductive organs.

  Pollinators documented to enter the flower are robust Euglossine or 'orchid bees'. Only female bees have the required strength to enter into the flower, in which they stay for up to 10–30 seconds, and leave with their thoracic surface covered with the pollen that is conveyed to the receptive stigma of the next flower they visit. Some of these vigorous and robust bees are able to fly distances up to 20 km – extremely important for the maintainance of gene flow among the plants in tropical forests.

- Euglossa bees are characterized by their large tongues, habitat of undisturbed forest, and lack of eusocial traits such as worker sterility, cooperative brood care and consequent absence of hives. In insects, chemical signals are frequently a part of mate location and recognition and chemical dichotomies can sometimes be a first clue in the differentiation of cryptic species. In order to acquire the pheromones required to attract a mate, male Euglossa bees of all species collect 'fragrances' from natural sources such as flowers, decaying vegetation and fungi and store them in voluminous pockets on their hind tibiae. Here they accumulate and develop into complex and species-specific blends of 'perfume' to be exposed during courtship displays – a function that, in the context of mate recognition, is indirectly supported by findings that chemical blends differ between species, particularly between closely related species.

In their task of achieving the above objective, the males of such bees visit, and in so doing pollinate, the *Coryanthes vasquezii* variety of orchid. This intricate association of male bees as pollinators of orchid flowers is yet another intriguing aspect in the symbiotic life cycle of *Bertholletia excelsa*.

- In the rainy season, some 15 months after the flower has been pollinated, mature fruits drop to the ground. These take the form of globe-shaped woody capsules 11–15 cm in diameter called pyxidia (seed-capsules that open so that the top comes off like the lid of a box). These do not split open to release seed, but have inward-opening lids and opening diameters narrower than their contained seeds. Tightly packed like segments of an orange, the 15–25 seeds are 3–4 cm long and angular, each with a hard, woody coat and a thin adhering protective covering. In botanical terms Brazil nuts are not nuts – a word used to refer to a specific kind of fruit – but the seeds of the tree.

- Neglected seeds left trapped inside mature pyxidia ultimately succumb to mortality through fungal attack and rotting. Successful germination of *Bertholletia* seeds thus appears to be entirely dependent on seed removal and dispersal by rodents of the *Dasyprocta* genus – agoutis, which have sharp chisel-like teeth that enable them to gnaw through the tough outer wall of the fruit and release the seeds. When an agouti has eaten its fill, it buries caches of the remaining seeds, and those that are not later eaten by it, or another seed predator, may remain in scattered caches and germinate after 12 to 18 months, into the next generation of trees. This behavioural pattern is typical of the scatterhoarding dispersal of other large seeds exercised by the various types of agoutis who appear to account for almost all Brazil nut seed dispersal.

This extremely complicated interrelated order is a clear illustration of ingenious complexity rather than an outcome of random events. Logically, it signifies the creation of an intelligent designer.

Flowers that trap insects

The wild arum, *Arum maculatum,* displays one of the most fascinating pollination mechanisms in the living world. Leaves appear in the spring followed by flowers borne on a poker-shaped inflorescence called a *spadix.* This spadix is partially enclosed by a leaf-like hood called a *spathe.* The inflorescence, hidden from sight, that is clustered around the base of the spadix consists of a ring of female flowers at the bottom and a ring of male flowers above them. Above the male flowers, a ring of hairs traps insects attracted to the spadix odour that mimics the smell of cow dung, and temperatures of up to 15° Celsius warmer than the ambient temperature. Flies with pollen on their bodies enter and fall down the spathe, which has a smooth slippery, oily surface and downward-pointing hairs – to be delivered to the female flowers at the bottom of the trap. As a ring of sterile flowers blocks their exit, they remain trapped there overnight. While they are trapped beneath the ring of sterile flowers, male flowers higher up the inflorescence axis mature and shed their pollen on to the trapped flies. The spathe then ceases to be slippery; its sterile flowers wither; the inflorescence ceases to be hot and fetid and flies, now dusted by the flower's pollen, are permitted to depart the trap to seek another fetid inflorescence.

In autumn the lower ring of (female) flowers forms a cluster of bright red berries that remain after the spathe and leaves have withered away.

Another example of 'intelligent design'!

Lightning's contribution to a fertile earth

While some might see lightning only as a destructive force, these electrical discharges are part of the 'intelligent design' that ensures the earth's fertility.

The main component of the nitrogen cycle starts with the element nitrogen, a relatively inert gas plentiful in air (about 78 per cent of the air being nitrogen). The intense energy from lightning breaks up nitrogen (N_2) and that enables its atoms and water (H_2O) to combine to form the nitrogen oxides – ammonia (NH_3) and nitrates (NO_3). Precipitation carries the ammonia and nitrates to earth where plants are able to assimilate them for their nutriment. Atmospheric nitrogen fixation probably contributes some 5–8 per cent of the total nitrogen fixed and is therefore an important feature of all organisms that depend on nutrients from the nitrogen cycle.

All life requires nitrogen compounds, e.g. proteins and nucleic acids. Air, which is 78 per cent nitrogen gas (N_2), is the major reservoir of nitrogen, but most organisms are not able to use nitrogen in this form. Plants need nitrogen in 'fixed' form, i.e. incorporated in compounds, such as nitrate ions (NO_{3-}), ammonia (NH_3), and urea $(NH_2)_2CO$. Animals secure their nitrogen (and all other) compounds from plants (or animals that have fed on plants).

Nitrogen in the air becomes a part of biological matter mostly through the actions of bacteria and algae in a process known as nitrogen fixation. Leguminous plants, such as clover, alfalfa and soybeans, form root nodules where nitrogen-fixing bacteria take nitrogen from the air and convert it into ammonia, NH_3. The ammonia is further converted by other bacteria, first into nitrite ions, NO_{2-}, and then into nitrate ions, NO_{3-}. Plants utilize these nitrate ions as a nutrient or fertilizer for growth. Nitrogen is also incorporated in many amino acids that are further combined to make proteins.

High-energy lightning, cosmic radiation and meteorite trail fixation accounts for about 8 per cent of the nitrate entering the nitrogen cycle. In contrast, biological fixation accounts for roughly 90 per cent of the fixed nitrogen in the cycle. In biological fixation, molecular nitrogen

(N_2) is split into two free N molecules. The N molecules combine with hydrogen (H) molecules to yield ammonia (NH_3).

In lightning flashes, nitrogen gas in super-heated air is converted to nitrate (NO_{3-}) and nitrite (NO_{2-}). Lightning may account for 1 to 50 pounds of plant-available nitrogen per acre per year.[26]

About 5 pounds of nitrogen per acre is deposited with precipitation each year although there are about 37,000 tons of nitrogen directly above each acre. The small quantity that falls is due to lightning action on nitrogen oxide compounds. Even though the amount added by direct deposition is small, most nitrogen used by crops originated in the atmosphere.[27]

We read in Qur'ān 30:24: 'Among His signs is that He shows you lightning that fills you with awe and hope, and He sends down rain from the skies and with it gives life to the earth after it has been lifeless. Truly, there are signs in this for those who apply their minds.' This incentive to apply our minds leads us to use all our faculties to examine in depth what we see in His creation, and to comprehend it more fully.

In *āyah* 13:12 we also read: 'It is He who shows you lightning [as a source of] fear and hope, and He raises clouds heavy with [fertilizing] rain.'

Atomic structure

The ancient Greek philosopher Leucippus and his pupil Democritus first proposed that all matter consists of invisible '*atomoi*', now referred to as atoms. They supposed that matter could be divided into smaller and smaller particles until they reached a point where they could no longer be divided. The fundamental truth of existence is that the universe is made up of atoms and that they are responsible for life on Earth.

We now know that atoms can be divided into subatomic particles – protons, neutrons and electrons – held together by electromagnetic force, and that these are the building blocks of all matter. Particle accelerators have helped scientists to break subatomic particles into even smaller units, some of which only exist for seconds. They classify subatomic particles as being either elementary or composite. Elementary subatomic particles, like quarks, are thought incapable of being divided into simpler particles while composite subatomic particles, such as hadrons, can be.

All subatomic particles share a fundamental property of 'intrinsic angular momentum', or spin. This means they rotate in one direction, just like planets, even when the particle is not moving. Subatomic 'fermion' particles, that can be either elementary or composite, contain a one-half integer spin.

- *Bosons.* These are groups of either elementary or composite subatomic particles that have a full integer spin. Unlike fermions, bosons obey Bose-Einstein condensation; this states that when the gas of an atom is cooled to its lowest state, the atoms gather in that lowest state, merging into a single wave. Several can occupy one quantum state at a time. Put another way, these atoms can act as one giant 'super-atom'.

  Bosons are famous for an entity known as the 'Higgs boson', believed to be the last missing particle – or set of particles – from the Standard Model. Proof of its existence would answer the questions: what exactly determines mass and why does gravity behave as it does?

- *Hadrons.* With a name derived from the Greek word for 'stout', hadrons are composite subatomic particles formed when quarks combine and are held together by a strong force. They have mass, a net integer charge, and live inside a nucleus. Protons and neutrons, two commonly recognized subatomic particles, are also hadrons. With the exclusion of protons, all hadrons undergo partial decay and transform into other elementary particles.

  Hadrons are divided into two groups or classes: baryons and mesons. What distinguishes these classes from each other is their respective quark allotment. Baryons are made up of three quarks: two up and one down. Mesons, on the other hand, consist of one quark and one anti-quark. Currently, research is being done into the possibility of a hadron composed of five quarks, known as the pentaquark – a new form of atomic matter said to live for less than one-hundredth of a billionth of a billionth of a second before decaying, making it extremely hard to observe.

- *Leptons.* Leptons, which are also fermions, are elementary particles which are a fundamental component of all matter. Unlike quarks, which always stay in groups, leptons are solitary. There are six types of leptons, and in terms of charges they are split down the middle: three have charges and three do not. After that straightforward division, things become a little more complicated.

  Being the first leptons to be identified, electrons are probably the most familiar of the charged leptons. Muons and taus are a little less well known. Like electrons, muon and tau leptons are charged. However, both have quite a bit of mass. These often decay quite rapidly or transform into something else such as a lighter lepton or quark. Like quarks and their anti-quarks, each charged lepton has a chargeless antineutrino. The neutrinos are much smaller than their charged counterparts. To understand lepton decay, scientists established three lepton families:

  1. electron and electron neutrino
  2. muon and muon neutrino
  3. tau and tau neutrino

  One particle of a decaying lepton must go into its neutrino while the others can transform into something else such as a quark or anti-quark. However, only the 'tau' have sufficient mass to decay into a hadron.

- *Quarks.* Matter is composed of protons and neutrons; and protons and neutrons are each made up of three quarks. Quarks are one type of elementary subatomic particle with a few unique features. Quarks are the only subatomic particles to undergo all four fundamental forces: electromagnetic force, gravitational force, strong interaction and weak interaction. They are also only observed in groups and are never found alone. Commonly called ‘flavours’, the six types of quark are usually regarded in pairs: up/down, charm/strange and top/bottom. Unlike protons and electrons, which have either positive or negative charges, quarks have a fractional electric charge. This means they have either a -1/3 or +2/3 of the charge carried by the proton. Quarks also have a colour charge: a term used to refer to its three charge aspects – positive, negative or neutral. As with everything in life, quarks have their opposites. For every quark, an anti-quark also exists.

- *Fermions.* These are subatomic particles that contain a one-half integer spin. They may be elementary or composite. Electrons, protons and neutrons are all fermions. Fermions differ from bosons in that that no two fermions in a single atom may exist in the same time and space – a fundamental property of all basic matter – for without this being so, and without fermions, electrons would collapse into the same exact energy states as all chemical elements and have precisely the same properties. Quarks, leptons and most composite particles fall into the fermion category. Quarks and leptons, along with most composite particles, also fall into the fermion category.[28]

As time passes, the application of the world’s scientists’ intellectual faculties seems, almost every day, to provide ever more evidence of the depth of complexity in the ‘intelligent design’ of the universes. Allāh tells us in Qur’ān 15:19: ‘We have spread out the earth with stabilizing mountains and caused everything to grow on it in proper measure.’ And in Qur’ān 55, after providing evidence of His powers, Allāh tells us: ‘Then which of the bounties of your Lord would you deny?’

Fingerprints

In the late seventeenth century, high levels of crime in London led to the state offering substantial rewards for the apprehension of suspects, with further payments becoming due if they were found guilty and convicted. Corrupt ‘thief-takers’ blackmailed criminals into paying protection money and encouraged gullible people to commit crimes so that they could then easily apprehend and prosecute them for the reward payment. Maliciously motivated prosecutions also occurred with no offence having ever been committed. This resulted in the release of many who were guilty and the hanging or imprisonment of many who were innocent.

Doubts regarding current practices and legal justice arose when cases with a similar profile were reported while the supposed offenders in these serial crimes were still incarcerated. Worldwide examples of probable injustices led to the birth of the scientific discipline now known as Crime Scene Forensics.

Fingerprints had been used as a means to positively identify people throughout history: clay-embossed fingertip impressions to record business transactions by ancient Babylonians; inked finger impressions on paper, for business and the identification of their children by the Chinese. However, they were not used for criminal identification until the nineteenth century.

The following timeline shows the developments that led to our current system of fingerprint identification:

1858 Sir William Herschel, a British District Administrator and Chief Magistrate in India, required fingerprints and signatures on civil contracts.

1880 Dr Henry Faulds (a Scottish doctor working in Japan) had his article on the use of printer's ink to record fingerprints, as a means of personal identification, published in the science journal *Nature*.

1891 Argentinian police official Juan Vucetich initiated the fingerprinting of criminals that was first applied in the Rojas Homicide case of 1892.

1892 Sir Francis Galton FRS, who had collected some 8,000 sample fingerprints to analyse, published the first book on the subject titled *Fingerprints*, which identified the unique fingerprint arches, whorls and loops that characterize individuality.

1896 The International Association of Chiefs of Police (IACP) established the National Bureau of Criminal Identification to exchange information.

1896–7 Between July 1896 and February 1897, Sub-Inspectors Azizul Haque and Hemchandra Bose, together with Inspector General of Police in India Sir Edward Henry, developed a system of fingerprint classification that enabled fingerprint records to be organized and searched with relative ease. Modern-day AFIS classification methods, up until the 1990s, were based on it.

The world's first fingerprint bureau was set up at Calcutta (now Kolkata) in 1897, mainly by their efforts. In addition, Bose invented the telegraphic code system for fingerprints that was published in 1916. Sir Charles Stockley Collins of Scotland Yard, still recognized worldwide as the originator of fingerprint telegraphic technique, published his findings in 1921, five years after Bose's publication.

1901 Scotland Yard established its first Fingerprint Bureau. The following year, fingerprints were presented as evidence for the first time in English courts.

1903 New York State prisons adopted the use of fingerprints, followed later by the FBI.

1905 US Military adopted the use of fingerprints, followed by police agencies.

1980 Development of the first computerized database of fingerprints that currently holds c. 70 million cards.

Interestingly, even identical twins have different unique pattern fingerprints and despite criminals burning or otherwise damaging their fingertips in attempts to conceal their identities, the new layers of skin that develop retain their unique patterns.

The significance of fingertip pattern confirms the miracle of intelligent design. Allāh tells us in the Qur'ān: 'Does man suppose that We shall not reassemble his scattered bones? Yes indeed, We are even able to recreate his fingertips.'[29]

Ants

Ants, social insects of the family Formicidae, occupy a broad range of ecological niches and exploit a wide range of food resources, as either direct or indirect herbivores, predators or scavengers. To date, more than 12,000 different species have been distinguished. E.O. Wilson, who is considered to be a leading authority on ants, has estimated that there are approximately 1 million ants for every human on Earth. An ant brain has about 250,000 brain cells and a human brain c. 10,000 million.

Scientists refer to insects that live in colonies of millions of individuals as being *eusocial* – showing an advanced level of social organization in which a single female's offspring of non-reproductive individuals cooperate in caring for them all. Despite eusocial insects representing less than 5 per cent of all insect life, they are the most successful species and outnumber the combined populations of all other insect species.

In sophisticated colonies such as those of the leafcutter ant, each individual has a dedicated 'specialist function'. There is only one queen, whose specialism and sole function is to produce eggs – up to 30,000 a day. She has no social dominance or ability to instruct, direct or order her offspring of female worker ants to undertake anything whatsoever. Although the eggs she lays – all fertilized during her departure from her birth home – are essentially the same, they yield the required number of ants of the different sizes and characteristics (castes) needed to carry out the various duties necessary for the colony to function. Once a year a colony will produce young queens and some males, the only time that this sex is ever raised. When mature, these castes of ant forsake the colony – the males to fertilize the queens and then die, the fertilized queens to strive to establish their own colonies. The multiple generations of other worker ants that undertake the wide variety of specialist duties required by the colony live out their lives as part of it. The specialist function of the large worker ants armed with heavy pincers ('soldiers') is to guard and protect the colony. Laboratory studies show that each one regularly patrols a specific area of the colony, some covering larger areas than others. When their colony is threatened, they all hasten to defend it. Some worker ants' specialist function is to keep the queen free from contamination, others to carry her newly laid eggs to brooding chambers, yet others to attend to the developing larvae and pupae. The specialist function of some is to take nest detritus to the 'rubbish tip' and dead ants to a 'cemetery' section. Yet other 'specialist' ants continually turn over waste to promote its breakdown.

As leafcutter ants feed exclusively on a fungus that is only found within their colonies, the specialist function of forager workers is to locate and bring leaf sections to the colony to fertilize the fungal growth that supplies the colonies with their sole nutriment. Larger worker ants specialize in cutting stalks, smaller ones in 'dicing' leaves, and the smallest in distributing this leaf nourishment to the fungus gardens.

Ants communicate with each other using pheromones, sound and touch. Some *stridulate* vigorously, that is, they produce shrill sounds by rubbing one part of their body against another, to inform or warn the others.

Sophisticated colonies, like those of leafcutter ants, are sometimes termed 'super-organisms' because their populations appear to operate as one entity. This leads us to ask the question: is all this sophisticated, elaborately controlled collective 'choreography' not the product of 'intelligent design'? Indeed, the clear scientific facts in all the above examples, the result of men and women utilizing their analytic intelligence to 'see how things work', points to the 'intelligent design' of the human brain itself.

The divided brain

In a ground-breaking, seminal, beautifully written, erudite and fascinating book – based on a vast body of recent experimental research – Iain McGilchrist, former Consultant Psychiatrist and Clinical Director at the Bethlem Royal & Maudsley Hospital, London, who has researched in neuroimaging at Johns Hopkins University Hospital, Baltimore, makes the case that the left and right hemispheres of our brains have differing insights, values and priorities. He elaborates on and explains this in 462 pages plus 55 pages of notes, the result of his 20 years of work and thought on this subject.

The brain is structurally asymmetrical, which probably indicates asymmetry of function. Hence the brain has to attend to the world in two completely different ways, and in so doing brings two different worlds into being. In the one, we *experience* the live, complex, embodied world of individual, always unique beings, forever in flux, a net of interdependencies, forming and reforming wholes, a world with which we are deeply connected. In the other we 'experience' our experience in a special way: a 're-presented' version of it, containing now static, separable, bounded, but essentially fragmented entities, grouped into classes, on which predictions can be based. This kind of attention isolates, fixes and makes each thing explicit by bringing it under the spotlight of attention. In doing so it renders things inert, mechanical, lifeless. But it also enables us for the first time to know, and consequently to learn and to make things.

> These are not different ways of *thinking about* the world: they are different ways of *being in* the world. And their difference is not symmetrical, but fundamentally asymmetrical. (pp. 30–31)
>
> . . . Ultimately what I have tried to point to is that the apparently separate 'functions' in each hemisphere fit together intelligently to form in each case a single coherent entity; . . . (p. 461)[30]
>
> McGilchrist's careful analysis of how brains work is a veritable *tour de force*, gradually and skilfully revealed. I know of no better exposition of the current state of functional brain neuroscience. [31]

To conclude, no matter what aspect is chosen for examination, we discover all of creation to be the product of 'intelligent design'.

3 The Teleological Argument

In Greek, *teleos* means end or purpose and *logos* means knowledge – thus teleology is the belief that every single thing in the world moves purposefully towards the goals that have been specified for it. This argument, because it refers to orderliness or purpose in the design of the universe, is also sometimes referred to as the Design Argument (that we have already discussed). As it tends to evoke spontaneous assent in the simple as well as in the sophisticated, it has also been the most popular theistic argument.

The Teleological Argument, being *a posteriori*, begins from experience of 'the world'. What we call 'the world' displays both intelligent order and purpose. We only know order and purpose as being brought about or given, not as the result of any accidental occurrence. So, we assume that there must be someone or something to bring everything into order. The Greek philosopher Plato (428–348 BC) expressed it in this way:

> On which grounds can one speak the truth in saying that gods exist? Why, to begin with, think of the earth, the sun, the planets and everything! And the wonderful and beautiful order of the seasons with the distinctions of years and months![32]

1 The Old and New Testaments

The same proposition is raised here:

> Bless the Lord, O my soul, O Lord my God, you are very great; you are clothed with honour and majesty . . . who laid the foundations of the earth that it should not be removed for ever . . . He sends the springs into the valleys, which run among the hills. They give drink to every beast of the fields . . . He causes the grass to grow for the cattle, and herb for the service of man: that he may bring forth food out of the earth . . . The trees of the Lord are full of sap . . . where the birds make their nests . . . He appointed the moon for seasons; the sun knows his going down. You make darkness, and it is night wherein all the beasts of the forest do creep forth.[33]

In one of his letters to the Romans, St Paul expounds Christian teaching thus:

> The invisible things of God from the creation of the world are clearly understood by the things that are made, even His eternal power and Godhead.[34]

Muslim philosophers such as Ibn Sīnā, Fārābi and Ibn Rushd frequently used this argument in discussing the existence of God. However, we suggest that, in reference to 'design', this should not be considered as separate from the Cosmological Argument. Nonetheless, it is appropriate to discuss here the part of the argument that focuses on the goal of existence – in order to align it with *teleos*.

2 William Paley

In the West, the contemporary approach to this argument is based on the presentation of William Paley (1743–1805 CE).[35]

Suppose that while walking in a desert place I see a rock lying on the ground and ask myself how this object came to exist. I can properly attribute its presence to chance, meaning in this case, the operation of such natural forces as wind, rain, heat, frost and volcanic action. However, if I see a watch lying on the ground I cannot reasonably account for it in a similar way. A watch consists of a complex arrangement of wheels, cogs, axles, springs and balances, all operating accurately together to provide a regular measurement of the lapse of time. It would be utterly unreasonable and improbable to attribute the formation and assembly of these metal parts into a functioning machine, to the chance operation of such factors as wind and rain. We are obliged to postulate an intelligent mind that is responsible for this phenomenon. The inevitable inference is that there is a watchmaker who designed the mechanism for a specific purpose, understood and achieved its construction.

In his analysis, Paley compared the watch to 'the world'.

- Even if we had never seen a watch before, we would still infer that watches are the product of human intelligence.
- Even if we had never seen a watch before, our inference from the watch to the watchmaker would not be invalid. We would always find ourselves obliged to postulate a watchmaker.
- Even if we do not understand how the mechanism works, it does not undermine our inference that there was a watchmaker.

If we consider the universe to be like Paley's watch, each component fulfils a specific function, designed with care and made with precision for each part to fit, integrate and work in harmony with all the other components that make up the whole. If we accept that the world is so designed, it automatically leads us to believe it must have a designer.

A more recent writer supports the Teleological Argument when he refers to the ozone layer in the atmosphere; this filters out enough of the burning ultraviolet rays of the sun to make life as we know it possible on the earth's surface.

> The ozone gas layer is a mighty proof of the Creator's forethought. Could anyone possibly attribute this system to chance evolution-

ary process? A wall which prevents death of every living thing, just the right thickness, and exactly the correct defence, gives every evidence of plan.[36]

3 Allāh's Signs

In Qur'ānic terminology, a thing that evidences the Design Argument is referred to as an *āyah* (pl. *ayāt*). In this terminology, everything in the universe is regarded as being a 'sign' or *āyah* of the Almighty Creator. Various *ayāt* of the Qur'ān, e.g. numbers 11, 13, 65, 67 and 69 in Surah 16, and numbers 7 and 8 in Surah 26, refer to the Argument from Design.

11 With it He produces for you corn, olives, dates, grapes and fruit of every kind: Truly, this is a sign for those who reflect.

13 And each of the varied hued things on this earth that He has produced is truly a sign for men who are mindful.

65 And Allāh sends down rain from the skies, and then enlivens the earth with it after its death: Truly, in this is a sign for those who listen.

67 And from the fruit of the date-palm and vine you obtain fortifying drinks and wholesome food: Truly, in this is a sign for those who are wise.

69 Then eat all the produce (of the earth) and follow the ways of your Lord submissively: there issues from within their bodies [the bee] a drink of varying hues, wherein is healing for people: Truly, in this is a sign for those who reflect.[37]

7 Do they not look at the earth, at how many noble things of all kinds that We have produced therein?

8 In this there is truly a sign: but most of them do not believe.[38]

Allāh tells us in the Holy Qur'ān,

> We shall soon show them our signs in the universe and in their own souls so that it becomes manifest to them that He is the Ultimate Truth.[39]

4 Purposefulness of Creation

To distinguish between the Teleological Argument and the Argument from Design we observe that the whole of creation, and humanity in particular, has a purpose. Aimlessness goes side by side with vanity and stupidity. As we will discuss later, one of the divine attributes mentioned in the Qur'ān is Wisdom (*Ḥikmah*). This indirectly negates every type of aimless vanity. Allāh tells us in the Qur'ān:

> Do you think We created you in vain and that you shall not return to us?[40]

> We did not create the heavens and the earth and what is between them as some game. Had We intended to amuse Ourself, We could surely have done so.[41]

However, Allāh Almighty explains the purpose of His creation as follows:

> I did not create Jinn and humanity other than for them to worship Me.[42]

In his elaboration on the above *āyah* Imām Ṣādiq عليه السلام said: 'Allāh created man and gave him faculties of observation and contemplation to enable him to acquire knowledge, so that they may understand the manifestation of His power and submit to Him.'

A *Ḥadīth Qudsi* informs us that Allāh said: 'I was a hidden treasure that wished to become known and created all creatures so that they may know me.'[43]

As Allāh Almighty is understood to be the manifestation of all goodness and perfection, all of His creation constantly struggles towards perfection. The end of the journey for all of us is to meet with the Lord in precisely the same manner in which every raindrop journeys through valleys and rivers to join and become part of the oceans.

Perfection here is an ontological attribute that is agreeable to an agent; it may sometimes be a result of a voluntary action, and at others be the result of a specific cause. That perfection derived as the effect of wilful action may constitute ultimate perfection is recognized by Muslim philosophers as 'Real Goodness (*Khayr Ḥaqiqi'*). While it may be agreeable to the agent, it may also be a source of harm to him. For example, a natural result of eating is satisfaction (of the vegetative faculty), as the need for nutrition is common to human beings, animals and plants. Philosophically, this may be referred to as 'goodness'. However, the pleasure derived from it is perfection in the view of the faculty that perceives it (one that humankind and animals have in common). At a higher level, eating to provide the energy to enable one to fulfil one's obligations to one's Lord is unique to human beings.

From the above example we realize that what is described as pleasure, perfection and goodness is based upon the fulfilment of a specific need. Since Allāh, by definition, is without need, we cannot imagine His purpose to create was to fulfil any of the above categories.

5 Concluding Comments

In comparing the above arguments for the existence of God we conclude that the following three are the most convincing:

1. The argument from contingency – to logically justify the need for an 'Eternal Existent'.

2. The argument from possibility – to logically justify the need for a 'Necessary Existent'.

3. The argument from design – to logically justify the need for an 'Intelligent Designer'.

4 The Methodology of the Error-Free Imāms عليهم السلام

In order to consider arguments for the existence of Allāh from the perspective of the Imāms of the Prophet's household عليهم السلام, we need to disregard the fact that they are successors to the Final Messenger صلى الله عليه وآله وسلم. Response to that status is dependent on him indeed being a divine messenger, and that itself depends on the existence of Allāh – and that constructs a circular argument. We need rather to consider their words from an entirely different perspective, namely that of historians' unanimous agreement that both friends and enemies of the Prophet's Household عليهم السلام regarded them as honourable, truthful, pious and learned throughout their lives. The examples of such views given below should suffice.

1 Imām ʿAli عليه السلام in *Nahj al-Balāghah*

Imām ʿAli عليه السلام said, 'Praise be to Allāh, whose proof of existence is through His creation and His being eternal through the contingency of creation.'[44]

He عليه السلام said, 'He did not create things from eternal sources, but created everything and then fixed limits for it all.'[45]

He said, 'His existence precedes time, His being precedes non-existence and His eternity precedes eternity . . . stillness and motion do not occur in Him – because how could something occur in Him which He himself made occur.'[46]

He described the design of the locust most beautifully: 'Look at the sun, moon, vegetation, plants, water, stone, the difference between night and day, the springing streams, the number of mountains, the height of their peaks, the diversity of language. Woe to those who do not believe in the "Ordainer" and deny the "Organizer". They believe themselves to be like grasses for which there is no cultivator, that there is no animator for life's diverse shapes . . . look, for example, at the tiny locust. Allāh gave it two red eyes with moonlike pupils, concealed ears, a keen sense, suitable mouth, two teeth to cut with and two sickle-like feet to grip with. The farmers are afraid of it because they cannot drive it away from their crops even though they join together. The locust attacks the fields and satisfies its hunger even though its body is smaller than a finger.[47]

His eloquence in his description of the design of the bat: 'An example of His wonderful creation is the bat that hides in the daylight that reveals everything else. Yet it is mobile during the night that shuts up every other living being. Its eyes are dazzled by light and cannot make use of that which reaches them. Allah has confined it to places of hiding and prevented it from moving in the brightness of the sun. In consequence, it keeps its eyelids down in daylight but treats the darkness of night as a lamp . . . He has given it wings of flesh which permit it to rise upwards in flight. It looks as though it has no feathers or bones, although one can see its veins quite distinctly. It has two wings neither so thin that they are not firm in flight nor so thick so that they are too weighty. Its young hold on to it for safety – they climb aboard when it flies and climb down when it lands.'[48]

So perfect is Allah's design that early aircraft designers, such as the Wright brothers, were inspired to incorporate batwing structural principles in aircraft wings. And despite the fact that many consider vampire bats to be rather repulsive, the medical world has recognized vampire bat saliva to be an anticoagulant that is able to prevent heart attacks and strokes.

Imām ʿAli عليه السلام on the human soul: The Commander of the Faithful, Imām ʿAli عليه السلام, said, 'Whoever knows his own self (*nafs*) knows his Lord.' Scholars have proposed 12 different meanings for this tradition.[49] Explained below are three that are the most appropriate to this work.

1. Inasmuch as the limbs and appendages of a body depend upon a central faculty to direct and guide them, and that the entire nervous system that extends throughout the whole body returns to a single point, and that none of this functions when a person dies and becomes devoid of their spirit, we conclude that matter alone is not sufficient to move a body. Further, and more crucially, it follows that matter is not able either to move the universe . . . and it follows that the material world is reliant upon an immaterial director, arranger and planner . . . namely Allāh.

2. Whoever knows that the soul exists before a body does, and continues to exist after the destruction of a body, knows that his Lord existed before He created creatures, and continues to exist after they perish. He was never non-existent nor shall He ever be.

3. As the body is limited by space and time, the soul is distinct inasmuch as it is subject neither to place nor constraint. This points to its participation, to some extent, in its absoluteness (*iṭlāq*) that is derived from the Source, i.e. Allāh Almighty.

Imām ʿAli عليه السلام on human will: Imām ʿAli عليه السلام said, 'Allāh is known by the annulment of resolutions, the unbinding of decisions, and the removal of harm and tribulation from those who purify their intentions.'[50]

The following wording has also been recorded, 'I knew Allāh by the annulment of resolutions and the frustration of plans.'[51]

Humans make up their minds about many things, resolve to undertake many things and determine to continue doing them until their end. However, they sometimes unexpectedly find themselves averse to their previous decisions, their resolutions voided and their previous determination dissipated.

Humans focus upon many things and prepare themselves, with all means at their disposal, to realize them; yet they discover their will thwarted when confronted by difficulties and obstacles that they are unable to overcome. This applies not only to weak, insignificant individuals but also to those who are powerful, influential and able to aspire to succeed in things that others are only able to dream about. For example: Shaddād (The king of Hūd's people), Nimrūd and Pharaoh. These were tyrants who had absolute power and control over entire nations. What became of them? Their stories illustrate that human will does not reign supreme, that there is a Higher Will that governs and controls the universe. For do any, other than Allāh, possess limitless, infinite power?

Shaddād sent agents using threats and intimidation to seize ornaments and jewellery in his kingdom, in order for all the gold, silver and jewels to be forged into towering pillars to adorn his magnificent palace. This was so that he would be seen to have outdone paradise, that is said to exist in the Hereafter. He persisted in transgression and aggression until his artisans finished crafting his worldly paradise, until the day his guards struck drums and bells and sang songs of celebration, the day when his people thronged the roadside to salute their mighty king. Then, in the midst of those festivities, as Shaddād placed his foot upon the chariot that would convey him, a Higher Will removed his spirit from his body to expose the magnificent event as the empty, worthless dream of the now dead and unmoving king. And so Allāh becomes known.

Nimrūd, who saw Ibrāhīm عليه السلام as the threat that would expose the falsity of his religion, determined to burn him alive. He called upon his people to protect the gods, to collect firewood and other fuel to be heaped up to make a fire in which Ibrāhīm عليه السلام, the destroyer of their idols, would be immolated and reduced to ashes. But a Higher Will transformed the fire into a cool place of safety, to the amazement of the onlookers who witnessed it. Yet another example of a plan thwarted and a will broken – so that Allāh could become known. We can all look at our own lives for examples of our hubris being thwarted.

2 Imām Ṣādiq عليه السلام and the Shipwrecked Man

Imām Ṣādiq عليه السلام was asked, 'O son of Allāh's messenger, please tell me about Allāh and what He is, for there are many disputes about Him that have perplexed me.'

Imām Ṣādiq عليه السلام responded with the question, 'O servant of Allāh, have you ever sailed in a boat?' To the affirmative response he عليه السلام then asked, 'And has it ever been wrecked in a manner in which no other boat could save you, nor any amount of swimming could bring you to safety?'

To an again affirmative response, he عليه السلام then asked, 'At that time did your heart hold out hope that there was something that could save you?'

To a yet again affirmative response, he عليه السلام then said, 'This "something" is Allāh, who is able to save and grant assistance when no one else can.'[52]

This life is an abode of ways and means by which people try to attain their aims and reach their goals. To do this, everyone must use whatever means are appropriate and whatever ways are able to convey them to their destinations. For example, if someone needs hot water they may utilize fire, if they need cold water they may utilize ice. If someone wants to travel by air, they may take an aeroplane to their destination; if by land, they may go in a car or a train; if by sea, then aboard a boat. And choices are available for whatever one is doing in any area of life.

When people meet problems they try to overcome them by conventional means. If they fall ill they consult doctors. If they need surgical procedures they go to hospitals equipped to undertake them.

If a boat one is travelling on sinks, one clings to a lifeboat, raft or driftwood – anything to save oneself from drowning. If there is nothing to cling on to one must swim and float for as long as one is able.

At the moment when all means at one's disposal are exhausted, when all hopes of being saved are lost, the human heart places all its hopes on a greater, a higher power – one above all natural means – to save it from the peril it is in. And this higher, greater power is nothing other than Allāh.

This phenomenon can be observed in all people, even those who deny belief in Allāh, when they are faced with perils that they have no hope of surviving by any normal means. This then is the means of salvation above and beyond all material means and that completely transcends them all. The Cause of causes, no doubt – the Creator of the universes!

3 Imām Ṣādiq عليه السلام in Tawḥīd al-Mufaḍḍal

Mufaḍḍal al-Joʿfi, perturbed by Abu al-ʿAwja' and his companions, voiced astonishment at the Prophet صلى الله عليه وآله being granted status on the basis of a supposed Creator, when everyone knows that nothing in the world needs any particular attention for it to be there. He discussed this with Imām Ṣādiq عليه السلام.

The Imām عليه السلام (702–765 CE) dedicated four consecutive days to providing Mufaḍḍal with teleological examples for the existence of Allāh – material that is now recorded in *Biḥār al-Anwār* – in order to dispel his unease and remove any doubts that he might have had. This is presented in four sections – the first part of each is presented below.

The creation of humankind

'Think first of the creation of the fetus in the womb, hidden in three dark areas: the dark of the abdomen; the dark of the womb; the dark of the placenta. Here it has no ability to look for food, to secure any advantage or avoid any injury. Indeed, its mother's blood flows through its body to nourish it, in the same way that water nourishes plants. When its formation has been perfected, when its body is robust, its skin able to exist outside the fluid of the womb, its sight capable of facing daylight, and its strength sufficient to endure the tumultuous upheaval of birth (which must be exceedingly shocking and uncomfortable for it), the baby is thrust from its secure, protected environment. At that time, its own blood is disconnected from its mother's blood, its sole source of sustenance, and to survive, it must seek out an entirely different source of nutrition – its mother's bosom. So, in addition to the deeply traumatic and unsettling experience of being born, the baby's sole nourishment changes from dark placental blood to the entirely different white maternal milk, that it is guided to suckle – a nourishment that is no longer continuously on stream, but is only available on demand. As the baby develops, grows and moves, it requires more solid food and so its teeth develop to allow it to chew. At puberty, males develop the hair that distinguishes them from boys and females, while girls retain the softness, beauty and freshness that attracts males to continue the species.

Mufaḍḍal, learn from the things that regulate males during these various states. Do you think that these are due to negligence or lack of attention? Do you not imagine that if blood did not circulate through the fetal body it would dehydrate and wither, as plants do without water? If its mother's birth labours did not discommode it when it had developed, would it not have preferred to remain in the womb, like an interred dead person? If, after birth, its mother's milk did not suit it, would it not die of hunger or try to eat inappropriate things that its body could not thrive on? If its teeth did not appear at the appropriate time, would it not be unable to chew and prefer to continue to suckle? And, if it did, would it grow strong, and would its mother not be so occupied with it as to be unable to attend to any other children? If its facial hair did not grow, would it not retain the characteristics of boys and women, devoid of masculine qualities? So who is it that takes care of the baby and supplies it with all it needs? Surely, none other than He who created and cared for it during its development into a human being? If negligence and lack of attention were able to establish such regulated processes, then their opposite, intention and estimation, might lead to error and impossibility. This is a horrid concept dreamed up by the ignorant: negligence does not establish correctness and contradiction does not create orderliness. Allāh Almighty is free from the things they ascribe to Him!'

The Imām عليه السلام then continued: 'If a baby was born with understanding and intellect, it would deny the world on the day of its birth, it would be perplexed when faced with what it did not know. We might liken such a baby to an intelligent person who has been transferred from one country to another. Such a person would likely be discommoded at not being able to read the literature of that country as easily as a person there of little intelligence could. If a baby was born with a developed intellect it would surely be discommoded by being carried, suckled, wrapped in cloth and placed in a cradle, despite needing such things at its age. It would not be cute, sweet and charming enough to engender warmth and pleasure in adult hearts in the manner that other babies do. So it is that a baby enters the world ignorant and heedless of its parents' possessions, incomplete in its knowledge and not discriminating about what it encounters. Its knowledge increases step by step, little by little, thing by thing, condition by condition, to progress steadily as it develops. It is completely unaware and unconcerned about the limit of its scrutiny; not baffled by what it will need to do to earn a livelihood; unconcerned about its intellect and ability to learn valuable lessons from events. It has no concept of obedience, disobedience, inattention or heedlessness.

From another point of view, if babies were born with developed intellects and were independent, then parental interest in their education might not exist and there would be none of the joys or pleasures in observing them develop and grow. There would be the option for parents to separate from their children after they were born and the result would be that children would not know their parents, with no way for them to avoid marrying blood relatives. In addition, a newly born baby with mature intellect would be forbidden to see its mother's bosom. We need to question how it is that everything in creation is established with precision, free from outlandish error?'

The Imām عليه السلام then mentioned that a child's crying contributes to its well-being and the development of its brain and sight.

He عليه السلام referred to the male and female pudenda being perfectly matched, citing reasons for their different shapes.

Mufaḍḍal said that others had made claim that all this had been created by nature, to which the Imām عليه السلام responded, 'Ask them about this nature: Is it a thing with knowledge and ability to create things or not? If they claim that it has such knowledge and abilities, then what prevents them from proving the Creator – for this is His attribute? And if they claim that it creates all these things without knowledge and purpose and its actions are correct and wise, then they should know that these actions belong to a Wise Creator, and what they refer to as nature is His law that He determined for all of His creation.'

Then the Imām عليه السلام spoke about food entering the body and how, once digested, nutriment is moved from the stomach to the liver via veins. How enriched blood is distributed throughout the body via the circulatory system. How waste materials are treated and voided.

He عليه السلام then discussed the various phases in the formation and growth of the body. The qualities that Allāh Almighty conferred upon humankind to distinguish them from lower orders of animals; the senses, their advantages, shapes and various functions. The reason why there are two of some organs and only one of others. He عليه السلام went on to speak about the blessing of food and water not resembling each another.

He عليه السلام ended by saying, 'If one sees a man's figure engraved on a wall and someone says, "that figure appeared autonomously, independent and free of external influence and control, no one made it", would you accept that statement? So, why would you refuse such a view concerning an engraving, yet accept it when it concerns living, talking beings?'

The creation of animals

Imām Ṣādiq عليه السلام began by saying that to understand animals and their formation one needs to understand the formation of the things that preceded them. 'Think of the body and shape of an animal. It is not solid like stone, for if it were it could not bend. Nor is it limp and spongy, for if it were, it would not have the ability to bear weight. Thus, it is created of pliable flesh that has the ability to bend; supported by solid bone, served by nerves, and veins to nourish it and ligaments to hold it together – with skin to cover it all. They are similar to models made of sticks: wrapped in cloth, tied by thread, and covered in gum, the sticks representing bones, the cloth the flesh, the threads the nerves and veins and the gum the skin. So, is it possible for a moving animal to appear out of negligence, inattention and without any maker, any more than it is possible for a model to appear out of negligence, inattention and without any maker?

Think about animal bodies. They too were created in the way that human beings were created. They have flesh, bones, nerves, ears and eyes. They were created in a manner that enables humankind to draw benefit from them. If they were blind and deaf humans would not be able to use them. If they did not have the disposition to obey people when tired from carrying heavy loads, they could not be used. If it is said that slaves, who have intellects, also obey when they are tired, the answer is: there are few slaves, some not willing to bear burdens in the way that animals do. In addition, it needs many people to undertake the work of a camel or a mule. If someone had to do their own fetching and carrying they would become exhausted and not have time or energy to do anything else.'

He ﷺ then spoke about the organs of the three types of animal: omnivores such as humans, carnivores and herbivores. The reason for eyes being prominent in faces, mouths unlike the human mouth that have split lower parts and so on. He continued by speaking about the behavioural habits of some creatures: the wiliness of the fox, who feigns death to lure prey to within its grasp; the ibex, that takes moisture from its food and does not drink water, yet will eat snakes. He then asked, 'Who has made the nature of these animals?'

The creation of the world

Imām Ṣādiq عليه السلام then spoke about the sky, the orbit of the heavenly bodies, weather conditions, geological formations, vegetation and the palm, providing proofs and lessons to be learned.

'Think about the colour of the sky and how it is regulated. Those with damaged sight are advised to look at it frequently, its colour being said to be beneficial for sight. Doctors also recommend those with weak sight to focus on green water containers. So why has Allāh given the sky that colour? Without doubt it does not harm eyesight and reason indicates there is a wisdom in its creation – believers take a lesson from it while those who do not believe do not even think of it.

Mufaḍḍal, think of the sun's rising and setting, that establish night and day. If day did not occur, people could neither continue their livelihoods nor manage their affairs. If the sun did not set, people would not find calm, tranquillity and rest, nor a time of inactivity for their food to be quietly digested. Eagerness for the pleasures of this life would drive them to work longer to acquire more, to collect more, to accumulate more, to the detriment of their health. Also, temperatures would increase so much under relentless sunshine, that intense heat would destroy many animal and plants. Thus, in His wisdom, Allāh ordained the sun to rise for a time and to set for a time. It is the lamp that illuminates the world in order for people to fulfil their needs, and it is extinguished for their peace and rest. Despite the contradiction between night and day, both are needed to regulate life.

Know, too, things are not ranked according to value. They might be valued differently in different markets. Some are cheap in commercial settings but expensive in scientific ones. Do not disregard anything that may be learned from a thing that has a low value. For example, chemists who value elements found in human faeces are prepared to pay handsomely for it.'

Calamities and catastrophes

'The ignorant might be pleased to cite epidemics, earthquakes, freak weather, swarms of locusts and other natural calamities and occurrences as evidence of there not being a Creator or any order in the world. We may ask them, "If there is no Creator and no Regulator, why are there not many more greater and more frequent catastrophes? Why does the sun rise each day? Why does the ocean not entirely cover the earth? Why do occasional catastrophes not cover the entire world and last forever? Can you not see that the world is protected from such enormous events, any of which would be able to destroy the world entirely? Rather, the occurrence of such catastrophes may be seen as being a sermon for humanity, and their end a mercy for them." The Muʿattilites and Manichean Christians say that if the world had a Compassionate and Merciful Creator such hateful things would not occur. Those who believe in this idea think that humanity ought to be able to live in the world without disturbance or discomfort. The danger, if this were to be so, is that humans would become so arrogant and insolent that no religion would be able to reform them. Think of the people of great status and wealth who live their lives in comfort, luxury and peace. Many forget that they are merely human beings, merely creatures, that an adversary could topple them or that harm might befall them. Thus deluded, they neglect to show mercy to the weak, to help the poor, to feel pity for the afflicted or empathy for those who are aggrieved. When misfortune strikes such people, they are provided with lessons to learn from, opportunities to realize that they have been arrogant and heedless. Those who object to and bewail the experience of painful misfortunes are like boys who reject bitter-tasting medicines, who become enraged when they are prevented from eating harmful food, who have an aversion to education and work, who always demand to be given food that they like, who choose to spend all their time playing. They do not appreciate that poor education and bad habits will result in them remaining unemployed. They do not want to be told about the harmful diseases that result from an overindulgence in over-rich food. Thus, they are not reformed and refined by education, nor cured by medicines prescribed for them.'

He عليه السلام then asked, 'How does Allāh order weak servants to recognize Him with gentle reason when He does not encompass them?'

He عليه السلام answered this by saying, 'Allāh has ordered people to recognize Him to the extent that they are able: to believe in Him, to put His instructions into effect, to refrain from what He has prohibited. He has not ordered them to encompass His characteristics. He is like a king who does not order his subjects to know if he is tall or short, white or brown. However, he requires them to yield to his authority and carry out his orders. Do you not think that a person who knocks on the door of his palace and says, "Show yourself to me or I will not listen to your words", is exposing himself to punishment? Similarly, those who do not believe in Allāh unless they have recognized His characteristics, expose themselves to Allāh's wrath.'

At the end of his lessons, Imām Ṣādiq عليه السلام said, 'Mufaḍḍal, learn what I have taught you, be among those who are grateful to Allāh, be among those who praise His favours and among those who obey His friends. I have provided you with some proofs regarding His creation and some examples regarding His precise regulations and purpose. Consider them carefully and learn lessons from them.'

Mufaḍḍal told others that he left his master, after having learned what no one had ever learned before.

Notes to Part One

1 Qur'ān 39:3.

2 Saint Anselm, born in Italy in the year 1033 CE, became a monk and later Abbot of Bec in Normandy before being appointed Archbishop of Canterbury in 1093. Philosophers know from his *Proslogium* that he was the propounder of the Ontological Argument for the existence of God. He said: 'If someone denies that God exists he is still able to understand the concept, "That than which nothing greater can be imagined".' Anselm argued that such a concept – for the greater to exist both in reality and in the mind – is greater than existence in the mind alone. For further information, refer to Hartshorne, C., *Anselm's Discovery* (La Salle: Open Court, 1965).

3 *Proslogium and Response to Guanilo,* in the series *Basic Writings* (1962).

4 *The Philosophical Works of Descartes*, ed. Haldane and Ross (New York: Dover, 1955).

5 Qur'ān 2:255.

6 Qur'ān 6:100.

7 Qur'ān 2:255.

8 Ibn Sīnā, born into a highly respected and important family in Afshana near Bukhara in the month of Safar 370 AH (August 980 CE) proved himself to be extraordinarily gifted. His bibliographer, Yahya Mahdavi, records that Ibn Sīnā wrote 242 works that covered the entire field of philosophy and sciences of the time. These deeply impressed the Islāmic East, and medieval West, where he came to be known as Avicenna.

While philosophical thought slumbered throughout the Islamic world, Ibn Sīnā's intellectual contribution elevated Shiʿite Islām to the apogee of philosophical awareness. His work *Kitāb al-Shifā* (The Book of Healing), is the most extensive philosophical encyclopaedia to have been authored by a single person. Ibn Sīnā propounded the Cosmological Argument – that the whole universe is created by a chain of causes, whose presence and continued existence has been brought about by a self-sustaining cause, that itself did not need to be caused.

As a philosopher, Ibn Sīnā adhered to the Muslim School of peripatetics that combined the principles of Islāmic belief with Aristotelian and Neoplatonic philosophy. His works discuss in depth all the arguments for the existence of God (the Cosmological, Ontological and Teleological), as well as the reality of Prophecy, use of the intellect and humankind's final return to Allāh, plus the methodology of *Kalām*. In addition to *Kitāb al-Shifā*, he wrote *Al-Ishārāt wal Tanbihāt* (Directives and Comments), and *Al-Ḥikmah al-Mashriqiyah* (Oriental Philosophy). His work on medicine, *Al-Qānūn fi al-Ṭib*, corresponds to the highest point of Islāmic medical research.

For further information refer to: Hourani, G. F., Ibn Sīnā on Necessary and Possible Existence, *The Philosophical Forum* 4 (1972) pp. 74–86; and Rahman F., Essence and Existence in Avicena, *Medieval and Renaissance Studies* 4 (1958) pp. 1–16.

9 *Al-Ishārāt wal Tanbihāt,* p. 29.

10 Ṣadr al-Din Shirazi's thought has left a lasting imprint at the highest level of Islāmic philosophy, Shiʿite consciousness and philosophical expression. He authored more than 45 works. His commentary on Suharwardi's *Ḥikmat al-Ishrāq* (Oriental Theosophy), provides a well-tested appraisal of the School of Illumination. Mulla Ṣadrā's masterpiece, *Al-Asfār al-Arbaʿah* (the Four Spiritual Journeys), has nourished Muslim philosophy and thought. His comprehensive commentary on *Uṣul al-Kāfi*, one of the fundamental books of Shiʿism, is a comprehensive exemplification of Persian Platonism combined with the authentic Prophetic philosophy of faith.

Mulla Ṣadrā focused on the existence of 'essences that exist'. His anthropology comprehensively supports Shiʿite Eschatology. After twenty-five centuries of bitter dispute between the two opposing schools of Greek and Islāmic philosophy, i.e. the School of Illumination and the School of Peripatetics, Mulla Ṣadrā's monumental work, *Al-Asfār al-Arbaʿah,* reconciled their opposing views and showed how humankind is able to comprehend truth and step towards the perfection of 'Ultimate Truth', to ascend from the world of creation (*Khalq*), towards the world of perfection (*Al-Haqq*), and then to descend and treat all of creation with measures of absolute and perfect action. Mulla Ṣadrā summarized his contribution to philosophy as follows:

a. harmony between Plato and Aristotle
b. harmony between philosophy and Prophetic teaching
c. harmony between intellectual reasoning and illumination
d. his four spiritual journeys to arrive at ultimate truth and then to live with it

11 Translated into English by W.M. Miller as *A Treatise on the Principles of Shiʿite Theology* (London: Royal Asiatic Society, 1928).

12 *Kashf al-Murād* is a commentary on *Tajrīd al-Iʿtiqād* of Nasir al-Din Ṭusi (1201–74), who is recognized to be the father of astronomy. That Nasir al-Din was adventurous in his youth is evidenced by his stay at the fortress of Alamut (the Ismāʿilī centre). The situation became dangerous when Mongols seized Alamut in 654 AH (1256 CE), but Nasir al-Din handled it so well that he became a respected advisor to Hulagu Khan and was able to intercede with him on behalf of Imāmite Shiʿites. It was he who persuaded the Mongol sovereign to build the great observatory at Maragheh in north-west Iran. He is also known as Khwajah Naṣir. Although primarily a mathematician and astronomer, he also wrote many books on philosophy. His commentary on Ibn Sīnā's '*Ishārāt*' was considered by Abd al-Razzāq Lāhijī, four centuries later, to be the best treatise on Ibn Sīnā ever written. Another work of Khwajah Naṣir's, on spiritual etiquette, is titled *Akhlāq-i Nāṣiri*. He was one of the teachers of Allamah Ḥilli, the great Shiʿite jurisprudent who died in 726 AH (1325 CE).

His famous work on theology, *Tajrīd al-Iʿtiqād* (Abstracts of the Creed) on which Ḥilli wrote a commentary, is still a text that is studied in many of today's Islāmic seminaries. Mudarris Raḍawi (1955) described Naṣir al-Din thus: '*Naṣir al-Dawlah wa al-Din* – The Sustainer of the State and the Faith,

Muḥammad Ṭusi, the unique . . . the like of whom the mother of time has not given birth'.

13 *Al-Babul Ḥadi 'Ashar,* pp. 11–12.

14 Immanuel Kant (1724–1804) was one of the most influential philosophers of modern times. In addition to his *Critique of Pure Reason*, he also authored *Foundations of the Metaphysics of Morals*, *Prolegomena*, *Critique of Practical Reason*, *Critique of Judgement* and *Religion within the Limits of Reason Alone*. In most of these works he attempts to answer three fundamental questions: 'What can I know? What ought I to do? What may I hope for?'

In his essays on religious matters, and particularly in his *Religion within the Limits of Reason Alone* (1793), Kant attempts to develop parallels between revealed religion and philosophical theology.

15 *The Complete Works of Aristotle*, revised Oxford Translation (Princeton University Press, 1984).

16 *Kitab al-Shifā* edited by M. Y. Mūsā and S. Zāyid, Introduction by Madkūr, 2 Volumes (Cairo, 1960).

17 In his *Tafsīr*, Al-'yyāshī refers to Imām Ṣādiq's report that, when the Prophet ﷺ was asked what was the very best of all that had been revealed to him, he ﷺ responded, *'Ayāt al-Kursi'* and went on to say, 'Compared with *Āyat al-Kursi*, all the galaxies and our earth are no more than a ring thrown into the vastness of a desert.'

Comparable narrations on the significance of *Āyat al-Kursi* are mentioned in Suyūṭi's *Al-Durr al-Manthūr,* and Al-Khaṭīb's *Tārikh Baghdad*. The deepest and clearest presentation of monotheism is to be found in that *āyah*.

The word *Kursi* in the *āyah* refers to the Almighty's absolute authority over all of creation. However, literalists insist that it attests to Him being physically seated on a throne, located somewhere in the heavens, an idea that has been challenged throughout the centuries. For further reading on the significance of *Āyat al-Kursi,* refer to Allamah Ṭabāṭabā'i's *Tafsīr Al-Mizān,* Vol. 2, pp. 336–341.

18 Qur'ān 2:255.

19 The Scottish empiricist philosopher David Hume is commonly considered to be the greatest philosopher to have written in the English language. His

Theory of Knowledge is a detailed elucidation of his claim that belief is 'more properly an act of the sensitive, than of the cogitative part of our natures'. To him, the mind has its own laws, namely those of association, where ideas lead on from one to another and are called forth by impressions. He concluded that our key beliefs are products of associative laws of imagination and not of reasoning, as rationalist philosophers suppose. He denies the Principle of Causality that is widely accepted in philosophy, chemistry, physics and other branches of science.

20 Muḥammad Ḥusayn Ṭabāṭabā'i was born into a family of scholars in Tabriz in north-west Iran in 1310 AH (1892 CE). He lost his mother when he was five years old and his father when he was nine. In 1925 he travelled to Najaf to attend the classes of Ayatollah Shaykh Muḥammad Ḥusayn Isfahāni and Ayatollah Nā'īni, where he studied jurisprudence and philosophy for six years. In order to specialize in philosophy, he also attended Sayyid Ḥusayn Badkūbi, the most renowned philosopher of his time. With him, Allamah Ṭabāṭabā'i studied the texts: *Manzuma* of Sabzawari, *Asfār* of Mulla Ṣadrā, *Shifa* and *Theology* of Ibn Sīnā, *Tamhid* of Ibn Tarka and the *Akhlāq* of Ibn Masquyah. He was introduced to mathematics in order to exercise his facility of systematic thought. His dedicated attention to analytical reasoning and its methodology enabled him to comprehend the works of earlier philosophers and establish his own.

Being impecunious, Allamah Ṭabāṭabā'i returned to Tabriz in 1935, where he remained for ten years. About that period he later wrote, 'I must really count this period in my life as one of spiritual barrenness because I was cut off from scholarship and reflection by the unavoidable involvement and social contact that is part and parcel of a farmer's survival.' In 1946 Allamah Ṭabāṭabā'i left Tabriz to settle in Qum and resume scholarly activities.

In Qum, where some jurists had objected to philosophy being taught, Allamah Ṭabāṭabā'i began to lecture openly on this subject. Contemporary experts in philosophy, such as Jawādi Āmuli, Ḥasan Zādeh Āmuli, Miṣbāḥ Yazdi and Jalāl al-Din Āshtiyāni, are but a few of his students of that time. We should not either forget the extended meetings between Allamah Ṭabāṭabā'i and Professor Henri Corbin that resulted in the latter's acquaintance with Islāmic Philosophy, facilitated by Professor Sayid Ḥusayn Naṣr.

In addition to his philosophical works, Allamah Ṭabāṭabā'i wrote a 20-volume commentary on the Qur'ān titled *Al-Mizan fi Tafsir al-Qur'ān* that is unique in its being the only exegetical work on the Qur'ān based upon the Qur'ān itself. Among his philosophical works, *Bidāyat al-Ḥikmah* appears in its English translation as *The Elements of Islāmic Metaphysics*, published by Islāmic College Press (London, 2003). Allamah Ṭabāṭabā'i died in Qum in 1402 AH (1981 CE).

21 *Uṣule Falsafah,* Vol. 5, p. 89. When so-called intellectuals adopted the wave of dialectical materialism that swept over Irān in the 1950s it resulted in many Islāmic beliefs, including the Existence of God, the Hereafter and the existence of the spirit being questioned. In response, Allamah Ṭabāṭabā'i wrote *Uṣule Falsafah wa Raweshe Realism* (Philosophical Principles according to the School of Realism), in order to explain the foundations of Islāmic Doctrine, refute materialism in general and dialectical materialism in particular. As the original work was extremely concise, Allamah's student, Murtaḍā Muṭahhari published a 5-volume commentary to elucidate its text.

22 Although historians record the existence of many Islāmic schools of theology, the main schools to have survived are: the Ashʿarite, Muʿtazilite and Twelver Imāmi Shiʿīte.

The scholars most influential in the spread of Ashʿarite doctrine were:

a. Abul Maʿālī Juwaynī, also known as *Imām al-Ḥaramain* – Imām of the two holy precincts. He was born in 419 AH (1028 CE) near the city of Nayshābūr and studied Ashʿarite *Kalām* under his father Abdullah ibn Yusuf and later Abul Qāsim Isfrāyinī. He was concerned with epistemological issues, particularly those that concern divine attributes. His famous work is titled *Kitāb al-Irshād.*

b. Abu Ḥāmid al-Ghazāli, was born in Ṭūs in the vicinity of Khurasān in 450 AH (1058 CE). His embrace of Ṣūfīsm, which introduced a new element into Ashʿarite *Kalām*, gained him the title 'The Founder of Philosophical Mysticism' that is traceable to *Iḥyā' ʿUlūm al-Din* – The Revivification of Religious Sciences. Ghazāli began his criticism of peripatetic philosophy in his book *Al-Munqidh min al-Ḍalāl* (Deliverance from Error). He then summarized Ibn Sīnā's views in his *Maqāṣid al-Falāsifah* (The

Purposes of Philosophers), and made his final assault on philosophers in his *Tahāfut al-Falāsifah* (The Incoherence of Philosophers).

c. ʿAḍud al-Din Ījī was born around 680 AH (1281 CE) in Īj, near today's city of Shiraz. His renown as an Ashʿarite theologian and Shāfiʿī jurist led to his being appointed chief judge to the Īlkhānīd king, Abu Saʿīd in 716 AH (1316 CE). His famous work *al-Mawāqif fi ʿIlm al Kalām* consists of epistemology, ontological principles, accidents and categories, substance, the soul, the intellect, then the divine essence and finally, eschatology.

d. Mīr Sayyid Sharīf Jurjānī, a great theologian and Ṣūfi of the Timūrid dynasty, was born in Gurgān in 740 AH (1339 CE). His famous work is a commentary on Ījī's *al-Mawāqif* that he titled *Sharḥ al-Mawāqif.* He dealt with the question of good and evil and their relationship to religious laws. He also concentrated on the doctrine of 'Unity of Being', usually associated with the school of Ibn ʿArabi and Suhrawardī's Illuminationist philosophy.

e. Saʿd al-Din Taftāzānī was born in 722 AH (1322 CE) in Taftāzān, Khurasān. He studied under Aḍud al-Din Ījī and Quṭb al-Din Rāzi. His major works include commentaries on Ījī's *al-Mawāqif* and Najm al-Din Kātibī's *Al-Risālat al- Shamsiyyah.* His views were well received by Indian Muslim philosophers and a few decades later, Siyālkutī, a prominent scholar, wrote a commentary on Taftāzānī.

Outstanding figures of the Muʿtazilite and Twelver Imāmi Shiʿīte schools appear in later notes.

23 Qur'ān 21:30.

24 In 1634 he was arrested for the crime of studying plants and other phenomena.

25 Qur'ān 41:53.

26 http://soiltesting.tamu.edu/publications/E-59.pdf

27 http://msucares.com/crops/soils/nitrogen.html

28 http://dsc.discovery.com/tv-shows/curiosity/topics/subatomic-particles-in-a-nutshell.htm/Joanna Burgess

29 Qur'ān 75:3–4.

30 *The Master and his Emissary: The Divided Brain and the Making of the Western World* (Yale University Press, paperback 2012, p. 461).

31 Professor W.F. Bynum, *Times Literary Supplement.*

32 Plato's *The Laws.*

33 Psalm 104:1–20.

34 St Paul's Epistle to the Romans 1:20.

35 *Natural Theology: Evidences of the Existence and Attributes of the Deity Collected from the Appearances of Nature* (Houston: St Thomas Press, 1972).

36 *Footprints Of God,* Arthur I. Brown, p. 102.

37 Qur'ān 16:11, 13, 65, 67, 69.

38 Qur'ān 26: 7, 8.

39 Qur'ān 41:53.

40 Qur'ān 23:115.

41 Qur'ān 21:16–17.

42 Qur'ān 51:56.

43 Majlisi, Muḥammad Baqir, *Biḥār al-Anwār* (Moassasat al-Wafā', Beirut, Vol. 87, p. 199).

44 *Nahj al-Balāghah*, Sermon 152.

45 *Ibid.*, Sermon 163.

46 *Ibid.*, Sermon 186.

47 *Ibid.*, Sermon 185.

48 *Ibid.*, Sermon 155.

49 Shubbar, Abdullah, *Maṣābīḥ al-anwār fī ḥall mushkilāt al-akhbār*, Vol. 1, pp. 204–5.

50 *Ghurar al-ḥikam wa durar al-kalim,* under the letter *'ayn.*

51 *Nahj al-Balāghah*, Maxim no. 247.

52 *Tafsir al-Imām al-'Askarī*, p. 7; *Ma'ānī al-Akhbār*, p. 4.

PART TWO

How to Know Allāh

5 Divine Attributes

In so far as affirmation of the existence of anything depends upon our ability to conceive of it, the question that presents itself is whether humankind is able to conceive of Allāh and then believe in Him.

One might say that to conceive of Allāh is impossible because in order to conceive of something we need to intellectually encompass it. However, the Divine Essence cannot be encompassed, nor is its true nature able to be known, whether in the mind or external to it. On this basis, the agnostic (*mu'aṭṭilah*) denies that we are able to know anything about Allāh or that reason is able to inform us of anything about His nature. The maximum level of such knowledge is a simple, naïve doctrine presented by the words: 'Follow the religion of old women.'

While some might imagine the above phrase to be a *ḥadīth* attributed to the Prophet ﷺ, investigation leads us to conclude that those are in fact the words of Sufyān al-Thawrī (d. 161 AH/778 CE).[1] Once, whilst 'Amr ibn 'Ubayd was talking about the Mu'tazilite doctrine of the 'intermediate position' (*al-Manzilah bayn al-Manzilatayn*), an old woman disputed with him by reciting a specific *āyah* of the Qur'ān. Sufyān, who was present during this, said: ' You should follow the religion of old women.'

However, Imām 'Ali (ع), the beacon of enlightenment on this as on many other matters, tells us: 'He may not have informed intellects of the nature of His attributes, but neither has He prevented them from attaining essential knowledge of Him.'[2]

Every 'qualified statement' (*Muqayyad*) expresses a collection of absolute concepts (*Muṭlaq*) that have been brought together to produce the qualified one. When a villager who is completely ignorant of everything outside his village hears that there is a great city called New York on the other side of the world, his mind conjures an image of a village that is many hundreds of times the size of his own. However, if we wanted to correct his mental representation, we would explain that 'New York is a city, but it is not like this one.' In the same way, we would tell a simple vendor: 'It is possible to measure weights down to 10 decimal fractions – but not with scales that are available to ordinary people.'

Al-Fāḍil al-Miqdād explained the above concept as follows: 'In truth, those attributes of His that we are able to understand are nothing other than negations and relations. And, as the nature of His essence and attributes is veiled from the gaze of dependants, no one knows what He is – other than He himself.'[3]

The Persian poet Saʿdī[4] wrote:

> O He exalted above imagination and chimerical analogies of intellects.
>
> Above the all-abundant chapters that we read about You.
>
> Our lessons are finished and our lives approach the times of their setting.
>
> Just as we began, we remain – still only beginning to describe Your beauty.

1 The Incomparability of Divine Attributes

Efforts to describe the Creator, or acquire knowledge of His attributes, call for concepts and terminologies that are beyond our ability to comprehend. Terms in common usage are not sufficient to describe that which is ineffable – for that is unutterable, indefinable and indescribable.

How can something that is finite encompass and describe that which is infinite? While we are embraced by time, space and measure,

Allāh Almighty is absolute – above and beyond such limits. Humanity, not having been created and fashioned to be perfect, cannot be expected to assess and describe 'the non-material', using the material means and methods at our disposal. As discussed earlier, every being in the world acquires its existence via 'the absolute and inherent Existent'. There is no similarity between that which is acquired and that which is inherent.

To quote Imām ʿAli عليه السلام, 'Those who attempt to compare or liken Allāh to material entities, or make reference to His sacred essence, have not in reality observed Him. Whatever is known of His essence must necessarily have been created. Allāh is the Creator and Fashioner – everything else has been caused and created. Allāh alone is only cause and not an effect.

He creates without means or instruments. He measures without need to think or reflect. He is free from need and does not draw benefit from anything. He is not bound by place or time, has no need for equipment or tools. His existence precedes time and His pre-eternity precedes all beginning.

He is not restricted by limits – for only phenomena that are perceived are defined by their own particular limits, and it is only bodies that indicate what they are like. His sacred Essence does not encompass concepts of motion and stillness – so how could it be possible for something created within phenomena to also exist in His being?

If there were motion or stillness in His essence, He would be exposed to mutation and change; would be divisible; and the pre-eternity of His being would be negated.'[5]

The fact that Allāh's attributes are entirely distinct from ours – and not able to be examined or analysed through comparisons with ours – leads us to understand that 'anthropomorphism' must be rejected for such purposes. For example, while we have abilities to perform certain tasks, these are in no way the same as Allāh's power; in our case, an attribute is one thing while the entity it describes is another. While we may boast of our knowledge, we are not one and identical with it. In our infancy there was no trace of knowledge or learning in our beings; later, through learning and experience we gradually acquire a certain amount of knowledge. Knowledge and power are two distinct aspects of our being; they are neither identical to our essence, nor integrated together with it into our being. Our attributes are accidental, our essences elemental; each one is independent of the other.

Divine attributes are fundamentally different. When we say Allāh Almighty is All-Knowing, All-Powerful, we mean that He is the source of all knowledge and all power – such attributes not being anything other than the entity they describe – despite their conceptual distinctions. In reality, His attributes are identical to His essence, for His essence does not constitute any substance to which accidents might adhere. He is 'absolute being', identical to knowledge, power, life, stability and realization; He is neither limited, nor subject to mental or external restriction.

Being nurtured in nature's focus we are at all times familiar with it, for all we see has dimension and shape within time and place, with the other properties associated with bodies. Because of our habituation to natural phenomena, we measure and assess all things through the criteria of nature, including our intellectual and rational concepts. The criteria of nature thus form the contextual background to all our scientific and philosophical investigations.

To imagine a being that has none of the properties of matter – who is 'other' than what our minds might conceive – and to understand that its attributes are inseparable from their essence, demands that we completely clear our minds of all 'material being' and progress with the utmost caution and precision.

Imām ʿAli عليه السلام, the Commander of the Faithful (*Amīr al-Mu'minīn*), spoke with feeling about humankind not imprisoning Allāh in their descriptions, saying: 'Pure monotheism and perfect faith depend upon all the attributes of created beings being excluded, negated and exempted from His sacred essence. Heaven forbid He be described by those attributes, because such descriptions misleadingly disconnect and detach His attributes from Him. If in their descriptions they add an alien imagined attribute to His essence, they make Him a partner to it and imply that He consists of two parts. Such attempts to describe Allāh are the result of ignorance and lack of awareness.'[6]

Anthropomorphism

There are a few Qur'ānic references that are utilized by those who support anthropomorphism, such as the *ayāt* that refer to Allāh's Hand, Face and Settlement on the Throne. The theologians who understood these to convey literal meanings did not think it problematic to believe that Allāh has a hand or a face. Others said that no intellectual analysis should be undertaken with regard to such *ayāt*.

The technical theological term used in discussions of narrated attributes (*Al-Ṣifāt al-Khabariah*) incorporates five different opinions on the subject.

Firstly, anthropomorphism: According to Shahristani, 'Anthropomorphists (*Ḥashawiyah*) believed that people are able to shake the hand of their Lord and that truly sincere Muslims will hug Him in this life and the next when they attain the highest point of spiritual development'.[7]

This astonishing opinion confronts common sense. As already discussed, human experiences and qualities have no bearing on divine attributes. Allāh has clearly stated: 'Nothing is able to be likened unto Him.'

Secondly, no questions of how: Abul Ḥasan al-Ashʿari[8] and his followers claimed that whilst we do not suggest similitude between the Creator and His creatures, we have no right to investigate belief in the Lord having a hand or a face. In other words, we have to 'put up and shut up'.

Al-Ashʿari said, 'Allāh Almighty has a face without anyone needing to ask how, for He has said, "The face of your glorious and gracious Lord will remain forever" [Qur'ān 55:27], and that He has two hands without anyone needing to ask how. For He has said, "I created [Adam] with both my hands" [Qur'ān 38:75].'[9]

Later, scholars including Abu Ḥanifah and Shafiʿi are reported to have said that Muslims must believe in such attributes and do not need to ask how. However, in view of the great deal of ambiguity regarding the above, Ghazāli (d. 505 AH) rejected it and considered those who literally believed Allāh Almighty has a hand, a face or descends to meet His servants on earth, to be worshippers of someone other than Allāh. He stated that when we hear a report that 'the city is in the hand of the governor', everyone with common sense understands the city to be under the full control of that governor, regardless of whether or not he has had a physical hand amputated.

Shaykh Muḥammad Abu Zuhrah, a contemporary scholar at Al-Azhar University, criticized the above opinion and rejected all physical and literal understandings of hand and face, saying that to stop questions of 'how' is to annul humanity's intellectual ability to ponder.[10]

Thirdly, leave it and do not get involved: Al-Fakhr al-Rāzi (d. 606 AH) considered narrated attributes to be an aspect of the equivocal *ayāt* of the Qur'ān (*Mutashābihāt*).[11] As Allāh Almighty has condemned those who intended to mislead others with misinterpretations of such *ayāt*, we have to leave the real meaning of such attributes to Him and not comment upon them.[12]

Fourthly, to interpret Allāh's physical attributes: Muʿtazilites are known to have applied logical reasoning to interpret all such physical attributes. Thus, they interpreted, for example, 'hand' as power or favour and 'settling on the throne' as indication of supreme authority over everything.

As the risk that flows from people interpreting the Qur'ān in accordance with their own understanding is not less than the risk of concocted similitudes between the Lord and His servants, we believe the more logical fifth opinion to be more likely to be sound.

Fifthly, criterion rather than apparent meaning: Depending on their usage, words may be understood by their literal meanings or by the metaphorical meaning they convey. As literal meanings do not necessarily convey the intended concept that flows from their use, we need to search for the meanings that are intended to portray the genuine value of something. For example, when we meet a person who has profound knowledge of a subject, then in our search for a word that will adequately convey its depth and breadth we might employ the word 'ocean'. None will understand the word 'ocean' in its literal sense despite it being used. Similarly, in describing a hero, the word 'lion' may be employed to emphasize their bravery, courage and resoluteness with no disagreement that those leonine characteristics are indeed applicable to them.

Those who presented the various opinions above seem to have forgotten the simple explanation: that in all languages, words are used sometimes to express their literal meaning and sometimes their metaphorical meaning. Thus, instead of being confused regarding 'Allāh being settled upon the throne' and stating that all have to believe it without any discussion, it is more logical to understand that the expression was used to convey Allāh Almighty's absolute, complete and perfect authority over everything. This is what is meant when the term 'criterion rather than apparent meaning' is used. In employing this methodology, Imāmi theologians have traced the usage of the various Qur'ānic words that might refer to anthropomorphisms and have examined each one separately.

Settling on the Throne

Allāh tells us in the Qur'ān that:

a. 'Your Lord is Allāh who created the heavens and the earth in six days and is firmly established upon the Throne . . .'[13]

b. 'It is Allāh who raised the heavens without pillars that you can see, then firmly established Himself upon the Throne [of absolute authority] . . .'[14]

c. ‘It is Allāh who created the heavens and the earth and all that is between them in six days, and then firmly established Himself upon the Throne [of absolute authority] . . .’[15]

Examining the *ayāt* that mention the word ‘throne’ leads us to conclude that all relate to the management and direction of the whole universe, i.e. the solar system, gravity, and the order and design that is evident in every aspect of life on and in it. If we understand the word ‘throne’, not in its literal sense but in the context of design and order, it is clear that it expresses Allāh’s absolute authority.

Allāh’s face

As quoted earlier, Al-Ashʿari said: ‘Allāh Almighty has a face without anyone needing to ask how, for He has said, “The face of your glorious and gracious Lord will remain forever.”’[16] However, as it is illogical to compare the Divine Being with human beings, no one may understand that the word ‘face’ represents the form and proportions of the features by which all human beings are recognized – namely our forehead, eyes, nose, mouth, cheeks and chin. Those who were confused by the expression ‘Allāh’s face’ resorted to banning all discussion about its real meaning saying that to discuss it is an innovation (*bidʿah*).

Some go so far as to state that a *ḥadīth* from the Holy Prophet صلى الله عليه وآله وسلم exists to claim that ‘Allāh created Adam in His own image’, upon which anthropomorphism was later based. Indeed, the true narration was reported by Imām ʿAli عليه السلام, who said: ‘When the Prophet صلى الله عليه وآله وسلم heard someone cursing another saying, “Ugly your face may be and the face of those who resemble you”, he صلى الله عليه وآله وسلم said, “Never say that because Allāh created Adam in that person’s image”’.[17]

Allāh’s hand

All clearly understand the word ‘hand’ to refer to that part of the human arm beyond the wrist, consisting of the palm, fingers and thumb. However, in a variety of languages, including Arabic, the word 'hand' may also be metaphorically employed to refer to power and favour.

Exegetes have variously interpreted the *āyah,* '[Allāh] said, O Iblīs, what prevents you from prostrating before what I have created with both my hands?'[18] Some interpreted 'hands' as power, others as favour. However, a question arises in regard to the use of the word 'hands', because even though the word 'hand' would have sufficed, most deeds and actions are accomplished by using both hands. Thus, the literal meaning of the word 'hand' would have been neither appropriate nor likely to direct attention to the actions of the agent – and the munificence of His favours – in the manner in which the plural word 'hands' does, even for acts that are not the product of any hand or hands.

Further, Allāh tells us in another *āyah*: 'Do they not see that We have created for them – out of what We fashioned with Our hands – the livestock that they own that we made subservient to them so that they may ride some and eat others?[19] This *āyah* emphasizes that Allāh Almighty is the Creator and Fashioner of all things, including the creatures mentioned in this *āyah*. It is not rational to think that Allah needed a pair of 'physical hands' with which to create them, as some apparently imagine.

The same conclusion may be drawn from the event at which people paid allegiance to the Prophet Muḥammad ﷺ. Allāh raises this in Qur'ān 48:10: 'Those who swear allegiance to you indeed swear allegiance to Allāh, Allāh's hand is above theirs. Those who break their oath break it to their own disadvantage, those who fulfil their covenants with Allāh will receive great reward from Him.' It is not logical to simplistically understand the phrase 'Allāh's hand is above theirs' as people's hands being placed upon the hands of one another, with Allāh's hand being finally placed above all of them.

2 Positive and Privative Attributes

The Muslim theologians (*mutakallimūn*) categorize Allāh's attributes as being either affirmative or privative.

The affirmative attributes (*Ṣifāt thubūtiyyah*) are:

1. power (*qudrah*)
2. knowledge (*ʿilm*)
3. life (*ḥayāt*)
4. will (*irādah*) and dislike (*karāhiyyah*)
5. perception (*idrāk*)
6. infinity, without beginning or end (*azaliyyah* and *abadiyyah*)
7. speech (*takallum*)
8. veracity (*ṣidq*)

While the majority of *mutakallimūn* consider there to be eight affirmative attributes, some deem that both 'will and antipathy' and 'infinity, without beginning or end' each consists of two attributes, and thus believe there to be ten in total.

The privative attributes (*Ṣifāt salbiyyah*) are:

1. 'He' is not composite (*murakkab*).
2. 'He' is not physical entity (*jism*), substance (*jawhar*) or accident (*ʿaraḍ*).
3. 'He' is not a locus of originated entities (*maḥall li al-ḥawādith*).
4. 'He' is not seen (*lā yurā*).
5. 'He' is without any partner (*sharīk*).
6. 'He' has no ideas (*maʿanī*) or states (*aḥwāl*).
7. 'He' is not in need of anything (*muḥtāj*).

While the reason for the categorization of the above attributes is immediately apparent, the attributes themselves, and their number, have not been determined in any clear Qur'ānic or *āḥadīth* statements (*naṣṣ*), but, rather, have emerged from implications of those attributes in Qur'ānic *ayāt* and authentic *āḥadīth*.

In order to be certain that all aspects of this topic have been covered, we also need to examine the following:

Is it appropriate to ascribe attributes to Allāh Almighty?

While this may at first appear to be a strange question, there are some who disapprove of such description.

The Ẓāhiri jurist and theologian of Umayyad Spain (383–457 AH/ 994–1064 CE), Ibn Ḥazm al-Andulusi,[20] author of some 400 works of which 40 are extant, said,

> [Allāh] has not explicitly used in His revealed word [the Qur'ān] the term 'attributes' [*ṣifāt*] or the term 'attribute' [*ṣifah*], nor has it been recalled from the Prophet ﷺ that Allāh has an attribute or attributes. Yes, indeed! And none of the Companions, nor their Successors, ever used such words, neither did any of the Successors of the Successors. Therefore, it is not permissible for anyone to pronounce such terms! And were we to say that there is a certain consensus [*ijmāʿ*] that we should renounce such terms, we would have spoken the truth. Therefore, it is not permissible for anyone to use the term 'attributes' nor believe in them, for it is a reprehensible innovation!' . . . [Then he said] . . . 'The term 'attributes' was devised by the Muʿtazilites, Hisham ibn al-Ḥakam and others like him of the leaders from the *Rāfiḍah* [an abusive term directed at the Shiʿah School of Law and its followers]. Their path was followed by a group of *mutakallimūn*, who abandoned the path of the righteous predecessors.[21]

The above statement entirely lacks scholarly precision, coming, as it did, from an exponent of the literalist school (*al-ẓāhiriyyah*), who insisted upon strictly literal interpretations of 'literal texts' (*ẓāhir*) of the Qur'ān and Sunnah, and vehemently opposed all exegesis, analysis, rationality, reflection and consideration.

It is clear that Allāh Almighty describes Himself as 'The Beneficent' (*al-Raḥmān*), 'The Most Merciful' (*al-Raḥim*), The 'Lord of the Worlds' (*Rabb al-ʿAlamīn*), 'The One Who is able to Satisfy All Needs' (*al-Ṣamad*), 'The Provider (*al-Razzāq*), The 'All-forgiving' (*al-Ghafūr*), 'Severe in Retribution' (*Shadīd alʿiqāb*), and 'The One Who splits seed and grain' (*Fāliq al-ḥabb wa al-nawā*).

Is there a single word in any language that could be used instead of 'attributes', to denote inherent characteristics, qualities or features? What motivates the paranoid delusion, suspicion, exaggerated self-importance and rigidity that would demand that intellects be denied the ability to convey meaning?

Are Allāh Almighty's attributes suprarational?

Some *mutakallimūn* argued that the human brain does not have the intellectual ability to distinguish between Allāh's perfective attributes (*Ṣifāt al-Kamāl*) and Allāh's privative attributes (*Ṣifāt al-Naqṣ*). When the Qur'ān and *āḥadīth* of the Prophet ﷺ and the error-free Imāms عليهم السلام inform us of His specific perfective attributes, we should affirm them. However, those not specifically referred to in these sources should not be affirmed.

Some Qur'ānic *ayāt* appear to allude to this, such as His saying:

> Immaculate is your Lord, the Lord Most High, above whatever they allege.[22]
>
> Immaculate is He, and greatly exalted above what they say.[23]

And the same is true for all *ayāt* that begin with phrases such as 'Immaculate is He!' (*subḥanahu*) or 'Exalted is He!' (*Taʿalā*), or 'So exalted is Allāh, the True Sovereign (*Al-Malik al-Ḥaqq*).[24]

Shaykh Muḥammad b. Yaʿqūb al-Kulaynī (249–329 AH/864–941 CE) included a section of 12 traditions, 'The prohibition on ascribing attributes that He did not ascribe to himself' (*Bāb al-nahy 'an al-ṣifah bi ghayr mā waṣafa bihi nafsahu*), in his encyclopaedic collection of *āḥadīth* called *Uṣūl al-kāfi*. Based upon this, a number of scholars accepted Allāh Almighty's attributes to be suprarational (*Tawqīfiyyah*), in having been provided by the Lawgiver Himself – a further reason for us not to apply names or attributes to Him, no matter how appropriate they may appear to be to us.

The reason behind Kulaynī's inclusion of that section stemmed from an accretion of 'questionable attributes' that were propounded, with no academic rigour, scholarly line of reasoning or rationality, during the period of the error-free Imāms عليهم السلام. He included it to end that practice and to retain the boundaries and limits of the Divine religion. One such narration from *Uṣūl al-kāfi* illustrates the point:

> ʿAbd al-Raḥīm b. ʿAtīk al-Qaṣīr narrates: I wrote to Abū ʿAbd Allāh via ʿAbd al-Malik b. Aʿyan: 'People in Iraq depict Allāh in images and drawings, so I would be most grateful to hear your explanation as to the correct doctrine of Divine Unity [*tawḥīd*].
>
> He wrote back: 'May Allāh have mercy upon you – you ask about Divine Unity and what these people believe. Allāh, to whom nothing is like, is All-hearing, All-seeing, is exalted above all the ascriptions of those who ascribe things to Him, who liken Him to His creation and fabricate lies about Him. So know – may Allāh have mercy upon you – that the correct doctrine of Divine Unity is based upon the attributes that Allāh has revealed in the Qur'ān. So remove from Allāh all falsehood [*buṭlān*] and all anthropomorphism [*tashbīh*], so that there is no privation nor similarity; He is Allāh, the Existent Unchanging [*thābit mawjūd*], Allāh is exalted above the ascriptions they ascribe to Him, and do not exceed the Qur'ān lest you do wrong after the matter has been made clear!' (*Uṣūl al-kāfi, al-Nahy 'an al-ṣifah bi ghayr mā waṣafa bihi nafsahu,* tradition no.1)

From this tradition we may conclude:

a. The reason for prohibiting the ascription of attributes to Allāh, that He has not Himself described, is to denounce those who propose corporealism and anthropomorphism.

b. Were Allāh's attributes truly suprarational – meaning that we may not describe Him as having attributes not found in the Qur'ān – how is the Imām able to describe Allāh as 'existent unchanging', when the Qur'ān contains no such description?

c. There is a difference between the suprarationality of the Divine Names (*asmā'*), and the suprarationality of the Divine Attributes (*ṣifāt*). Thus, even though we might accept that Allāh's Names are suprarational, it does not follow that this suprarationality extends to all His attributes.

To argue that Allāh's Names are suprarational some quote the *āyah*: 'To Allāh belong the Best Names, so beg Him humbly by using them, and abandon those who commit sacrilege in His names.'[25] They claim that the definite article in 'the Best Names' shows them to be 'a specific set' of names, and that 'sacrilege' means going beyond this set that has been arrived at via scripture.

There is no evidence of the definite article being used in this way, nor is such an assertion supported by the context of the *āyah,* other than in oral reports that enumerate 'the Best Names'. Indeed, 'the Best Names' is a plural attached to the definite article to indicate generality and signify that every 'best name in existence' belongs to Allāh – and that no other can lay claim to them! The word 'sacrilege' implies inclination away from the path of moderation towards extremism.

What is the appropriate manner in which to acquire knowledge of Allāh's Names?

When we contemplate an attribute, our minds naturally turn to attributes of created beings (rather than of the Creator who caused them) because we have derived such attributes from created beings. For example, when we imagine perfection, we imagine it in human form. Should we wish to apply such an attribute to Allāh as well, it would be an attribute shared between Him and His creatures. The Qur'ān explicitly states that 'there is nothing like Him'[26] and an authentic *ḥadīth* records that 'no matter what "precise meanings" for a thing you distinguish through your suppositions, they are your constructs and return to you. For example, a bee might imagine Allāh has antennae.'

This may possibly cause one to imagine that there is no way for us to know Allāh's attributes, or that attributes which have come down to us via revelation must be denied their common meanings and explanations or be reduced to privative attributes. However, distinctness and precise definition make a great contribution to the alleviation of this situation – we do not deny that there is nothing like Allāh, nor do we fail to remember what has already been said regarding the impossibility of understanding the nature of the Divine Essence. However, this in no way means that we must deny the Creator every attribute that might possibly be applied to a created being. **The great difference between Creator and created is ontological**: necessity and contingency, eternity and temporality, infinity and finitude, self-sufficiency and dependency.

For example, Allāh is All-Knowing (*'alim*). Humankind are also 'knowing'. For to know something means to encompass it and uncover it. However, Allāh's knowledge is necessary, while humankind's knowledge is contingent.

Allāh's unlimited knowledge encompasses all past, present and future universes, and all things within them, down to their tiniest subatomic particles – it encompasses all things. Humankind's knowledge is limited.

Allāh's knowledge is infinite, humankind's finite.

Allāh knows by virtue of His inherent Essence, humankind only acquires knowledge from things outside themselves.

Such differences are sufficient to nullify any similarities or equivalences (*nidiyyah*) between Allāh and His creation, without any need to affirm them.

The objection to any references to His attributes stems, without doubt, from confusion between 'concept' (*mafhūm*) and 'its substantiation' (*miṣdāq*), namely, that the external existence of creation differs from the existence of the Creator. However, this does not mean that a concept that has validity when applied to creatures cannot also be applied to the Creator.

What do we mean by Privative Attributes?

When we consider Allāh to be the 'source of all perfection', how can we possibly deprive Him of any perfection? Privative attributes are comprehended as being 'deprivation' of imperfection and need when they are associated with Him. With reference to this, al-Sabzawārī said: 'If a Muslim believes Allāh to be without imperfection [*laysa nāqiṣan*], that is sufficient for belief in the Privative Attributes – and there is no need to know each of the seven such attributes in detail because all seven stem from a single attribute.'[27]

Further, there is no need for the Privative Attributes to begin with a prefix that indicates negation, such as 'not' (*la*), or 'He is not' (*laysa*), for they are more general than that. The concepts of 'holiness' (*qudūsiyyah*) and 'immateriality' (*tajarrud*) do not include any explicit prefixes of negation.

In an attempt to establish the basis for divine attributes in the Qur'ān (being categorized as affirmative or privative) some scholars cite the *āyah*, 'Blessed is the Name of your Lord, possessed of Majesty and Magnificence'[28] as evidence. They intend privative attributes to fall under the description of 'majesty' (*jalāl*), and affirmative attributes under that of 'magnificence' (*jamāl*).

How are Divine Attributes classified?

The most common classification of divine attributes is 'affirmative' and 'privative'. However, al-ʿAllāmah al-Ṭabāṭabāʾī suggests that the three categories listed below for Allāh's attributes should be used.

The affirmative attributes of essence (Al-Ṣifāt al-Dhātiyyah al-Thubūtiyyah)

These are attributes and perfections that, when analysed, are seen to relate to 'existence' (*wujūd*), and are affirmed qualities of the Creator, such as knowledge, power, life, etc. And in so far as need and limit are deprived from being associated with the Divine Essence, every 'perfective' attribute (*ṣifah kamāliyyah*) has necessarily to be consistent with it in every detail, for perfection cannot be realized outside the Essence that is completely free of limitation, conditionality and need. These affirmative aspects are subdivided as being:

a. 'purely relational' (*iḍāfiyyah maḥḍah*), i.e. power

b. 'purely essential' (*haqīqiyyah maḥḍah*), i.e. life

c. 'essential with relational aspects' (*haqīqiyyah dhāt iḍāfah*), i.e. knowledge of other beings

The privative attributes (Al-Ṣifāt al-Salbiyyah)

These are attributes that, when analysed, are seen to relate to 'non-existence' (*ʿadam*), such as ignorance (*jahl*), impotence (*ʿajz*), evanescence (*ḥājah*), being caused (*maʿlūliyyah*) and dependency (*iḍṭirār*). All of these attributes are characterized as not being associated with Allāh.

The relative attributes (Al-Ṣifāt al-Nisbiyyah)

These are attributes that are external to the Divine Essence, such as 'creating' (*khalq*), 'fashioning' (*ṣunʿ*), 'giving life' (*iḥyā'*), 'causing death' (*imātah*) and 'granting sustenance' (*irzāq*).[29]

3 Divine Attributes of Essence and Divine Attributes of Action

Attributes of essence (*Ṣifāt al-dhāt*)

These are attributes whose opposites can never properly be applied to Allāh, nor deprived of being associated with Him under any circumstances, i.e. knowledge, power and life.

Attributes of action (*Ṣifāt al-fiʿl*)

These are attributes that can be applied to Allāh in one set of circumstances, and their opposites to Him in another, i.e. creating and granting sustenance. As it may be said, 'Allāh created X but He did not create Y.'[30]

Mystics (*ʿurafā'*) employ two further categories by which to classify divine attributes. The first refers to that which is 'graceful' (*luṭfiyyah*) and 'forceful' (*qahriyyah*), the second to that which is 'immanent' (*tashbhiyyah*) and 'transcendent' (*tanzīhiyyah*).

Graceful attributes include 'mercy' (*raḥmah*), 'grace' (*luṭf*), 'kindness' (*iḥsān*), 'forgiveness' (*maghfirah*), etc. Forceful attributes include 'wrath' (*ghaḍab*), 'vengefulness' (*intiqām*) and 'retribution' (*ʿiqāb*), etc.

Transcendent attributes – that are restricted to Allāh alone – include 'holiness' (*qudūsiyyah*) [defined theologically as being devoid of, and thus not limited or restricted by the 'quiddity' (*māhiyyah*) that is characteristic of everything else], 'lack of need' (*ṣamadiyyah*), 'absolute simplicity' (*baṣaṭah maḥḍah*) [defined theologically as being unencumbered by components or limitations], and, 'being without beginning and without end' (*qidam dhātī*). The immanent attributes that are present in all His creatures include 'seeing' (*baṣar*) and 'hearing' (*samʿ*).[31]

Are all attributes part of the Divine Essence?

Profound theological debate during the second and third centuries AH, concerning the relationship between Allāh's essence and attributes, served to confuse many Muslims.

Whilst all scholars agreed on Allāh being eternal, i.e. beyond space and time, they disagreed about His attributes being eternal. The first point of dispute concerned 'Allāh's speech' – the Holy Qur'ān accepted by all as representative of His speech. Some scholars claimed that 'not only the content of the Qur'ān, but even the paper and ink upon which it is written, are eternal!' Others pointed out that 'whilst the eternal entity does not change over time, the utterances and recitations of revelation that occur do provide evidence that what was revealed in year 2 AH is different from what was revealed in year 3 AH.'

During the time of the Abbasid caliph Al-Ma'mūn the second opinion was decreed to be the official point of view, with judges who held the first opinion not being permitted to preside over any Court of Law, nor the testimony of witnesses who held that view being accepted – stipulations that continued throughout the reign of Al-Muʿtaṣim. However, during the time of Al-Mutawakkil that decree was changed to support of the first opinion. The above is recorded in Islāmic histories as 'The crisis of the Qur'ān being created' during which period there was bloodshed and torture.

To clarify the various opinions about this, they are summarized below:

1. Ashʿarites believe divine attributes to be additional to divine essence, but as they occur alongside it they are co-eternal.
2. Muʿtazilites believe divine essence represents all of His attributes.
3. Karāmiyah believe divine attributes to be additional to divine essence but that they are only transitory.
4. Imāmiyah believe divine attributes fall within three categories:
    a. As privative attributes negate imperfection from the divine essence, these need to be referred to as being affirmative of His perfection.
    b. Attributes of action – not part of His divine essence – are relative. This means that they may or may not apply. Speech, creation and provision are examples that fall under this category.
    c. Affirmative attributes of essence (*Al-Ṣifāt al-Dhātiyyah al-Thubūtiyyah*), that uniquely coexist with His essence, are omniscience (knowledge), omnipotence (power) and life. These three attributes express the perfection and absoluteness of His existence.

4 The Significance of the Supplication (*Duʿa*) *Jawshan Kabīr'*

Communication with our Lord (*dhikr*) is acknowledged to be a formidable tool by which to attain spiritual advancement. Indeed, to develop and attain salvation the soul needs careful nurture and exercise.

Supplications developed and practised by the greatest exemplars of the faith are utilized to guide wayfarers on their spiritual journey. *Al-Ṣaḥifah al-Kāmilah al-Sajjādiyah* by Imām Zayn al-ʿAbidin ʿAli ibn al-Ḥusayn عليه السلام is one such repository of effective practices for spiritual improvement and training, on how to communicate with the Almighty. It contextualizes His Glory and Might in relation to our own insignificant helplessness.

This section focuses upon the supplication known as 'The Ultimate Protection' *(Jawshan Kabīr)*, narrated by the same Imām, as reported by both Kafʿami in *Al- Balad al-Amīn* and Shaykh Ṭūsi in *Miṣbāḥ al-Mutahajid*. In the same way that armour provides physical protection, this supplication provides ultimate spiritual protection, when articulated with absolute humility, sincerity and concentration.

It is the tradition of 'Twelver Shiʿahs' to recite this supplication on the Nights of Destiny and Measure (*Laylat al-Qadr)* during the holy month of Ramaḍan. It comprises 100 paragraphs, in each of which 10 beautiful names of Allāh are called upon – a total of 1,000 appeals. Some names appear by themselves and some are expanded.

All theological argument regarding the existence of Allāh and His divine attributes, i.e. the Ontological, Cosmological and Teleological methodologies (see Part One), find support in a variety of paragraphs of this supplication. Believers experience relief, peace and tranquillity in every line of this beautiful *duʿa*.

Mullā Hādi Sabzawārī (d. 1289 AH/1878 CE), who revived the theosophy of Mullā Ṣadrā in his *Sharḥ al-Manẓumah,* provided a commentary on the above supplication in his work *Explanation of the Most Beautiful Divine Names (Sharḥ al Asmā' al-Ḥusnā).* Sabzawārī disclosed in his introduction: 'At times I include some paragraphs from this *du'a* in the *Qunūt* of my prayers and am indebted to it for providing me with a deep appreciation of *Tawḥid*.'

To focus concentration on the content of this *du'a* is to refresh one's spirit at the divine fountain of life.

There follow some relevant references from the Holy Qur'ān and *āḥadīth*.

Qur'ān

In the holy Qur'ān Allāh emphasizes 'His remembrance' as the means to acquire eternal salvation via comprehension of the goals of creation.

1. Those who remember Allāh, standing, sitting and reclining, who reflect upon and contemplate the creation of the heavens and the earth, [say]: 'Our Lord! You have not created [all] this in vain! Glory be to You! Save us then from the torment of the fire.'[32]

This *āyah* clarifies that remembrance of Allāh does not need to be done in a particular place or with any specific posture, but rather that it should be a constant exercise. A believer may enjoy this communication with the Lord even when jogging, sitting on a bus or eating a meal.

2. The hearts of those who believe find satisfaction in the remembrance of Allāh: for without doubt, it is in the remembrance of Allāh that hearts find satisfaction . . .[33]

There are times when everyone feels concerned or worried about some worldly affair or other. It seems that stress and lack of well-being are trademarks of contemporary life. It is at these times that the utmost tranquillity can be found in the remembrance of the Lord.

3. O you who believe! Let not your riches or your children divert you from the remembrance of Allāh . . .[34]

An excuse often proffered is that people are extraordinarily occupied with their employment and family concerns so that they have absolutely no time for anything else. The above *āyah* stresses that remembrance of the Lord is of greater importance than all the concerns of this world.

4. O you who believe, remember Allāh more frequently.[35]

Some feel that five to ten minutes a day is a sufficient amount of time to devote to the remembrance of the Lord. However, this *āyah* illustrates that one should always strive to do more! It is clear that the term 'more frequently' is a relative statement. For those who are concerned about the amount of time, Imām Ṣādiq عليه السلام pointed out that it would only take the *tasbiḥāt* after the five daily prayers to constitute 500 instances of remembrance; he عليه السلام considered this the minimum.

5. . . . and remembrance of Allāh is, without doubt, the greatest good.[36]

6. So remember the name of your Lord and devote yourself to Him wholeheartedly.[37]

Even though this *āyah* was addressed to the Prophet Muḥammad صلى الله عليه وآله وسلم, Muslim scholars regard the advice, for all Muslims to follow in the footsteps of their exemplar, to be valuable.

7. So, therefore remember Me, and I will remember you; and be grateful to Me and do not reject faith.[38]

It is inspiring for believers to know that remembrance of the Lord is a two-way system. When one opens the lines of communication, one receives instant response!

8. Invoke your Lord humbly and in secret, He indeed does not like aggressors.[39]

Based upon this *āyah*, it is clearly not always necessary to articulate remembrance of the Lord for it to be valid. Even sitting on a garden bench or at a public meeting, silent, concentrated communication with one's Lord may bring awareness of His presence and illumination to a believer's heart.

Aḥādīth

The Prophet ﷺ, in his capacity as role model and deliverer of the Divine Message, detailed the Qur'ānic concept of remembrance and invocation in his sayings and actions. Below are some examples.

1. The Prophet ﷺ said, 'There is no action more loved by Allāh, or more effective in protecting His servant from the evils of this life and the next, than remembrance of Allāh.'

   Someone asked him ﷺ, 'What about striving in the way of Allāh?' The Prophet ﷺ answered, 'Striving (*Jihād*) was ordered to guarantee remembrance of Allāh.'[40]

2. The Prophet ﷺ was once asked: 'Who has the greatest merit in the eyes of Allāh?' He replied: 'Those who remember Allāh most often and remain obedient.'[41]

3. The Prophet ﷺ said, 'Every single hour which passes without Allāh being remembered will be regretted on the Day of Judgement.'[42]

4. The Prophet ﷺ said, 'Whoever remembers Allāh when shopping – while others concentrate on their own affairs and profits – will receive a thousand rewards from Allāh, who, on the Day of Judgement, will forgive them with a forgiveness the like of which no one can imagine.'[43]

5. Imām ʿAli عليه السلام said, 'Remember Allāh with perfect remembrance, and you will live the best of lives and be led to the path of salvation.'[44]

6. Imām ʿAli عليه السلام said, 'Continuous remembrance lightens both heart and brain.'[45]

7. Imām ʿAli عليه السلام said, 'Remembrance of Allāh is a believer's capital, the profit of which is protection from Shaytan.'[46]

8. Imām ʿAli عليه السلام said, 'Allāh is He whose name is a remedy and His remembrance a cure.'[47]

9. Imām ʿAli عليه السلام said, 'When you face your enemy in battle, reduce your talk and increase your remembrance of Allāh.' He عليه السلام then referred to Qur'ān 8:45.[48]

10. Imām Ṣādiq عليه السلام said, 'Uttering *'Lā ilaha illa Lāh'* is the price of Paradise.[49]

11. Imām Ṣādiq عليه السلام said, 'All things have a limit other than remembrance of Allāh. Allāh is not content with a little and demands ever more.' He عليه السلام then recited Qur'ān 33:41.[50]

12. Imām Ṣādiq عليه السلام said, 'The Prophet Mūsa عليه السلام said, "O my Lord, I sometimes find myself in a position in which I feel it inappropriate to remember You." Allāh Almighty's response was: "Remember Me in all circumstances".'[51]

13. Imām Baqir عليه السلام said, 'Three actions are of utmost importance: being fair to people, helping brothers and sisters in faith and remembering Allāh in all circumstances. In particular, remember Him when about to commit a sin, for remembrance of Allāh will prevent it from being committed.'[52]

14. The Prophet صلى الله عليه وآله said to his companions, 'Reach out and hasten to the Gardens of Paradise.' When asked where those gardens are, He replied, 'They are the "circles of invocation".'[53]

Ṭasbiḥ: Glorification of Allāh

Dhikr and *Ṭasbiḥ* are opposite faces of the same coin. Since the latter is repeated at the end of each section of the supplication of 'The Ultimate Protection', let us investigate its variety.

Allāh Almighty tells us: 'There is not a single thing that does not celebrate His glory and praise Him, but you do not understand their glorification.'[54]

Subḥan Allāh is used to describe two concepts: one an exclamation of awe and wonder at the magnificence of His work, the other to underline that Allāh is inexpressibly greater than the thing that has been described. When a physical attribute is used to attempt to convey an aspect of Allāh, people will often utter '*Subḥan Allāh*', to emphasize that such analogy bears no resemblance to Allāh Almighty – who is far beyond what has been described.

The word *Ṭasbiḥ* is also used to describe *Subḥah* – Islamic prayer beads. The verb *Yosabiḥu*, in its different tenses, is used 34 times in the Holy Qur'ān and the word *Subḥana* 41 times. Allāh Almighty tells us:

> Therefore glorify the name of your Lord, the Supreme.[55]

And this, the Prophet ﷺ ordered Muslims to do while bowing in prayer. While bowing in *ṣalah*, Muslims therefore recite, *'Subḥana Rabbi al-ʿaẓīm wa bi Ḥamdih'* – 'Glory to my Sustainer the Supreme whom I praise.'

Allāh Almighty also tells us:

> Glorify the name of your Guardian Lord, most High.[56]

And this, the Prophet ﷺ ordered Muslims to do in prostration. While prostrating in *ṣalah*, Muslims recite, *'Subḥana Rabbi al-aʿlā wa bi Ḥamdih'* – 'Glory be to my Guardian Lord most High whom I praise.'

Prostration is the closest physical expression a believer can make to portray their position in relationship to that of their Lord. This is reflected in believers' diminishing their physical presence while remembering the Lord 'Most High'.

The following *āḥadīth* explain how everything glorifies Allāh:

1. Imām Ṣādiq عليه السلام said, 'Whenever the Prophet Dāwūd عليه السلام recited the psalms, Zabur, the mountains, rocks and birds recited with him.'[57]

   This refers to the *ayāt* of the Qur'ān in which Allāh tells us: 'And We subdued the mountains and the birds to sing our praises with Dawūd.'[58]

2. Imām Ṣādiq عليه السلام said, 'The movement of every thing is a glorification of Allāh Almighty.'[59]

3. The Prophet صلى الله عليه وآله said, 'Those who recite *Bismillah ar-Rahman ar-Rahim* with certainty have every mountain echo it despite their not being able to hear it.'[60]

4. Saʿid bin Musayib said, 'I saw Imām Zayn al-Abidin عليه السلام offer two *rakʿāt* midway between Makkah and Madinah. While in prostration he glorified Allāh and all the trees and rocks echoed his glorification with him.'[61]

The interrelation between Dhikr Allāh and Ṭasbiḥ

Allāh tells us what the connection between *Dhikr Allāh* and *Ṭasbiḥ* is:

> Truly, in the creation of the heavens and the earth and the alternation of night and day, are signs for those who understand.
>
> They who remember Allāh while standing, sitting or reclining, and reflect and contemplate the [wonders of the] creation of the heavens and the earth [say], 'Our Lord! You have not created all this in vain. Glory be to You! Protect us from the torment of the fire.'[62]

Just as it is not those who come away from art exhibitions with faint memories of pretty pictures who appreciate or understand the stature and achievement of an artist, those who grasp the significance of the work and appreciate an artist's achievements are the only ones who truly understand and esteem their work. And it is only those who grasp the significance of the signs of creation, of the heavens and the earth, who are the ones who really glorify Allāh Almighty and remember Him.

The fruits of remembrance

1. *Dhikr Allāh* (Remembrance) is the key to prosperity.[63]

2. *Dhikr Allāh* (Remembrance) is nourishment for the soul.[64]

3. *Dhikr Allāh* (Remembrance) illuminates the heart.[65]

4. *Dhikr Allāh* (Remembrance) is a remedy.[66]

5. *Dhikr Allāh* (Remembrance) keeps Shaytan away.[67]

6. *Dhikr Allāh* (Remembrance) prevents hypocrisy.[68]

7. *Dhikr Allāh* (Remembrance) leads to the love of Allāh.[69]

8. *Dhikr Allāh* (Remembrance) satisfies the heart.[70]

Disadvantages of neglecting to remember Allāh

1. The lives of those who turn from My remembrance will be circumscribed and they shall be blind when they are raised on the Day of Judgement.[71]

2. For those who withdraw themselves from the remembrance of The Most Gracious, We will appoint a devil to be their intimate companion.[72]

3. Satan's plan is to create hostility and hatred between you via intoxicants and gambling, in order to hinder you from the remembrance of Allāh.[73]

The significance of Lā ilāha illal Allāh

In this supplication, two phrases are repeatedly combined 100 times after each paragraph – *Subḥanaka, Lā ilāha illā Ant'*. As we have already discussed *Ṭasbiḥ*, we now need to consider *Lā ilāha illal Allāh*.

This first part of the *shahādatain* (normally referred to as *Tahlīl*) plays an important role in the declaration of the faith in Islām. Kulaynī narrates upon the authority of the Prophet ﷺ that, 'the most meritorious act of worship is constant repetition of *Lā ilāha illal Allāh'*.[74]

Imām 'Ali عليه السلام said, 'There is not a Muslim who utters *Lā ilāha illal Allāh* without stripping away all veils and obstacles to their ascendance to the celestial realm. This utterance does not encounter sin without nullifying it.'[75]

Imām Ṣādiq عليه السلام said, 'Utterance of *Lā ilāha illal Allāh* is the entrance fee to paradise.'[76]

Al-Bayhaqi (384–458 AH) in his *Al-Asmā' wal Ṣifāt* quotes Ibn ʿAbbās saying that 'the following *ayāt* all refer to *Lā ilāha illal Allāh*:

> . . . let them fear the Lord and speak the right words.[77]
>
> . . . do you wish to purify yourself?[78]
>
> Allāh send down his tranquillity to His Messenger and believers, binding them to the word of piety.[79]
>
> Truly, angels descend to those who say Allāh is our Lord.[80]
>
> . . . those who speak the truth.[81]
>
> Those who do good receive the best, and more . . . ,[82]

Lā ilāha illal Allāh in poetry

Shaykh Muḥammad ʿAli Mu'adhin, an Iranian Ṣūfī of the eleventh century AH, illustrates this in the following lines:

The intimate companion of the soul in loneliness
  Is Lā ilāha illal Allāh
The life of the soul and the body
  Is Lā ilāha illal Allāh.
Like the Sweet song of nightingales,
  sing from the bottom of your heart
  with a hundred thousand tongues
  sing Lā ilāha illal Allāh.
Like intoxicated lovers who have lost their intellect
  and are drunk with [divine] love
  make invoking Lā ilāha illal Allāh
Like second nature to your tongue
  take the path of the men of the truth and like the pious people
  constantly invoke Lā ilāha illal Allāh.
All guardians of the abode of sanctity,
  intoxicated by divine love, profess divine unity saying Lā ilāha illal Allāh.

I swear by the religion of Aḥmad and the sayings of ʿAli,
whose station is exalted and is the intercessor of all the people of the world,
there is nothing but Lā ilāha illal Allāh.
You shall be saved from the evils of the carnal soul
If you only utter Lā ilāha illal Allāh.
You shall find your way to the realm of Allāh's Unity
If you only utter Lā ilāha illal Allāh.
O Mu'adhin! Keep your hope up at the time of death by declaring
Lā ilāha illal Allāh.[83]

Names used singly/expanded

The structure of *Jawshan Kabīr* is that in 25 paragraphs out of the 100 the Most Beautiful Divine Names appear singly, while in the remaining 75 they are either contrasted with all of creation or expanded upon.

The paragraphs in which these names appear singly are: 1, 5, 9, 13, 17, 21, 25, 29, 32, 36, 40, 44, 49, 53, 57, 61, 65, 69, 73, 77, 81, 85, 89, 93 and 97.

However, it needs to be clarified that in the paragraphs in which comparisons are made, these do not refer to Divine Essence or Attribute, because Allāh clarifies in Qur'ān 42:11 that, 'there is nothing whatever that resembles Him.'

Chapters that deal with 'The Incomparability of Divine Attributes' are included in all books on Islāmic theology.

A few examples of each of the above categories are given below.

Single attributes

Al-ʿAdl. The Just: Humankind's greatest benefit arises from accepting Allāh Almighty's justice, for His plans, decrees and actions are just, whether they correspond with our will or not. In the same way as patients accept the medication that doctors prescribe to alleviate physical and mental suffering, our acceptance of Allāh's divine and absolute justice alleviates the suffering that stems from objecting to and resisting Allāh Almighty. Absolute faith lies in acceptance of what He has ordained with absolute justice.

Al-ʿAfūw. The Pardoner: One of the recommended forms of remembrance (*Dhikr*) by which to seek purification and divine inspiration is, while in prostration, to repeatedly call upon *'al-ʿAfūw*. In Islamic teaching, there is a firm link between the concepts of pardon and repentance. Our share in this quality lies in our pardoning others. Thus, in one of his supplications, Imām ʿAli ibn Ḥusayn عليه السلام says, 'O Allāh, you ordered us to pardon those who have wronged us; we have now wronged ourselves and have no one other than You to pardon us.'

Al-ʿAliyy. The Most High: Being Most High (*Al-ʿAliyy*) refers to difference in rank rather than to difference in spatial height. Rational grading is mere perception. One is above another in that it is the 'cause', the other below in that it is 'contingent' on the former. Thus it is that the cause of all existence holds the highest rank. Everything in existence holds a lower or inferior rank to Allāh the Most High – *Allāh al-ʿAliyy.*

Al-ʿAzīz. The Eminent (The Almighty): While a scarce gemstone might be referred to as being precious or rare (*ʿIzzah*) or (*Nudrah*), *ʿAziz* refers to one who is distinguished or noble. *Al-ʿAziz*, when associated with Allāh, is translated as Eminent because it is the highest degree of nobility, preciousness and rarity. To be *al-ʿAziz* requires four related qualities: being rare, being needed, being difficult to approach and being Almighty. Difficulty of access is related to greatness of need and remarkableness of quality. So, while all life depends on sunlight, sunlight is not considered eminent because it is readily accessible. And, notwithstanding the sun's uniqueness for earth, there are apparently millions of suns in the universes.

Absolute rarity depends upon uniqueness in actuality, as well as possibility. The ultimate degree of being needed lies in being needed by all creatures, both for their attributes and for their existence and survival. Only Allāh Almighty fulfils these qualities.

Al-Bāqī. The Everlasting: Allāh is the pure and perfect Existent, whose existence is inherent and not acquired. He is beyond time, space and limit. He is the Creator of the whole universe and, since time is related to motion, it is easy to comprehend that before there was anything in the cosmos, there was no motion and, consequently, no concept of time. While all physical and material beings have an end, Allāh, who is beyond time and material measure, is eternal and everlasting.

All creatures, including human beings, exist within the boundaries of their limitations while Allāh Almighty exists without boundary. He is Omnipresent in the sense that the whole universe is merely the result of an act of His, and an expression of His grace and bounty.

Al-Baṣīr. The All-Seeing: The attribute that *Al-Baṣīr* represents is the perfection of seeing and witnessing all things. For *Al-Baṣīr*, everything is visible, be it as yet undisclosed, distant, secreted, concealed, or in the future. His sight, without eyes, pupils, or lenses, is free from distortion and has such clarity that both the inner and the outer appearance of things are obvious to Him.

In comparison, human sight is deficient and sometimes fails us completely. Our sight, concerned only with the outer appearance of things, is not equipped to glimpse that which is interior and secret, or even, at any distance, the detail of things.

Dhul-Jalāl wal-ikrām. The One Full of Majesty, Bounty and Honour: According to Islāmic theology and creed (*ʿIlm al-Kalām*), Allāh Almighty's attributes are of two types: attributes of affirmation such as knowledge, power, wisdom and life; and attributes of privation, such as not having a body, not having any needs and not occupying space. For Qur'ānic reference for these types of attributes, some theologians refer to Qur'ān 55:78. Here, *Al-Jalāl* refers to His privative (not being associated with) attributes and *Al-Ikrām* to His affirmative or affirming attributes. '*Dhu*' in Arabic simply indicates ownership. *Dhul-Jalāl wal-Ikrām* thus refers to Allāh Almighty possessing both affirmative and privative attributes. On the affirmative side He is the owner of bounty and honour; on the privative, He is so beyond imperfection as to be truly Majestic. Here, being privative of imperfection affirms His perfection. In other words, His is the most perfect existence.

Al-Hādī. The Guide: The simplest level of guidance is that which helps every creature meet the requirements of its life. Thus, it is He who guides the infant to the breast once it has left the womb, the chick to peck for food when it emerges from the egg and the bee to build hexagonal combs, without any of these creatures needing to learn such things.

We need guidance, not only to obtain knowledge of the theory and practice of the doctrines we believe in, but also to perceive the extraordinary truths that open new and wider spiritual horizons.

Al-Ḥāfiẓ. The Best Preserver: Allāh, *Al-Ḥāfiẓ,* preserves all that is in the heavens, the earth and everything that lies between them. He preserves and perpetuates existence by:

1. Sustaining: preserving, as in sustaining the heavens, earth and all therein.
2. Safeguarding: preserving by safeguarding orderly arrangement and identity, e.g. water from being permanently transformed into steam or ice, fresh water from being permanently transformed into salt water.
3. Reconciling: Preserving by reconciling the balance between inimical forces, i.e. between heat and cold, moisture and dryness, etc.
4. Reinforcing: preserving by reinforcing to overcome a condition, i.e. when coldness or moisture are overtaken by heat and dryness, cold moist rain is sent to reinforce, revive and re-establish those conditions.
5. Equipping: preserving by equipping creatures with protective instincts, senses, limbs and memory so that they may perceive danger, learn how to defend themselves, fight or escape, and acquire and accumulate knowledge to promote their progress and survival.

Al-Jalīl. The Majestic: The Arabic word *Jalla* means to be exalted and sublime. When *Jalla* is associated with anything, it indicates that it is far above and beyond everything else. For example, to afford a King or Queen the highest respect within society, he or she is referred to as *Ṣāḥib al-Jalālah* (his or her majesty). Thus, the most appropriate translation for *Al-Jalīl* is 'The Majestic'.

Every attribute of majesty is distilled in *Al-Jalīl*, the Supremely Majestic Being. For *Al-Jalīl* is immeasurable in might, dominion, knowledge, wealth, power, space, time and existence. He has power over every atomic particle in the universes of His creation. His mercy, generosity, compassion and treasures are without limit.

The majestic amongst humankind are the intelligent and the learned, who are distinguished by their generosity, discernment, compassion and nobility of spirit, despite not having temporal power.

Al-Karīm. The Generous, The Noble: *Al-Karīm* represents infinite generosity and infinite nobility – infinite generosity in that He generously grants His creation absolutely everything it requires for its existence; infinite nobility in that it is He that has originated all Creation.

Our generosity is limited to those to whom Allāh – The Most Generous – has specifically granted this quality. They are not content when not able to give to or assist others. It is Allāh, Lord of the Throne of Honour, who determines who is born of noble and pure lineage and who will work justly and tirelessly out of love for Him. It is not those who lay claim to the illusory status of inherited wealth, land owned, or their connection with those in ruling positions, but those to whom Allāh has granted that quality, who are truly honourable and noble.

Al-Malik. The King (Sovereign): The Arabic root for both this name and the one immediately above is 'M-L-K', which may indicate several different meanings:

1. *Malik* refers to the King or supreme authority.

2. *Mālik* refers to the owner of something.

3. *Malak* refers to an Angel (plural *Mala'ikah*).
4. *Melk* and *Mulk* both refer to land, property or other material things owned.

The common thread behind all the above is power and authority.

Al-Malik is the one who is sovereign of all that is in the universes, who does not need any of His creation, despite all of it needing Him.

It was previously thought that humans who claimed sovereignty submitted to Allāh's rule alone and needed nothing other than Him. History, however, records few kings who served Allāh in preference to their own egos. Now, at the dawn of the twenty-first century, it is clear to most that kings, queens and rulers are themselves dominated by political/economic powers at home or abroad.

Examples of those ruled by Allāh alone may, thus, only be found amongst the Prophets and error-free Imāms who, guided by Him, in turn guided others.

To aspire to the quality of *Al-Malik* is to focus one's life on Allāh alone and not to be ruled by desire for any of the things of this world.

Al-Muṣawwir. The Fashioner: The Fashioner describes the aspect of the Almighty that orders the quality and finish of individual components, as well as their integration and coordination, in order that they may work together to fulfil their function and discharge their obligations.

So fine is the order of everything in the heavens and earth that, if any part should be altered, all order would be abolished. This applies on both a macrocosmic and a microcosmic scale. The greater one's understanding of its detail, the greater one's comprehension of the organization of the universe, its arrangement and the name *Al-Muṣawwir.*

As all knowledge exists in a form that corresponds to the thing known, those souls who aspire to the quality of *Al-Muṣawwir* must, according to their ability, acquire the disposition, organization, arrangement and 'form' of all material and spiritual things that exist in the heavens and earth.

Al-Nūr. The Light: Light is an attribute of Allāh and a symbol of guidance. It is manifested in both creation and legislation. Allāh is the light through which every creature comes into existence and through which every creature is guided towards its final goal. This goal – the fruit of true guidance – is salvation, bliss and satisfaction. In Qur'ān 24:35 'light' illuminates the surroundings. 'Niche' (*mishkāt*) refers to the point at which Allāh's names and attributes become manifest. The *mishkat* is a recess in a wall, high above the ground, and the Divine light, according to this parable, is located in it above everything that has been created (i.e. above all the universes). The lamp, the core of real illumination, is inside glass and protected from all outside interference. Like a bright star, this illumination shines in a world in which all understand that illumination depends upon a power source. To indicate the source of that light, the above *āyah* refers to it being generated from the oil of a blessed olive tree.

Mulla Ṣadrā Shirāzi elaborates on this attribute and the *āyah* of the same name in his commentary, translated and annotated by Latimah Parvin Peerwani, published by ICAS Press (London, 2004).

Al-Raḥim. The Most Merciful: *Al-Raḥim* represents the perfection of mercy in both this world and the next. Allāh is prepared to extend mercy to the deserving as well as to the undeserving, and it is only He, the Most Merciful of the Merciful, who is able to meet every need.

To aspire to reflect the quality of *Al-Raḥim* is to intend to be merciful to those in need, even when not able to meet their need; it is to aspire to, not to turn from; it is to help all to the extent of one's ability.

Al-Raḥmān. The Beneficent: To aspire to reflect this quality of goodness may lead us to attempt to protect others from the potential consequences of their own actions. Such desire to be of service requires one to behave with consideration, not contempt, and to offer wise and gentle counsel.

Al-Raḥmān relates to the 'all-encompassing' mercy bestowed upon believer and unbeliever alike. This is the most frequent meaning of this word in the Qur'ān and the reason for the prayer taught by Imām ʿAli ﷺ to Kumayl, beginning, 'O Allāh, I beseech you by Your Mercy which encompasses all things.'

Mercy, when used as one of the 'Most Beautiful Names of Allāh', has nothing to do with people's emotional feelings but is rather an encouragement to humanity to accept His invitation to seek Him. When Allāh in His wisdom shuts one door, it is out of His mercy that He opens another for His servants.

Al-Razzāq. The Provider: *Al-Razzāq* is the Creator of sustenance and of all whom He sustains (i.e. He is the source of sustenance as well as of the creatures that benefit from it). Sustenance may serve to nourish a body while it is on earth, or nourish a soul for eternity,

> He increases or restricts sustenance to whomever He wills . . .[84]

The ability to reflect this attribute stems from knowing its essential reality, comprehending that all sustenance comes from Allāh Almighty alone, and that we cannot rely on any other than Him. Following this, Allāh grants knowledge to guide us, speech to teach us and hands to write and 'do good'. When Allāh loves someone, He makes His other creatures depend on them to the extent that those whom He loves become intermediaries between Him and His creation. It is in enabling His sustenance to reach people that we may reflect this attribute. Thus, when a father financially supports his dependants, the actual provider is Allāh because it is He who uses the family breadwinner as the channel for His provision to his dependants.

Attributes accompanied by comparisons

Paragraph 33 of *Jawshan Kabīr* includes, 'O Grandest of the Grand, O Most Magnanimous of the Magnanimous, O Most Merciful of the Merciful, O Most Knowledgeable of the Knowledgeable, O Most Wise of the Wise, O Most Ancient of the Ancient, O most Great of the Great, O Most Benign of the Benign, O Most Magnificent of the Magnificent, O Most Mighty of the Mighty.'

The use of these superlatives underlines that whatever is imagined or attained, in terms of perfection achieved in this world, is indeed insignificant in comparison to His Absolute and Unlimited Perfection.

Paragraph 95 includes, 'O Best Rememberer and Remembered, O Best Appreciator and Appreciated, O Best Praiser and Praised, O Best Witness and Witnessed, O Best Inviter and Invited, O Best Responder and Responded, O Best Comforter and Consoler, O Best Friend and Companion, O Most Desired and Sought after, O Most Affectionate and Loved.'

6 Theistic Concept of God

1 Being/Life

Al-Ḥayy is mentioned in the Qur'ān five times as one of Allāh's Most Beautiful Names. It literally means 'alive, lively, active or energetic', but in reference to Allāh, it means 'The Ever-Living'.

Two types of thing exist: one is the type whose condition does not necessarily change while it exists, for example, stone and other mineral matter. The other type develops and changes while it exists, for example, plant and animal life. After some time, this second group also deteriorates. For everything of this type, a specific moment is reached when its life on this earth comes to an end. As animals such as human beings sometimes lose consciousness while they are still alive, we realize that there is something other than our senses that keeps us alive, something that is the source of all our senses and perceptions. Its presence is referred to as 'life' and its absence as 'death'. It is this that is the source of perception and power.

If we go a step further, we realize that 'real' life, as opposed to 'temporary' life is life that cannot be overtaken by death. That the life of the hereafter is not overtaken by death, unless Allāh so wishes, shows that real life is that for which non-existence is impossible. It is, in other words, essential being. Allāh tells us in the Qur'ān, 'Rely only on the ever-living who does not die'.[85]

Ever-living, as a divine attribute, refers to pure, perfect and unlimited existence for which non-existence is impossible.

Many Muslim theologians consider life as a theistic attribute, the logical conclusion of His being omniscient and omnipotent. In the words of Allamah Ḥilli, 'It goes without saying that the One who is omniscient and omnipotent is impossible not also to be alive.'[86]

Indeed, who could be better than 'the Life Giver of everything' to be recognized as being alive?

In *Āyat al-Kursi*, the attribute of 'life' is combined with another divine attribute, *Al-Qayyūm*, which means, 'the One who Maintains the Existence of All Reality'. In precisely the same way as gravity maintains planets in their various trajectories, it is Allāh Almighty who maintains the existence and function of all reality. When a mind full of thoughts ceases to concentrate, all thoughts dissipate. Similarly, if Allāh were to withdraw His attention from the universe, everything manifest would disappear. This is the concept behind the name *Al-Qayyūm*.

Some translators infer that the name *Qayyūm* means the self-subsistent, by whom all subsist.

Imām Muḥammad al-Baqir عليه السلام elaborated on the above attribute in saying, 'Allāh Almighty existed when nothing other than Him existed, He is Light without any darkness, Truth without any falsehood, Knower without any ignorance and Life that is unassailable by death.'[87]

2 Omniscience

The Qur'ānic term for Omniscience is *Al-ʿAlīm* – the One who comprehends and has perfect knowledge of all things: the first and the last; the manifest and the hidden; the large and the small; origin and culmination. It is His knowledge that preceded the infinity of things. Everything is simply a flowering of His inherent knowledge, the source from which all existence has been derived. Perfect knowledge is disclosed with perfect clarity, and it is not possible for human beings to conceive of anything with such a degree of perfection.

Many contemporary philosophers compare this divine attribute with what human beings comprehend from their own experience. To these, we must clarify that our knowledge differs from the knowledge of *Al-ʿAlīm* in four distinct ways:

1. Our knowledge is derived from things. It is not the knowledge from which things are derived. Allāh's knowledge precedes creation, ours is the result of creation. For example, while the acquired knowledge of those who devised the game of chess may be said to have been the 'cause' of that game, the fact that there is now a game called chess is itself the 'cause' for people acquiring 'knowledge' of that game.

2. Our knowledge is based on deliberation, careful consideration, attention, reflection and contemplation; His is based on things being in His presence. He has no need to search for them. The former is defined as 'acquired knowledge' (*ʿIlm Ḥuṣūli*) and the latter as 'knowledge by presence' (*ʿIlm Ḥuḍūri*). We may recognize the difference between these two types of knowledge by examining the manner in which each of us has a clear idea of her/his organs, physical body and awareness of their inherent character. Muslim philosophers define the first type of knowledge, acquired through our physical senses, as *ʿIlm Ḥuṣūli* and our awareness of our innate character and personal qualities, such as being courageous or cowardly, generous or mean, etc., as *ʿIlm Ḥuḍūri*.

3. Despite our knowledge being vast and wide-ranging, it is finite, and not infinite. Thus, while humanity has lived on this earth for thousands of years we are still studying and trying to understand its climatic, environmental, ecological and life forms. Nor do we know all that has happened in the past or what is to happen in the future.

4. Despite being clear, the clarity of our knowledge is limited, and not limitless. Thus, despite it being clear to us that all creatures have to eat to live, we are not always clear about the result of eating a particular thing, as 'Mad Cow Disease' or Bovine Spongiform Encephalopathy clearly illustrates.

With knowledge being an attribute of our Creator, those who are recognized to be knowledgeable authorities acquire distinction, the degree of which relates directly to their level of academic achievement. It is undoubtedly knowledge of Allāh Almighty that secures the greatest distinction of all. The highest degree of knowledge is the knowledge of Allāh Almighty that enables one to come closer to Him and acquire even deeper knowledge of Him.

Allāmah Ḥilli elaborated on 'omniscience' in the following manner:

> He performs actions that are firm (*muḥkam*) and perfect (*mutqan*), and everyone who does this is of necessity knowing.[88]

In his commentary on the above, Al-Faḍil al-Miqdād made the following points:

> Among His positive qualities is His being Knowing and the Knowing One is He to whom all things are clear in such a way that what is present in Him does not become absent.
>
> And a firm and perfect act is that which includes matters strange and wonderful and unites many characteristics.
>
> There are two proofs that He is Knowing.
>
> 1. He is a free agent, and every free agent 'is knowing'. [In the terminology of 'Logic', the first premise is considered to be the minor premise of an argument, as was affirmed in our earlier discussion of the Argument from Design.] As for the major premise, know that the acts of free agents are purposeful, and it is impossible for them to be purposeful without knowledge.
>
> 2. He has performed firm and perfect acts, and everyone who does the like is necessarily omniscient. That He performs such acts is manifest to whoever considers His creation: the heavenly bodies on whose movement the characteristics of the four seasons are arranged, as explained by science; the things on earth in which wisdom appears, revealed in the three kingdoms (mineral, vegetable and animal), in the precise design

embraced by them, and in the wonderful characteristics that they possess. And if there were nothing else other than the structure of humankind, certainly the wisdom deposited in that creation and the orderliness of its structure and its senses and the benefits that depend on them would be sufficient [to demonstrate the perfection of Allāh's acts], as is indicated in the word of Allāh, 'Have they considered that Allāh has not created the heavens and the earth and all that is between them without purpose?' [Qur'ān 30:8]. And among the wonders of humankind's physiology we find that every organ/system incorporates four powers: attraction (*jādhibah*), retention (*māsikah*), digestion (*hāḍimah*) and excretion (*dāfiʿah*).

With regard to attraction, since the body constantly undergoes biological degradation, it needs the power of attraction to replace what has been degraded from it [the constant replacement of cells]. It needs the power of retention because ingested food is viscid (*lazij*), as are the organs. Hence it must have the power of retention in order for digestion to take place. Digestion is needed in order for ingested food to be broken down within the body, into forms that may be readily assimilated to nourish the body. Excretion is the expulsion of matter not needed by the body.

In consequence of the above we may conclude that everyone who performs actions that are **firm and perfect** must encompass the maximum capacity of knowledge.

Allāh's knowledge incorporates microscopic detail

Muslim theologians differed over the exclusivity of Divine knowledge: whether Allāh Almighty's knowledge encompasses the microscopic detail of every thing in His creation's past, present and future, or if His knowledge is concise and brief.

ʿAllāmah Ṭabāṭabā'ī mentions ten different viewpoints concerning this, of which we here examine only seven:

1. The Divine Being has knowledge of its own Essence but not of its effects, because while its Essence is eternal, the existence of every effect is contingent upon its cause.

   This view is rejected because awareness of consequences does not necessarily imply the existence of such consequences at any previous time.

2. **Muʿtazilites** believe quiddities have some sort of objective subsistence during their state of nothingness (*ʿadam*) and it is to this that Allāh's knowledge pertains.

   This view is rejected on the grounds of it being illogical for nothingness to incorporate any degree of existence.

3. It is ascribed to **Ṣūfis** that contingent quiddities (*māhiyyāt mumkinah*) have an epistemic substance that is subsumed in His Divine Names and Attributes prior to their creation, and Allāh's knowledge encompasses such substance.

   It is proven in Islāmic philosophy that existence is fundamentally real but that quiddities only derive from that which exists. Thus, suggestions for the existence of any quiddities, prior to the attainment of any identity, are highly illogical.

4. It is ascribed to **Plato** that God's detailed knowledge of things consists of immaterial ideas and divine archetypes that possess all the perfections of their species.

   This opinion is refuted because (1) the existence of Platonic Forms is not established; (2) if it is posited that such forms are not imaginary and do actually exist, while they might possibly provide images for knowledge that relate to contingent beings, they do not provide knowledge that relates to the Divine Essence.

5. **Suhrawardi** (549–587 AH; Head of the School of Illumination in Islāmic Philosophy) believed that all material or immaterial contingent beings are present with Allāh by virtue of their existence not being hidden from Him.

The problem with this view is that materialistic being is only compatible with our physical senses (*ʿIlm Ḥuṣūli*) and has no relation whatever to 'knowledge by presence'.

6. **Thales of Miletus** held that God knows the First Intellect, which is the first effect by virtue of the presence of its essence for Him. All other things are known to Him via reflection of their forms in the First Intellect.

   This opinion is refuted because:

   a. While it is suitable for *ʿIlm Ḥuṣūli,* it does not fit with 'knowledge by presence'.

   b. It negates the Divine Essence's Omniscience (in relation to all other things).

7. **Peripatetic philosophers** (Aristotle, Farabi and Ibn Sīnā) state that God's knowledge of things prior to their creation is by their quiddities being present in His Essence not by way of union (*ittiḥād*) nor penetration (*dukhūl*), but as universals that are sustained by the Essence through mental subsistence. His knowledge is universal in the sense that it does not change with the changes of known things. Hence, it is a foreknowledge (*ʿilm ʿInāʿi*) wherein cognitive apprehension is accompanied by its objective realization.[89]

Conclusion

Having covered the above opinions, we can conclude:

1. It is matter that causes obscurity, while immateriality (*tajarrud*) is the source of immediate knowledge/knowledge by presence.

2. Allāh knows all contingent beings before they exist, at the level of His Divine Essence. This knowledge is identical to His Divine Essence, and not at the level of contingent beings, such that one might object that there is nothing known before that object comes into existence. The Commander of the Faithful, Imām ʿAli عليه السلام, alluded to this when he said, 'He knew them before He initiated them.'[90]

3. Positing Allāh's brief knowledge (*'ilm 'Ijmāli*) rather than His detailed knowledge (*'ilm Tafṣili*) of things prior to their existence implies that the Divine Essence lacks perfection of knowledge. This is contrary to Allāh being Pure Existence that lacks no perfection whatsoever.

4. The presence of material/contingent beings with Allāh is illogical because matter is exclusive of immediate knowledge (*'Ilm Ḥuḍūri*).

5. A variety of Qur'ānic *ayāt* evidence that Allāh knows both 'Universals' (*Kulliyāt*) and 'Particulars' (*Juz'iyyāt*):

   - 'Not even an atom's weight, in the heavens or the earth, is hidden from Him.'[91]
   - 'With Him are the keys [treasures] of the unseen. None other than He knows about them, and He alone knows what is on the land and in the sea. Not a leaf falls without His knowledge, and not a grain exists in the darkness of the earth, nor anything dry or fresh that is not clearly accounted for.'[92]
   - 'Say, [O Muḥammad] If you conceal or disclose what is in your heart, Allāh knows it. He knows all that is in the heavens and the earth, Allāh has power over all things.'[93]
   - 'Allāh knows what every female will bear and what will not be accomplished.'[94]
   - 'We created humankind and know the [dark secrets] that his soul whispers to him for We are nearer to him than his jugular vein.'[95]

All-Hearing, All-Seeing

In 42 *ayāt* of the Qur'ān Allāh Almighty describes Himself as All-Hearing and All-Seeing, and thus aware of everything we utter and do. Such understanding encourages moral habits and conduct, and polite, obliging and courteous behaviour.

Muslim theologians have debated whether these two attributes should be considered aspects of His Omniscience, or themselves unique attributes? As we suggest that All-Hearing and All-Seeing is elaborative of nothing being concealed from Him, it is preferable to consider them aspects of His Knowledge.

A few Qur'ānic references to His hearing and seeing are listed below.

> . . . know that Allāh is both hearing and knowing.[96]

> . . . He is with you wherever you may be and He sees whatever you do.[97]

> . . . Allāh hears everything that you say to each other – truly Allāh is All-Hearing and All-Seeing.[98]

The error-free Imāms عليهم السلام refer to the attributes in the above *ayāt* as not being able to be compared with human physical sight and hearing.[99]

3 Omnipotence

He is Powerful (*qādir*) and Free (*mukhtār*). We begin with His being Powerful, because creation requires power (*qudra*).

'Powerful and Free is He who, if He wills anything done it is, and if He wills anything to be left it is – who acts with purpose (*qaṣd*) and will (*irādah*).' A mechanical cause does not have such abilities because of the numerous differences that exist between the free agent (*mukhtār*) and a mechanical cause (*mūjib*). For example:

1. The free agent is able to act or cease to act while a mechanical cause does not have that capability.
2. Actions of the free agent are the consequence of knowledge, purpose and will; the effect of a mechanical cause is not a consequence of knowledge, purpose and will.

3. It is possible for the act of the free agent to become manifest at some future time; the effect of a mechanical cause is not able to be separated from its cause; for example, the sun providing light and fire burning.

Allāh's omnipotence rests upon His being the infinite and unlimited existent. Inability, in its general sense, stems from one of the following three factors:

a. a shortcoming of the agent

b. a shortcoming of the object

c. obstacles that prevent the efficacy of the agent's will

Factor (a) is negated because the perfection of every aspect of the absolute existent (Allāh Almighty) excludes all possibility of deficiency.

Factor (b) is negated by Allāh Almighty's being able to grant greater capacity and abilities to enable objects to respond to His will.

Factor (c) is negated because Allāh is able to remove all obstacles that hinder His will.

In different methodology the following argument is sometimes employed: If there were something that Allāh was not able to do, is it possible to conceive of another being able to do it? If the response is that there is no such being, it signals that that action is impossible (self-contradictory). If the response is that there is another agent that is powerful enough to undertake that task, it follows that there is something more perfect in its every aspect than Allāh. However, it has already been established that the necessary being does not lack any existential perfection whatsoever.

The universality of His power

In researching the views of Muslim theologians, we uncover restrictions in their work.

1. Philosophers claim that Allāh is only able to accomplish one thing because 'the One has only one effect'.

   The above statement would only be valid if it meant that cause and effect both resemble and are compatible with each other. However, this statement is not to be understood as a numerical reference.

2. Dualists[100] believe that Allāh is not able to produce anything that is evil because He is Pure Good.

   Evil is not an essential quality of anything and is only realized in relation to that which is good. This relative concept will be elaborated upon under the heading 'Theodicy' (see chapter 7).

3. Naẓẓām[101] (Ibrāhīm ibn Sayyār, d. 231 AH) believed that Allāh is not able to produce anything that is evil.

   To respond – Evil stems from deficiency or ignorance, neither of which it is possible to associate with the absolute perfection of the Divine Essence. Our discussion here relates only to the possibility of the existence of evil.

4. Abul Qasim al-Kaʿbi (also known as Balkhi, d. 317 AH) believed that Allāh is not able to act in the same manner as His servants because their abilities only encompass obedience or disobedience, neither of which it is possible to ascribe to Allāh Almighty.

5. Abi ʿAlī Jubbā'i (d. 303 AH)[102] and his son Abu Hashim (d. 321 AH) believed that Allāh is not able to produce the same acts as His servants.

However, having explored all the evidence regarding the universality of Allāh Almighty's omnipotence, the above opinions are easy to refute.

4 Omnipresence

It is an essential principle of Islāmic faith that Allāh Almighty is everywhere and not restricted to any specific place. To Him, the whole world is manifest, with nothing whatever hidden from Him. Only that which is materially existent is able to occupy a specific space and it is illogical to imagine such existents occupying two different spaces simultaneously. However, Allāh Almighty tells us in Qur'ān 2:115, 'Wherever you turn, the face of Allāh is before you.' And in Qur'ān 57:4, 'Wherever you are, He is with you.' And in 50:16, 'We are nearer to you than your jugular vein.'

Since Allāh Almighty is an immaterial being, occupying space is not applicable to Him. As will be seen later, past, present and future are merely measures of our understanding; however, for Allāh Almighty, all things are always present – that is what is meant by the term Omnipresence.

To illustrate this concept: Prior to the invention of the digital camera, photography utilized 'film stock' on which the sequence of all the photographs 'shot' were recorded, one after another. Imagine photograph number 5 in a sequence. Clearly, all of the preceding photographs are considered to have been **past** in comparison to number 5, with all the further ones being **future**. However, once the film is developed one sees all the photographs present, none of them being past or future. Likewise, all the photographs on a smartphone.

Now for some of the science vis-à-vis time. Theoretical physicists and cosmological theoreticians utilize complex mathematics in their study of the cosmos that are not areas of expertise of the author of this book.

In a 536-page book that includes 43 pages of notes, *The Fabric of the Cosmos*: *Space, Time and the Texture of Reality*, Brian Greene, American theoretical physicist and string theorist, and professor at Columbia University, permits readers 'to walk the path of discovery and gain not just knowledge of physics' current worldview, but an understanding of why that worldview has gained prominence'.

> Yet science is still struggling to understand what space and time actually are. (p. ix)

> Einstein's paper can now be viewed as among the first to point out that quantum mechanics – if taken at face value – implies that

something you do over here can be instantaneously linked to something over there, regardless of the distance. (p. 11)

During the first decades of the twentieth century, Albert Einstein made two deep discoveries. . . . When he was done, time had become so enmeshed with space that the reality of one could no longer be pondered separately from the other. (p. 39)

A less than widely appreciated implication of Einstein's work is that special relativistic reality treats all time equally. (pp. 131–2)

. . . because it takes time for light to reach your eyes. Anything you see now has already happened. (p. 133)

But as Einstein once said, 'For us convinced physicists, the distinction between past, present and future is only an illusion, however persistent.' (p. 139)

A particular moment can no more change in time than a particular location can move in space: if the location were to move, it would be a different location in space: if a moment in time were to change, it would be a different moment in time, . . . Einstein said that the problem of the now worried him seriously. He explained that the experience of the now means something special for man, something essentially different from the past and the future, but that this important difference does not and cannot occur within physics. . . . Is science unable to grasp a fundamental quality of time that the human mind embraces as readily as the lungs take in air, or does the human mind impose on time a quality of its own making, one that is artificial and that hence does not show up in the laws of physics? (p. 141)

Even though experience reveals over and over again that there is an arrow of how events unfold in time, this arrow seems not to be found in the fundamental laws of physics. (p. 145)

Again, since the underlying laws of physics are time-reversal symmetric, there is no way for them even to distinguish between what

> we call the past and what we call the future. And since the laws of motion are responsible for how things change both toward what we call the future and toward what we call the past – the statistical/probabilistic reasoning between the second law of thermodynamics applies equally well in both temporal directions. (p. 160)
>
> Physicists have come to realize that mathematics, when used with sufficient care, is a proven pathway to truth. (p. 162)
>
> Time itself is intimately entwined with symmetry. (p. 220)
>
> We are bound to planet earth and its vicinity. And yet, because of translational symmetry, we can learn about fundamental laws at work in the entire universe without straying from home, since the laws we discover here are those laws. (p. 223)
>
> From our modern perspective, symmetries are the foundation from which laws spring. (p. 225)
>
> After centuries of thought, we still can only portray space and time as the most familiar of strangers. They unabashedly wend their way through our lives, but adroitly conceal their fundamental makeup from the very perceptions they so fully inform and influence. (p. 492)[103]

Allāh Almighty is Knower of both all that is manifest and all that is unseen. Qur'ān 6:73, 9:94, 13:9, 23:92, 62:8 and 64:18.

Whilst human beings mainly have access to manifest things (via their five senses) and only occasionally to that which is unseen (via the purification of their souls and the illumination Allāh permits to their hearts), for Allāh no such distinction exists as His knowledge is ever-present (*Ḥuḍūri*).

St Anselm's argument, 'God exists in no place and no time', may contradict His being everywhere in every place. Anselm distinguished two senses (being in a place and being present at a place) to conclude that God is in every place in the sense of His being present in every place. According to Edward R. Wierenga, 'Anselm said very little explicitly to make it clearer.'[104]

5 Goodness

In chapter 1 on the Ontological Argument, it was clarified that Allāh Almighty is the 'Necessary Existent'. That is, He is the source of every existent and the sole manifestation of perfection and completeness – perfection in the sense that He is not in any need of anything whatever, and completeness in the sense that every aspect of goodness is incorporated within His being.

The Arabic word for goodness (*Khair*) expresses two concepts: goodness itself and, when added to an adjective, the superlative quality of 'Being The Best'. However, our focus here is on the first concept – goodness itself. Allāh tells us in the Qur'ān:

> Every goodness lies in His hands.[105]

> Allāh comprehensively encompasses all the qualities of goodness . . .[106]

> When Allāh wishes something good for you, no one is able to deflect it.[107]

> Allāh is the ultimate and everlasting good.[108]

We are thus led to conclude that all of Allāh's 'Most Beautiful Names' exemplify the complete and perfect goodness that is inseparable from His Divine Essence. Everything that is beautiful, elegant, graceful or good is but a reflection of His goodness.

The 'Dawn' supplication of Imām Zayn al-ʿAbidin ʿAli ibn al-Ḥusayn عليه السلام begins with the following phrase, 'O Lord, how would it be possible for me to access any goodness that does not stem from you?'

Another divine attribute to correspond with 'His being the source of all goodness' is *Al-Barr. Birr* means kindness, especially in actions and manner. *Barr* describes devoted kindness and, at the same time, indicates a person who is replete with every type of goodness. This attribute may apply to Allāh as well as to His honourable messengers. This is why ʿIsa's behaviour towards his mother is described in Qur'ān 19:32

as being *Barr,* and in Qur'ān 19:14 the same is said of Yahya's conduct towards his parents. Furthermore, Qur'ānic terminology utilizes the plural of the word *Barr* (*Abrar*), to identify those who are righteous,

> Truly, the righteous shall drink a cup tempered with camphor that contains water from the spring that Allah's servants drink from . . .[109]

6 Simplicity/Negation of the Concept of Trinity

The peoples of the Arabian Peninsula were overwhelmingly preoccupied with the worship of idols. The Kaʿbah was itself surrounded by well-known idols such as *Lāt, ʿUzzā, Manāt, Yaʿūq* and *Nasr.* The very first declaration the Prophet Muḥammad ﷺ made at the start of the message of Islām was, 'Say that there is no deity other than Allāh if you wish to achieve salvation'. This is summarized in *Surah al-Ikhlās*:

> Say, 'He, Allah, is Unique,
> It is upon Allah that all depend.
> He fathers none nor has Himself been fathered.
> And there are none like Him'.

Three aspects stem from simplicity being a divine attribute: negation of the concept of the Trinity, negation of anything being associated with Allāh and negation of the concept that He is a compound being, that is, His being indivisible.

Simplicity is one of the most important challenges for Muslim theologians and philosophers. If a cause is supposed to contain its effects within itself, in the form of potentiality, it then follows that God must have contained within Himself all that exists. We will deal with these three aspects in greater detail, starting with the concept of Trinity.

The Prophet ﷺ wrote to call people to embrace Islām, including those in Najran, an important centre of Christianity. In response they sent a delegation that included an eminent scholar of the Christian faith and another renowned for his sagacity and wisdom. As their response to being asked if they would embrace Islām was that they were indeed already Muslim, they were asked, 'How can you be when you eat pork, worship the Cross and consider ʿIsā to be the Son of God?' When they admitted that they did believe the *Masīḥ* to be the Son of God, the Prophet's response was, 'The likeness of ʿIsā to Allāh is precisely the same as Adam's – He created them both from dust . . .' they were then asked why they did not call Adam عليه السلام Son of God when their belief was that he was not conceived by parents? A debate ensued until the *āyah* was revealed:

> But whoever disputes with you in this matter after what has come to you of knowledge say, 'Let us summon our sons and your sons, and our women and your women, and ourselves and yourselves, then let us humbly pray and invoke Allāh to curse those who lie.'[110]

The Prophet ﷺ had at first employed logic and reason in his attempt to establish the invalidity of ʿIsā عليه السلام being the Son of God. However, after rational argument failed, Allāh ordered that he challenge them to have the truth revealed via imprecation (*mubāhalah*).

Note: Imprecation, included in the Psalms, is accepted by Christians because Jesus is recorded (in Luke 24:44) to have said, 'These are my words that I spoke to you while I was still with you – that everything written about me in the Law of Moses, the prophets and the psalms must be fulfilled.'[111]

We need a little background information to understand why and how the concept of the Trinity came to be officialized by the Church, and the consequences that flowed from that process.

The Shorter Oxford Dictionary includes the definition of the word Gospel as 'The record of Jesus's life and teaching, contained in the first four books of the New Testament.'

Pertinent to this subject are (a) scholarly evidence of gospels being composed in the name of every apostle, including Thomas, Bartholomew and Philip; and (b) based upon dating difficulties and other problems, many scholars and researchers over the centuries having become convinced that the four gospels were not written by the people to whom they are ascribed. There are places in the New Testament that imply the books were written long after purported events and that the four gospels that are included were not mentioned or named as such by anyone until the time of Church Father Irenaeus, Bishop of Lyon (c. 120/140–c. 200/203 AD/CE).[112]

The 52 Christian texts, including gospels and secret documents, hidden for nearly 2,000 years until they were discovered at Nag Hamadi in Egypt in 1945 are evidence that during the spread of Christianity adherents in different areas held a variety of radically different beliefs and practices. Some of the discovered gospels, thought to have been written before those of Mathew, Mark, Luke and John, include traditions older than the New Testament. To counter such writings, which he claimed were being widely circulated from Gaul through Rome, Greece and Asia Minor, Irenaeus, bishop of the church in Lyon, wrote several volumes entitled *The Destruction and Overthrow of Falsely So-called Knowledge* (c. 180 CE). His, and other attacks on these types of texts were part of a struggle that was critical for the formation of early Christianity. When the Roman Emperor Constantine converted to Christianity and stopped the persecution of Christians, the thus-empowered bishops condemned non-orthodox writings as heretical, ordered them burned and made their possession a criminal offence.[113]

The reason for the convocation of the Council of Nicaea in 325 CE was to establish official Christian doctrine. It addressed the nature of the Holy Spirit and its relationship to the Father and Son in the Trinity – in other words, how to maintain the unity of God while insisting on the deity of someone who is distinct from God the Father. This was referred to as the Arian problem, after Arius, who used logic to argue essentially that the Son was distinct from the Father and a creature created by Him. He said that if the Father had begotten a son, then the Son began to exist, and therefore there was a period before this when he did not exist. The Father, on the other hand, is the absolute transcendent, the One without source who is the source of all reality.

While the Council of Nicaea was felt to have settled the first two persons of the trinity, the Council of Constantinople was convened in 381 CE to expand on the first two, and complete the doctrine of the third person of the Trinity, the 'Holy Spirit'. The Councils of Nicaea and Constantinople resulted in the establishment of the Nicene Creed with 'either of two formal statements of Christian belief, (a) a rare one drawn up by the first Nicene Council; (b) one drawn up at the first Council of Constantinople in AD 381, in regular use in Eucharistic worship.' (SOED)

In its fervent desire to maintain regulatory control over this officialized Christian belief, the Church strove to (a) eliminate all opinion and doctrine that countered its orthodoxy, and (b) actively spread its beliefs via universal evangelization. Hence the setting up of a judicial institution for the persecution of heresy: the Inquisition and its concomitant torture. The crusades were wars instigated by the Church for alleged religious ends; and colonial conquests were ostensibly to preach orthodox Christianity and redeem the souls of 'savage peoples' from false non-Christian belief, etc.[114]

In spite of there being only four specified gospels in the New Testament, some scholars have highlighted scriptural inconsistencies that question the official concept of the Trinity.

The New Testament sometimes suggests very little difference between the persons. It is not always easy to tell when God as Spirit is the intended reference and when the Holy Spirit; the Gospel of John often moves indifferently between Father and Son. At other times quite a sharp distinction is applied: the Son praying to the Father; the Resurrection as a unique experience of the Son, as Pentecost is of the Spirit; references to the Spirit making possible an experience of the relation between Son and Father (Romans 8:14–15; Galatians 4:6–7). . . .[115]

Alexander Hislop (1807–65) Free Church of Scotland minister and for a time editor of the *Scottish Guardian* newspaper, authored the *Two Babylons*: *Or, The Papal Worship Proved to Be the Worship of Nimrod*, released in 1858 and still popular among some fundamentalist Protestant Christians. In it he provides evidence to support his allegation that the Roman Catholic Church is a continuation of the Babylonian pagan mystery cult of Semiramis (queen and wife of Nimrod). He claims that in the spread of her cult her name was changed by different cultures but that she remained central to its prayers and that it, and its concept of Trinity, became established as 'official Christian belief' during the reign of Constantine.[116]

Modern non-Trinitarian Christian groups or denominations include Christadelphians, Christian Scientists, The Church of Jesus Christ of Latter-Day Saints (Mormons), Dawn Bible Students, Friends General Conference, Iglesia ni Cristo, Jehovah's Witnesses, Living Church of God, Oneness Pentecostals, Members Church of God International, Unitarian Universalist Christians, The Way International, and the United Church of God (Armstrongism).[117]

The idea of the Trinity is not one that is found in the Bible. Far from being part of the same being, God and Christ are quite separate. Consider the following verse, 1 Timothy 2:5: 'For there is one God, and one mediator between God and men, the man Christ Jesus.' A mediator is a go-between. For Christ to mediate between God and men, he must be separate from God, just as he is separate from the individual people he mediates for; if Christ is part of God then this verse would be nonsense.

1 Corinthians 8:6 also speaks plainly of God and Christ as separate: 'But to us there is but one God, the Father, . . . and one Lord Jesus Christ'. If God the Father and Christ were part of the one being, why would these words have been written? If they were part of the Trinity, why is there no reference to the Holy Spirit here? The only reasonable answer is that God the Father is a totally separate being from Jesus Christ.

There are two passages from the New Testament that are often used to prove the Trinity, John 1 and Luke 1:35. In reality, both of these show that the Trinity does not exist.

John 1:18 plainly states, 'No man hath seen God at any time'. It does not say 'No man hath seen God the Father' at any time, but that no man has seen GOD at any time. It is obvious from the Gospels that people saw Jesus: therefore Jesus cannot be God, or any part of God. The verse goes on to say ‘the only begotten Son, which is in the bosom of the Father, he hath declared him.’ Some other translations of this passage, which are based on other Greek manuscripts, have ‘the only begotten God’ where the Authorized Version has ‘only begotten Son’. The Greek words for ‘son’ and ‘god’ in this context are very similar, and it seems likely that ‘son’ becoming ‘god’ was a simple slip of the pen when the early manuscripts were copied. The phrase ‘only begotten God’ is also at odds with the doctrine of the Trinity. Something that is begotten has a definite beginning, and a cornerstone of the Trinity is that ‘God the Son’ has always existed.

‘And the angel answered and said unto her, The Holy Ghost shall come upon thee, and the power of the Highest shall overshadow thee: therefore also that holy thing which shall be born of thee shall be called the Son of God’ (Luke 1:35). Let us suppose that this passage does speak of the Trinity. It would seem then that the Holy Spirit is the Father of Christ, which would give a trinity of ‘God the Father & Holy Spirit, God the Son, and God the Redundant’! The more logical interpretation of this passage is that the Holy Spirit is simply the power of God.

Christ stands out in the Bible as being a sinless individual; this is a truly great achievement for a man. Sin is simply acting contrary to the will of God; therefore, for Christ’s sinlessness to be an achievement he must not be part of God.[118]

Is God a Trinity? Many Christian denominations teach that God is indeed a Trinity. However, note what the Encyclopaedia Britannica states: ‘Neither the word Trinity nor the explicit doctrine appears in the New Testament . . . The doctrine developed gradually over several centuries and through many controversies.’ In fact, the God of the Bible is never described as being part of a Trinity. Note these Bible passages:

> Jehovah our God is one Jehovah. (Deuteronomy 6:4)

> You, whose name is Jehovah, you alone are the Most High over all the earth. (Psalm 83:18)

> This means everlasting life, their taking in knowledge of you, the only true God, and of the one whom you sent forth, Jesus Christ. (John 17:3)
>
> God is only one. (Galatians 3:20) [119]

Is Jesus Almighty God? Jesus's opposers accused him of making himself equal to God (John 5:18; 10:30–33). However, Jesus never claimed to be on the same level as Almighty God. He said: 'The Father is greater than I am.' (John 14:28)

Jesus's early followers did not view him as being equal to Almighty God. For example, the apostle Paul wrote that after Jesus was resurrected, God 'exalted him [Jesus] to a superior position.' Obviously, Paul did not believe that Jesus was Almighty God. Otherwise, how could God exalt Jesus to a superior position? (Philippians 2:9)[120]

Negation of anything being associated with Allāh

This subject, referred to by Muslim theologians as *Tawḥīd,* expresses Allāh's 'Oneness'. Serious debate remains with regard to the appropriateness of this attribute being ascribed to Allāh Almighty, because 'One' (*Wāḥid*) is a numeric concept that is applied to materialistic beings. This is why in *Surah al-Ikhlās* He is described as 'Unique' (*Aḥad*) rather than 'One'.

The aim of this discussion is not to prove that the essence of the Necessary Existent is one, because no one has ever posited the existence of two infinitely necessary existents; nor is the Qur'ān concerned with proving such an idea. Discussions of polytheism and monotheism are in reality debates about whether there is only one object to worship and seek favour and grace from, or many.

Over the years, Muslim philosophers have explored a variety of arguments to prove Allāh's 'Oneness'.

The first argument

The oneness of the universe indicates the oneness of its creator.

This argument comprises four premises that need to be clarified.

1. The universe is properly attributed oneness in both reality and nature.
2. There is no universe other than our own.
3. A single effect is the product of a single cause.
4. The Necessary Being is necessary from every aspect and modality.

We may arrive at the **first premise** once we have examined the three theories that concern the connection between the various parts of the universe.

1. There is no connection between the different parts of the universe. The term 'The Universe' is nothing more than an expression of the sum total of the assorted parts and particles in existence that have no real connection one to another. It is like a box into which various items are put. If there is any connection between the parts of this universe, it is only between a series of successive events, some of which are the causes of others. There is no connection either between the physical components of the universe, that are perceived to be individual corporeal entities. What follows is that if we would posit the non-existence of some of these parts, or a complete change of their states or positions as the result of an external agent, such change would not effect any alteration in the universe itself.
2. The bodies that make up the universe are connected in the same manner as the parts of a machine. Machine components work in harmony with one another in accordance with their specific arrangement; each performs a unique and necessary function in the production process. Any change, addition or subtraction of these parts will affect the efficiency of its operation. Based upon this, if we posit the non-existence of some parts of the universe, the stability of the whole universe would be affected.

The law of gravity exerts enormous influence over the connectivity of various parts of the universe. Similarly, it is proven scientific fact that any change of a planetary body in the solar system affects the whole system.

3. The connectivity between the different parts of the universe is finer and deeper than that of parts of a machine; it is more akin to the connection of the limbs and organs of a single body. Thus, a single life, a single personality, governs the universe.

   In examining the above, we conclude that philosophers incline towards the third theory and reject the others. Thus, the first premise is: The universe is properly attributed oneness in both reality and nature.

The **second premise** is explained here in the words of Blaise Pascal (French scientist and religious philosopher, 1623–62 CE), 'The universe is an infinite sphere, the centre of which is everywhere, the circumference nowhere.' Thus, it is not possible to imagine the existence of any universe other than our own.

Cautionary note: In theological terminology the word 'universe' refers to everything other than Allāh Almighty, and in this context is not to be misunderstood to mean 'planets'.

The **third premise** (a single effect is the product of a single cause) is an established and generally accepted precept in philosophical discourse.

The **fourth premise** (the Necessary Being is necessary from every aspect and modality). This is necessarily true, for if it were not so, it would lead to a contradiction in terms – The Necessary Being would have to be viewed as being contingent and thus not the Necessary Being.

The second argument

Multiple creators are mutually contradictory.

This argument – technically referred to as *Burhān al-Tamānuʿ* – is alluded to in, 'Had there been gods other than Allāh they [heaven and earth] would surely have collapsed.'[121] This may be expressed:

(a) *In simple terms*. If there were more than one creator, conflict and contradiction would arise between competing wills, with each one having the potential to obstruct the others. In such situations the will of one would have to overpower or negate the will of the others. The first position is impossible because the Necessary Being is perfect; it is not possible for that perfection to be overpowered.

The second position would lead to the destruction of the universe because none of their wills would be guaranteed effective. A clash of interests would occur, either as the result of self-centredness and the pursuit of personal interest, or from ignorance and inability to understand – all qualities that it is illogical to apply to the divine being.

(b) *Philosophically* – based upon the analysis of three premises. The **first** of these is that the Necessary Being is necessary from every aspect and modality. It follows from this that all attributes of the Necessary Being are actual and not potential. Thus, when we definitively state that He is Omniscient, we mean that He is actually and necessarily 'All-Knowing'. And when we describe Him as Omnipotent, we mean that He **is** 'All-Powerful', not that He has the potentiality of so becoming. The obvious conclusion from the above is that it is impossible to imagine an acquiring existent not being obtained from the Inherent Existent.

The **second** premise: the philosophical definition of 'causation' is that the realization of everything is dependent upon its cause. Thus, an effect does not have two modalities, one being 'existence', and the other 'dependency upon a creative cause'. Rather, the existence of an effect is nothing other than its dependency upon its cause.

The **third** premise: it is illogical for an action or effect to move 'from potentiality to actuality' without the motivation of an external agent or cause. In other words, it is not possible for a melon seed to develop into an actual melon without intervention by an agent, be that human or mechanical.

According to the first premise, when conditions are met for the existence of any contingent being, the necessary consequence is for it to acquire the property of existence. However, if it were hypothetically posited that the Necessary Being is a multiple existent, each of them would be in the position to grant existence. According to the second premise, once existence is granted by an agent (its creator) there is no longer any need for another agent to grant existence to the same effect. As for the third premise, there is no imaginable precedent of any creator over others. Having explained the above, we may **conclude** that multiple creators would lead to nothing at all being created and this is the core understanding of *Burhān al-Tamānu*ʿ.

The third argument

In addressing his son Imām Ḥasan, Imām ʿAli عليه السلام said,

> My son, know that, had your Lord had a partner, that partner's messengers would have come to you. You would thus have seen the effect of that partner's sovereignty and power and would know their acts and attributes. But there is only One God who has described himself – and none oppose Him in His sovereignty.[122]

A concomitant of divinity is for prophets and messengers to be sent to guide humankind. Thus, it would not be unreasonable to expect that had there been a deity other than Allāh, that deity too would have sent messengers, and those who received revelation would have realized that revelation had two different sources. However, searches throughout written history have not provided a single such example; indeed, all the evidence from such searches refers only to the existence of ONE true god.

Negation of the concept that He is a compound being

The doctrine of simplicity in regard to this aspect of *Tawḥīd* is focused on the negation of spatial or temporal particles being incorporated in the Divine Being. No Divine Attribute can be understood in material or physical terms because His existence is beyond space, time and measure. This has already been discussed under the heading 'The Incomparability of Divine Attributes' (chapter 5).

It follows then that no real distinction can be made between the Attributes of Essence and the essence itself. Omniscience, omnipotence and life are logically not separable from the concept of divine necessary and perfect existence. In Qur'ānic terminology this is explained as Allāh being 'The First' and 'The Last'.

Another logical consequence regarding simplicity is: If it were posited that the Divine Being is of a compound nature, it would follow that He would need assistance from the particles of His composition to accomplish His wishes. However, by definition, the Divine Being is without need.

7 Eternity

Our comprehension of the concept of 'time' is based upon the rotation of the earth around its axis and its orbit of the sun. From the latter it is unanimously agreed that this orbit be divided into 365 days; and from the former, that each day be subdivided into 24 hours and broken down further into minutes and seconds. Without such motion it is unimaginable for time to exist.

Before the solar system, galaxies and planets came into being, or more precisely were created, there was no motion and consequently no concept of time. It follows that a timeless God can have no past, present or future, and thus it is illogical to imagine that He has any human characteristics – He does not forget, regret, feel relief or cease to act.

Now, to focus on the above-mentioned Divine Attributes, the First (*Al-Awwal*) and the Last (*Al-Ākhir*).

> He is the First, and He is the Last.[123]

It is He who gives life and causes death. The beginning was established by His existence and to Him is the last return and destination.

It is He who is eternal and who is the focus of those with spiritual aspirations.

By its very definition, the eternal is self-existent; it could never have been non-existent nor can it ever be terminated. It has no beginning because if we were to suppose a beginning for it, we would have to admit that it was non-existent before that. In the same way, eternal can be neither a compound nor a mixture, because compounds or mixtures depend for their existence upon their constituent parts. Therefore, if we accept that eternal is self-existent, we cannot accept that its existence is dependent upon any component or part.

The eternal cannot be subject to change, because change would render it either better or worse. If a change made it better it would imply that the eternal was not perfect prior to that change. We have, however, already concluded that that which is eternal is perfect and not in need of anything. Equally, if the change were for the worse, it would imply that the eternal had been in need of something to make it perfect.

Because Allah is eternal and everlasting, He is beyond both time and space. The concept of time is related to motion, a characteristic of matter. However, as it is clear in Islāmic theology that Allāh Almighty is neither a body nor a substance, motion, change or alteration are not relevant to Him. Everything perishes, while it is He alone who is everlasting, eternal. Thus, He is The Last and nothing is able to exist after Him.

Imām ʿAli عليه السلام explained the above in the following way:

> He commences creation without means or instruments. He measures without recourse to thought or reflection. He is free of all need and derives no benefit from anything. Time and place do not accompany Him and tools and instruments do not aid Him. His existence precedes all time, and His pre-eternity precedes all beginning.[124]

8 Will

One of the divine attributes traditionally included in Theistic Concepts is that Allāh Almighty both 'Wills and Dislikes'. However, Muslim theologians have differed as to what the two words, 'Will' and 'Dislike', actually mean. Abul Ḥasan al-Baṣri said: 'In this context, Will signifies that Allāh knows the benefit of an action (*Maṣlaḥah*), and it is this benefit of that action that triggers its being performed.' Al-Balkhi[125] said: 'Will, in the context of divine acts, means His knowledge of them, and in the context of the actions of others, it means His commanding them.'

Muslim theologians debated as to whether 'will' is an Attribute of Essence or an Attribute of Action. The Ashʿarites, Karramites and a group of Muʿtazilites claimed 'will' to be a quality that is extra to Divine Essence – that it is itself separate from power and knowledge (by the fact that He is Omnipotent and Omniscient). Sayyid Niʿmatullāh Jazā'iri (d. 1112 AH) said: 'Imāmi theologians employ rational argument to prove that Divine Will is identical to Divine Essence, even though it is transmitted in various *āḥadīth* as being one of the Attributes of Action.'[126]

For a deeper understanding of the subject we need to look at the following *āḥadīth:*

1. ʿAṣim ibn Ḥamīd narrates that he asked Imām Ṣadiq عليه السلام, 'Is Allāh always willing?' To this he عليه السلام responded, 'One does not will, unless there is something that is to be willed – Allāh is always knowing and powerful and thus, He wills.' What we gather from this *ḥadīth* is that Divine Will is a relational attribute (*Ṣifah iḍāfiyyah*) and, as explained earlier, it is not possible for relational attributes to be identical to the Divine Essence. In brief, Knowledge and Power are both pre-eternal while Will is originated.

2. Muḥammad ibn Muslim narrates that Imām Ṣādiq عليه السلام said, 'The Divine Will is originated.'

3. Sulaymān ibn Jaʿfar al-Jaʿfari narrates that Imām Riḍā عليه السلام said, 'Wanting (*Irādah*) and Willing (*Mashiyyah*) are Attributes of Action. Whoever claims that Allāh is eternally wanting and willing is not a monotheist.' This *ḥadīth* underlines the importance of accurately describing/classifying attributes.

4. Abu Saʿid al-Qammāṭ narrates that Imām Ṣādiq عليه السلام said, 'Allāh created Divine Will – and then created everything else through it.' We thus conclude that nothing exists in the universe that has not obtained its existence via Divine Will. Therefore, Divine Will is understood to be the medium through which all things emanate.

Shaykh Ṣadūq concluded from all the above that Divine Will is one of the Attributes of Action. He said. 'Neither wanting nor willing, nor satisfaction nor anger, nor any attribute that resembles these should be included in the Attributes of Essence. Allāh is eternal in His power and Knowledge but not necessarily eternal in His will.[127]

Distinguishing knowledge from will

Bukair ibn Aʿyan asked Imām Ṣādiq عليه السلام: 'Are Allāh's Knowledge and Will always in mutual agreement, or do they sometimes differ?' His عليه السلام response was that knowledge differs from will. For example, one might well say, 'I will do such and such if Allāh so wills', but never, 'I will do such and such if Allāh knows.' He concluded by saying, 'Allāh's knowledge precedes His will.'

We should note that the words *Irādah* (Wanting) and *Mashiyyah* (Willing) are frequently treated as synonyms in both the Qur'ān and the *āḥadīth*. However, some sources indicate that they in fact differ from one another. Muʿallā ibn Muḥammad asked Imām Ṣādiq عليه السلام how Allāh knows. His عليه السلام response was, 'He knows, wills, wants, determines, decrees and enacts . . . thus knowledge precedes will, will comes second, wanting third and it is His determination that leads Him to decree that something be enacted.'[128]

In-depth examination of the term Will discloses that it may be used to convey two different meanings.

The **first** is 'wanting', as opposed to disliking, or, put in another way, liking as opposed to disliking. This meaning cannot appropriately be applied to Allāh's Essence because, as explained earlier, Will is a relational attribute. In instances in which 'willing' is referred to as an attribute of action, it is employed to convey the understanding that no creature is emanated from anything other than Divine Will. The **second** meaning is that the Divine Essence is indeed the source of all manifest things. Allāh knows the perfect design and order for all things; thus, knowledge (Omniscience) is an immediate inference to His Essence.

9 Speech

All Muslims believe the Holy Qur'ān to be Allāh's word. Indeed, Allāh refers to the Qur'ān as being His speech (see Qur'ān 9:6). As will be later explained, revelation is considered to be direct communication between Allāh and His Messengers عليهم السلام. Fierce disagreement arose between **Muʿtazilites** and **Ashʿarites** regarding Allāh's speech (the Qur'ān) being created or eternal.

Qāḍi ʿAbdul Jabbār[129] (a famous Muʿtazili theologian, d. 415 AH) stated that, 'in reality, speech is nothing other than well-organized alphabets enunciated by the human voice. Allāh Almighty graces His creatures with bounty and provision and similarly created His speech, to be articulated outside of His Essence – and not in any way as a part of it.'[130] The Muʿtazilites argued that:

1. Speech is directed to an audience and audiences are clearly not eternal. If it is to be claimed that Allāh's speech is eternal, it would follow that the audience too would be eternal. Take, for example, Allāh's words, 'establish prayer' – had these been eternal it would follow that those who acted upon them would also be eternal. Clearly, none other than Allāh Almighty is eternal.

2. Divine messages delivered, specific to the nations being addressed, are different from the divine messages delivered to other nations by other prophets. It is not possible for the Divine Essence to be subjected to differences and changes.

3. We know that the Holy Qur'ān was revealed to the Prophet Muḥammad ﷺ over a period of 23 years. It is thus clear that Allāh

Almighty communicated with His Final Messenger at different times and places. Had any of these specific communications been eternal they could not have been revealed at different times.

The Muʿtazilites also relied upon a variety of Qur'ānic *ayāt* to support their opinions:

1. 'When your Lord told the angels, "I am going to appoint a vicegerent upon the earth . . ."'[131] The word 'when' is an adverb that relates to time, meaning that Allāh's words to the angels were spoken at a particular moment and such an occurrence cannot be interpreted as being eternal.
2. '. . . [this is] a book whose verses were arranged in a specific order, and then elaborated upon by the One who is All-Wise, All-Aware.'[132] The adverb 'then' indicates that the *ayāt* were successively revealed.
3. 'If any idolater seeks your protection, grant it to him until he hears the word of Allāh . . .'[133] For the 'word' of Allāh to be heard, combinations of vowels and consonants – represented in non-eternal man-made alphabetic constructs used for written language – need to be vocalized.
4. 'Indeed, We sent it down on the Night of Measure.'[134]
5. 'Whatever *ayāt* that We abrogate or cause to be forgotten, We bring [in its place] one that is better than it, or like it.'[135] We cannot imagine abrogation ever to have taken place if it is not originated, because an eternal entity is not subject to change and alteration. For example, Allāh Almighty ordered believers, who sought private meetings with the Prophet ﷺ, to give alms prior to their appointments. This proved difficult for the companions to comply with. Historical records inform us that the only one to act upon this Qur'ānic instruction was Imām ʿAli عليه السلام. In order to remove what was seen to be a burden, Allāh later abrogated this ruling.[136]

However, the Ashʿarite theologian Al-Ījī (d. 756 AH) commented

> on the above, saying: 'We do not deny what the Muʿtazilites believe regarding Divine Speech; indeed, we call it verbal speech. However, we prove that there is another speech that is eternal.'[137]

Abul Ḥasan al-Ashʿari propounded the idea of 'internal speech' (*Al-Kalām al-Nafsī*) in order to escape the fact that speech is nothing other than well-organized alphabetic enunciations by a human voice. He supported his statement by citing the poem:

> Indeed speech arises in the mind.
> And is then articulated by the tongue.

History confirms that the Abbasid Caliph Al-Ma'mūn adopted **Muʿtazilite** opinion and supported the idea that the Qur'ān had been created. In his insistence that this opinion should remain integral to all aspects under his dominion, he ruled that no judge in any court within his realm was to be allowed to hold any opposing opinion: a ruling that resulted in the dismissal of many judges. Furthermore, witnesses' opinions on the subject of the Qur'ān being eternal or created were required to be established prior to their being granted permission to testify before the courts. This situation continued throughout the reign of Al-Muʿtaṣim until Mutawakkil reigned and overturned that ruling in favour of the **Ashʿarite** view: that the Qur'ān is eternal. Some of their extremists even claimed that not only the words of the Qur'ān, but even the paper and ink it is written upon are eternal!

Aḥmad ibn Ḥanbal[138] (d. 241 AH) expounded: 'The Qur'ān is Allāh's speech that has not been created. Whoever claims it to have been created is not a believer (*kāfir*), and any who claim the Qur'ān to be Allāh's speech – without characterizing it as being created or not – is worse than the one mentioned previously.' He went on to say: 'Whoever does not consider these people *kāfir* is not different from them.' He referred to Allāh Almighty speaking to Mūsa ﷺ, saying: 'Mūsa directly heard Allāh's speech and was given the *Torāh* from His hand.'[139]

The head of the Ashʿari School of Theology (Abul Ḥasan al-Ashʿari, d. 330 AH) similarly stated, 'We say that the Qur'ān is Allāh's speech and that it has not been created. Whoever believes it to have been created is a *kāfir*.'[140]

Abul Ḥasan al-Ash'ari also said that Abu Ḥanifah was a *Mushrik*, one who associated others with Allāh, and that he believed in the Qur'ān being created, until he was examined by Ibn Abi Layla and repented in order to save his life.[141]

As **Imāmiyah** theologians consider speech to be an attribute of action and not of Divine Essence, it follows that all attributes of action are created and not eternal.

10 Wisdom

> 'Glory be to You. We have no knowledge other than that which You taught us. Truly You alone are the All-Knowing, The All-Wise.'[142]

Since *'Ḥikma'* is wisdom, *Al-Ḥakīm* is The Wise. In the Qur'ān, this divine attribute is combined with *Al-'Alīm* (The Omniscient) 38 times and with *Al-'Aziz* (The Eminent) 47 times. It also appears with *Al-Khabīr* (The Most Aware) four times.

Al-Ḥakīm represents the perfection of unlimited wisdom – wisdom of the highest rank that uniquely comprehends Allāh and all His attributes; wisdom which is all-seeing, all-hearing and all-knowing. Perfect wisdom that ensures absolute justice is all-encompassing and entirely independent. It is the wisdom that originated and sustains universes; that understands the function, purpose and interrelation of every atom and element; that maintains the mind, body and soul of His creatures; and the wisdom that knows who is faithful and who is faithless.

Only those with knowledge of Allah, the Highest and Most Sublime, may be considered to be truly wise. They alone benefit from the reflection of His knowledge. Those who are wise do not concern themselves with temporal advantage but with the benefits of the world to come.

With regard to ethical values, the one who is wise is the one who behaves in a proper and appropriate manner. The Wise, as one of the

Beautiful Names of Allah, refers to the fact that His decisions to give or withhold are based on the appropriateness of Him doing so.

Appropriateness and inappropriateness

Muslim theologians differed over the source and criteria by which acts are classified appropriate or inappropriate. The Ashʿarites believed that the only source for the above lies in religious texts. However, the Imāmiyah and Muʿtazilites held an opposing view. For them, it was human intellect (*ʿAql*) that, prior to any divine revelation, guided people as to what was appropriate or not. To elaborate, we need to discuss various aspects of appropriateness.

There are three different aspects to be established and considered:

1. Things that are harmonious and consistent with human nature are considered to be both good and appropriate. A practical consequence of this is that things which are not harmonious and consistent with human nature are considered inappropriate and unacceptable. For example, beautiful scenery, pleasant fragrances, pleasing voices and the aroma of appetizing meals are consistent with human nature as they all elicit favourable responses. In contrast, the revolting stench of rotting flesh, the braying of an ass and call of a peacock, which are thought disagreeable and unpleasant by most, are not harmonious and consistent with human nature and are thus considered to be inappropriate and unacceptable.

   Clearly, such aspects are not included in theological discussions regarding wisdom as a divine attribute.

2. Signs and indications of perfection and enhancement are considered to be appropriate, while those that point to low character or moral and intellectual debasement are considered inappropriate. An example of the former might be knowledge and, of the latter, fecklessness and ignorance.

   This aspect too has nothing at all to do with theological discourse.

3. Actions worthy of intellectual approval are considered appropriate; those that warrant intellectual condemnation are thought inappropriate. An example of the former is justice and fair treatment of others, of the latter, injustice and transgression. This aspect has been the subject of fierce debate between the Ashʿarites, on the one hand, and the Muʿtazilites and Imāmiyah on the other.

   In such theological debates, the Ashʿarites refute that the human intellect has the ability to differentiate between appropriate and inappropriate behaviour. For them, this can only be determined via available texts. However, Muʿtazilites and Imāmiyah believe that even with texts – that (hypothetically) do not mention this subject – divine guidance provides sufficient information for us to intellectually derive, by a process of reasoning, the appropriateness of justice and fairness and the inappropriateness of transgressions and injustice.

In-depth examination points to there being a conformity between reason and religion, in that reason distinguishes honesty to be intrinsically good, without regard to people being Muslim or not, or professing religious or secular viewpoints. In other words, the processes of reasoning and rational judgement conclude that honesty constitutes appropriate behaviour, and, conversely, that dishonesty constitutes inappropriate behaviour. This applies to all religions, faiths and cultures, all of which value justice and condemn its being transgressed.

Ashʿarite views pay scant regard to the above, their stance being that what the Law Giver approves of is appropriate and what He disapproves of is not. Thus, reason plays no part whatever in their judgements. Ashʿarites do not consider it problematic for Allāh to (hypothetically) direct all prophets and righteous people to the punishments of Hell and direct all sinners to the rewards of Paradise. Thus, if one were to argue that this would be unjust, their response would be that whatever Allāh does is both beautiful and appropriate.

So how do they respond to the question: what if Allāh the All-Wise's promise to reward just behaviour with the assurance of good outcomes in paradise is later broken by His countermanding that promise? A question that is clearly too illogical, irrational and indeed nonsensical to be considered for even a nanosecond.

Abul Ḥasan al-Ashʿari (d. 330 AH), in an apparent attempt to circumvent this nonsensicality, said: 'It is not inappropriate to believe that Allāh will punish all believers and reward all disbelievers, but He is not going to do so because He is not a liar.'[143]

Is it possible that Allāh places unbearable burdens on His servants?

Having discussed Wisdom as a divine attribute, we now need further discussion.

Can we suppose that Allāh commands His servants to do things that are beyond their capacities and abilities? Logically, it is both inappropriate and impossible for the Lawmaker to demand that people do things that He has not equipped them to do, for example, to fly without having been given the means to achieve flight. Similarly, it would be impossible to demand that a thick rope be threaded through the eye of a needle.

The above is confirmed in many Qur'ānic *ayāt* such as: 'Allāh does not impose upon souls duties that are beyond their abilities.'[144]

In spite of the above, Ashʿarites deem that there is no problem whatever in the Almighty imposing His rulings upon humankind, notwithstanding these being beyond their abilities. This is evident from Abul Ḥasan al-Ashʿari's work.[145] To support their view, Ashʿarites referred to a few Qur'ānic *ayāt,* such as, 'When [on the Day of Resurrection] the shin bone is laid bare and they [all sinners] are called to prostrate themselves they will not be able to do so.'[146] They claim that if, on the Day of Judgement, sinners are ordered to do what they are unable to do, it is also possible in this life for something to be imposed that is beyond people's abilities.

One may argue that comparisons between this life and the hereafter are not valid as this life is the time for effort and striving, and the hereafter, the time to receive rewards or punishments for what one has done during one's lifetime. Indeed, this is explained in the *āyah* that follows the one above, 'They had indeed been called to prostrate while they were in perfect health.'[147]

Another *āyah* that Ashʿarites claim supports the appropriateness of Allāh placing unbearable burdens on His Servants is, 'If you fear that you will not be able to act justly [in regard to polygamy] only marry one [wife].'[148] However, in *āyah* 129 of the same Surah Allāh tells us. 'You will never be able to observe justice between women [your wives] even if you are eager to do so . . .' They claim that this *āyah* indicates that despite men's inability to act justly in these circumstances, they have nevertheless been ordered to do so.

Our understanding of the command to treat wives equally is that the husband is to meet all his wives' financial, psychological and physical needs. Nonetheless, they are still advised to refrain from favouring one wife above the others so that none feel ignored, marginalized or suspended from favour.

7 Challenges to the Rationality of Theistic Belief

1 The Problem of Evil/Theodicy

Theodicy can be defined as 'the vindication of divine providence in relation to the existence of evil'.

Philosophers claim that the existence of evil is a problem for those who believe in an omnipotent and wholly good God. Expressed simply, the problem states that because God is omnipotent and wholly good, believers have to account for the existence of evil.

There is evil in the world, so either God could not prevent it (even though He is, by definition, omnipotent), or He did not choose to do so (even though He is, by definition, benevolent).

One solution put forward for solving the problem is to argue that evil is merely the absence of good and thus not truly real. Another solution is to attribute all defects to the 'free will' of humankind. (Creatures with free will are thought to be more like God and thus more perfect than creatures without such freedom.) Yet another solution put forward is that evil is an illusion of the human mind. However, because within the Bible there is no attempt to regard evil as anything but dark, menacingly ugly, heartrending and crushing, then for people with Biblical faith there can be no doubt that evil is entirely real and in no sense illusory.

Unlike scientific problems that may be solved by observation, or practical problems solved by decision or action, the reconciliation of contradictory beliefs poses a problem of logic.

If any two of the three hypotheses are true (evil exists, yet God is omnipotent and wholly good), then the third must be false. This is seen to be both illogical and contradictory. Philosophers demand that theologians adhere to all three, and then call them illogical and inconsistent when they do.

One may, of course, also pose the question, 'Is God a dictator who controls every breath and forbids every comment or challenge, or is He a tolerant God who permits people to choose their own actions while He retains ultimate authority?'

The question still remains: evil may be a lack of goodness, but why is there a lack of goodness if God is All-Powerful and All-Wise. Could He not have created a perfect world? Wasn't He clever enough or was He not powerful enough to do so?

Some Greek philosophers tried to answer these questions. Plato (c. 428–348 BCE) argued that all things are imperfect copies of their 'Forms' and that such imperfections are a feature of everything. Aristotle, on the other hand, divided all possible existents into five logical probabilities:

1. that which is completely good and has no trace of evil
2. that which has much good but has a little evil
3. that which has much evil but has a little good
4. that which has equal proportions of good and evil
5. that which is completely evil and has no trace of good

He then suggested that the last three do not exist within this universe in which only the first two may be observed.[149]

There were other answers to this question such as the Augustinian, the Anselmian and the Irenaean; however, the focus of our subject relates to Islām.

The Islāmic answer to the problem of evil

The Islāmic response to what others regard as the problem of evil and suffering may be discussed in the following ways.

Must creation be absolutely good and perfect?

We can posit that Allāh Almighty had four possible options vis-à-vis Creation:

a. not to create anything

b. to create only that which is absolutely good and perfect

c. to create only that which is absolutely evil

d. to create variety within creation with differing capacities for goodness

The **first possibility** – that Allāh did not create anything – cannot logically be true. It contradicts His being Omnipotent and being able to evidence His Power, Wisdom and Greatness everywhere. For example, if a poet, lauded because he is at the height of his profession and thus has the capacity to express himself with the greatest eloquence, is asked to demonstrate his artistry by reciting a line of his poetry, but is not able to do so, how can he possibly be described as a poet, let alone a leading one.

The **second possibility** is also illogical. For Allāh to create only absolute good and perfection contradicts the belief that perfection and absolute existence are His alone. Had He, despite it being possible for Him to do so, only created that which is absolutely good and perfect, and eliminated every shortcoming and darkness from the universe, His creation would have been as perfect as He Himself is.

The **third possibility** is both illogical and nonsensical. How could the 'Source of Mercy and Every Good', who cares for all of His creation, produce only that which is evil?

The **remaining possibility**, and only logical one, is that Allāh created the whole universe, including humankind, allotted certain measure to each and distributed 'shares and dividends' according to their different capacities and abilities. It is human beings who imagine differences to be shortcomings or suffering.

Shortcomings are not evils

It is ridiculous to claim a fighter plane to be the equivalent of a passenger plane. To assume fighter aircraft carry the same number of passengers as jumbo jets is apparent nonsense. Each is good and fit for its own purpose, environment and circumstances.

Since the whole universe is finite (ruled by time, space and measures) it falls within 'limits'. This means that every part of creation is limited, including human beings, who are not able to achieve perfection. Human beings' knowledge is limited and their powers bounded by limitations.

Everything created has its own degrees of goodness. A racehorse and a heavy horse are both of the same species. Yet, despite insurance companies being prepared to insure some racehorses for millions of pounds, they are not prepared to insure heavy horses for similar amounts. Is it reasonable to expect every horse on earth to win races?

We need horses and we need ponies. We need camels and we need oxen. Each has its own purpose and function. A bat's blindness may be considered a shortcoming, but not an evil. The All-Knowing and All-Wise Creator provided it with extraordinary abilities to enable it to 'see', not by sight but by determining the position from which its own sounds are reflected back to it.

Furthermore, evil is not an absolute philosophical concept but a relative one. This being so, it is only by making comparisons between one thing and another that either can be considered to be an evil. If one omits such relative considerations, there is no longer any evidence of evil.

Plato described the non-existence of evil in the following way: Killing with a sword is not evil because it is the result of the sharpness of the blade, the strength of the one who slays, that person's boldness, and the vulnerability of a neck. All these evidence perfection. The only thing that might be imagined to be evil is the loss of life of the deceased that results. This illustrates that evil does not exist as an entity.

A balance between good and evil

Some say that evil contradicts goodness. However, it is possible to suggest that evil and good function in tandem rather than in conflict. To act without regard to danger is foolhardy. Bravery is overcoming fear and acting in the face of an understood danger. People cannot comprehend generosity until they witness neediness. That people bear difficulties with patience and tolerance cannot be understood without foreknowledge of calamity or atrocity. One cannot establish honesty and integrity without also affording the possibility for dishonesty or lack of integrity. To express it in another way: sunshine is most appreciated during times of cloudiness.

This does not stop with values and ideas; it applies equally to experiences and feelings. One enjoys a cool drink most when it quenches extreme thirst. Marie Antoinette's statement, 'Let them eat cake', illustrates that she lacked comprehension of poverty and hunger.

'Life' is not appreciated without awareness of the possibility of 'death'.

The lesser of two evils

Allāh tells us in the Holy Qur'ān that He destroyed Nūh's people via a flood. The punishment of Lūṭ's people and the drowning of Pharaoh and his cohorts exemplify choice of the 'lesser of two evils'. For example,

- The first evil – permitting evil-doers to live allows them to afflict the innocent.
- The second evil – the destruction of a few to protect society from a greater evil.

Most legal systems claim imprisonment to be a means by which to rehabilitate criminals. It is considered a benefit for society rather than an act of revenge. For example, when children are abused by those in positions of trust such as parents, carers or teachers, society has no option other than to imprison the abusers to prevent the continuation of their evil behaviour.

Imām ʿAli ﷺ refers to the results of bad actions:

> Allāh Almighty tries His creatures in respect of their evil deeds by decreasing fruits, holding back blessings and closing His treasury of good, so that those who wish to repent may repent, and those who wish to turn away from evils may turn away. Allāh the Glorified has made seeking His forgiveness a pouring down of livelihood and mercy on people – as Allāh has said,
>
> 'Seek forgiveness of your Lord, truly, He is ever most forgiving. He will send you abundant rain from the heaven, will help you with wealth and sons, will make for you gardens and will make for you rivers.'[150]
>
> Allāh may shower mercy on those who repent, give up sins and hasten to perform good acts before their death.[151]

We conclude, the removal of a diseased organ may save a patient's life.

A clash of interests

It is arrogant to expect others to obey you. All who exist in the universe have their own interests and goals. All try to manage their lives and environment. However, some want to change the circumstances of others simply to further their own interests.

If on a cloudy day one leaves home without an umbrella, only to discover on the way back that it is raining and muddy everywhere, is it reasonable to object to the universal order on account of one's shoes being muddy and one's clothes wet? Indeed, such a person has to accept responsibility for not having taken suitable precautions. Divine wisdom decrees rainfall to benefit all, including those who complain about it.

Often, the view of a thing being evil is the result of a lack of perspective. Human beings expect fire to burn in their fireplace but not to affect their clothes. They expect rain to prevent drought but not damage buildings. They want wind to blow only at the command of the sailor. They want fire to be fire and yet not to be fire at one and the same time. And this is so for all the elements.

Ailments

Complaints about evil and suffering are often the result of physical or mental challenges or ailments. People who are deprived tend to hold God responsible for their misery. Many ailments result from people's own lack of precaution: lung cancer, food poisoning, cirrhosis of the liver, etc. If one goes to places described as being 'high-risk' due to the presence of malaria, yellow fever, tuberculosis, meningitis etc., and does not take the necessary precautions, then any resulting illness is one's own fault NOT God's. Despite ailments being regarded as evils from God, they can clearly be seen to be the 'evil' results of actions of humanity.

Certain ailments are known to cause a body's immune system to develop antibodies that block specific infections. Is this an evil thing?

To some extent Allāh compensates those afflicted by loss of sight and hearing via greater acuity of the other senses, memory or development of intuition. Such things are NOT a punishment from on high, but simply each one's share in the bounties granted by the Almighty.

Death

When we lose a loved one we are saddened. We miss them and are concerned about the future without them. The Islāmic understanding of death is that it is not the end of life itself, but simply the transformation from a lower life to a higher one. We will discuss this more fully when we discuss 'The Day of Resurrection' (see Part Five).

However, if every generation did not ever depart this life, one might imagine an overcrowded world in which succeeding generations could not be afforded the opportunity to mature, obtain nourishment, employment or housing.

Why does Allāh allow evil?

This seems a reasonable question if we believe Allāh to be Merciful, Ever-Giving of His bounty with manifestations of His favour and goodness everywhere. So, why does He allow humankind to be seduced and to diverge from the 'Right Path'?

The answer is simply that we cannot laud a deaf and dumb person for not telling lies or slandering others, as they do not have ability or opportunity to do such things. While seeking election, politicians promise to act justly, to treat others fairly and to work only for the common good. However, once they gain power many conveniently forget their promises. While every student may claim to be the best student in the class, the end of year examinations make clear who actually is, just as hurdles reveal the best steeplechaser. Thus, without temptation it is not possible to establish or distinguish the truly pious and righteous from those who falsely claim so to be.

We conclude from the above points that theodicy to justify evil, and Allāh permitting it, has no firm basis.

2 Can We See Allāh?

One might ask: if Allāh exists, why is He not seen? In other words, how can I believe in a god that I am not able to see? Such questions are answered in the following ways:

There are many things that do exist that we are not able to see. In the same way, there are things that we might see that are not themselves real. For example, physicists have demonstrated that subatomic particles such as electrons and quarks do exist despite our not being able to see them. Here are a few examples of mistakes our eyesight might influence us to believe:

1. We see a lifelike image reflected in a mirror, but it has no external existence of its own.

2. Passengers on a train see mountains and trees rushing past them, while it is they that are moving at great speed.

3. Standing on a train track, we see the two parallel metal rails meeting each other in the distance, which in reality they do not.

4. In hot climates people see mirages of water in the arid distance.

5. Physicists tell us that the universe has four dimensions, yet we are only able to perceive three.

6. In winter, if we touch a wooden door and a steel door we might imagine the latter to be colder than the former, while they are actually both at the exact same temperature.

7. In many scientific experiments, if it were not for the availability of laboratory equipment and advanced systems for physical measurement, our physical senses would not be able to detect many things at all.

From the above, we conclude that **our senses are not the only measure by which to evidence things**. On the other hand, there are many things that we are not able to see despite the fact that they do exist. For example:

1. When someone is in pain, even without our being able to see what has caused it, we accept the fact of their pain.

2. Everybody watching a sunset deduces the sun is rising somewhere else in the world, despite not being able to see and witness it.

3. The world is spherical even though people do not experience this.

4. Radio waves permeate the space that surrounds us, despite our not being able to see or sense them.

5. Human beings are able to distinguish sound waves between the frequencies of 20 and 20,000 Hz, while those above or below these frequencies are not heard by the naked human ear.

6. The naked human eye can detect light – electromagnetic radiation between the wavelengths of 458 million and 727 million nanometres. It does not see infrared, ultraviolet or microwave electromagnetic radiation, which fall outside this spectrum.
7. We know that energy exists but are not able to sense it, and no one knows what it is.

These are just some facts, not subject to the human senses, that have been exposed by modern scientific enquiry. It is abundantly clear from them that it would be absolutely incorrect to make sensory perception the criterion by which to determine what is real and what is not.

What we perceive is corporeal

We only observe things that belong to physical bodies, which are corporeal. All bodies are limited either by height, breadth and width, or by time. It is self-evident that time and the three physical dimensions are created and not eternal.

Allāh, the Absolute Existent and Infinite Being, is not limited in any regard. This being so, it is not possible to locate precisely any place where He is. Once we rule out space and place, distance and nearness are beyond comprehension. When we rule out the existence of time, terms such as fast and slow are meaningless, as are the concepts of past, present and future.

For example, if we were able to travel faster than the speed of light we would arrive yesterday as opposed to today. While this sounds impossible, it is nonetheless a serious point of discussion in modern physics.

From the above, it should be clear that whatever we are able to sense is one kind of body or another, for we are only able to sense things that are finite and limited. The Absolute Being is both unlimited and infinite.

Everything has its own measure

It is self-evident that all things have their own measures and that there are specific ways and means to arrive at them. We cannot rationally expect an astronomer to employ 'astronomic tools' to investigate microbiology, nor a microbiologist to employ 'tools appropriate to microbiology' to study the moons of Jupiter. Similarly, it is inappropriate to attempt to answer metaphysical questions by scientific methodologies, or to expect to examine the Creator through a microscope.

We measure distances in kilometres, weights in kilograms, temperatures in degrees and pressures in isobars. But we are not able to learn anything about Allāh Almighty using these measurements, nor can we use them as the basis for reasoned argument.

Arguing the basic effects

Looking for the effects (*āthār*) of a thing is the appropriate manner by which to deduce its existence. This is why theologians assiduously apply themselves to the development of *a posteriori* proofs for the existence of Allāh Almighty, that is, proofs in which the existence of a cause is demonstrated by the existence of its effects. This approach is inspired by the *āyah*, 'Soon We shall show them Our signs in the horizon of their own souls, until it is clear to them that He is The Ultimate Truth.'[152] This has been extensively covered in 'The Design Argument' (see chapter 2).

Proofs presented by the Imāms عليهم السلام

Some illuminating answers to questions on the subject of seeing Allāh Almighty:

> Dhiʿlib al-Yamānī asked Imām ʿAli عليه السلام, 'O Commander of the Faithful, have you seen your Lord?'

He ﷺ responded, 'Would I worship something that I could not see?'

'But how do you know what He is like?'

'The eyes do not perceive Him in their vision; rather, it is hearts that perceive Him through the realities of faith. He is near to things, without being amongst them; He is far from them, without being apart; He speaks, without need to first consider what He wants to say; He Wills whatever He wants, without any need to resolve to do so; He fashions, without the use of limbs; He is subtle, but cannot be described as being small; He is awesome, but cannot be described as being huge; He is Seeing, without the sense of sight being ascribed to Him; He is Merciful, but cannot be described as being soft of heart.'[153]

We find that all the error-free Imāms عليهم السلام place great emphasis upon 'Inner Sight'.

Imām Ṣādiq عليه السلام was once told, 'Some claim that it is possible to see Allāh.'

He عليه السلام responded, 'The light of the sun is one-seventieth of the intensity of that of 'The Seat' [*kursi*], the light of 'The Seat' is one-seventieth of the intensity of that of 'The Throne' [*ʿarsh*], the light of The Throne is one-seventieth of the intensity of that of 'The Curtain' [*ḥijāb*], the light of 'The Curtain' is one-seventieth of the intensity of that of 'The Veil' [*satr*]. So if they speak the truth, let them fill their eyes with the sun on a cloudless day.'[154]

The Russian author Leo Tolstoy's story, 'I Want to See God', employs the same line of argument as the final sentence of this *ḥadīth*.

Abū Hishām al-Jaʿfarī narrates that he said to Imām Baqir عليه السلام, 'The eyesight cannot apprehend Him yet He apprehends the eyes?' [As this is part of Qur'ān 6:103, he meant to ask the Imām عليه السلام to elaborate upon it.]

> He عليه السلام responded, ‘O Abū Hishām, the imaginings of the heart are more discerning than the sight of the eyes. In your heart you may perceive Sindh and India and other countries that you have never visited or seen. And if your heart’s imaginings cannot perceive Him, then how can your eyes.’[155]
>
> This calls to mind the Prophet Mūsa عليه السلام asking the Lord, ‘My Lord, please reveal yourself to me so that I may see.’ Allāh Almighty responded, ‘You are **never** going to be able to see me, but look at the mountain; if it remains firm in its position you may see me.’ However, when the Lord manifested His Glory the mountain crumbled into a heap of dust and Mūsa fainted. When he recovered he said, ‘Glory be to You, I have repented and am the first one to believe.’[156]

ʿAllāmah Ḥilli commented upon the word never (*lan*) saying, ‘It is the eternal negative according to lexicographers, and as Mūsa عليه السلام did not see Him, certainly no one else has seen Him.’[157]

3 Theism and Technology

Since the Biblical exposition of God being ‘Thinker and Creator’, many contemporary philosophers have faced the extremely serious problem of how to match their faith with ever-expanding technological progress. For example, Norris Clarke writes,

> God is at once contemplative and active. He has not only thought up the material universe, with all its intricate network of laws, but He has actively brought it into existence and supports and guides its vast pulsating network of forces. God is both a thinker and a worker, so to speak. So, too, man should imitate God his Father by both thinking and working in the world.

He goes on to point out that the Biblical creation story includes the human vocation to co-create with God. The first humans significantly before the Fall were given a garden to 'Till and keep' (Genesis 2:15) – the incarnate god-man was depicted as a tool user.[158]

A similar discussion is to be found by Jacques Ellul (in 'Theology and Technology').[159] This topic will be analysed in depth in our discussion regarding 'Miracles' and how to explain them within scientific/natural laws (see chapter 9).

8 Predestination and Free Will

1 Introduction

The question of free will is passionately debated, as some believe it is key to the understanding of human nature as a whole. In his *Social Contract* Jean-Jacques Rousseau claimed that the fundamental difference between man and animals is not the former's understanding or ability to think, but rather his free will and ability to choose.

In our discussions on predestination and free will we will focus on the following question: Can our actions be entirely and properly attributed to our own will and volition, or are they caused by Allāh's power and thus not affected by humankind's own whims? Those who incline towards the former view are labelled 'delegationists' (*mufawwiḍah*) and those who incline towards the latter view 'determinists' (*mujabbirah*).

2 Various Viewpoints

Many different opinions have emerged in response to this question. Scholars tally as many as 17 different theological and philosophical views on the subject. We summarize below the most popular.

Absolute predestination

According to this theory, the ascription of actions to human beings is no different from the ascription of actions to inanimate objects or plants, in so far as both humans and the latter have no will in regard to movement or behaviour. Therefore, humankind is nothing other than the tool of a 'higher will' – 'a feather on the Breath of God'.

This theory is also referred to as 'philosophical predestination', or, more precisely, 'philosophical necessity'. This means that, in the presence of a complete cause of something, its effect **must** immediately follow. For example, wood that is not wet, fire-proofed, or located some way away from a fire, will almost certainly catch light. However, with a distance between a cause and its effect, or the wood being protectively covered with asbestos, the possibility, but not the necessity, exists for it to catch fire and burn. Philosophically, the relationship between the complete cause and its effect is **'a must'** while the relationship between an incomplete cause and its supposed effect is **'a might'**. Such relationships, in terms of human actions, define the former as predestination and the latter as free will.

Another aspect of predestination may be suggested by genes – the units of heredity transmitted from parent to offspring that control or determine a single characteristic in their offspring. For example, those who commit evil actions may attempt to escape accountability by claiming that their 'behaviour was genetically inherited' – 'I was born to be like this.' This position is also put forward in regard to same-sex marriage. However, Dr Alan Sanders, associate Professor of Psychiatry at Northwestern University, who led a study on the genetic basis of male homosexuality, reported in the *Telegraph* newspaper on 13 February 2014,[160] said that it was an 'oversimplification' to suggest that there was a 'gay gene'. Dr Bailey, a psychologist who worked with him on the study, said environmental factors were likely to have the biggest impact on homosexuality. The complete article may be seen on the *Telegraph* website.

Acquisition

This theory was introduced by Abul Ḥasan al-Ashʿarī, founder of the Ashʿarite school of *Kalām* (d. 330 AH/941 CE). According to his view, while people possess both the power and the will connected to their actions, neither their will nor power play any role whatever in their acts, because the real 'cause' of those acts is Allāh, and people merely acquire them.

Al-Bāqillānī (d. 403 AH) explained acquisition (*kasb*) as an act undertaken by people, that assumes its external appearance in accord with their intention to achieve a goal. While the good or evil classification of an act is determined by its acquired 'hue', the act itself originates from Allāh. Thus, if a person strikes an orphan, it may be done with the intention of disciplining the orphan, in which case the action assumes the hue of commendability, or it may be done with the intention of hurting the orphan, in which case it assumes the hue of reprehensibility.

As the theory of *kasb* is surrounded by ambiguity, many Ashʿarite theologians are not able to provide a comprehensive or precise definition of it. For this reason some say, 'There are three illogical things posited by theologians: *Ḥāl* (an intermediate state between existence and non-existence), *Ṭafrah*, according to al-Naẓẓām, and *kasb*, according to the Ashʿarites.' In reality, while supporters of the above view have attempted to escape the problem of predestination via this theory, they have fallen into the very trap that they attempted to avoid.

The Muʿtazilites

This school of thought asserts that human action emanates from humans and is properly attributed to their power and will. Allāh's power has absolutely no impact on human activity and there is no need for any external motivation to set a person's will in motion. A dissenting voice in this matter is Abul Ḥusayn al-Baṣrī (d. 436 AH/1044 CE), who stipulated that there had to be a motivation for a will to emerge.

Pantheism

This is the belief that no distinction should be made between Allāh and other beings, because Allāh encompasses all entities – each entity being merely a distinctive manifestation of Allāh. According to this view, predestination and free will have no meaning because Allāh and humanity are really a single entity, and thus there is no need to determine whether people's actions are their own or Allāh's.

Al-Zamakhsharī's theory

This is identical to all other Muʿtazilite ideas except that Al-Zamakhsharī believed that there is no necessity for a motive to support people's will.

Al-Fakhr al-Rāzī

Al-Fakhr al-Rāzī (d. 606 AH/1209 CE) believed that while it is true that people's actions depend upon their own power, will and motive, these causes and their effects exist only by virtue of Allāh willing them.

Muslim peripatetic philosophers

Peripatetic philosophers (*mashshā'ūn*) believe that when the causes for action, i.e. the power, will and all necessary impulses, are present, an action is ready to enter the realm of existence. However, the potentiality for such actualization depends upon the will of Allāh.

Some Muslim 'illuminationist' and peripatetic philosophers

These believe that all occurrences are ultimately effusions from Allāh, with the varied agents and causes that lead to actions being merely subsidiary factors.

Some Ṣūfīs

Some Ṣūfīs believe that voluntary actions have two attributions, one being essential, the other conventional. The former is attributed to Allāh, the latter to humankind.

The Imāmiyah

The Imāmiyah assert that human beings' power, and the tools that enable them to act, all stem from Allāh Almighty. However, the manner in which those tools are utilized depends on those who employ them. This is the doctrine of the intermediate position (*Al-Amr bayn al-Amrayn*), which is explained below in greater detail.

Having explained the various viewpoints regarding free will, we now analyse the most widely believed doctrines of three schools.

3 Refutation of Predestination

Even the most simple-minded of souls can understand the difference between actions that they are able to control and actions over which they have no control whatever. Had humans been compelled to do everything that they do, such distinction would not exist. As a practical example: a person picks up a piece of food, puts it into their mouth, then chews and swallows it. All those actions are under their control – they may choose to do them or choose not to do them. However, once the food has been swallowed, enzymes are released to break it down, whether they will this to be done or not; their intestines will compress and move the food, whether they will this to be done or not; and ultimately, the waste material from the digestive processes will be expelled from their body, whether they will this to be done or not. The same may be said of all the functions of the body's other internal organs.

Voluntary actions encompass going to work, to a library or to a market, to sit or stand, study or play, etc. We can exercise our will and make definite choices or decisions whether to undertake such courses of action or not.

We can all distinguish the difference between using a staircase or elevator to travel down to the ground floor, and jumping out of a window. In the former case we have the option to cease our further descent; in the latter, we have no free will and must thus continue to descend through the air until the ground stops further progress. Is this so difficult to comprehend?

Abu al-Hudhayl al-ʿAllāf[161] (d. 235 AH/841 CE), criticized the claim of 'proponents of predestination' – that their actions were not under their control – saying, 'A man's donkey is cleverer than its owner, for if he takes it to a large river, even if he beats it, it will not even attempt to leap over it and will certainly look for a way around it instead. Even a donkey can tell the difference between what it can jump over and what it cannot. However, some human beings seem unable to tell the difference.'

The difference between being good and being evil

It is a human instinct to respond warmly to those who treat them well and feel animus towards those who treat them badly. Children will readily smile at those who give them a sweet, and cry if someone slaps their cheek. Society displays similar reactions in regard to philanthropists and those who disregard societal well-being. All legal systems have similar responses to law-abiding citizens and those who disregard the law. If all human action was solely motivated by the will of Allāh Almighty, one would not be able to distinguish between those who behave well and do good, and those who do not.

Your Lord is not tyrannical towards His servants

Assertion of the doctrine of predestination characterizes Allāh Almighty as unjust, in the face of His having created humankind to be morally accountable for their actions. Throughout history, His messengers have enjoined people to 'do good' and forbade them to 'commit evil'.

Had He tried to compel them to do so, it would have constituted an unjust act on His part.

When Abu Ḥanifah came to Madinah together with Abdullah ibn Muslim, the latter told him, 'Here there is a famous scholar from the household of the Prophet ﷺ so we should visit him to learn from him.' When they arrived they found themselves amongst a gathering of followers awaiting his appearance. When a teenager entered, people stood up in respect and Abu Ḥanifah asked his friend who this boy was. Abdullah told him that it was Mūsa, the Imām's son.

Abu Ḥanifah said, 'By Allāh, I will humiliate him in the presence of this crowd.' Abdullah responded, 'You will not be able to!'

Abu Ḥanifah replied, 'I most certainly will.' He turned to Mūsa and said, 'O boy, where can a stranger set down his load in your land?' (This was a reference to defecation.) Mūsa replied, 'Let him go behind a wall, avoid neighbours' eyes, the banks of rivers and the shade of fruit-bearing trees, let him not face the *Qiblah* nor turn his back to it. Then he can set down his load whenever he pleases.'

Abu Ḥanifah then asked, 'O boy, from whom comes disobedience?' Mūsa replied, 'O Shaykh, there are three possibilities: Either it comes entirely from Allāh, in which case the Wise One does not punish His servant for something he did not do; or it comes from the servant and Allāh together, but as Allāh is the stronger of the two partners it is not right for the stronger partner to punish the weaker one for his wrong-doing; or it comes from the servant alone, in which case Allāh may punish or forgive as He sees fit.'

At this eloquent response, Abu Ḥanifah fell silent. Seeing this, Abdullah ibn Muslim turned to Abu Ḥanifah and said, 'Did I not warn you not to try to take on the descendants of Allāh's Messenger ﷺ?'[162]

A critique of the arguments used by determinists

Having covered the various opinions regarding free will and predestination, we now need to discuss the main arguments used by those Muslim theologians who believe in predestination.

The first argument

The proponents of predestination think that because we ascribe absolute 'creatorship' to Allāh, it follows that no creational ability may be ascribed to any other than Him. However, if it were claimed that human beings create their own actions it would contradict the doctrine that 'nothing affects existence other than Allāh'. The obvious conclusion from this is that if human beings lack free will, they are obliged to act.

Many Qur'ānic references state that Allāh Almighty is the Creator of all things. See for example: 6:102, 7:54, 13:16, 35:3, 39:62 and 59:24.

Response to the above: In addition to Allāh Almighty's confirmation that He is the Sole Creator, He frequently also refers to the function of natural causes in the growth, order and continuity of life – for example, water being necessary for the growth of vegetation in Qur'ān 32:27, His confirmation that He has ordained water to fulfil this function. He also tells us in Qur'ān 13:4, 'On earth there are fields that are side by side with vineyards and areas of corn and date palms, some [plants] have multiple roots, some single roots, all irrigated by the same waters, yet We have made some fruits more excellent than others. Truly, in this there are signs for those who reflect.'

In Qur'ān 30:48 Allāh tells us, 'It is He who sends winds to raise clouds, that He scatters over the skies as He wills. You see their raindrops falling upon whichever of His servants He pleases.' It is clear from this that the winds have been ordained to effect the important dissemination of clouds.

In Qur'ān 2:261, the immense possible benefit from charity offered by believers is likened to the grain that produces seven ears, each one with 100 grains within. Allāh Almighty considers that the grain that produces 700 in no way contradicts His being the Sole Creator

While Muslims unanimously agree that every human being is the creation of Allāh, they do not deny that an act of a man and a woman is necessary to bring about the fertilization of new life.

To conclude: acknowledgement of the impact that nature has does not contradict or negate the fact of Allāh being the Sole Creator.

Causality: As a consequence of the above-mentioned argument, some Muslim theologians have completely negated the principle of causality. For them, a believer is not permitted to say that fire itself burns, nor that water itself quenches thirst. They base such statements on no agent other than Allāh having any impact on anything in the world.

Response to this: While Allāh Almighty tells us in Qur'ān 39:42, 'He causes death and takes souls', in Qur'ān 6:61 He informs us that He has allocated that duty to His angels (the Angel of Death). Similarly, in Qur'ān 4:81, where He declares Himself the Recorder of all that people do, in Qur'ān 43:80 He informs us that He has allocated the keeping of such records to His angels. While in Qur'ān 26:80 remedy and cure are recognized to be 'Acts of God', in Qur'ān 16:69 He informs us that He has allocated these functions to 'the honey that is produced by bees'. All the above clearly shows that belief in Allāh being the Sole Creator does not negate the roles played by those to whom He has allocated a variety of duties.

The second argument

Those who support the concept of predestination claim that whatever people do has been either willed by Allāh or has not been willed. If He has willed something it follows that He is the Creator of their deeds, and if He has not, nothing whatever will occur. To make this claim appear logical and reasonable they state that faith requires absolute submission and surrender to Allāh's will, for when He ordains something it occurs and when He does not, nothing happens. They support this with one Qur'ānic reference that appears at first glance to confirm their ideas – Qur'ān 37:96, 'Allāh has created you and what you make.' Sayyid Sharif Jurjāni, an Ashʿarite theologian, depended upon this *āyah* for his conclusion: 'all human deeds are committed by Allāh.' He then confirmed this to be 'doctrine' put forward by the master of this school, Abul Ḥasan al-Ashʿari.[163]

Response: It is not appropriate to quote any *āyah* out of context. The *āyah* quoted above refers to the incident in which the Prophet Ibrāhim ﷺ destroyed the idols of his nation. When those who worshipped them condemned him, he responded, 'Do you worship that which you yourselves have carved? While Allāh has created you and [the sculpted images] that you have made.'

However, for a meaningful discussion about the will of Allāh, we need to be conscious of the difference between 'creative will' (*Irādah Takwiniyah*), and 'legislative will' (*Irādah Tashri'iyah*).

All Muslims concur that without a 'creative will' nothing could have come into being. Allāh willed the entire universe to exist, from its most minuscule particles to its largest planets, and thus its every aspect is the result of His creative power. 'Natural Causes' – the fields of study of chemistry, micro-, macro- and theoretical physics, biology, physiology and other sciences – are the means by which Allāh's 'creative will' is manifest.

His 'legislative will' is manifested by the commands and prohibitions that have been brought to us by His Prophets and Messengers ﷺ. This legislative will is entirely free of compulsion. Human beings have free choice: to strive to obtain worldly merits and perfections by following the guidance delivered via His messengers, or to ignore the guidance and concomitant consequences that flow from that decision.

Allāh informs us in Qur'ān 76:3 that He has shown humankind the right path to tread but has left it entirely to each individual to be grateful for it or not. In Qur'ān 90:10, He refers to two paths [good and evil] that make evident to us that we are at a bifurcation and must select which route to follow to the future.

The third argument

Some supporters of determinism refer to a divine foreknowledge of human actions. They claim that 'if Allāh has foreknowledge of all of our actions, it follows that we are predestined to perform them'. A literary expression of the consequence of our not doing that is found in the famous quatrain of 'Umar Khayyām, Persian poet and astronomer

(d. 525 AH/1131 CE) that contains the lines, ‘Allāh Almighty knew from pre-eternity that I am going to drink wine. If I stop drinking now, Allāh will be seen to have been ignorant.’

Response:

1. If the connection between Allāh’s knowledge and our actions were such that it necessitated the occurrence of predestined acts, it would mean that Allāh’s knowledge of His own acts would necessitate their predestined occurrence. There is not a single Muslim theologian to agree with this.

2. Allāh is completely aware of our actions and the preparatory steps we take to achieve them. This includes the aspect of our free will, cited in Qur’ān 76:3 and 90:10. The Almighty has known from pre-eternity that His provision includes the ability for us to choose the direction we wish to take.

3. Let us imagine a teacher who uses the most proficient methodology to teach mathematics and regularly tests students to monitor their progress. Based upon their level of skill this teacher is able accurately to predict pupils’ final grades. Is it logical to imagine that the pupils who achieved the top marks did so as the result of their teacher’s knowledge rather than their own intelligence and diligent work throughout the course? Similarly, is it logical to claim that those who failed did so as the result of the teacher’s knowledge and not their lack of effort or inability?

   The saying, ‘A bad workman blames his tools’, comes to mind! All are accountable for their own efforts and achievements, despite the wish of others to predict results.

4 The Muʿtazilite Concept of Free Will

Contrary to the Ashʿarite view that supports the concept of predestination, Muʿtazilite doctrine claims that Allāh Almighty created human beings to have the capacity to act and administer their own affairs without His intervention. This doctrine is technically referred to as (*Tafwīḍ*). After having ridiculed Ashʿarite beliefs, Qāḍi Abdul Jabbar (d. 415 AH), argued that without such free will it would not be possible to make any distinction between those who commit good acts and those who commit evil ones. Indeed, Muʿtazilite belief in divine justice being a principle of faith requires negation of the idea that human actions have anything whatever to do with Allāh.[164]

Response: In their reaction to one extreme opinion, Muʿtazilites appear to have adopted its opposite extreme. However, there are many *ayāt* in the Qur'ān indicating that nothing occurs without Allāh's permission.

> And they followed [instead] that which the evil ones practised during Solomon's reign – for it was not Solomon who denied the truth, but those who were evil denied it and taught people the sorcery that came via the two angels in Babylon, *Hārūt* and *Mārūt,* even though neither of these two ever informed anyone about it without first stating, 'We are but a temptation to evil: so do not disbelieve [Allāh's] truth.' Yet people learned from them how to create discord between man and wife. Regardless of their being unable to harm anyone without Allāh's permission, they acquired a knowledge that harmed themselves and gave them no benefit, in spite of their being aware that those who acquire such [knowledge] shall not share the good of the life to come. That for which they sold their souls is indeed vile – had they but known.[165]

> And when *Talūt* (Saul) set out with his forces, he said, 'Be forewarned, Allāh is to test you at a river: those who drink from it will no longer belong to me, but those who refrain from drinking will. However, those who scoop up a single handful to taste will be forgiven.' Despite this all but a few quenched their thirst.
>
> When they had crossed the river, those who had not kept faith with him said, 'We do not have the strength today to [face] *Jalūt* (Goliath) and his forces. However, those who knew they were

> destined to meet Allāh responded, 'How often has a small force **with Allāh's leave** overcome a great host, for He is with those who are patient in adversity.'[166]

> And **with Allāh's leave** they thereupon routed them. *Dāwūd* (David) slew Jalūt and Allāh bestowed upon him dominion and wisdom and imparted to him the knowledge of whatever he willed . . .[167]

> And no human being can leave this life **without His leave**. Those who desire the rewards of this world shall have it granted; and those who desire the rewards of the hereafter shall have that granted.[168]

> No human being can ever attain faith other than **by Allāh's leave** . . .[169]

It is clear from the above Qur'ānic references that regardless of our determination and exertion, nothing occurs without Allāh's leave. It follows that Muʿtazilite doctrine regarding our determined acts being independent of Allāh's intervention cannot possibly be valid.

> Whatever good happens to you is from Allāh and whatever evil befalls you is from yourself.[170]

This *āyah* clarifies that Allāh enables us to achieve good characteristics and practices, while leaving each human being responsible for their own nonconformity with divine guidance and the wrongdoings that they enact. This plainly negates the Muʿtazilite concept of *Tafwīḍ*.

Imām Ṣādiq عليه السلام clearly considered the concept of *Tafwīḍ* an attempt to weaken the sovereignty of Allāh when he said, 'With regard to predestination, people fall into three groups: (1) those who claim Allāh predestines His servants' sins, (2) those who claim Allāh leaves it up to His servants to determine their decisions on their own, and (3) those who believe Allāh commands His servants to act within their abilities and does not hold them accountable for anything beyond that. When this third group do good deeds they thank Allāh and when they commit evil acts they seek His forgiveness. As the first group does Allāh an injustice and the second weakens His sovereignty, both are wrong and it is only the third group that tread the right path.'[171]

5 Imāmiyah Doctrine

As explained earlier, the Imāmiyah assert that all 'tools' available to humankind stem from Allāh Almighty. However, the manner in which they are used depends upon each individual. To arrive at this conclusion the Imāmiyah have examined and compared two groups of Qur'ānic statements: those that indicate that human beings possess free will and those that clarify that nothing whatever occurs without Allāh's leave.

Qur'ānic references regarding free will

With every legal system throughout the world based upon individual accountability, all understand that they are answerable for their own actions. Thus it is no surprise to find many Qur'ānic *ayāt* refer to personal accountability:

> Those who commit good deeds benefit themselves while those who commit evil deeds burden their souls. The Lord is not unjust to His servants.[172]

> We will unite believers with the children that follow them in faith. We will not decrease any of their [good] deeds. **Each person is to be held responsible for what they have done.**[173]

> Beyond doubt many have joined together to falsely accuse others of unchaste behaviour. [But you who have been wronged] do not consider this to be a burden for it is a benefit. **Every one of them [is to be held accountable] for what they earned from this sin . . .**[174]

> There is nothing for people other than what they strive for. Their striving shall soon become apparent. They will then be fully compensated with its maximum worth.[175]

Say [O Muḥammad]. The truth [has now come] from your Lord so **let those who wish believe it; and let those who wish reject it . . .**[176]

It matters not to Allāh if you deny the truth [and are ungrateful]. Nonetheless, while He does not approve of His servants' lack of gratitude, He is pleased when they are grateful. **None will bear the burdens of others.** All must return to their Lord, at which time He will permit them to [fully] understand all that they did [during their lives].[177]

We have, beyond doubt, shown them the way [and it rests with them to prove themselves] grateful or not grateful.[178]

Beyond doubt this is a reminder. Therefore, let those who will set out on their way to the Lord.[179]

By the soul and that which perfected it, inspired it [with the faculty to discern between] what is evil and what is good. Those who purify it succeed, and those who corrupt it fail.[180]

Qur'ānic references regarding Allāh's leave

Without the Lord of the Worlds' permission you will not be able to make a choice.[181]

. . . regardless of not being able to harm anyone **without Allāh's permission.**[182]

And **with Allāh's leave** they thereupon routed them. Dāwūd (David) slew Jalūt (Goliath) and Allāh bestowed upon him dominion and wisdom and imparted to him the knowledge of whatever he willed . . .[183]

No human being can ever attain faith other than **by Allāh's leave . . .**[184]

Conclusion

Belief in there being no contradictory statements in the Holy Qur'ān is an essential principle of faith. So how do we justify the differences between the above two groups of Qur'ānic quotations?

In answer, let us consider the following:

a. Quadriplegic patients require assistance, and while state-of-the-art equipment may help them overcome disadvantages, they still need continual attention from carers. Unless they wish to effect a specific action, their carer is not in a position to help them achieve it. Conversely, without their carer's continual attention, the patient is not in a position to have their wishes fulfilled. This leads us to acknowledge the importance of the mutual relationship that exists between patient and carer.

b. Imagine a father bequeaths a million pounds to his two sons. One is astute enough to invest his share profitably, and in time to grow his share threefold. The other spends his inheritance in vainglorious activities and ends up bankrupt. Clearly, the success of one is the result of both his inheritance and his astute investments; the failure of the other is entirely due to his own profligacy.

Having understood the above, we can understand too those Qur'ānic references that indicate that nothing takes place without Allāh's permission – and also those that emphasize humanity's free will and accountability for their own actions. In other words, such an understanding negates the Muʿtazilite concept of *Tafwīḍ* and the Ashʿarite concept of predestination. This outlines precisely the doctrine of the intermediate position (*Al-Amr bayn al-Amrayn*) propounded and advocated by the Imāmiyah. Human beings depend upon the ceaseless grace of their Lord to grant them life, power and the ability to function, without which they would cease to exist. Similarly, we have been granted free will to choose to walk the path of obedience or not.

Imāmi theologians quote many *āḥadīth* from the error-free Imāms عليهم السلام

to clarify the above. Shaykh Ṣadūq narrates from both Imāms Baqir and Ṣādiq عليهما السلام that 'Allāh Almighty's mercy towards His creatures is more principled than to compel them to sin and then punish them. He is more magnificent than to will something that does not occur.' When they were asked, 'Is there another stance other than *Jabr* (predestination) and *Qadar* (fate)?' they both answered in the affirmative.

In another report, Shaykh Ṣadūq narrates from Imām Riḍā عليه السلام that when people discussed *Jabr* and *Tafwīḍ* in his presence, he asked them, 'Shall I inform you of a principle that will provide an accurate understanding of faith and help you overcome the arguments that propound predestination?' After they had expressed their desire for him to do so he عليه السلام said, 'Allāh Almighty is not reluctantly obeyed nor disobeyed by being overcome. He is the absolute owner of all that humanity has and is Omnipotent over all that He has enabled them to do. When they decide to commit a sin He may put obstacles in their way; however, when He does not intervene in their plans He is seen not to compel them.'[185]

It is interesting to observe that some famous Ashʿarite theologians such as Al-Fakhr al-Rāzi (d. 606 AH), after having explained both the Ashʿarite and Muʿtazilite schools' understanding of free will, supported the doctrine of the intermediate position (*Al-Amr bayn al-Amrayn*), that he said is advocated by 'Some religious leaders' without telling anyone which. He then used the following parable: 'A rock that is being cut by a chisel questions it, why? The chisel's response: Ask the man hitting me.'

Notes to Part Two

1 Sufyān al-Thawrī was born in Kufah in the year 97 AH. In recognition of his eminence in the field of *ḥadīth*, the Abbasid caliph al-Manṣūr requested he accept the position of *Qāḍi*. He declined the offer and left Kufah in the year 144 AH to settle in Makkah and Madinah. He is known to have had a very sharp memory and is quoted as saying, 'I have never forgotten anything that I memorized.' He died in Baṣrah in the year 161 AH.

2 *Nahj al-Balaghah,* Sermon 49.

3 *Al-Nāfiʿ yawm al-Ḥashr fi Sharḥ al-Bāb al-Ḥādi ʿAshr,* p. 21.

4 Shaykh Muṣliḥ al-Din Saʿdī, one of the most important Persian poets, was born in Shiraz in 571 AH (1175 CE). His legacy rests on two famous anthologies, one being *Gulistān* (Rose Garden), the other *Būstān* (Garden). He studied in Baghdad at the Niẓāmiyah College founded by Niẓām al-Mulk and later joined Ṣūfi circles, particularly that of Shihāb al-Din Suhrawardi.

Saʿdī's Rose Garden presents in story form ethical lessons and advice in verse and prose, supported by *āḥadīth* quotations from the holy Prophet ﷺ. The quotation given here appears in his introductory lines to *Gulistān*.

5 *Nahj al-Balaghah,* Sermon 181.

6 *Ibid.,* Sermon 14.

7 *Al-Milal wal Niḥal,* Vol. 1, p. 105.

8 Abul Ḥasan al-Ashʿari was born in Baṣrah in the year 260 AH. He was a descendant of Abu Mūsā al-Ashʿari, who played a role in the arbitration between Imām ʿAli عليه السلام and Muʿawiyah during the battle of Ṣiffin. He studied

jurisprudence under the Shāfiʿi teacher Abu Isḥāq in Baghdad and theology under the Muʿtazilite teacher Abu ʿAli Jubbā'i until the age of 40 – an important turning point in his life. As the result of debate between him and his Muʿtazilite teacher regarding the purposefulness of Divine Acts, he rejected the school of 'Defenders of Reason' and established his own school of 'Textual Sources' that was eventually adopted by the majority of Sunnis, who thereafter became known as Ashʿarites. While we should not forget the essential role that Al-Ghazāli played in strengthening the foundations of Ashʿarite thought, it is traditionally accepted that Abul Ḥasan is the father-figure of that movement.

It has been reported that Abul Ḥasan al-Ashʿari, after having been deeply affected by Muʿtazilite teachings, faced unanswered questions in the field of theology. He thus decided to pray two *rakʿāt* to request divine guidance before he retired. In his dream that night he saw the Prophet ﷺ and complained to him about the confusion in his mind, to which the Prophet ﷺ responded, 'Hold fast to my Sunnah.' After getting up the next morning he abandoned his previous ideas to accept whatever the Qur'ān literally says. This dream appears in Ibn ʿAsākir's *Tabyīn Kidhb al-Muftarī fi Mā Nusiba ilā al-Ashʿari*, p. 40.

According to Dr Ahmad Mahmūd Ṣubḥi, despite that dream not being acceptable historical evidence, it is a psychological manifestation of perplexity. Refer to *Fi ʿIlm al-Kalām*, Vol. 2, p. 49.

As described by Ibn Khillikān, Abul Ḥasan al-Ashʿari attended the mosque one day to announce, 'Those who know me know me, but for those who do not, I now introduce myself. I am so and so son of so and so, I used to believe in the Qur'ān being created, and that the eyes cannot see Allāh, and I am accountable for my own evil acts. However, I now repent absolutely and reject all the nonsense of the Muʿtazilites. See *Wafayāt al-Aʿyān*, Vol. 2, p. 446.

His famous works are: *Al-Ibānah ʿan Uṣūl al-Diyānah, al-Lumaʿ* and *Maqālāt al Islāmiyīn.*

9 *Al-Ibānah,* p. 18.

10 *Tarikh al-Madahib al-Islāmiyah,* Vol. 1, p. 220.

11 On the subject of *Muḥkam* and *Mutashābih* we refer to Qur'ān 3:7: 'It is He

who has sent down the Book to you. Parts of it consist of *Muḥkamāt*, that comprise the "Mother of the Book", while other parts are *Mutashābihāt*. Individuals of perverse character delight in misleading others with understandings of *Mutashābih,* informed by their own misinterpretations of them. However, it is only Allāh who knows those meanings. People firmly grounded in knowledge say: we believe in it, the whole is from our Lord.' Exegetes differ in their understandings of the above *āyah*, particularly in regard to the definitions of *Muḥkamāt and Mutashābihāt*. Ibn Ḥazm al-Ẓāhirī and others are of the opinion that, with the exception of the *Muqaṭṭa'āt* – single alphabets that appear at the beginning of 29 Surahs – there is no *Mutashābih* in the Qur'ān. Others maintain that Qur'ānic references that draw resemblance between Allāh and men such as 'The hand of Allāh', 'His face' and 'His eyes' are also *Mutashābihāt.*

Muḥammad Hāshim Kamāli claims, 'The correct view is that *Muḥkam* is the part of the Qur'ān that is not open to conjecture and doubt, whereas the *Mutashābih* is open to conjecture and doubt.' He translates *Mutashābih* as 'intricate'. See *Principles of Islāmic Jurisprudence*, Islamic Texts Society (Cambridge, 1997).

Allāmah Ṭabāṭabā'ī, in his *Tafsīr al-Mizān,* Vol. 3, pp. 31–42, refers to 16 different opinions regarding the definition of *Muḥkam* and *Mutashābih,* and after analysing each one thoroughly, rejected them all and concluded, 'Rather than indicate ambiguity in their wording, *Mutashābihāt* are able to be simply understood by laymen to convey that which is closer to their intellect. It is those whose hearts swerve, who interpret such *ayāt* to meet with their own ill-intentions. Thus, all disputes and rifts throughout Islāmic history are the result of such misinterpretations.'

In his further discussion of this subject, Allāmah Ṭabāṭabā'ī elaborates on the meaning of 'Mother of the Book', the appropriate method of 'Interpretation' and the reasons for the existence of *Mutashābih* in the Qur'ān.

Al-Fakhr al-Rāzī, on the other hand, explores five different advantages for there being *Mutashābih* in the Qur'ān.

12 *Asās al-Taqdīs,* p. 223.

13 Qur'ān 10:3.

14 Qur'ān 13:2.

15 Qur'ān 32:4.

16 Qur'ān 55:27.

17 Shaykh Ṣadūq, *The Book of Monotheism* (*Tawḥīd*), p. 152.

18 Qur'ān 38:75.

19 Qur'ān 36:71.

20 Ibn Ḥazm al-Andulusī, known to have been the head of the Ẓāhirī School of Islāmic Law, rejected every aspect of intellectual reasoning in the field of *Ijtihād* because, according to him, the main source of *Shari'ah* is the apparent meanings of the Qur'ānic *ayāt* and *āḥadīth*. There is a consensus of agreement that when the lesser harm, of disrespect to parents, is prohibited (as is clearly indicated in Qur'ān 17:23), it is logical to conclude also that any greater degree of harm is also prohibited – despite it not being included in the *āyah*. However, according to the Ẓāhirī School, such logic is considered unacceptable. His work of 11 volumes on the subject of Islāmic Law is titled *Al-Muḥallā*.

21 Al-Sha'rānī's annotations on *Sharḥ Uṣūl al-Kāfī* by al-Māzandarānī, Vol. 3, p. 313.

22 Qur'ān 37:18.

23 Qur'ān 17:43.

24 Qur'ān 21:116.

25 Qur'ān 7:180.

26 Qur'ān 42:11.

27 Mullā Hādi Sabzawāri: *Asrār al-Ḥikam*, p. 46.

28 Qur'ān 55:78.

29 *Uṣūl al-Falsafah*, Vol. 5, pp. 138–143.

30 *Al-Bayān fi tafsīr al-Qur'ān*, p. 432, translated into English as *The Prolegomena to the Qur'ān*.

31 Sabzawārī alludes to these divisions in his *Asrār al-Ḥikam*, pp. 28–39.

32 Qur'ān 3:191.

33 Qur'ān 13:28.

34 Qur'ān 63:09.

35 Qur'ān 33:41.

36 Qur'ān 29:45.

37 Qur'ān 73:8.

38 Qur'ān 2:152.

39 Qur'ān 7:55.

40 *Kanz al-'Ummāl,* Tradition 3931.

41 *Biḥar al-Anwār,* Vol. 93, p. 164.

42 *Kanz al-'Ummāl,* Tradition 1819.

43 *Biḥar al-Anwār,* Vol. 103, p. 102.

44 *Ibid.,* Vol. 78, p. 38.

45 *Ghorar al-Ḥikam.*

46 *Ibid.*

47 Kumayl ibn Ziyād al-Nakha'ī is a devoted companion of Imām 'Ali عليه السلام who is frequently mentioned in *Nahj al-Balāghah*. It is he who memorized the words of his master's profound, eloquent and pious communication with the Almighty. Throughout the centuries this has been, and still is, recited all over the world each and every Thursday night by those who follow the *Ahl al-Bayt* عليهم السلام.

48 *Biḥar al-Anwār,* Vol. 93, p. 154.

49 *Al-Kāfi,* Vol. 2, p. 485, and *Biḥar al-Anwār,* Vol. 93, p. 196.

50 *Biḥar al-Anwār,* Vol. 93, p. 161.

51 *Ibid.,* Vol. 80, p. 176.

52 *Ibid.,* Vol. 93, p. 379.

53 *Ibid.,* Vol. 93, p. 15.

54 Qur'ān 17:44.

55 Qur'ān 56:74.

56 Qur'ān 87:1.

57 *Tafsīr Nūr al-Thaqalain,* Vol. 3, p. 444.

58 Qur'ān 21:79.

59 *Biḥar al-Anwār,* Vol. 60, p. 179.

60 *Al-Durr al-Manthūr,* Vol. 1, p. 10.

61 *Tafsīr Nūr al-Thaqalain,* Vol. 3, p. 445.

62 Qur'ān 3:190–191.

63 *Biḥar al-Anwār,* Vol. 77, p. 199.

64 *Ghorar al-Hikam.*

65 *Ibid.*

66 *Kanz al-ʿUmmāl,* Tradition 1751.
67 *Nahj al-Balāghah,* Sermon No. 2.
68 *Biḥar al-Anwār,* Vol. 77, p. 290.
69 *Ibid.,* Vol. 93, p. 160.
70 Qur'ān 13:28.
71 Qur'ān 20:124.
72 Qur'ān 43:36.
73 Qur'ān 5:91.
74 *Al-Kāfi,* Vol. 2, p. 485, and *Makārim al-Akhlāq,* Vol. 2, p. 82.
75 *Thawāb al-Aʿmāl,* p. 21, and *Biḥar al-Anwār,* Vol. 93, p. 195.
76 *Al-Kāfi,* Vol. 2, p. 485, and *Makārim al-Akhlāq,* Vol. 2, p. 83.
77 Qur'ān 4:9.
78 Qur'ān 79:18.
79 Qur'ān 48:26.
80 Qur'ān 41:30.
81 Qur'ān 78:38.
82 Qur'ān 10:26.
83 *Tuḥfah yi-ʿAbbasi,* by Shaykh Muḥammad ʿAli Mu'adhdhin, trans. Dr Faghfoory (2008), p. 162.
84 Qur'ān 42:12.
85 Qur'ān 25:58.
86 *Kashf al-Fawā'id fi Sharḥ Qawā'id al-ʿAqa'id,* p. 46.
87 Shaykh Ṣadūq in his book *Tawḥīd,* p. 141.
88 *Al Bāb al-Ḥādi ʿAshar,* p. 19.
89 *The Elements of Islāmic Metaphysics,* pp. 141–143.
90 *Nahj al-Balāghah,* Sermon 1.
91 Qur'ān 34:3.
92 Qur'ān 6:59.
93 Qur'ān 3:29.
94 Qur'ān 13:8.
95 Qur'ān 50:16.
96 Qur'ān 2:244.
97 Qur'ān 57:4.
98 Qur'ān 58:1.

99 *Nahj al-Balāghah,* Sermon 155.

100 Ancient Persian religious belief was that there were two opposing divinities, one good, and one evil, and that no evil could emanate from the creator of good and no good could emanate from the creator of evil.

In metaphysics, dualism refers to the existence of two types of reality: finite and infinite, matter and form, matter and spirit, relative and absolute. In the 'philosophy of mind', dualism refers to the concept that human beings consist of two radically distinct constituents, i.e. body and soul.

101 Ibrāhīm ibn Sayyār al-Naẓẓām is recognized by most biographers as being the most outstanding Mu'tazilite scholar. To ensure he would have a sound education, his father prevailed upon Al-Khalīl ibn Aḥmad al-Farāhīdī, the first Arabic lexicographer, to accept him as a pupil. He further widened his knowledge base and understanding by his later visits to most of the centres of excellence in Muslim-majority countries. After studying Christianity, Zoroastrianism and Greek heritage, he went on to Kufah to meet the great Shi'ah theologian of his time, Hishām ibn Al-Ḥakam.

He believed the holy Qur'ān to be the eternal miracle of the Prophet Muḥammad ﷺ, not, as thought by many, because of its high degree of eloquence, but because, in spite of people's ability to produce something similar, Allāh Almighty prevents them from doing so. This idea drew harsh Ash'arite attacks that Naẓẓām was thereby falsifying Allāh's word, 'If human beings and Jinn work together to produce the like of the Qur'ān they will never succeed, no matter how hard they strive.' (Qur'ān 17:88)

Naẓẓām also denied that analogy (*Qiyās*) is a valid method by which to deduce Islāmic law.

Naẓẓām died in the year 231 AH. For further reading see Dr Muḥammad Abdul Hādī Abū Rīdah in *Ibrāhīm ibn Sayyār al-Naẓẓām wa Ārā'uhu al-Kalamiyah al-Falsafiyah* (Cairo, 1946).

102 Abū 'Ali Jubbā'i (d. 303 AH) and his son Abū Hāshim (d. 321 AH), both highly respected Mu'tazilite theorists, experienced severely harsh treatment levied by ten contemporary Abbasid caliphs. They witnessed the turning point of Al-Mutawakkil, during which time Mu'tazilite favour was overturned by an ascendency of Ahlul Sunnah. The shift from the School of Reason, supported by Abū 'Ali, to the School of Tradition, supported by

his stepson Abul Ḥasan al-Ashʿari, had a dramatic impact on their severe mistreatment.

It is reported that Abū Hāshim had 29 major disagreements with his father, to the extent that the followers of both camps took every possible opportunity to denounce each other.

103 Brian Greene, *The Fabric of the Cosmos: Space, Time and the Texture of Reality* (Allen Lane, 2004).

104 *A Companion to the Philosophy of Religion*, p. 286.

105 Qur'ān 3:26.

106 Qur'ān 3:198.

107 Qur'ān 10:107.

108 Qur'ān 20:73.

109 Qur'ān 76:5–6.

110 Qur'ān 3:59–61.

111 *The Holy Bible*, New Revised Standard Version, Minster Text Edition (Cambridge University Press, 1992).

112 Extracted from: http://stellarhousepublishing.com/gospel-dates.html.

113 Extracted from *The Gnostic Gospels* by Elaine Pagels (Pelican Books, 1982).

114 See *The Bible and Colonialism: A Moral Critique* by Michael Prior, CM (Sheffield Academic Press, 1997).

115 'Trinity' by David Brown, in *A Companion to the Philosophy of Religion*, edited by Philip L. Quinn and Charles Taliaferro, pp. 527–528 (Blackwell, 1997).

116 http://www.ldolphin.org/PDFs/The_Two_Babylons-Alexander_Hislop.pdf.

117 http://en.wikipedia.org/wiki/Nontrinitarianism.

118 http://www.christadelphian.org.uk/wcb/notrinit.html.

119 http://www.jw.org/en/bible-teachings/questions/trinity/.

120 http://www.jw.org/en/bible-teachings/questions/is-jesus-almighty.

121 Qur'ān 21:22.

122 *Nahj al-Balāghah*, Letter number 31.

123 Qur'ān 57:3.

124 *Nahj al-Balāghah*, Sermon 186.

125 Abul Qāsim al-Balkhi is known to have been the head of the Muʿtazilites of Baghdad. His theological views supported Shiʿism. Aḥmād ibn Yaḥyā ibn

al-Murtaḍā praised him as being an outstanding figure in theology, jurisprudence and Arabic literature. When Al-Balkhi was mentioned in the presence of Abu ʿAli Jubbā'ī, the latter held him to be more learned than his teacher al-Khayyāṭ. See *Ṭabaqāt al-Muʿtazilah*, edited by Suzannah Diviled (Istanbul, 1960).

126 *Wasilat al-Wasā'il fi Sharḥ al-Rasā'il.*

127 Shaykh Ṣadūq, *The Book of Monotheism – Tawḥīd,* pp. 146–338.

128 *Ibid.*, p. 344.

129 ʿAbdul Jabbār ibn Aḥmad is recognized as being the last of the truly outstanding Muʿtazilite scholars. He adhered to Shāfiʿi jurisprudence and Ashʿarite theology until he was 24 years old, when he met Ibrāhīm ibn ʿAyyāsh al-Basri, a close colleague of Abū Hāshim Jubbā'i, and, as a result, became a Muʿtazilite.

After Al-Ṣāḥib ibn ʿAbbād, vizier of the Buyād Mu'ayyid al-Dawlah, appointed him to the highest position in the judiciary in the year 367 AH, he became known as Qāḍī al-Quḍāt. He remained in that august position until he was dismissed by Fakhr al-Dawlah in the year 385 AH.

Abul Ḥusayn al-Basri, Abu Rashid al-Naysābūri, Abdul Salām al-Qazwini, Abul Qasim al-Busti and Abul Qasim al-Tanūkhi are but a small selection of his most famous students. Although he wrote many books on Qur'ānic studies and Principles of Jurisprudence, his works on theology, particularly those that elaborate on Muʿtazilite teaching, received the greatest accolades. His famous work, *Al-Mughnī fi Uṣūl al-Dīn,* consisted of 20 volumes, of which only the 14 that were found in the Yemen have been published. Many biographers have claimed that al-Sayyid al-Murtaḍā (d. 436 AH), a famous Ithnā ʿAshari Shiʿah scholar, studied under him despite there being no solid evidence to support it. Further, al-Murtaḍā's four-volume work *Al-Shāfī fi Al-Imāmah* is a refutation of Qāḍī ʿAbdul Jabbār's *Al-Mughnī*. Some time later, Shaykh Ṭūsī summarized his teacher's book in his *Talkhīs al-Shāfī* published in Najaf by Maktabat al-ʿAlamayn: Al-Ṭūsī wa Baḥr al-ʿUlūm.

Another of Qāḍī ʿAbdul Jabbār's works on theology, *Sharḥ al-Usūl al-Khamsah*, challenges Ashʿarite claims regarding predestination.

130 *Sharḥ al-Usūl al-Khamsah*, p. 528.

131 Qur'ān 2:30.

132 Qur'ān 11:1.

133 Qur'ān 9:6.

134 Qur'ān 97:1.

135 Qur'ān 2:106.

136 Qur'ān 58:12–13.

137 *Sharḥ al-Mawāqif,* Vol. 1, p. 77.

138 Aḥmad ibn Ḥanbal, after whom the Hanbali school of Islāmic Law is named, was born in Baghdad in the year 164 AH. He pursued knowledge in Kufah, Baṣrah, Makkah, Madinah, Syria and Khurasān and compiled 30,000 Prophetic *āḥadīth* into a six-volume work titled *Musnad*. When the Abbasid caliph al-Ma'mūn demanded all scholars within his realm accept the belief that the Qur'ān is created and not eternal, Aḥmad ibn Ḥanbal declined to give in to his demand. After al-Ma'mūn's demise, the caliph al-Muʿtaṣim imprisoned him for 28 months for failure to comply with this belief. He was released in the year 220 AH, to be later acknowledged and highly regarded by al-Mutawakkil.

139 *The Book of Sunnah,* p. 49.

140 *Maqālāt al-Islāmiyīn,* p. 321.

141 *Al-Ibānah,* p. 72.

142 Qur'ān 2:32.

143 *Al-Lumaʿ fi al-Radd ʿala Ahl al-Zaygh wal Bidaʿ,* p. 116.

144 Qur'ān 2:286.

145 *Al-Lumaʿ fi al-Radd ʿala Ahl al-Zaygh wal Bidaʿ,* pp. 99, 113 and 114.

146 Qur'ān 68:42.

147 Qur'ān 68:43.

148 Qur'ān 4:3.

149 *Al-Asfār al-Arbaʿah,* Vol. 7, p. 68.

150 Qur'ān 71:10–12.

151 *Nahj al-Balāghah,* Sermon 143, Vol. 1, p. 524.

152 Qur'ān 41:53.

153 *Nahj al-Balāghah,* Sermon no. 180.

154 *Al-Wāfī (commentary on al-Kāfī),* Vol. 1, p. 84.

155 *Ibid.,* Vol. 1, p. 85.

156 Qur'ān 7:143.

157 *Al Bāb al-Ḥādi 'Ashar,* p. 36.

158 *Philosophy and Technology* (New York: Free Press, 1972, p. 252).

159 *Essays in Christian Analysis and Exegesis,* pp. 123–37.

160 http://www.telegraph.co.uk/science/science-news/10637532/Being-homosexual-is-only-partly-due-to-gay-gene-research-finds.html.

161 Abū al-Hudhayl al-'Allāf, born in Baṣrah in the year 135 AH, was the scholar most favoured by Abbasid caliphs al-Ma'mūn, al-Mu'taṣim and al-Wāthiq, and highly respected by both branches of Mu'tazilitism, i.e. those in Baghdad and those in Baṣrah. The middle of the second and third centuries was a decisive period vis-à-vis debate and dialogue between followers of the various schools of theology, and during this time it was Abū al-Hudhayl who appears to have had the greatest ability. It is reported that while he was 15 years old, a Jewish scholar challenged Muslim scholars by saying, 'You Muslims and we Jews are in agreement about Mūsa being a messenger of Allāh but are not in agreement in regard to the Prophethood of Muḥammad. We thus accept our point of agreement but deny that in which only you believe.' As Abū al-Hudhayl's teacher Uthmān al-Ṭawīl made no comment, the Jewish scholar asked the youth, 'Have you observed how your masters are not able to make any response to this?' To which Abū al-Hudhayl said, 'Leaving that aside, either you ask me or I ask you.' The Jewish scholar then repeated his question, to which Abū al-Hudhayl then responded, 'What you said about the prophet Mūsa refers either to the one who gave glad tidings about the coming of the Prophet Muḥammad and approved of him, or it refers to a Mūsa who did not give such glad tidings. If you meant to refer to the former, I recognize and respect him fully, but if you meant to refer to the latter, I do not recognize that Mūsa and cannot believe that Allāh appointed him a messenger.' At this point the Jewish scholar made an impolite response, regarded by the audience to be so offensive that circumspection determined he depart from Baṣrah. See *Tārikh Baghdad,* Vol. 3, p. 367. The glad tidings of Prophets Mūsa and 'Isā عليهما السلام are discussed in the section on Prophethood (see chapter 9).

As Abū al-Hudhayl was known to have been interested in Greek philosophy, Abul Ḥasan al-Ash'ari asserted that his ideas of Divine Attributes had come from Aristotle. Al-Naẓẓām was one of Abū al-Hudhayl's most famous students. This theologian died in Baṣrah in the year 235 AH. For further reading see: Richard Frank in *The Metaphysics of Created Being According to Abū al-Hudhayl al-'Allāf.*

162 *Biḥar al-Anwar,* Vol. 5, p. 27.

163 *Sharḥ al-Mawāqif,* Vol. 8, p. 146.

164 *Sharḥ al Usūl al-Khamsah,* pp. 332–372.

165 Qur'ān 2:102.

166 Qur'ān 2:249.

167 Qur'ān 2:251.

168 Qur'ān 3:145.

169 Qur'ān 10:100.

170 Qur'ān 4:79.

171 *Biḥār al-Anwār,* Vol. 5, p. 10.

172 Qur'ān 41:46.

173 Qur'ān 52:21.

174 Qur'ān 24:11.

175 Qur'ān 53:39–41.

176 Qur'ān 18:29.

177 Qur'ān 39:7.

178 Qur'ān 76:3.

179 Qur'ān 73:19.

180 Qur'ān 91:7–10.

181 Qur'ān 81:29.

182 Qur'ān 2:102.

183 Qur'ān 2:251.

184 Qur'ān 10:100.

185 *The Book of Monotheism* (*Tawḥīd*), p. 360.

PART THREE

Prophethood

9 The Concept of Prophethood

The Arabic word for Prophethood (*Nubuwwah*) is derived from the word *Naba'* (to inform or to bring news). In its technical sense *Nubuwwah* refers to revelations from Allāh Almighty being received via supernatural means, to enable His guidance for salvation to be delivered to individuals and societies. ʿAllamah Ḥilli defines 'prophet' as 'A man who brings a message from Allāh The Most High, without the mediation of any human being'.

In his commentary, Al Fāḍil al-Miqdād explains that, 'by the term "man" angels are excluded, and by the term, "a bringer of a message from Allāh", everyone is excluded who brings a message from any besides Allāh.'[1]

Allāh Almighty provided human beings with two sources of guidance: one internal, the other external. In Islāmic teaching, the internal is referred to as 'intellect' and the external as 'the Prophets'. As discussed earlier (see p. 4), intellect or innate instinct (*fiṭrah*) directs the soul to recognize 'virtue' and to differentiate between vice and virtue.

1 Is Intellect not a Sufficient Guide?

As human beings are provided with both intellect and desire, there is always a possibility that natural desires may overwhelm and corrupt intellectual judgement. While a person might instinctively know that misappropriation of the wealth of others is wrong and constitutes a transgression, if greed and ill desire overcome logical recognition, it may lead them to ignore all ethical values. In other words, there is a continuous challenge between intellect and desire over how one should behave in specific circumstances. Thus **Divine guidance** appears to be an essential reinforcement of intellectual judgement.[2]

2 Prophets as Role Models and Guides

Allāh tells us that the disbelievers in Makkah were not prepared to accept Muḥammad ﷺ as Allāh's Messenger without supranatural evidence to support his claim to be the Prophet of God. They said to him, 'We will not believe you [O Muḥammad] until you make a spring of water gush forth for us from this [arid] land. Or until you have a garden of palms and vines or generate rivers to suddenly surge through it. Or you cause, as you threaten, the heavens to shatter and drop upon us; or you bring Allāh and the Angels face to face before us. Or you have a house of gold, or ascend into the heavens; and we will not believe you have been there unless you bring us back a book that we may read. Say then [O Muḥammad], "Glory to my Lord. I am only a mortal who has been sent as a Messenger."'[3]

The reason for the above *ayāt* being revealed was because a group of well-known members of the Quraish tribe (including Walid, the son of Mughirah and Abu Jahl) had gathered near the Kaʿbah to request the Prophet Muḥammad ﷺ to open discussions with them. The Prophet ﷺ attended in the hope of guiding them towards the right path. The Makkan spokesperson began by listing the many changes Muḥammad ﷺ had wrought to the traditions and customs of their tribe. He concluded: 'You have disrespected our gods, ridiculed our religion, annulled our ambitions and created disunity. If your purpose is to gain wealth, we are prepared to help you achieve that; if you are after political power, we are willing to establish you as the head of the tribe; if you are suffering from anything, we will assist you in any way we can.'

Muḥammad's response was: 'I seek none of these; the truth is that Allāh has sent me as a Messenger and revealed His Divine scripture for me to deliver to you. If you accept it, you will gain the prosperity of this life and the life hereafter. If you reject it, I will patiently persevere until Allāh passes His Judgement between us.'

The spokesperson replied: 'If you persevere, you will not find any place more disagreeable than our city – so ask your Lord to move these mountains and make rivers flow in our land like those of Syria and Iraq.'

The Prophet Muḥammad ﷺ responded, 'I was not sent to do such things.' They said, 'Then ask your Lord to send down Angels to certify your status and to bestow upon you castles of gold within lush gardens.'

The Prophet ﷺ said, 'I was not sent to do such things. I brought you what has been sent with me and what I have been ordered to deliver. If you do not accept this, I must leave the matter with Allāh.'

They then said, 'Then cause, as you threaten, that the heavens shatter and drop down upon us.' He ﷺ said, 'That is up to Allāh.'

The Prophet ﷺ then left. Abdullah, the nephew of ʿĀtikah and Abu Umayyah, went with him saying, 'O Muḥammad, they made you a generous and fair offer yet you refused them. When they challenged, you declined to accept their challenges, so we will not believe you until you ascend into the heavens and bring us back a book to read.'

Abu Jahl threatened, 'If he does not cease disrespecting our gods and ridiculing the customs of our ancestors, I will have a rock dropped on him when he prostrates.' The Prophet ﷺ had expected them to follow the right path and was disturbed by the incident until the above *ayāt* were revealed.

If they thought all this would end the Prophet's claim to Prophethood, he ﷺ disappointed them. The Prophet's twofold response to Makkan suggestions designed to safeguard idol worship and existing traditions was:

1. Allāh Almighty is glorified and above puerile requests.
2. That he, like them, was human, while the supranatural incidents and miracles they demanded are under the sole control of Allāh Almighty and can only be brought about with His permission.

The Holy Prophet ﷺ, sent as a teacher of humankind, shared their joys and sorrows, mingled with them and was acquainted with their doings. He was merely a human being who had been inspired with Divine wisdom. There would have been no point in Allāh sending angels as messengers, for had they been sent they would have caused confusion rather than understanding. The nature of a messenger needs to be comprehensible if it is to identify characteristics that are understood by people as being of use to them. This is not possible unless feelings, emotions and desires have a similar basis. If the Messenger of Allāh had no idea about anger, greed, jealousy, self-centredness or other human emotions, how could he have been in a position to propose solutions for them?

Familiarity with the hardships, difficulties and sufferings of ordinary people provides the eligibility for a leader to empathize with them and make realistic proposals. For example, Imām ʿAli عليه السلام wrote to his governor in Baṣrah after he learned that the latter had attended a banquet,

> Remember, people emulate their role models. Be informed that your leader [ʿAli himself] has contented himself with two shabby garments out of all the comforts of the world – and only two loaves for his daily sustenance. It is unlikely that you will be able to do the same, but at least support me by remaining pious, chaste and upright. By Allāh, I have no treasure of gold in this world, nor have I plentiful wealth . . . Should I be content with being called Commander of the Believers if I do not share with them their lives' hardships? I try to keep myself engaged in piety so that I am secure on the Day of Judgement and steady on the slippery path. If I had wished, I could have found my way to pure honey, fine wheat and silken clothing – but I dare not allow passions to lead me to greed.[4]

To conclude, Allāh's Messengers are human beings who share the same qualities as all other human beings. Notwithstanding this, they have been inspired by Divine Will and, at Allāh's discretion, present miracles and supranatural evidence of His existence.

3 Revelation

A distinctive and exclusive characteristic of prophets is their connective relationship with the Almighty, by which His communications are received immediately by them. This process, known as revelation (*waḥy*), is unique to prophets. It is in no way comparable to 'eureka' moments of rapture and triumphant joy at a sudden discovery, without necessarily knowing precisely how it was arrived at. This is referred to as inspiration or 'disclosure' (*mukāshafah*).

In the language of the Qur'ān, Allāh employs the word revelation (*waḥy*) in five different ways:

1. *Vis-à-vis guiding creation to fulfil its duties*. Allāh tells us, 'Then He made seven heavens in two days and **revealed** to each heaven its task'.[5]

   Thus it is that we believed that Allāh created the heavens in two days. However, this is not to be understood as two 24-hour periods of time – between the sun's rising one day and its rising on the following day. It refers to an entirely different understanding of the word 'day', as is evidenced by the fact that the concept of time as discrete units is related to motion. This is itself dependent upon the existence of the universe. It follows that, prior to the creation of anything, time, movement and the unit called a day, in the sense in which we currently use this word, did not exist. Thus the Qur'ānic use of the word 'day' refers to stages in creation. From our previous discussion we understand that Allāh has the power to command and create, so the expression **'revealed to each heaven its task'** indicates that He guided His creation to the purposes for which they were created. The word used for 'establishing order' in this *āyah* is 'revelation' (*waḥy*).

The same usage of the word 'revelation' is found in the Qur'ān: 'The day the earth is shaken by a terrible quake that sends forth everything hidden under it, causing human beings to fear what will happen next, will be the day the earth discloses what its Lord had **revealed** to it.'[6]

2. *Vis-à-vis animal instincts.* We understand that animals, insects and birds are guided by innate instincts, and not by reason, wisdom or planning in the manner that free-willed human beings are.

   Allāh refers to the instincts that facilitate animal performance as revelation (*waḥy*). As, for example, 'Your Lord **revealed** to the bee, saying, "Make hives in mountains, in trees and in that which they [humankind] build".'[7]

   Such 'creative revelation' (*waḥy takwīnī*) is the innate and instinctive guidance received by animals.

3. *Vis-à-vis inspiration of the heart.* This is a third meaning for the word 'revelation' used by Allāh in the Qur'ān. For example, 'We revealed to Mūsa's mother "Nurse him".'[8]

   This refers to the time when Pharaoh, told by his soothsayers and astrologers that a child to be born in his kingdom would one day overthrow him, ordered that every new-born boy child in his kingdom be killed. As Allāh had willed Mūsa ﵇ to be protected, He inspired in Mūsa's mother's heart the drive to succeed in her efforts to save her son.

   This same usage is also employed in, 'I revealed to the disciples, "Believe in Me and My messenger [ʿIsā]" and they responded, "We believe and bear witness that we submit to Allāh".'[9] Not being prophets, the disciples clearly did not receive revelation in the sense that it is technically understood – rather, the word 'revelation' used here refers to their hearts being inspired.

4. *Vis-à-vis subtle communication.* This is a fourth meaning for the word 'revelation' that Allāh uses in the Qur'ān. For example, Allāh

tells us, 'Indeed, devils inspire their allies to dispute with you' (Qur'ān 6:121). Subtle communications to inspire allies of Shayṭān are referred to as revelation because, in the Arabic language, the original meaning of the word **'revelation'** was: communication in a manner not easily grasped, understood, or perceived, in order to elude observation or analysis – so that it can take effect imperceptibly and insidiously. It refers to Shayṭān inspiring non-believers to deny the existence of Allāh.

The above four meanings for the word 'revelation' are not what is being referred to in our theological discussions of 'Divine Revelation' with regard to prophethood. 'Revelation' in this context relates to the communication between prophets and the higher realms of existence.

5. *Vis-à-vis Allāh Almighty's connective relationship with prophets.* This connection affords to prophets continuous awareness and understanding of Allāh; its existence ensures that a revelatory suffusion can come down to pervade their hearts, filled with all the meanings of awe, understanding, wisdom, intellect and reflection. It is such revelatory outpourings of wisdom and comprehension that make it possible for prophets to guide others to wisdom, admonition, learning and self-development. The technical term for the word 'revelation' is very different to that of those mentioned above.

   Prophetic revelations may manifest themselves in a variety of ways:

   a. Through dreams, for example when Ibrāhīm عليه السلام dreamed that he had to slaughter his son Ismāʿīl عليه السلام.

   b. Through the direct transference of Divine Knowledge, Wisdom and Divine Law to the Prophet's heart, i.e. complete revelation (*waḥy kāmil*): 'With it came down the Trusted Spirit upon your heart [O Muḥammad] that you may be a warner'.[10]

   c. Aurally, as in, '. . . and Allāh spoke directly to Mūsa'.[11]

> However, the best-known types of revelation are those in which Jibrā'īl or another angel brings down revelatory messages. These three states of revelation are covered in the Qur'ān: 'It is not given to man that Allāh should speak to him other than through revelation, from behind a veil or via a messenger being sent to reveal, by His permission, whatsoever He wills. Truly, He is The Most High, The All-Wise.'[12]

We have covered above definitions of 'revelation' found in the books of Islāmic doctrine and *Kalām*, and its etymology and usage in the Qur'ān. To reiterate, four types of Qur'ānic usage of this word are not relevant to the context of our discussion of doctrine; thus we have identified the only one that is.

It is clear that great triumphs of science do impinge on our lives with an almost daily increase in our understanding of the laws and patterns of matter, energy, space and time. However, as these do not afford us any knowledge of the reality that transcends the world of science, they do not prevent us needing the divine wisdom instilled into the mind, heart and wisdom of the Prophet ﷺ.

Some social scientists claim revelation to be a form of genius – from the Greek verb *gignesthai,* to come into being – defined here as natural aptitude, talent or inclination, a gift possessed by a tiny minority of intelligent people. To consider this we first need to explore what factors, if any, contribute to it.

Most of those in the worlds of science, the arts and philosophy are content to accept that the first factor to motivate genius is probably love, as they consider this state to be the strongest motivational force in the development of the human intellect. This is because intense love leads to passion and enthralment, and those who become enthralled focus on nothing apart from the object of their love, and become annihilated in their beloved. Thus love is most probably the strongest motivational factor to drive the body and mind to innovate, to display genius, advance learning and produce wonderful discoveries and inventions. There are many examples of this in history.

The second factor sometimes mentioned is suffering, for when people experience lengthy periods of suffering, oppression and maltreatment, they are motivated to think and innovate in order for their intellectual output to be recognized as being equal to, if not greater than, that of those who are more advantaged than themselves – and thereby to gain acceptance as citizens of equal worth. There are, too, many examples of this.

The third factor mentioned is membership of a minority community, for they too seek to become accepted as citizens of equal worth.

The fourth factor is a stable childhood background. Within a milieu of psychological and physical stability a child's character may be nourished and allowed to flourish. It is within a secure home that the contented child is free to explore, think, reflect, question and innovate.

The fifth factor is quietude and repose – the ability to lead a quiet, calm and tranquil life in which extraneous activity may be avoided, and physical and mental powers and abilities refreshed.

The sixth factor is primary education. This is an extremely important factor in the shaping of early thought and understanding of the world, in preparation for later flowering of abilities.

We may agree on the above six identified points being contributory factors to genius. They may, together or singly, encourage innovative thought in the fields of literature and science that leads to great discoveries and advancements – hailed as being works of genius – that elevate otherwise ordinary people to that acclaimed position. However, despite their great accomplishments, geniuses are not comparable to prophets other than in their also being human. While their achievements are undoubtedly the result of much endeavour, often in pursuit of hypotheses that they attempt to justify retrospectively, this work is not necessarily undertaken in the spirit of objectivity or scientific inquiry. For example, Freud did not study different human activities and then, on the basis of those findings, explain the variety of behaviours that led to his positing that man's primary motivation is sexual enjoyment. Rather, after having decided that sexual motivation was the most powerful driver of human behaviour, he affirmed it to be true, and only then searched for examples that would support this hypothesis.

Scientists assume that every single phenomenon must have a material explanation. They have no regard for ascension to perfection, nor for a being divested of the properties of matter, place and time. Thus, if they do try to study revelation, it is shorn of all connection to the Divine and to the abundance of existence from the Divine. They do not accept that Allāh's will does not need to be bounded by natural laws.

There is no likeness between geniuses and prophets in regard to their connection with Allāh, nor in the perfections, qualities and moral excellence that they display in their service to humanity. Whatever geniuses produce is connected only to themselves and their thoughts, and has no connection with the First Cause or His unseen knowledge. On the other hand, what prophets arrive at is attributable to Divine revelation and not to the prophets themselves, and thus they do not apply to register patents to secure for themselves any benefit from what they bring.

To conclude, as revelation is not a product of genius, there is no valid reason to confound prophethood with genius.

4 Immunity from Error

According to Imāmiyah theology, immunity from error and sin (*ʿIṣmah*) are essential aspects of Prophethood. All Imāmi scholars concur that this covers the characteristics of prophets that relate to their personal lives – in addition to everything that relates to their receiving revelation and conveying it to people. However, most Sunni scholars deem it only necessary for prophets to have such immunity with regard to the transference of the messages they receive.

The Muʿtazilite theologian Abu ʿAli Jubbā'i did not consider major sins committed by a prophet, prior to being appointed a messenger, to be a matter of any concern, but viewed sins committed after such appointment in a different light. While another Muʿtazilite scholar, Qāḍi Abul Jabbār, believed that prophets should not ever commit major sins, he did consider minor sins to be acceptable, so long as they did not result in the public shunning the prophet.[13]

In quoting all the scholars of his school, the famous Ashʿarite theologian Al-Īji declared: 'There is no problem whatever if prophets commit major or minor sins.'[14]

The main line of reasoning for Imāmiyah doctrine may be summarized as set out below.

1. Prophethood is a covenant with Allāh. The Almighty tells us, 'When his Lord tested Ibrāhīm with specific trials over which he successfully prevailed, He said, "I am making you the Imām of humankind". Ibrāhīm asked, "What about my descendants?" Allāh said, "My covenant does not extend to those who do wrong".'[15] Clearly, committing sins is known by Shariʿah to constitute wrongdoing. Those who commit wrongful acts not only wrong themselves but also their 'messages' and the people to whom they have been sent. It follows, according to the above *āyah*, that the divine covenant is not extended to them.

2. If Prophets were not immune from error there would be no reason for their existence, as any potential inaccuracies might well lead others astray. People tend to follow only those whom they hold in high esteem and in whom they have unequivocal trust. It follows that they would be unlikely to accept 'guidance' from those without such a quality and would most probably disregard whatever they said. As already stated, prophets are role models for the whole of humanity and the possibility that they could behave badly and commit errors would completely negate that function.

3. It is a religious duty that is incumbent upon all Muslims to enjoin good and forbid evil. If a prophet were to sin or err, would it be appropriate for the members of their community to exercise their religious duty and advise them? If answered in the affirmative, such a 'divinely sent guide' would need the guidance of those who had

not themselves received divine guidance, whereas the specific function of prophets is to guide others.

There are Qur'ānic references to acts prophets have committed that, at first glance, appear to negate the above doctrine. The Imāmi scholar, Al-Sayyid al-Murtaḍā,[16] painstakingly analysed all such *ayāt* and presented precise interpretations for each in his book.[17]

To conclude, all people of sound mind agree that in order to educate and advise others, those in charge need to practise what they preach if they want others to follow their advice. In spite of this being obvious, Allāh Almighty commands us: 'O you who believe, why do you say what you do not yourselves do? This is a most heinous error.'[18]

Does ʿIṣmah indicate an inability to err?

If prophets were unable to go astray there would be no reason to consider them virtuous. One does not laud the blind for not ogling the opposite sex, something prohibited by Islām.

Sane pedestrians, aware of the hazard posed by traffic, obey the 'rules of the road'. Aware of potential danger, parents protect children from strangers. As prophets sent to guide people were without doubt aware of the consequence of sinful behaviour, their exemplary conduct was clearly based upon freedom of choice and not inability. Indeed, there are examples of Qur'ānic references regarding the hypothetical (not actual) possibility of them sinning, 'We chose them [the prophets] and guided them to the right path . . . had they associated any other with Him, all their good actions would certainly have been in vain.'[19] From this it is clear that the choice to associate something with Allāh was not negated but that it was Allāh's guidance that prevented their doing so. Another example concerns the appointment of a successor. Allāh Almighty commanded His messenger to deliver what He had revealed to him at that particular moment, with the clear warning, 'And if you do not do so, it will be tantamount to your not having delivered any part of your Lord's message at all.'[20] This signifies that if

Muḥammad ﷺ had (hypothetically) not complied with that order, his every effort over the previous 23 years would have been of no worth. Thus, it was clearly his choice to comply or not to comply.

5 Miracles

The essence of a miracle is that it is a demonstration of the truthfulness of a person's claim to prophethood. Anyone who announces that they have been appointed Allāh's messenger and earthly representative is obliged to provide irrefutable proof to back that claim. Thus, miracles (*Muʿjiz*) constitute an essential aspect of prophethood. There are three requirements for a thing to be considered a miracle:

1. *A miracle is something supranatural.* 'Supranatural' does not mean that the impossible suddenly becomes possible. Rather, it means that, while in the normal course of events things occur gradually over periods of time, in miracles time is dramatically foreshortened so that things appear to occur almost instantly. For example, a small snake grows into a large snake in the space of weeks or months. However, if a staff carried by a man called Mūsa عليه السلام is transformed into a serpent and swallows all before it (i.e. the ropes and sticks made to appear to be snakes), it clearly indicates something supranatural has occurred. Similarly, ʿIsā عليه السلام modelled a bird out of clay and blew life into it by Allāh Almighty's permission.

   During the time of Pharaoh and Mūsa عليه السلام spectacular magic competitions were routinely organized during which, among other things, sticks and ropes were made to appear transformed into serpents. Not believing Mūsa عليه السلام to be a divine messenger, Pharaoh accused him of being a common magician. To make evident to all that that was the case, he arranged for the best magicians to compete with Mūsa عليه السلام. However, Allāh provided Mūsa عليه السلام with the supranatural power to demonstrate His status.

   At the time of ʿIsā عليه السلام the Children of Isrā'il were preoccupied by material advancement and development and not in the least interested in spiritual matters. Thus ʿIsā's miracles were focused on evidencing the supranatural via the transformation of a model bird into a live one and in restoration of the dead.

The eloquence and the beauty of Arabic literature and poetry were well known to the peoples of Arabia. When the unlettered Muḥammad ﷺ produced the apogee of Arabic eloquence it was not believed to be his work but rather some kind of supranatural production. However, Muḥammad ﷺ challenged the masters of Arabic poetry and literature to match the Qur'ān, or even its shortest Sūrah. This subject will be discussed in greater detail in chapter 10 (Specific Prophethood).

2. *Those who perform miracles claim to represent Allāh.* Ambassadors have to present diplomatic credentials before they are accepted, and Allāh Almighty's messengers have to demonstrate their Divine credentials through miracles in order to be accepted by their nations.

   No matter how impressive mystics' extraordinary abilities might be, they cannot be considered divine miracle workers.

3. *Ordinary people are not able to perform anything that resembles miracles.* And as miraculous as they might appear, the most advanced technologies and techniques in the various fields of science and medicine are not on the same level as divine miracles. In order to claim Prophethood, two elements must by definition be present – a challenge to others to effect a similar wonder, and their consequent inability to do so. As neither of these applies to advanced technologies, they are not in any way comparable.

While some might assume that miracles dismantle physical causality, that cannot be so as natural causes are nothing other than channels through which Divine Will is manifest; without it, such causes could not function. For example, a house may be completely rewired to meet all current regulations, but unless it is connected to the electricity supply none of its appliances are able to function.

10 Specific Prophethood

1 Beginning of the Message

There are two versions of how the Prophet Muḥammad ﷺ first heard the divine command to bear responsibility for conveying the message of Islām. One is presented by Sunni theologians and the other by Imāmi scholars.

Both Ṭabari and Ibn Hisham report that revelation began when the Prophet Muḥammad ﷺ, asleep in the cave called Ḥirā, saw the Archangel Jibrā'il appear and command him, 'Recite'. The Prophet answered in surprise, 'What do you want me to recite?' He felt the angel strangle and then release him, before once more commanding him 'Recite'. Muḥammad ﷺ asked, 'What do you want me to recite?' He again felt the angel strangle and release him. When this occurred a third time, fearful that he would be strangled to death, he pleaded, 'What is it that you want me to recite?' The angel then answered, 'Recite in the name of your Lord, the Creator, who originated humanity from a clot of blood. Recite! Your Lord is most gracious. It is He who taught humanity through [the use of] the pen.'

This report continues: the panic-stricken Prophet ﷺ then stood up to ask himself, 'What is it that I have seen? Am I being possessed by the devil?' He glanced to right and left but saw nothing and for a while remained frozen in awe and fear. When home again, he told his wife Khadijah what had occurred and she suggested they consult her religious cousin, Waraqah ibn Nawfal, about it. After being told what had occurred Waraqah said, 'Holy, Holy! By Him who dominates Waraqah's soul, if your report is true this must be the "great spirit" that spoke to Moses.'[21]

Similar reports are to be found in Ibn Kathīr.[22]

Critique: The above report points to the Prophet ﷺ being deeply submerged in oceans of fear, worry and desperation. On the one hand, it insinuates that an evil spirit had taken possession of him, on the other that he had suffered a delusional experience. Thereafter, the succour and advice of a monk was considered necessary to assuage his fear, resolve his dilemma and inform him that he had been appointed a messenger. What an outrageously disrespectful portrayal!

In discussions that relate to the commencement of revelation, Imāmi theologians and historians refer to Qur'ānic references such as, 'Truly it [the Qur'ān] was brought from the Lord of the Universes to your heart by the trusted spirit [the archangel Jibrā'il], so that you may warn people in clearly expressed Arabic.'[23]

Imām ʿAli عليه السلام, the Prophet's closest companion, describes the beginning of the message as follows:

> From the time he was weaned, Allāh ordered a mighty angel to care for him day and night, and guide him along the path of high character and good behaviour. I would follow him like a young camel following the footprints of its mother. Every day he would show me signs of his moral virtues and ordered me to follow them. Every year he sought seclusion in the hill of Ḥirā, where no one but I saw him. In those days, Islām did not exist in any house other than in that of Khadijah and Allāh's Prophet ﷺ where I lived as the third person.[24]

2 Muḥammad ﷺ Allāh's Final Messenger

Those who follow the Messenger, the Prophet, the unlettered one (*Ummi*) mentioned in the *Tawrāt* and the *Injīl* (the Old and New Testaments); the one who commands good, and forbids evil, makes all good things lawful and only prohibits those that are impure, relieves people of burdens and the yokes that lie upon them – those who believe in him, and honour him, and help him, and follow the light sent down with him, are those who achieve success.[25]

Qualities of Allāh's final messenger صلى الله عليه وآله

According to the above *āyah* he has the following qualities.

1. *The Messenger.* The Prophet صلى الله عليه وآله, while worshipping in the cave of Ḥirā outside Makkah was suddenly shaken by the summons: 'O Muḥammad', followed by the command, 'Recite'. That was how revelation began. A swell from the limitless ocean of divinity rose to rend the Prophet's breast and fill the cup of his spirit to the brim. Consequently, he carried the message from the Almighty to guide all humankind to the right path.

2. *The Prophet.* The difference between Prophet and Messenger is that a Prophet brings news from Allāh to humankind, while a Messenger delivers a book of rulings (*Sharīʿah*) and invites all to practise what he teaches.

3. *The unlettered one (Ummi).* Among its various meanings, the word *ummi* describes one who retains unchanged (without need of identifiable training or education) the endowments that they were born with. The final Prophet صلى الله عليه وآله is regarded as *ummi* in the sense that the wisdom needed to fulfil his mission had been divinely implanted. He did not need to attend lessons or lectures or undergo other training to learn to read and write. It would be absurd to think of him as being illiterate in its sense of being unenlightened, or that the Creator had chosen an ignoramus to teach people 'wisdom' and 'the book'.

   > Allāh has revealed to you the book and the wisdom and taught you that which you did not know . . .[26]

If one wonders why the Prophet Muḥammad ﷺ was unlettered, Allāh Almighty explains it in the following *āyah*, i.e. to avoid future allegations that he had copied previous scriptures:

> You did not recite any book before it [the Qur'ān] nor did you transcribe one with your right hand, for then, those who utter falsehoods might have tried to create doubts.[27]

4. *Mentioned in the Tawrāt and the Injīl.* Many exegetes refer to the Comforter in John 14:16, 26, 30 and 15:26, to highlight the Almighty's promise to send the Prophet Muḥammad ﷺ as the final messenger to humankind. Here are some references from both the Old and New Testaments:

> 18 And Abraham said unto God, O that Ishmael might live before thee!
>
> 20 And as for **Ishmael**, I have heard thee: Behold, I have blessed him, and will make him fruitful, and will multiply him exceedingly; **twelve princes** shall he beget, and I will make him a great nation.[28]
>
> 10 The sceptre shall not depart from Judah, nor a lawgiver from between his feet, until Shiloh come; and unto him shall the gathering of the people be.[29]
>
> 15 The Lord thy God will raise up unto thee a Prophet from the midst of thee, of thy brethren, like unto me; unto him ye shall hearken;
>
> 18 I will raise them up a Prophet from among their brethren, like unto thee, and will put my words in his mouth; and he shall speak unto them all that I shall command him.
>
> 19 And it shall come to pass, that whosoever will not hearken unto my words which he shall speak in my name, I will require it of him.[30]
>
> 16 And I will pray the Father, and he shall give you another **Comforter**, that he may abide with you forever;[31]

26 But the **Comforter**, which is the Holy Ghost, whom the Father will send in my name, he shall teach you all things, and bring all things to your remembrance, whatsoever I have said unto you.[32]

30 Hereafter I will not talk much with you: for the prince of this world cometh, and hath nothing in me.[33]

26 But when the **Comforter** is come, whom I will send unto you from the Father, even the Spirit of truth, which proceedeth from the Father, he shall testify of me:[34]

Allāh tells us in Qur'ān 61:6, "ʿIsā son of Maryam said, "O children of Isrā'il, truly I am the messenger of Allāh sent to you to confirm the Torah that was sent out before me, and the good news of the messenger to come after me, whose name is Aḥmad."'

The name Aḥmad was employed as a translation of *Periclytos* in all Arabic versions of the New Testament. Muir and Sale say Aḥmad or Muḥammad, the praised one, is almost a translation of the Greek word *Periclytos*. The word 'Comforter' in the English version is for the Greek word *Paracletos* that means Advocate, or one who is called to the help of another.

5/6. *Commands the good/Forbids evil.* An essential teaching of the Holy Qur'ān is to command good and forbid evil. This refers to moral values recognized by all humankind of pure nature, that exemplify good conduct, honesty, caring, helping one another, being truthful and the maintenance of justice and fairness in all situations. It refers also to the reciprocal values: preventing corruption, mischief, insult, assault and harm to others that must necessarily be avoided. Indeed, every Muslim is obliged to be a societal advocate of moral values and to advise their fellow Muslims to eschew all vices. The Muslim nation is described as being the finest exemplar of morality. In Allāh's words, 'You are the best nation ever brought forward from humankind for you enjoin good and forbid evil.'[35]

7/8. *Endorses the wholesome as lawful/Decrees what is foul to be unlawful.* In the Qur'ān the terms *Ṭayyib* and *Khabīth* are used to express the wholesome and the foul. In 7:58, Allāh compares lands of luxuriant vegetation with barren land whose yield is, if anything, poor in quality and quantity. In 7:32, Allāh describes wholesome provision from which people benefit. However, according to Allamah Ṭabāṭabā'i, both *Ṭayyib* and *Khabīth* may refer to anything that is immaculate and beneficial, or their opposites vis-à-vis judgement, conduct and characteristics. For example, logical and beneficial advice is described as *Kalām Ṭayyib.* Similarly, Arabs pronounce delicious food to be *Ṭaʿām Ṭayyib.*

To conclude, Qur'ān 7:157 indicates that all the rulings of the Prophet Muḥammad ﷺ guarantee maximum soundness and benefit to humanity regardless of whether they refer to dos or to don'ts. This wider concept may be observed in a variety of ways:

- Acts of Worship benefit the spiritual, psychological and physical needs of humanity. They purify souls and secure their healthy state.

- The higher objectives of Islāmic legislation are to benefit both individual and societal interests. Whilst the happiness of individuals is a matter of concern to them, the soundness and health of society as a whole is a matter of concern to all.

- An analysis of what is prohibited in Islām indicates that all kinds of food and drink that are beneficial to health are considered to be lawful, with all things harmful to health being considered unlawful. For example, intoxicating beverages are prohibited on the ground of alcohol being a toxin (e.g. it is used to kill microorganisms in order to sterilize instruments), a toxicity that is worsened in that, to be cleared from the body it has to be metabolized to acetaldehyde, an even more toxic substance. Further, intoxicating beverages impair cognition, increase the risk of dementia, have the potential to be addictive, severely damage the brain, heart and liver, and increase mortality risk. Illicit drugs and other poisons are also unlawful. Blood products and carrion [that may carry bacteria] are deemed to be unlawful as well.

9. *Relieves burdens*. The Prophet ﷺ said, 'I bring a religion that is easy to follow and one in which there are many advantages.'[36]

   According to Qur'ān 7:157, before the Holy Prophet ﷺ the duties and injunctions of believers had been most demanding. The Message of Islām came to remove difficulty and to relieve humankind of burdens. Allāh Almighty teaches us how to communicate with Him:

   > O our Lord! Do not burden us as you burdened those before us. O our Lord! Do not impose upon us that which we have not the strength to bear.'[37]

   In the field of Principles of Jurisprudence, scholars discuss 'Islāmic Law does not occasion unbearable hardship' that is based upon the above considerations.

10. *Light was sent down with him*. Light may be interpreted as 'Guidance', 'Knowledge' or the Qur'ān itself. The Prophet ﷺ faultlessly delivered all the above.

Conclusion: Thus, 'any who seek to achieve salvation and prosperity should believe in the Prophet Muḥammad ﷺ, honour him, help him, and value his teaching.'

Qur'ānic descriptions of the Prophet Muḥammad ﷺ

Four aspects are described in the Qur'ān.

a. **What Allāh tells us regarding his merits:**

   1. Allāh Almighty elevated him, 'And [have We not] elevated you to pre-eminence?'[38]

2. In spite of Allāh's punishment of previous nations, 'Allāh did not choose to chastise [your people] while you were still among them . . .'[39]

3. '[O Muḥammad] I avow by your life that it is their delirium [of lust] that causes them to blindly stumble to and fro!'[40] No record exists of the establishment of such an oath by Allāh vis-à-vis the life of any other prophet.

4. After having informed him that He and His angels offer their salutations to him, Allāh commanded Muslims to do so too: 'Verily Allāh and His angels bless the Prophet: [hence,] you who have attained faith, bless him and submit to [his guidance].'[41] Authentic sources evidence that the Prophet ﷺ taught Muslims to include also his progeny in their salutations.[42]

5. 'You indeed exemplify divinely inspired ethical behaviour.'[43]

6. 'The Messenger of Allāh [Muḥammad] is undoubtedly the exemplar for those who believe in Allāh and the last day.'[44]

7. 'Say [O Muḥammad] if you love Allāh then follow me, for Allāh will love you and forgive you your sins as He is both forgiving and merciful'.[45] This suggests Allāh's love is inchoate until the Prophet ﷺ is followed.

8. 'Those who obey the Messenger obey Allāh.'[46]

9. Allāh Almighty raised the Prophet ﷺ to the celestial arena to disclose to him what no human ever saw before. '[His] eye did not waver or stray, and he truly witnessed his Lord's most profound signs.'[47]

10. 'He does not speak on his own behalf, but only to pass on what has been divinely revealed to him.'[48]

b. **Refutation of Makkan allegations:**

1. Allāh's refutation of the allegation that he was a poet: 'And it is not – however little you may [be prepared to] believe him – the

word of a poet.'[49] And, 'We have not imparted to this [Prophet] the gift of poetry, nor would [poetry] have been suitable for this [message]; it is but a reminder to clarify truth lucidly.'[50]

2. Allāh's refutation of the allegation that he was a soothsayer: 'And neither is it – however little you may [be prepared to] take it to heart – the word of a soothsayer.'[51]

3. As they continued to deny his being Allāh's messenger, He instructed him to say, 'None are able to bear witness between us as Allāh does; and [none can bear witness as] those who truly understand this divine injunction.'[52]

4. Allāh's refutation of the allegation that he was insane: 'Have none of them been able to discern that he does not exhibit any symptoms of mental disorder? That he is but a plain warner?'[53] And, 'By the grace of Allāh, you are not [O Muḥammad], mentally deranged!'[54]

5. 'We are fully aware that they say, "It is only another human being who imparts this to him!" The person to whom they [falsely] ascribe that is not a native of this land, while this is articulated in clear [pure and unadulterated] Arabic.'[55]

6. Allāh's refutation of the allegation that he was a sorcerer: 'All of Our previously sent messengers have been portrayed as either having the ability to cast spells or being of unsound mind.'[56]

7. As it might have been difficult for them to observe a Messenger of Allāh lead a normal life, they questioned, 'What kind of messenger is a [man] who eats food [like other mortals] and goes about the marketplaces? Why has no [visible] angel been sent as a warner together with him?'[57] Allāh's response: 'Even before you [O Muḥammad], we never sent any message-bearer who was not a [mortal man] who ate food [like other human beings] and went about the marketplaces – for We cause you [human beings] to be a means of testing one another.'[58]

8. As Makkan society regarded only male offspring to be their descendants, subsequent to the death of all of the Prophet's sons they considered him to be *abtar* (without offspring). Allāh refuted this in saying, 'It is certainly your enemy's lineage that will cease to exist!'[59] Further, authentic sources report that the Prophet ﷺ said, 'The lineage of every prophet is continued via his loins but mine is continued via ʿAli and Fatimah.'[60]

9. When a few days' break occurred between revelations being received, Makkans imagined the Prophet to have been forsaken by Allāh. The divine response to this was, 'Your Lord has neither forsaken you, nor is He displeased by you.'[61]

10. Allāh's refutation of the allegation that what he said merely reiterated assertions made by previous societies: 'Say [O Muḥammad], He who knows the mysteries of the heavens and the earth has revealed this [Qur'ān] to me!'[62]

c. **Allāh's solicitude in the fulfilment of his mission.**

1. As the Prophet's message was met with complete uninterest and negative comment, he ﷺ grew increasingly frustrated by the seeming hopelessness of fulfilling his mission. However, Allāh reassured him, 'Ṭā Hā, We did not bestow the Qur'ān on you from on high to cause you distress.'[63]

   Ṭā Hā is one of the names by which the Prophet Muḥammad ﷺ is known.

2. 'Perhaps you are disheartened by their not being willing to believe this message?'[64]

3. 'Do not agonize over them, for Allāh is certainly fully aware of all that they do!'[65] This emphasizes the Prophet's disheartenment at their being indifferent to the light that he invited them to.

4. 'Indeed, a messenger from among you has come to you. His concern about what you might suffer weighs heavily upon him in light of his compassion and mercy.'[66]

To emphasize the unpredictability of divine guidance being accepted, Allāh told His messenger:

1. 'You certainly will not be able to guide all those whom you strive to guide. For, it is Allāh who guides those whom He wishes.'[67]
2. [O Prophet] continue to urge them, for your mission is to encourage – you cannot compel them to believe.[68]
3. But if they turn away [from you, remember that] your duty is only to deliver the message clearly.[69]

d. **Benefits to be drawn from his Message:**

1. His hoped-for intercession: 'And forsake sleep for [part] of the night in order to offer additional prayers, for your Lord may well raise you to an honourable position [of intercession on the Day of Judgement].'[70]
2. He leads humankind from darkness into light: 'It is He who bestows, from on high, clear messages to His servant to guide you out of the deep darkness [of infidelity] into the light [of faith], for Allāh is most compassionate and merciful towards you.'[71] Indeed, those who believe in the Prophet Muḥammad ﷺ, support him and follow the light that has been sent down with him will be triumphant.[72]
3. He invites to the reality of life: 'O you who have attained to faith! Respond to Allāh and His messenger who invite you to life.'[73]
4. Submission to his authority: 'By your Lord! They do not [truly] believe until they request you [O Prophet], to pass judgement on all that they dispute amongst themselves – that their hearts so willingly accept, they completely submit to it.'[74]

Imām ʿAli عليه السلام describes the Prophet ﷺ

The easiest way in which to discover the characteristics of another is to ask those who know them well. Who better than ʿAli عليه السلام to disclose what the Prophet ﷺ was really like:

1. ‘As I breathed the scent of Prophethood I would observe the brilliance of divine revelation and message.

   When revelation descended on Allāh’s Prophet ﷺ I heard Shayṭān moan. I asked, “O Prophet of Allāh, what is this moaning?” and he replied, “That is Shayṭān who has lost all hope of being worshipped. O ʿAli, you see all that I see and hear all that I hear although you are not a prophet – you are vicegerent (*Waṣiy*) and surely on (the path of) virtue.”

   I was with him when a party of Quraish came to him saying, “O Muḥammad, you have made a big claim which none of your forefathers nor any of your own family have made. We ask you one thing: if you answer us and show it to us, we will believe you are a prophet and messenger; but if you cannot, we will know you are a sorcerer and a liar.”

   The Messenger of Allāh said, “What do you ask for?” They said, “Ask this tree to move, together with its roots, and stop before you.” The Prophet responded, “Truly, Allāh has power over everything. If Allāh does it for you, will you then believe and stand witness for truth?” They answered, “Yes.” He then said, “I will show you whatever you want, but I know you will not incline towards virtue, and that among you there are those who will be thrown into the pit and those who will form parties [against me].” Then the Holy Prophet said, “O tree, if you believe in Allāh and the Day of Judgement and know that I am the Prophet of Allāh, then with His permission, come up with your roots and stand before me.” By Him who entrusted the Prophet with truth, the tree moved itself, and with a great humming and flapping like wings of birds, came with its roots, to stand before the Messenger of Allāh. I was on the Prophet’s right side and some of its twigs brushed my shoulders.

   When the people saw this they said with pride and vanity, “Now order half of it to come to you and the half of it remain [in its place].”

The Holy Prophet ordered the tree to do that and half the tree advanced towards him in an amazing manner and with great humming. It was about to touch the Prophet of Allāh when they, in disbelief and revolt, said, "Ask this half to go back to its other half and be as it was." This the Prophet ordered and it returned. I then said, "O Prophet of Allāh, I acknowledge that with the permission of Allāh the Sublime, the tree did what it did in testimony to your Prophethood and to heighten your word." Upon this, all the people shouted, "Rather a sorcerer, a liar; it is indeed a wonderful wizardry that he is very adept in. Only a man like this [pointing to me] can stand testimony to you in your affairs."'[75]

2. 'Allāh Almighty had brought out the Prophet Muḥammad ﷺ from the supremely distinguished origin and (lineal) tree from which He had brought forth other Prophets. Muḥammad's descendants are the best descendants, his kinsmen the best of kin and his lineal tree the best of trees. It grew in esteem and rose in distinction. It has tall branches and unapproachable fruit. He is the leader (*Imām*) of all who exercise fear (of Allāh) and the light for those who seek guidance. He is a lamp whose flame burns, a meteor whose light shines and a flint with bright spark. His conduct is upright, his behaviour exemplary, his speech decisive and his decision just. Allāh sent him after an interval from the previous Prophets, when people had fallen into errors of action and ignorance. May Allāh have mercy upon you.'[76]

3. '. . . burdened with responsibility [of Prophethood] he bore it standing by Your commands, advancing Your will, without shrinking nor weakened determination, listening to Your revelation, preserving Your testament, continuing to spread Your commands till he had lit fire for its seeker and illuminated the path for those who groped in the dark.

   He guided troubled hearts. He introduced clear guiding signs and shining injunctions. He is Your trusted trustee, the treasurer of Your treasured knowledge, Your witness on the Day of Judgement,

Your envoy of truth and Your Messenger to the people. O Allāh, prepare a large place for him under Your shade and reward him by multiplying Your bounty.

O Allāh, elevate his status above all others, heighten his position with You, grant perfection to his brilliance and perfect his light. In reward for his discharging Your mission, grant him that his testimony be admitted and his speech be liked, for his speech is just and his judgements clear-cut.'[77]

3 The Universality of His Message

1. 'We have not sent you but as a bearer of glad tidings and a warner to the whole of humankind'[78]

   Allāh's revelation through the Holy Prophet was not meant for one family, one tribe, one race or one set of people. It was meant for all humankind, for whom, if they turn to Allāh, it is a message of glad tidings of His mercy, and if they do not turn to Him, a warning against disobedience and inevitable punishment.

   Even though most people do not appreciate the universality of Allāh's final Prophet's mission, He tells us in the Qur'ān that it was revealed to endow humanity with awareness of their full dynamic potential.

2. 'We sent you not but as a mercy unto the worlds.'[79]

   Throughout the ages Allāh Almighty has sent Prophets to every nation and tribe. Prophethood culminated with the Holy Prophet ﷺ being sent to deliver Allāh's Universal Message to all of humanity. His Eternal Mercy, the Qur'ān, revealed the perfected and completed religion as law and guidance for all humankind until the end of time.

3. 'It is He who sent His messenger with guidance and the religion of truth, that He may make it prevail over all religions, even though the polytheists may detest it.[80]

Throughout the centuries insincere teachers and preachers have attempted to benefit themselves with false statements and distortions of Allāh's message. However, through the Holy Prophet and his progeny, Allāh has shown His true religion to be a sign of success. For the people with understanding, the true teaching of Islām provides a model code of law for human society. The ultimate triumph of Islām will be witnessed when Imām al-Mahdi, the final true successor of the Holy Prophet, reappears by Allāh's permission. It is he who will unite humanity into a single community, guided by Divine law, to live in peace and harmony, freed from injustice, exploitation and polytheism.

The laws given to earlier Prophets were divinely perfected and completed and called Islām. In both theory and practice, Islāmic teaching surpasses all others.

4. 'Say (O Muḥammad), O People, truly I am the Messenger of Allāh to whom belongs the kingdom of the heavens and the earth.[81]

As the message of Islām is universal, the Prophet sent letters to the Emperor of Persia, Caesar in Rome, the King of Egypt and the Ruler of Abyssinia, to invite them to embrace Islām.

Was the Prophet Muḥammad forgetful?

As already discussed (see p. 194), prophets are role models, to exemplify the behaviour and conduct that need to be emulated by those who seek guidance on their road towards perfection. All ethical merit found in their personality and character is based not upon what people would love to see in their leaders (as is claimed by some orientalists) but on what has been established by the Almighty: 'Truly you [O Muḥammad] are the exalted example of sublime morality.'[82]

All historians confirm that even before he received the message, the Prophet Muḥammad was renowned for truthfulness and honesty, as is evidenced by Imām ʿAli's words regarding his personality. Nonetheless, there are reports that allege the prophet was not always mindful, with assertions that he once shortened the noon prayer to two *rakʿāt* (cycles). It is claimed that a companion then asked if that prayer represented a new ruling or if it was simply that he ﷺ had forgotten how many he had already offered. Turning to the congregation the Prophet ﷺ is then said to have asked, 'Is this true?' When they confirmed it was, he offered two further *rakʿāt* plus two extra prostrations to make up for his error.[83]

Another incident, reported by Bukhāri, Muslim and Abu Dāwūd on the authority of ʿImrān ibn Ḥuṣain, is that once while on a journey the Prophet ﷺ did not arise for morning prayers until the sun's heat woke them all.[84]

Having investigated the above claims it may be concluded that:

1. The holy Qur'ān confirms that Allāh Almighty protected the Prophet Muḥammad ﷺ from forgetfulness: 'We make you read so that you will not forget.'[85] That He did not grant similar protection to other prophets is witnessed vis-à-vis Adam[86] and Mūsa.[87]

2. Shaykh Al-Ḥurr al-ʿĀmili narrates many *āḥadīth* that evidence the Prophet Muḥammad ﷺ being protected from forgetfulness. The authenticity of these *āḥadīth* is considered to be stronger than those that make claim to the contrary.[88]

3. Further, those *āḥadīth* that claim him to have been forgetful are invalidated by an absence of logic. Any possibility of forgetfulness would destroy the 'trust' that people need to have before they agree to follow any leader.

4. Discrepancies in the detail of reports by Bukhāri, Muslim and others weaken their validity. Some claim that the Prophet ﷺ forgot *Salāt al Fajr*, others that it was the *Ḍuhr* prayer. Some claim he ﷺ offered two *rakʿāt* instead of four, yet others, purporting to refer to the same incident, assert he offered five *rakʿāt*. Whilst some reports claim that he ﷺ prayed *ʿAsr* prayer in three *rakʿāt* and then went home, others claim that he then leant on the wood at the entrance of the mosque.

The above four points sufficiently illustrate the improbability that tales of the Prophet's supposed forgetfulness are true.

4 The Eternal Miracle

The Prophet Muḥammad ﷺ effected both temporary and eternal miracles. The temporary were of limited time and effect, such as when pebbles in his hand glorified Allāh (see: *Biḥar al-Anwār* Vol. 17. p. 296), and when a limited amount of food proved more than sufficient to feed 40 people (see: The summoning of his family, page 240). Another temporary miracle is recorded by Imām ʿAli ؑ when he describes the Prophet ﷺ (see: p. 218).

His eternal miracle, the challenge to all to effect something similar, is the Holy Qur'ān. Despite Arab claims that their poetry represents the ultimate in eloquence (they would proudly hang their most famous works *Muʿallaqāt* on the walls of the Kaʿbah), no Arab poet was able to meet this challenge. Those who attempted it had ridicule heaped upon their efforts. Had they been able to produce anything similar to the Qur'ān they would not have risked their lives in waging war against the Prophet ﷺ.

The various stages of the challenge

Allāh first challenged the Arabs to produce the likeness of the entire Qur'ān: 'If both humankind and Jinn laboured to produce the like of this Qur'ān they would not succeed, even if they successfully managed to cooperate with each other.'[89]

The second stage was when they were challenged to produce only 10 Surahs like those of the Qur'ān: 'Do they say he has fabricated it? Say, then fabricate 10 Surahs like it and invoke whomever you can besides Allāh should you be truthful'.[90]

The third stage, after they have proven unable to meet either of the above challenges, was to produce a single Surah like it: 'If you are in doubt concerning what We have sent down to Our servant, then bring a Surah like it, and invoke your helpers besides Allāh should you be truthful.[91]

This challenge remains valid until people no longer exist on this earth.

Some believe the inimitability of the Qur'ān refers to its literary form, eloquence and style, others that it refers to its meaning, arrangement and consistency. Nonetheless, its inimitability is evidenced by:

1. The Qur'ān guarantees spiritual guidance in addition to physical and material effects.

2. All generations may benefit from the Qur'ān in accordance with the depth of their understanding.

3. The holy Qur'ān uses the most simple of devices, namely the letters of the alphabet, to establish its miraculous nature.

The above points are elaborated on below:

To end allegation and speculation that the Qur'ān – revealed to a person known not to have received any formal education – could possibly be the construct of the human intellect, Allāh Almighty challenged human beings to compose even one Surah in the style and manner of His Divine Revelation.

In what respect then is the Qur'ān an unchallengeable miracle, and how is it the proof of its own truthfulness? In answer to these questions the following opinions have been raised:

1. The Qur'ān's universal message of guidance is in a language and style appropriate to address every aspect of human life and endeavour: individual and social, economic and political, physical and spiritual. Allāh Almighty challenged the poets and orators of the *Jāhiliyyah* to match the eloquent and unique rhetorical style of the Qur'ān. In failing this challenge, some chose to confront Allāh's final Messenger, and sacrifice their life and dignity.

2. The Qur'ān's powerful and fascinating tone has the ability to touch the human mind and heart. This is acknowledged by the comments

of early opponents of Islām. They advised their fellow citizens of Makkah not to go near the Prophet – for fear of being bewitched, for they claimed his Qur'ānic recitation wove magical spells over people. Some tried to block their ears, but were not able to resist their hearts being touched and their lives being transformed once they heard it. The following incidents elaborate on the above:

a. When the Quraish observed a dramatic increase in the number of people who joined the Prophet ﷺ, ʿUtbah, son of Rabiʿah addressed his people and, pointing to the Prophet sitting alone in the mosque, asked them, 'Shall I go to Muḥammad and suggest he discontinue his efforts?' With their approval he went to him and said, 'My nephew, you have greatly damaged your community – you have created disunity amongst them and ridiculed their gods – so I propose that we appoint you king and collect for you substantial capital in order for you to cease your current divisive activity.' To this came the answer, 'Have you finished?' He ﷺ then asked ʿUtbah to hear him out and proceeded to recite the first five *ayāt* of Surah 41. Moved by the words, ʿUtbah continued to listen to the Prophet's recitation until he reached *āyah* 28, in which prostration is ordered. After the Prophet ﷺ had prostrated and raised his head, he said to ʿUtbah, 'Now that you have heard you may decide.'

   When he returned to his colleagues they found him altered and asked him why this was so: 'I heard something that I have never heard the like of, by god it is not poetry nor magic, nor prophecy, so, people of Quraish, leave this man alone as I see he will greatly alter your future.'[92]

b. The famed Arab celebrity Walīd, son of Mughirah, renowned as a connoisseur and authority on Arabic poetry (and invariably a judge at their competitions), resolutely insulted the Prophet ﷺ until he had occasion to hear the Prophet ﷺ recite:

   Ḥā Mim The revelation of the Book from Allāh the Almighty the Omniscient. Forgiver of sin, Accepter of repentance, severe in

> chastisement, Lord of Bounty. There is no deity but He, He is the ultimate end [of life's journey]. No one disputes the signs of Allāh save those who disbelieve. So, [O Muḥammad] let not their wandering in the cities deceive you. The people of *Nūḥ* before them and the confederate tribes after them belied [Our signs] and every people plotted against their messenger in order to seize him, and dispute by means of false arguments to refute truth, so I seized them. How terrible was then My retribution? Thus, the word of your Lord proved again to be true against those who disbelieved and who are inmates of the fire.'[93]

Walīd is reported to have admitted to his friends, 'By God, I heard Muḥammad recite something that is the speech neither of human nor Jinn. There is a particular sweetness and brightness to it, the highest register is so fertile and the lowest of such depth that it overcomes all other speech – there is nothing at all like it.'

3. Muḥammad's gift of prophecy foretold, for example, the 'Roman' victory over the Persians.[94] Between 614 and 616 CE the Persians defeated the Emperor Heraclius and gained many of his lands. While Muslims were saddened by the Persian victory, Makkan pagans were overjoyed that Fire Worshippers had overcome followers of Divine scripture, and taunted Muslims saying that they would ultimately suffer the same fate. Allāh, however, revealed in the Qur'ān that Rome would gain ultimate victory.[95] This was fulfilled when Heraclius defeated Persia in the year 624 CE and when, at the Battle of Badr, the Muslims defeated the disbelievers of Makkah. It is interesting to note the different reactions of the Emperors of Byzantium and Persia to Muḥammad's letters. The former received his graciously and responded with valuable gifts while the latter is reported to have torn it up.

4. The extensive Islāmic legal structure in which rulings, based on Qur'ānic teaching, provide comprehensive, accurate and appropriate legislation to cover every aspect of human activity. This discipline is referred to as 'Principles of Jurisprudence'.

5. The scientific facts presented in many *ayāt* of the Holy Qur'ān that cover the order of the universe, celestial bodies, the laws of nature and other subjects that could not have been known during the Prophet's lifetime other than via Divine revelation. For example, in the Qur'ān Allāh discloses that everything that grows in the earth has a specific weight. If any change of weight were to occur in the parts of plants, for example, it would form a different organism: 'The earth We have spread out, and placed therein firm hills and caused each thing to grow therein, well proportioned.'[96] In another *āyah* Allah alludes to the need for various species to be pollinated by wind in order to blossom.[97] Another unknown scientific fact at the time unveiled by the Qur'ān is the movement of the earth. In this regard Allāh Almighty tells us, 'It is Allāh who has appointed the Earth as a cradle'[98] – a cradle being a device that oscillates on rockers or swings on pivots to induce movement.

A further unknown fact disclosed in the Qur'ān 14 centuries ago was the existence of another continent,[99] in which Allāh refers to the two easts and the two wests, where sunrise and sunset times are different.

To conclude, the Holy Qur'ān is not a human construct but a precise revelation.

Notes to Part Three

1 *Al-Nāfi' Yawm al-Ḥashr fi Sharḥ al-Bāb al-Ḥādī 'Ashr,* p. 54.

2 In Hinduism, Brahman connotes the highest Universal Principle, or the Ultimate Reality in the universe. Hindus claim to recognize one God, Brahman, the eternal origin who is the cause and foundation of all existence. However, different Hindu communities may have their own divinities whom they worship, but these are simply different ways of approaching the Ultimate. They recognize three principal gods:

- Brahma, who creates the universe
- Vishnu, who preserves the universe
- Shiva, who destroys the universe

In some temples, a sculpture of one head with three faces symbolizes the above ideas.

3 Qur'ān 17:90–93.

4 *Nahj al-Balāghah,* Letter No. 45.

5 Qur'ān 41:12.

6 Qur'ān 99:1–5.

7 Qurān 16:68.

8 Qur'ān 28:7.

9 Qur'ān 5:111.

10 Qur'ān 26:193–194.

11 Qur'ān 4:164.

12 Qur'ān 42:51.

13 *Sharh al-Uṣūl al-Khamsah,* p. 573.

14 *Al-Mawāqif,* p. 359.

15 Qur'ān 2:124.

16 ʿAli ibn Ḥusayn ibn Mūsa (355–436 AH), also known as Al-Sharīf al-Murtaḍā, studied under the renowned Shiʿah scholar Al-Shaykh al-Mufīd. His residence in Baghdad was a centre of scholarship attended by hundreds of students including Al-Shaykh al-Ṭūsi. His library is known to have contained 80,000 manuscrpts.

Ibn Ḥajar claimed him to have been the very first scholar to dedicate his residence to such extensive scholarly endeavours. He was later appointed Head Hashemite of his time. Najāshi recorded that he was the author of 71 manuscripts.

17 *Tanzīh al-Anbeyā',* Najaf: Al-Ḥaydariyah Press, 1372 AH.

18 Qur'ān 61:2–3.

19 Qur'ān 6:87–88.

20 Qur'ān 5:67.

21 *The Life of Muḥammad,* by Muḥammad Husein Haykal, pp. 73–77.

22 *The Life of the Prophet Muḥammad,* by Ibn Kathīr, translated by Dr Trevor Le Gassick, Vol.1, p. 292.

23 Qur'ān 26:192–195.

24 *Nahj al-Balāghah,* Sermon 192.

25 Qur'ān 7:157.

26 Qur'ān 4:113.

27 Qur'ān 29:48.

28 Genesis 17:18, 20.

29 Genesis 49:10.

30 Deuteronomy 18:15, 18, 19.

31 John 14:16.

32 John 14:26.

33 John 14:30.

34 John 15:26.

35 Qur'ān 3:110.

36 *Kanz al-ʿUmmāl, Ḥadīth* numbers 900 and 5422.

37 Qur'ān 2:286.

38 Qur'ān 94:4.

39 Qur'ān 8:33.
40 Qur'ān 15:72.
41 Qur'ān 33:56.
42 *Ṣaḥiḥ al-Bukhāri*, Vol. 4, p. 178 and *Faḍl al-ṣalāt ʿalā al-Nabī*, pp. 56, 57, 62 and 64.
43 Qur'ān 68:4.
44 Qur'ān 33:21.
45 Qur'ān 3:31.
46 Qur'ān 4:80.
47 Qur'ān 53:17–18.
48 Qur'ān 53:3–4.
49 Qur'ān 69:41.
50 Qur'ān 36:69.
51 Qur'ān 69:42.
52 Qur'ān 13:43.
53 Qur'ān 7:184.
54 Qur'ān 68:2.
55 Qur'ān 16:103
56 Qur'ān 51:52.
57 Qur'ān 25:7.
58 Qur'ān 25:20.
59 Qur'ān 108:3.
60 See: Ibn Ḥajar in *Lisān al-Mizān*, Vol. 3, p. 429;
Al-Ḥākim al-Naishābūri in *Al-Mustadrak ʿala Ṣaḥiḥain*, Vol. 3, p. 164;
Al Qundūzi in *Yanābiʿ al-Mawaddah*, p. 266;
Al-Muttaqi al-Hindi in *Kanz al-ʿUmmāl*, Vol. 6, p. 152.
61 Qur'ān 93:3.
62 Qur'ān 25:6.
63 Qur'ān 20:1–2.
64 Qur'ān 18:6 and 26:3.
65 Qur'ān 35:8.
66 Qur'ān 9:128.
67 Qur'ān 28:56.
68 Qur'ān 88:21–22.

69 Qur'ān 16:82.

70 Qur'ān 17:79.

71 Qur'ān 57:9.

72 Qur'ān 7:157.

73 Qur'ān 8:24.

74 Qur'ān 4:65.

75 *Nahj al-Balāghah,* Sermon 192.

76 *Ibid.,* Sermon 94.

77 *Ibid.,* Sermon 72.

78 Qur'ān 34:28.

79 Qur'ān 21:107.

80 Qur'ān 9:33.

81 Qur'ān 7:158.

82 Qur'ān 68:4.

83 *Jamiʿ al-Uṣūl,* Vol. 6, p. 350.

84 *Al-Tāj al Jāmiʿ lil Uṣūl,* Vol. 1, p. 120.

85 Qur'ān 87:6.

86 Qur'ān 20:115.

87 Qur'ān 18:61, 73.

88 *Al-Tanbīh bil Maʿlūm min al-Burhān,* pp. 26–44.

89 Qur'ān 17:88.

90 Qur'ān 11:13.

91 Qur'ān 2:23.

92 *Biography of the Prophet,* by Ibn Hishām, Vol. 1, p. 293.

93 Qur'ān 40:1–6.

94 The Byzantine or Eastern Roman Empire (terms created after the end of the realm) was the predominantly Greek-speaking continuation of the eastern part of the Roman Empire. It survived and continued to exist after the fall of the Western Roman Empire and during most of its existence was the most powerful economic, cultural and military force in Europe. Under the reign of Heraclius (610–641 CE) its military and administration were restructured and adopted Greek for official use instead of Latin. Thus, it continued the Roman state and maintained Roman state traditions, and its citizens and neighbours continued to refer to it as the *Roman Empire* and to themselves as Romans.

95 Qur'ān 30:3.
96 Qur'ān 15:19.
97 Qur'ān 15:22.
98 Qur'ān 20:53.
99 Qur'ān 55:17.

PART FOUR

Divine Leadership

11 Divine Leadership/ Succession

Shiʿah Muslims believe Divine leadership (*Imāmah*) to be one of the five principles of religion (*Uṣūl al-Din*) – Sunni Muslims regard it as a 'branch' (*furūʿ*) rather than a 'principle' of religion. This results in Shiʿahs' acknowledgement of Imāmah being 'Universal Leadership in regard to all matters of religion and life' and the Sunnis' view that it relates only to the succession of the Prophet and the establishment of 'good practice'. Thus, while Sunnis might regard succession to be a historic matter that has little relevance to contemporary life, for Shiʿahs, succession is the essential underpinning and crucial aspect of faith (*ʿAqidah*) and practice (*Shariʿah*).[1]

If this matter had only been of secondary importance, one would understandably be surprised by Shahrestāni's statement vis-à-vis the schism between Muslims, 'The greatest dispute within the Muslim nation is in regard to Imāmah. No sword has been raised in Islām concerning any religious matter, in any generation, as occurs in regard to Imāmah.'[2]

We need first to establish what the Prophet's major responsibilities were before we can attest to the need for someone to continue that mission. For a brief outline:

1. **To elucidate ayāt of the Qur'ān and reveal their hidden depths:** This is clarified in the Qur'ān:[3] 'We sent to you the reminder [the Qur'ān] so that you may make it clear to humankind what has been sent

down to them.' Thus, the mission of the Prophet ﷺ was not merely to recite the words of the Qur'ān but to elaborate and clarify their message.

All those familiar with Qur'ānic methodology know that some of its statements are explicit and others implicit. Some are revealed in their universal sense, others in a specific sense. Some exist to abrogate, while others have been abrogated. Some are unequivocal, others are ambivalent. The ultimate authority to clarify all of these was none other than the Prophet himself.

After the Prophet's death, who was supposed to fill the gap that he had left? Was there any member of the then Muslim community who had the ability to deal with such clarification? History records several occasions on which the Prophet's companions were not able to answer questions regarding specific Qur'ānic *ayāt*. They were unsure about what was precisely meant in the *ayāt* of *wuḍū* (ablution), *al-sāriq wal sāriqah* (male and female thieves), and *kalālah* (distant heirs).

Is it logical to assume that such clarifications would no longer be able to be provided? Would it not be irrational to imagine that the Almighty Lawmaker was indifferent to the vital necessity for His Message to be comprehended?

It is naïve to imagine that Allāh's Final Messenger did not entrust the divine knowledge that had been revealed to him to a trustworthy, reliable successor.

2. **To deliver Islāmic rulings on issues as they arose:** Each day the Prophet ﷺ was confronted by questions regarding personal, social and political matters. What is the Islāmic viewpoint regarding X, Y or Z?

   Such questions continued to require clarification even after he had passed away, and so the appointment of a successor acquainted with all Sharʿi matters was irrefutably a necessity.

3. **To meet all the challenges made by atheists** who argued with the Prophet about: the existence of God, his being a messenger of such

a God and his claim regarding resurrection and life after death. Christians confronted the Prophet about ʿIsā ﷺ being born without having a father – his response being that that was no more difficult than Ādam ﷺ being born without any parent at all.

History also informs us of ʿUmar being confronted by Jews and Christians relating to the Islāmic view on shared theological issues and Muʿawiyah being sent questions from Rome. Such challenges continue to this day. Who is knowledgeable enough to respond with accuracy and clarity?

To conclude, the appointment of the most highly qualified, competent person to deal with the wide-ranging tasks and responsibilities after the Prophet ﷺ departed this temporary life, was most certainly a necessity. Such a person could not be anyone other than the Imām.

1 Imāmah: a Divine Covenant

It was only when the prophet Ibrāhim ﷺ had successfully overcome the trials imposed upon him that Allāh ordained him *Imām*. When he ﷺ asked if his progeny would also be entitled to that position Allāh responded, 'My covenant does not embrace the unjust.'[4] This divine covenant, by which Allāh ordained him Imām, had nothing whatever to do with Ibrāhim's Prophethood, as some Sunni exegetes like to claim, because Ibrāhim ﷺ was only granted offspring in his old age, long after he had been appointed a prophet and messenger. This is evidenced in 'Praise to Allāh who granted me Ismāʿil and Isḥāq despite my old age.'[5]

Further evidence for Ibrāhim ﷺ being a messenger prior to being granted offspring is found in the Qur'ān,[6] in which angels descend to inform him ﷺ that he will soon become a father. There is neither evidence nor mention, in the corpus of Islāmic reference, of any Muslim scholar having ever asserted, implied or suggested that angels communicate with beings other than prophets.

2 Explicit Texts Regarding Divine Appointment

We need also to inform ourselves of the measures undertaken by the Prophet ﷺ that affirm he was well aware of the necessity for sound leadership to continue after him. Those measures clearly demonstrate that it was never his policy simply to leave it to the public to choose a leader from amongst them.

The summoning of his family

In the early days of Islām, the Prophet Muḥammad ﷺ was ordered to invite his kinsfolk to Islām.[7] To this end, he ﷺ invited approximately 40 of the family's menfolk to dine with him. Those present included his uncles Abu Ṭalīb, Hamzah, ʿAbbas and Abu Lahab. At the end of the meal the Holy Prophet ﷺ addressed his guests: 'O children of ʿAbd al-Muṭṭalib, I do not know any amongst the Arabs who has given his nation a better gift than that which I now present to you [i.e. Islām]. As Allāh has ordered me to invite you to Islām, I now offer you the 'good' of this life and that of the one to come. I will regard whichever one of you is willing to help me convey the faith of Islām to the people as my brother, the executor of my Will and my successor.'

All the reporters observed, after all the guests had satisfied themselves, that the meal of one leg of lamb and a bowl of yoghurt appeared not to have been touched. One guest stood up to declaim, 'Muḥammad has bewitched you all.'

The only one present to respond was ʿAli ؑ, the youngest person present. He immediately arose to announce that he was ready and willing to share the Prophet's burdens. The Messenger of Islām ﷺ placed his hand on ʿAli's shoulder and said, 'This is my brother, the executor of my Will and my successor, so listen to what he says and obey him.'

The family considered this outrageous and said to Abu Ṭalīb, 'Now you are being ordered to listen to and obey your own son.'

It is evident from this event that from the very earliest days of his mission, the Prophet Muḥammad ﷺ had concerned himself with the matter of his succession. As he had made it clear to all his relatives that 'Ali ﷺ had been appointed to take over this position, subsequent to that event all of them were aware that 'Ali ﷺ would eventually take charge of the Muslim nation. It was for this reason that they taunted Abu Ṭalīb for being ordered to listen to and obey his son.[8]

It is clear from the above *ḥadīth* that the Prophet ﷺ was concerned about the continuation of his mission, and needed to appoint a suitable person to take charge of the affairs of the Muslim community. He titled this person his successor and the executor of his will. In other words, the announcement of his message needed to proceed hand in hand with the appointment of the leader who was to follow him.

His ﷺ appointment of deputies

Meticulous study of the history of Islām shows that the Prophet ﷺ never left Madinah without leaving an appointed deputy to take charge of Muslim affairs in his absence. This was so even when he planned to be away for a single day or to go on a short journey, such as to *Uḥud*.

1. When he left Madinah in the year 2 AH, he appointed Sa'd bin 'Abadah to be in charge in his absence.

2. When he left for the Battle of Bowaṭ in year 2 AH, he appointed Sa'd bin Ma'ath.

3. When he left for the Battle of Badr, he appointed Ibn Um Maktūm.

4. For the Battle of Bani Qaynaqa and Sawiq, he appointed Abu Lubabah al-Anṣari.

5. When he went to Salim and Ghaṭfan in year 3 AH, he again appointed Ibn Um Maktūm to be in charge.

6. He appointed 'Uthmān bin Affan when he left for Dhi Amr.

7. He appointed Ibn Um Maktūm when he left for Uḥud, Bani al-Naḍīr, Dawmat al-Jandal and Aḥzāb.

8. When he left Madinah for Bani al-Musṭalaq, he appointed Zayd bin Ḥarithah.
9. He appointed Abu Ruham al-Ghifari when he left for Bani Quraydah.
10. When he left for Khaybar he appointed Siba' bin 'Arfaṭah.
11. He appointed Abu Ruham al-Ghifari while he took charge of the conquest of Makkah.
12. The only occasion on which 'Ali عليه السلام was ordered to take charge in Madinah was when the Prophet ﷺ left for Tabūk.

The above facts confirm that the Prophet ﷺ never neglected to appoint a deputy when he knew he was not going to be present. It would have been contrary to his customary practice, and quite out of character for him to leave the Muslim nation without having appointed a deputy and successor. It is misleading to claim that this is what occurred.

It is reported by all Muslim historians that Jibrā'il would revise the Qur'ān with the Prophet ﷺ once each year. However, it was towards the end of year 10 AH that the Prophet said, 'This year Jibrā'il revised the Qur'ān with me twice, and I consider that to indicate that I am soon to depart this world.' With this in his ﷺ mind, it is not rational to imagine he would have been indifferent to the future success of the Muslim nation.

Further, history records that Abu Bakr appointed 'Umar to succeed him and 'Umar appointed a council of six to deal with the matter of his succession. It is a fantasy to believe that Allāh's Prophet and Messenger ﷺ did not attend to such an important matter while Abu Bakr and 'Umar both did!

It is specious scholarship to disregard the evidence of the Prophet's appointment of a successor – and utterly reprehensible then to infer that he ﷺ was incompetent and had not appointed a successor to guide the Muslim nation after him!

Ghadīr Khum

Ghadīr Khum lies near Joḥfah between Makkah and Madinah. On the Prophet's journey home from his final pilgrimage, Jibrā'īl delivered this urgent command from Allāh:

> O [My] Messenger, deliver what has been sent down to you from your Lord for if you do not, you will have failed to deliver His message [completely]. Allāh will protect you from the people.[9]

The Prophet ﷺ immediately drew to a halt and ordered those ahead of him to be called back while he waited for the stragglers to arrive. Acacia thorns were swept away, cloaks spread underfoot and overhead as protection from the heat and a platform, constructed of camel saddles, was raised. When all were present, the Prophet ﷺ ascended this makeshift structure to address them as follows:

> O people, know well that Jibrā'il has come down to me several times with the Most Merciful Lord's order to halt here to inform all, white or black, that ʿAli, son of Abu Ṭalīb is my brother, my successor, my caliph and the Imām that has been appointed to follow me. His position in relation to me is as that of Hārūn to Mūsa, except that no prophet is to follow me. ʿAli is your master after Allāh and His Prophet.

In most reports, the Prophet ﷺ also informed them of his approaching demise and called them to witness that he had faithfully discharged his duties. He then asked:

> 'Do I not have more authority over you than you have yourselves?' They responded that he certainly did have greater rights over them than they themselves had. The Prophet ﷺ then said, 'Whoever I am master over [*mawlā*] ʿAli is also *mawlā*.' He ended with the prayer, 'O Allāh, love those who love ʿAli and oppose those who are ʿAli's enemies.

When he had finished, the following *āyah* was revealed:

> This day I have perfected your religion for you, granted you my bounties and approved Islām as your faith and way of life.[10]

Three important aspects need to be examined regarding the above reports:

a. their authenticity

b. the general meaning of the word *mawlā*

c. the specific meaning of the word *mawlā* as used in this context

Authenticity

ʿAllamah Amini recorded a comprehensive 11-volume study of this subject entitled *Al-Ghadīr*. In it he lists the chains of narration throughout 14 centuries of Islāmic history and traces every Arab poet whose work mentions the events at Ghadīr.

In his book *ʿAbaqat al-Anwār*, Sayyid Ḥamid Ḥusayn presents all the chains of narration on Ghadīr that include comprehensive details, confirmed in dozens of Sunni books, of each narrator and their reliability.

In the first volume of ʿAllamah Amini's *Al-Ghadīr*, the names of 110 of the Holy Prophet's companions who narrated *aḥādith* on this subject are listed. Only those companions whose names start with the letter *alif* are included below:

1. Abu Layla al-Anṣāri
2. Abu Zaynab ibn ʿAwf
3. Abu Fadhalah al-Anṣāri
4. Abu Qudamah al-Anṣāri
5. Abu ʿAmra ibn Muḥasin
6. Abu al-Haytham ibn al-Tayyihān
7. Abu Rafiaʿ

8. Abu Dhuwayab
9. Usamah ibn Zayd
10. Ubayy ibn Kaʿb
11. Asʿad ibn Zurarah
12. Asmaʿ bint ʿUmays
13. Um Salamah
14. Um Hanī bint abu Talib
15. Anas ibn Mālik
16. Abu Bakr
17. Abu Hurayrah

ʿAllamah Aminī also includes the names of 84 of the generation that followed the companions (the *tābiʿūn*) followed by succeeding generations. In referring to scholars and writers who include this *ḥadīth* in their works, ʿAllamah Aminī lists 360 scholars throughout the 14 centuries of the Hijri calendar.

In his book *The Right Path*, ʿAllamah Sharafuddin quotes Al-Ḥākim al-Nishaburi, Imām Aḥmad ibn Ḥanbal, Al-Nissaiʿi and many others, who included this *ḥadīth* in their works.

Interestingly, Imām ʿAli ﵇ asked companions to affirm that at Ghadīr Khum they had heard the Prophet ﷺ make a declaration regarding his authority. Indeed, Aḥmad ibn Ḥanbal narrates, on the authority of Abdul Raḥman ibn abi Layla, that he said, 'I saw ʿAli, may Allāh be pleased with him, invite those who had attended Ghadīr Khum to stand up to inform others of what they had witnessed.' Twelve people stood up to say, 'We saw the Prophet holding ʿAli's hand while he appealed to Allāh, "O Allah, love those who love ʿAli, be an enemy of those who are ʿAli's enemies, support those who support ʿAli and forsake those who forsake him"'.[11]

General meaning of the word mawlā

As Sunni Muslims cannot deny the authenticity of the Ghadīr *ḥadīth*, they downplay its significance with claims that the word *mawlā* in this *ḥadīth* means 'friend' – that the Holy Prophet ﷺ simply wanted to announce, 'Whoever's friend I am, ʿAli is also their friend.' The problem with this assertion is that not a single person present at Ghadīr understood that to be the case. Ḥassān ibn Thabit, famously regarded as being the Prophet's poet, composed a few lines before the audience present at Ghadīr. In these he clearly described the occasion on which the Prophet ﷺ said, 'Arise O ʿAli, for I am pleased to appoint you Imām and Guide after me.'

The fact that, at that time, no one objected to Ḥassān's words confirms that those present had all understood *mawlā* to denote that ʿAli was their Master and Guardian. This comprehension is confirmed by the phrase that ʿUmar ibn al-Khaṭṭāb used to congratulate ʿAli ؑ: 'Congratulations O son of Abu Ṭalīb. This morning you have become the *mawlā* of every believing man and woman.'

Not only was ʿAli ؑ known to be friendly to all, it is clear that no congratulatory declaration would have been apposite if the Prophet ﷺ had stated, 'Those to whom I am a friend, ʿAli is also friends with.'[12]

While it is true that Arabic lexicons make reference to 22 different meanings for the word *mawlā,* what defines the specific meaning of all homonymous words is the context in which they are used. Thus, depending on the context, *mawlā* may mean:

Owner	Lodger/guest
Master	Partner
Slave	Son
The one who frees another	Uncle
The one who has been freed	Cousin
The benefactor	Nephew
The beneficiary	Son-in-law
Friend	Relative
Companion	Follower

Protector	Helper
Neighbour	One who holds authority

Specific meaning of mawlā in the Ghadīr context

To examine the meaning implied by *mawlā* in the context of the Ghadīr *ḥadīth*, we find scores of 'associations' that point clearly towards 'Master' being the only meaning to fit that context. Here are some such 'associations':

1. The question that the Holy Prophet ﷺ asked prior to his declaration is: Do I not have more authority over you than you have yourselves?' When they responded in the affirmative, the Prophet ﷺ declared, 'Whoever I am master over (*mawlā*) ʿAli is also *mawlā*.'

   The word *mawlā* used in this declaration has the same meaning as *awla bikum* ('having greater authority over you') in the preceding question. At least 64 Sunni scholars have quoted the above question that the Prophet ﷺ asked, including Aḥmad ibn Ḥanbal, Ibn Majah, Al-Nisāʿi and Al-Tirmidhi.[13]

2. The prayer that the Holy Prophet ﷺ offered just after this declaration is: 'O Allāh, love those who love ʿAli and oppose those who are ʿAli's enemies. Help those who help ʿAli and forsake those who forsake ʿAli.' From this it is clear that on that day ʿAli was entrusted with a responsibility that by its very nature would arouse the enmity of those eager for that position.

3. The Prophet ﷺ declared, 'I am soon to depart from this world in response to Allāh's call.' This points to his confirming his arrangements for the leadership succession after his departure.

4. The expressions of joy of the congratulatory companions leave little room to doubt the meaning of the word *mawlā* in the context of the Prophet's declaration.

5. Consider the nonsensicality of the Holy Prophet ﷺ halting his, and nearly 100,000 travellers' journey at midday, to assemble together

in a thorn-strewn area and erect a platform of camel saddles – in the relentless sun of the Arabian desert – simply to tell them that ʿAli ﷺ is their friend?

Ḥadīth al-Thaqalain

It has been reported through reliable chains of narrators that the Prophet ﷺ said, 'I am leaving behind two precious things that, as long as you cling to both, will prevent you ever being led astray: The Book of Allāh [i.e. the Qur'ān] and my progeny – my household. Allāh Almighty informed me that these are to remain inseparable until they meet me at the pool. Take care of how you behave towards them after my demise.'

The Prophet ﷺ repeated this on several occasions including: when he ﷺ returned from Ṭāif; the day of ʿArafah during his farewell pilgrimage; the day of Ghadīr Khum; from the pulpit of his mosque in Madinah and in his own house just prior to his death.

Some 25 of his companions, many from the next generation (*tābiʿūn*), and hundreds of narrators over the centuries have recorded this to be an authentic narration.[14] Sayyid Ḥāmid Ḥusayn, a renowned scholar from Lucknow in India, compiled six enormous volumes of all the chains of narrators of this *ḥadīth,* verifying the reliability of each one from Sunni references. The Cairo 'Centre for Proximity between the various Islāmic Schools of Law' (*Dār al-Taqrīb bayn al-Madhāhib al-Islāmiyah*) published one volume that records all the references regarding *Ḥadith al-Thaqalain.*

The following facts are established by this *ḥadīth*:

1. That the Qur'ān and the Prophet's progeny will remain inseparable until the Day of Resurrection.
2. To cling to both, rather than only one, is a guarantee of immunity for communities and individuals.
3. The Prophet's progeny alongside the Qur'ān are free from error.

4. From the moment that this was declared, till the Day of Judgement, a member of the Prophet's progeny must be existent as the source of divine guidance. The Book of Allāh and the progeny of the Prophet ﷺ being inseparable until that 'Day' is evidence of the reality of the Twelfth Imām عليه السلام.[15]

Progeny or Sunnah?

Sunni scholars claim that the two entities entrusted by the Prophet ﷺ were, 'The Book of Allāh and my Sunnah.' However, painstakingly in-depth research confirms that this so-called *ḥadīth* first made its appearance in the *Al-Muwaṭṭa'* of Imām Mālik ibn Anas, without any accompanying support of a chain of narrators between his and the Prophet's lifetime. Malik simply recorded, 'I was informed that the Prophet said . . .' It is imperative for there to be a verifiable chain of those who narrated this report, from the time of the Prophet ﷺ to Imām Malik's lifetime, for it ever to be considered an authentic *ḥadīth*. There is a gap of 150 years which, in *ʿIlm al-ḥadīth*, constitutes five generations of missing narrators. (Reports that are unable to be verified as authentic are considered unsound or weak.)

With Islāmic scholarship's well-established methodologies to verify the authenticity of reports, it is beyond belief why this spurious statement is ever cited in opposition to the exceedingly well-authenticated *Ḥadīth al-Thaqalain*. Such brazenly transparent attempts at deception bankrupt the academic status and scholarship of their authors.

What is meant by 'Progeny' and 'Household'?

1. Tirmidhi narrates that Saʿd ibn Abi Waqqāṣ said, 'When the *āyah* "Let us summon our sons and your sons, and our women and your women . . ."[16] was revealed, the Prophet ﷺ summoned ʿAli, Fatimah, Ḥasan and Ḥusayn and said, "O Allāh, these are my **household**".'

2. He also narrated Um Salamah, saying, '*Āyah* 33:33 [Allāh intends to keep every kind of uncleanliness away from you, O you people of

the house, and to purify you thoroughly], was revealed in my house. I was sitting by the door and asked the Prophet, "O Allāh's Messenger, am I not amongst the people of your house?" He ﷺ responded, "You are an exceedingly good lady and a Prophet's wife". He then covered ʿAli, Fatimah, Ḥasan and Ḥusayn with his cloak and said, "O Allāh, these are my **household**".'

3. Muslim narrates that he asked Zayd ibn Arqam, 'Are the Prophet's wives considered to be a part of his household?' To which he responded, 'By Allāh, women may stay with their husbands for many years and then get divorced and return to their own families. On the other hand, the Prophet's household comprises his progeny who are not entitled to receive alms [*ṣadaqah*].'

4. According to many authentic reports, after *āyah* 33:33 was revealed, the Prophet ﷺ went at each prayer time to knock on the door of ʿAli and Fatimah's house and call, 'O people of the house, it is now time for prayer'. He continued this practice for six months according to one report, nine months according to another and 10 months according to a third.[17]

To conclude, the Prophet's clarification made clear to whom he was referring when he spoke about 'his household' and 'people of the house'. As he had distinctly expressed what he ﷺ meant, nothing further can be said.

Charity given during prayer

One of the strongest Qur'ānic texts to evidence Imām ʿAli's authority is *Ayāt al-Wilayah,* that refers to his giving his ring to a beggar while still bowing during prayer. Al-Nisā'i in his *Sunan*, Al-Thaʿlabi in his *Tafsīr* and Aḥmad Ibn Ḥanbal in his *Musnad*, in addition to many others, report that *Ayāt al-Wilayah* was revealed in praise of that charitable act.

> Truly, full authority over you lies with Allāh, His Messenger and those who believe and give charity while they are still in *rukū'*.[18]

The famous companion Abu Dharr al-Ghifari said, 'May my ears turn deaf and my eyes blind if I lie. I heard the Holy Prophet ﷺ say, "'Ali is the guide of the righteous and the slayer of the infidel. He who helps him will be victorious and he who abandons him forsaken." Once, while offering prayer in the company of the Holy Prophet ﷺ, a man in the *masjid* unsuccessfully begged for help. 'Ali, while still in *rukū'* pointed to his ring, which the beggar then took from his finger. Upon this the Holy Prophet ﷺ implored Allāh with the words, "O Allāh, my brother Mūsa begged You saying, My Lord, delight my heart and ease my task by untying the knot in my tongue so that they may understand me, and appoint from among my kinsmen my brother Harūn as my vizier to strengthen my message and glorify You." After quoting Mūsa the Prophet continued, "Delight my heart and ease my task by appointing from among my kinsmen 'Ali as my vizier to strengthen my message." [Abu Dharr continued], By Allāh, the Holy Prophet ﷺ had not completed his supplication before the trustworthy Jibrā'il descended with the above *āyah*.'

The authentication of this āyah

Many exegetes, theologians and traditionists from the *Ahl al-Sunnah* report that the above *āyah* was revealed in praise of Imām 'Ali عليه السلام, including:

1. Ḥāfiḍ 'abd ibn Ḥumaid (d. 249 AH) on the authority of ibn Abbas.[19]
2. Ibn Jarir Ṭabari (d. 310 AH) on the authority of Suddi and 'Utbah ibn Abi Ḥakīm.[20]
3. Ibn abi Ḥātam al-Rāzi (d. 327 AH) on the authority of Salamah ibn Kuhail.[21]
4. Ḥāfiḍ Ṭabarāni.[22]

5. Ḥāfiḍ Abu-Bakr al-Jaṣṣāṣ (d. 370 AH).[23]

6. Ḥāfiḍ Abul Ḥasan al-Wāḥidi (d. 468 AH).[24]

7. Ḥāfiḍ Abul Qasim ibn ʿAsākir Dimashqi (d. 571 AH).[25]

8. Ḥāfiḍ Abul Faraj, ibn al-Jawzi (d. 597 AH).[26]

9. Ibn al-Athīr al-Jazari (d. 606 AH).[27]

10. Al-Bayḍāwi.[28]

Indeed, ʿAllamah Aminī provides a list of 66 Sunni scholars who narrated that the above *āyah* was revealed in praise of Imām ʿAli's charitable act.[29] It is thus surprising that ibn Taymiah, who had all the above references available to him, asserted that **no** scholar had narrated anything regarding the circumstances surrounding the revelation of this *āyah*.[30]

In order to comprehend *Ayāt al-Wilayah* and its being applied to Imām ʿAli عليه السلام, we need to examine the following:

- the article (*innamā*) at the beginning of the above *āyah*
- the meaning of *waliyy*
- why a believer who offered charity during prayer is referred to in the plural
- the sequence between the three entities mentioned in the *āyah*

Article (*innamā*). Scholars unanimously agree that in Arabic, 'the article' (*innamā*) relates to exclusivity. That which refers to full authority over the Muslim nation thus applies **only** to those mentioned in the above *āyah*.

The meaning of waliyy. Regardless of our clarification above that the word *mawlā* can be understood in several different ways, the context of *Ḥadīth Al-Ghadīr* makes clear that only 'Authority' and 'Mastership' are being referred to. However, with regard to the word *waliyy* in the above *āyah*, no meaning other than authority can possibly be logically applied. Lexicographers concur that one who is recognized to be a guardian with full authority is the *waliyy* of that person.

Why is the individual Imām ʿAli referred to in the plural? There are several *ayāt* in the Qur'ān, including this one, in which individuals are referred to in the plural form, for example:

- 'Those to whom **the people** said, "Be fearful, large forces are being mustered to oppose you!" They responded, "Allāh is sufficient support for us."'[31] Both exegetes and historians concur that the one to announce that was Naʿim ibn Masʿūd, after Abu Sufyan had given him ten camels to weaken Muslim morale following their defeat on the battlefield of Uḥud. Despite this, he is referred to in the Qur'ān as **the people**.

- 'O you who believe, remember Allāh's bounties when **some people** determined to stretch forth their hands against you and He withheld their hands from you.'[32] This *āyah* refers to the occasion in which Allāh thwarted ʿUmar ibn Jaḥsh's attack, when he had drawn his sword to strike the Prophet ﷺ. Yet again, the plural form is used to describe the action of an individual.

- Allāh refers to the Prophet Ibrahīm عليه السلام as '*Ummah*' (nation) despite him being an individual.[33]

It is clear from the above *ayāt* that it is not infrequent for the Qur'ān to refer to individuals in the plural form.

Is the sequence of the three entities lateral or hierarchical? Full authority over all creatures lies with Allāh Almighty, who brought everything into existence and who provides every creature with all their needs, and who bestowed creation and guidance on human beings.[34] The Prophet Muḥammad ﷺ, His final Messenger, was given full authority over the Muslim nation.[35] It is thus incumbent upon all Muslims to obey His Messenger. Having understood this, *Ayāt al-Wilayah* clarifies that after Allāh Almighty, the Prophet Muḥammad ﷺ holds that authority. After him, it is only The Commander of the Faithful, ʿAli ibn Abu Ṭalib عليه السلام, who has been granted that authority.

12 Twelve Successors/Amirs

The number 12 has significance in Judaeo-Christian scripture in terms of being a unit for the passage of hours in a day and the months of both the lunar and solar calendars. Allāh confirms this number in the Qur'ān.[36] For example, He tells us that 12 tribes followed the Prophet Mūsa عليه السلام and that 12 springs of water gushed forth in order for each tribe to have its own water source.[37] In another Qur'ānic reference, 'Allāh took a covenant from the Children of Isrā'il, from whom We raised 12 chiefs . . .'[38] We know also from the life of the Prophet ʿIsā عليه السلام that he chose 12 disciples. Ismaʿil too had 12 successors as stated below.

> 12 Now these are the generations of Ishmael, Abraham's son, whom Hagar the Egyptian, Sarah's handmaid, bare unto Abraham:
>
> 13 And these are the names of the sons of Ishmael, by their names, according to their generations: the firstborn of Ishmael, Nebajoth; and Kedar, and Adbeel, and Mibsam,
>
> 14 And Mishma, and Dumah, and Massa,
>
> 15 Hadar, and Tema, Jetur, Naphish, and Kedemah:
>
> 16 These are the sons of Ishmael, and these are their names, by their towns, and by their castles; twelve princes according to their nations.[39]

Does this number have any significance in relation to the succession of the Prophet Muḥammad ﷺ?

a. Bukhāri narrates on the authority of Jabir ibn Samurah that the Prophet said, 'There will be 12 Amirs,' and then he ﷺ said something I could not hear; however, my father told me that he had said, 'All are from the Quraish'.[40]

b. Muslim narrates on the authority of Jabir ibn Samurah that the Prophet said, 'This religion will continue its dignity while 12 successors continue to exist.'[41]

c. Tirmithi narrates on the authority of Jabir ibn Samurah that the Prophet said, '12 Amirs will follow after me, all from the Quraish.'[42]

d. Ahmad ibn Ḥanbal narrates on the authority of ʿAbdullah ibn Masʿūd that when someone asked him, 'Did you ask Allāh's Messenger how many Caliphs are to rule over this nation?' He replied, 'No one has asked me such a question since I arrived in Iraq, but, yes, we did ask him ﷺ about this, to which he responded, "There will be 12, the same number as the chiefs of Mūsa's tribes."'[43]

e. Al Hākim al-Nishabūri narrates on the authority of Abu Juḥaifah that he said, 'I accompanied my uncle to meet the Prophet ﷺ and heard him say, "The affairs of my nation will continue to remain upright while 12 successors continue to exist." He ﷺ then whispered, but I later checked with my uncle what he had said and he told me that it was, "All are from Quraish".'[44]

f. Al Muttaqi al-Hindi narrates that the Prophet ﷺ said, 'There will be 12 successors to administer the affairs of this nation, they will not be affected by those who forsake them, all of them are from the Quraish".'[45]

Thus, one may realistically conclude that the Prophet ﷺ clearly informed his companions that 12 successors would administrate all the affairs of the Muslim nation, as is confirmed by the major sources of

Sunni *āḥadīth*. Some scholars have tried to present this as being the number of caliphs, by adding the first four so-called 'Rightly Guided Caliphs' to a few Umayyad Caliphs whom they do not claim to be 'Rightly Guided'. However, they completely ignore the criterion specified by the Prophet ﷺ – that 'all are from the Quraish'.

1 Twelve Successors/Imāms in Shiʿah Sources

We have already provided references from *Ḥadīth al-Thaqalain* to clarify that the authority and value of the Prophet's progeny has equivalence with that of the Holy Qur'ān. Affirmation of there being twelve successors is reported, on the authority of Imām Ṣādiq via his forefathers عليهم السلام, the descendants of the Holy Prophet ﷺ, that he ﷺ said, 'There are to be twelve Imāms to follow after me, of whom the first is ʿAli and the last *al-Qā'im* (the one who rises), they are my successors and vicegerents.'[46]

2 Summarized Biographies of the Twelve Imāms

First Imām – ʿAli عليه السلام

The few *ayāt* and *āḥadīth* cited above affirm the divinely appointed leadership (*Imāmah*) of the Prophet ﷺ and error-free Imāms عليهم السلام. There is a plethora of such texts, all of which denote Imām ʿAli عليه السلام as being the Prophet's immediate successor. Pangs of birth, during his mother's circumambulations of the Kaʿbah, drove her to seek privacy within the House of Allāh, in which she gave birth to ʿAli on the 13th Rajab in the year 23 BH.

His father, Abu Ṭalīb, financially straitened by the Quraishi boycott of the Muslim community, gratefully accepted the Prophet's suggestion that his young son ʿAli come to live with him and his family. Thus ʿAli عليه السلام grew up, developed and matured under the influence and personal supervision of the Prophet Muḥammad ﷺ. He later recounted that the Prophet ﷺ had never sought to criticize the things he said or did and would often give him big hugs of affection. He, in return, adored his cousin whom, in his own words, he 'used to accompany like a young camel following in the footprints of its mother. Each day, he said, the Prophet ﷺ would draw his attention to one or another virtue that he would encourage him to emulate.'[47]

During the 23 years of his stay with him, the Prophet ﷺ would often tell his companions of ʿAli's development, doings and character:

- His position described in relation to the Prophet, as that of Harūn to Mūsa.
- ʿAli being referred to as 'The Gate to the City of Knowledge'.
- That ʿAli is always with the Qur'ān and that the Qur'ān is always with ʿAli. They will not separate until they meet me at the pool.
- That ʿAli was the first to believe and confirm his Prophethood.
- That ʿAli is to me as my head is to my body.
- That the characteristic of true believers is their 'love of ʿAli'.
- That the believers love ʿAli but that the hypocrites hate ʿAli.
- That until the Day of Judgement, the blow struck by ʿAli during the battle of Khandaq is of greater consequence than any other act of my nation.
- That the Prophet established brotherhood between himself and ʿAli at the same time as he established the brotherhood between the *Muhājerūn* and *Anṣār*. That he ﷺ then said, 'O ʿAli, you are my brother in this life and in the hereafter.'
- That remembrance of ʿAli is an act of worship.[48]

His leadership

As discussed earlier, from the time that he announced his Prophethood and commenced his message, the Prophet صلى الله عليه وآله emphasized and repeatedly reconfirmed that ʿAli عليه السلام was to succeed him. The first time that he did so was when he صلى الله عليه وآله summoned his family (see p. 240), the final time at Ghadīr Khum on his way home after his farewell pilgrimage. To ensure that those who had followed him to Madinah would be welcomed and accepted into homes there, shortly after his arrival in Madinah the Prophet صلى الله عليه وآله established formal bonds of brotherhood between the *Muhājerūn* and *Anṣār,* and used the opportunity to declare his صلى الله عليه وآله brotherhood with ʿAli عليه السلام. He restated his bond of brotherhood with ʿAli عليه السلام at the Battle of Tabūk in the year 9 AH when he صلى الله عليه وآله said, "ʿAli's connection to to me is exactly the same as Harūn's was to Mūsa.' According to Qur'ān 7:142, Harūn was Mūsa's successor.

Despite this, as his صلى الله عليه وآله temporary stay on earth drew to a close in the year 11 AH, both the *Muhājerūn* and *Anṣār,* seeing this as their opportunity to grasp leadership and power, vied with each other to seize the big prize, with no consideration at all being given by either to the Prophet's clear and repeated statements that ʿAli عليه السلام was to succeed him. ʿUmar and Abu ʿUbaydah Al-Jarraḥ, who claimed they represented the *Muhājerūn,* triumphed in their temporal leadership bid, appointed Abu Bakr caliph and demanded that all pay him allegiance. Nonetheless, before Abu Bakr died he appointed ʿUmar as caliph, who in turn established a council of six to appoint Uthmān caliph after him. History records that there was such great dissatisfaction and unrest over that caliphate that it ended in Uthmān being assassinated in the year 35 AH. By common consensus the public then implored Imām ʿAli عليه السلام to accept temporal leadership. That he has always retained spiritual leadership of both Shiʿāh and Sunni Islām is evidenced by all of today's *Ṣūfī Ṭuruq* who, with one exception, trace their spiritual inheritance to him.

During the caliphates of Abu Bakr, ʿUmar and Uthmān (11–35 AH), Imām ʿAli's legal opinions were relied upon to determine rulings on the wide variety of issues that they found too complex to pass judgement on. The most lucid explanation for this is to be found in a sermon Imām

ʿAli ﷺ delivered (listed as number three in *Nahj al-Balāghah*), in which he explains that, regardless of those three caliphates' lack of validity, he considered the availability of jurisprudential capacity to meet the needs of the Muslim community to have greater importance than a fight to establish his rightful position.

Imām ʿAli ﷺ moved the centre of his caliphate from Madinah to Kufah in Iraq and, throughout his ﷺ five years as caliph, exemplified Islāmic leadership and upheld Qur'ānic principles in their entirety. In spite of this, three catastrophic wars were waged against him. The first was Ayesha's claim to revenge the death of her cousin Uthman, in which she wrongly accused Imām ʿAli ﷺ of abetting the assassination of Uthman; the second, led by Muʿāwiyah; and the third, by the *Kharijites*. These wars are respectively known as *Jamal*, *Ṣiffīn* and *Nahrawān*. While leading the *Fajr* prayer on the 19th day of Ramaḍān in the year 40 AH, the *Kaharijite* Abdul Raḥmān ibn Muljim struck Imām ʿAli ﷺ on the head with a poisoned sword – the injury that resulted in his becoming a martyr two days later. Thus both his birth and his death are indelibly linked to the 'House of Allāh'.[49]

Sermons and maxims

The edifying sermons Imām ʿAli ﷺ delivered in the Kufah mosque during the five years of his caliphate were later collected and promulgated by a wide variety of Islāmic scholars. Al Nisā'i (d. 303 AH) presented what the Imām had recounted from the Holy Prophet ﷺ.[50] Al-Āmidi (d. circa 520 AH) concerned himself solely with the maxims.[51] Abu Isḥāq al-Waṭwāṭ (d. circa 553 AH) collected together the Imām's speeches.[52] However, the most extensive compilation of the Imām's sermons, maxims and letters is presented by Al-Sharif al-Raḍī (d. 404 AH).[53] As doubt was cast on the authenticity of what was attributed to Imām ʿAli ﷺ, many scholars dedicated themselves to the research and verification of each and every quoted reference. For example, Sayyid Abdul Zahra Husayni's four-volume work traces the source of every scholarly citation for each of the years that preceded Al-Sharif al-Raḍī's birth in 349 AH.[54]

A few of Imām ʿAli's reflections are listed below.

1. In times of strife be like a calf – a creature with a back that cannot be ridden and no udder that can be milked.
2. When the world turns towards someone, they are afforded the merit of others, but when it turns away from them all merit is annulled, even their own.
3. Generosity is what one is motivated to give; that which is requested is surrendered out of embarrassment, shame or rebuke.
4. Those who consider themselves leaders should be exemplars, not just privileged by being in charge, so that others can emulate their conduct and not merely be obliged to obey what their tongues utter.
5. On passing the graves outside Kufah as they returned from the battle of Ṣiffīn, the Imām عليه السلام addressed them saying, 'O people of desolate abode, of empty shops, of dark tombs! O people of dust, of exile, of isolation, O people of gloom! You have departed before us and we are to follow. Your houses have been reoccupied, your spouses remarried, your wealth distributed. This is the news from our side – what is it from yours?' The Imām عليه السلام then said to his companions, 'Had they permission to respond they would tell you that the best provision for your journey is piety.'
6. Friendship is not true unless it protects friends in three circumstances: in misfortune, in absence and at the time of their death.
7. O son of Adam, do not inflict on your life worries over your future needs, for Allāh is there to ensure your provision.
8. You are in control of your words until they are uttered, but once they are out, you are under their control. So guard your tongue as you guard your gold, for one word may snatch blessings and bring adversity.
9. The Imām was once asked, 'Does justice or generosity have greater value?' His response: 'Justice gives things their equitable right;

generosity removes them from their circumstances. Justice is a common public guide; generosity a special boon. So justice is the more noble and the superior of the two.'

10. Someone commented on the Imām ﷺ being observed to be wearing a patched garment. The Imām countered, 'Hearts grow docile and egos humble as believers accept a different state. This world and the next are irreconcilable enemies – diametrically opposite paths. Those who love and befriend this world detest the concept of the hereafter and deem it their enemy. Every step that brings us closer towards one is a step that takes us further away from the other.'

11. There is no wealth greater than knowledge and no poverty worse than ignorance. There is no heritage finer than a good upbringing and no support better than consolation.

12. It is possible that one meal can prevent one from having others.

Second Imām – Al-Ḥasan عليه السلام

On the 15th of Ramaḍān in the year 3 AH, the Prophet's household was filled with joy at the birth of his first grandson. Ḥasan عليه السلام was firstly assigned the title 'Master of the Youth of Paradise' and was later divinely appointed Imām.

Imām Ḥasan عليه السلام was brought up by his father Imām ʿAli 'The Commander of the Faithful' and his mother 'The Lady Faṭimah' عليهما السلام, and he and his younger brother Imām Ḥusayn عليه السلام were nurtured by both their grandfather and their parents. Historians report that when his grandchildren were present the Prophet would prolong his prostrations to let the two little boys clamber over him.

It is reported that once, while the Prophet ﷺ addressed his companions, the little Ḥasan, toddling toward the *minbar*, stepped on the hem of his garment and toppled over, upon which the Prophet immediately descended to pick him up and console him.

The following *āyah* was revealed, 'But whoever disputes with you in this matter [ʿIsā's not being an aspect of Godhood] after what has come to you of knowledge, say, "Let us summon our **sons** and your sons, and our women and your women, and ourselves and yourselves, and then let us humbly pray and invoke Allāh to curse those who lie".'[55] When that event occurred, the Prophet ﷺ took both Ḥasan and Ḥusayn, whom he considered to be his own sons.

Imām Ḥasan ؑ participated in all of the three battles imposed upon his father, namely *Jamal*, *Ṣiffin* and *Nahrawān*. After the martyrdom of ʿImām ʿAli ؑ, all but one of the companions accorded him their allegiance. The one who declined to do so was Muʿāwiyah, who took it as an opportunity to declare himself Caliph of Damascus and wage war upon the Prophet's grandchild. Imām Ḥasan ؑ encouraged the Muslim population of Kufah to confront this challenge and join the troops he led out of Kufah to the battlefield. It is regrettable that Muʿāwiyah's incentives successfully enticed some of Imām Ḥasan's key commanders to desert him. This unhappily led to a treaty being signed between Imām Ḥasan and Muʿāwiyah by which both agreed to the following commitments:

Article 1 Muʿāwiyah covenanted to comply with the guidelines of the Holy Qur'ān and Sunnah of the Prophet ﷺ.

Article 2 Muʿāwiyah covenanted to uphold Imām Ḥasan's and his brother Imām Ḥusayn's rights to the Caliphate, and not to appoint any successor.

Article 3 Muʿāwiyah covenanted to cease cursing Imām ʿAli during the *qunūt* of his prayers.

Article 4 Muʿāwiyah covenanted to compensate the families of those killed on the battlefields of *Jamal* and *Ṣiffin* and not access *Bayt al-Mal* funds in Kufah but to reserve them for the benefit of all.

Article 5 Muʿāwiyah covenanted to accept the rights of all the people to the protection they were entitled to, regardless of social

> status or being domiciled in Shām, Iraq, Hijaz or Yemen, and not to discriminate or pass judgement on anyone's previous views or actions – in particular, not to disadvantage in any way or prosecute those who had sworn allegiance to Imām ʿAli.[56]

It is clear from the above that the Imām's intention was to publicly announce that his agreement to that treaty being drawn up was to save the blood of the Muslim community and to limit the spread of Muʿāwiyah's corruption. Despite Muʿāwiyah covenanting his acceptance of all the articles of the treaty, he shamelessly denounced it in the very first speech he made after ratifying his agreement to its terms. In his address to the people of Kufah he said, 'Do you imagine that my fight with you was about prayer, *zakāt* and *hajj*? I already knew that you pray, pay *zakāt* and go on pilgrimage – no, I fought you explicitly to take the reins of power and hold authority over you. Allāh has favoured me in spite of you. Thus, I now say publicly before you all that every one of my covenanted commitments to the articles in the treaty with Imām Ḥasan have from this moment forth no legal validity. They are null, void and as dust under my feet.'[57]

To further emphasize his contempt, Muʿāwiyah ended his speech by insulting both Imām ʿAli and Imām Ḥasan عليهما السلام. Imām Ḥasan's response was to remind all present of the Islāmic principles of love and unity that had been promoted by his grandfather the Prophet Muḥammad صلى الله عليه وآله وسلم, and then to contrast the characteristically exemplary conduct of his family with the markedly different attitudes and behaviour of Muʿāwiyah's family. He said, 'O you who insult ʿAli! I am Ḥasan and my father is ʿAli, while you are Muʿāwiyah and your father is Ṣakhr. My mother is Fatimah and yours is Hind. My grandfather is Allāh's holy messenger and yours is ʿUtbah son of Rabiʿah. My grandmother is Khadijah and yours is Futailah. May Allāh curse the one whose family is the most despicable, the one who each day becomes more deeply enmeshed in evil, the one whose family has the longest history of disbelief, hypocrisy and lack of empathy with others.'[58]

Those who objected to the treaty

In retrospect it is not surprising that some of ʿImām ʿAli's supporters expressed distress at such a treaty being drawn up. Qays, son of Saʿd ibn ʿAbādah, whom Imām ʿAli عليه السلام had appointed governor of Egypt, was wretched when he learned about it but was somewhat soothed to hear the Imām's account of the circumstances that had brought it about and his عليه السلام recounting what Imām ʿAli عليه السلام had said vis-à-vis followers of both camps: 'I wish I could replace my followers with those of Muʿāwiyah and exchange ten of mine for one of his.'[59] And on another occasion: 'It is most painful to see that you are not united despite following the right path while Muʿāwiyah's followers are united despite their not following it.'[60]

Another life-long supporter loyal to the Prophet ﷺ and Imām ʿAli عليه السلام, Ḥijr the son of ʿAdiy (later beheaded by Muʿāwiyah), expressed his opposition to the treaty by saying, 'I wish we all had died prior to having to witness such a humiliating event. They gained everything and we lost everything.' To which the Imām's response was, 'O Ḥijr, I was only seeking to protect you all.'

Imām Ḥasan's address to the people

'O people, Muʿāwiyah has claimed I am not eligible to be Khalifah and that he is. By Allāh, he is a liar. Based upon the Holy Book and the declarations of Allāh's messenger, I have the greater entitlement to lead others. Had the people sworn allegiance to me and obeyed and supported me, they would most certainly have benefited from the blessings that would have accrued to them, and no thought of leadership would have even entered Muʿāwiyah's mind. The Prophet ﷺ said, "If a nation elects a leader when someone of greater learning, capability and eligibility is available to lead them, their fate will be similar to that of those who worshipped the calf."'[61]

On jurisprudence

During the Khilafah of Abu Bakr a Bedouin asked him about the rulings that applied to the following circumstances, 'While still in the state of

Iḥram I found a nest of ostrich eggs that I later fried and ate.' As Abu Bakr was not aware of any rulings regarding such circumstances he advised him to ask ʿUmar. He in turn sent him to ʿAbdul Raḥmān ibn ʿAwf. As none of them was aware of any, Abu Bakr then referred the Bedouin to Imām ʿAli عليه السلام. When he came to him, the Imām posed the question to his two sons. It was Imām Ḥasan who asked the Bedouin, 'Do you own camels?' When he responded that he did, Imām Ḥasan عليه السلام ruled, 'Allow your male camels to mate as many times as the number of eggs you ate and then donate the resulting calves to the service of the Kaʿbah.'[62]

Imām ʿAli's advice to his son

After returning from the battle of Ṣiffin, Imām ʿAli عليه السلام gave his son Ḥasan the luminous advice, now recorded in *Nahj al-Balāghah* as letter Number 31, of which this is a brief summary:

- O my son, be balanced in your dealings with others. You should seek for them what you yourself want, and consider unpalatable for them all you yourself consider to be unpalatable. Do not be oppressive, as a reflection of your own wish not to be oppressed, and be good to them, as a reflection of your own desire for good. Do not talk about what you do not know, even if you have a vague knowledge of the subject.

- He who owns the treasures of heaven and the earth has given you permission to pray to Him and has promised that He will accept your prayer . . . He regards abstinence from sin a virtue, but while He reckons every sin to be a single one, He reckons every virtue to be ten. He has placed the keys of His treasury in your hands so that whenever you wish, you can use the key of prayer to open the doors to his favours and access the abundance of His mercy.

- Do not be deceived by people's rush towards worldly attractions, for like barking dogs and carnivores, they loathe each other. The stronger eat the weaker and the larger trample the smaller.

- O my son, livelihoods are of two kinds: one that you seek and the other that seeks you. If you do not strive to attain it, it will rush to you.
- Make inquiries about the character of travel companions prior to embarking on a journey, and neighbours prior to buying a house. Do not speak about things that may rouse laughter, even someone else's quote.

Imām Ḥasan's advice to Junādah

In his عليه السلام final days, after being poisoned by a fatal toxin, his companion Junādah, son of Abi Umayah, came to him for advice. Despite the severity of his condition Imām Ḥasan's edifying response encompassed several topics that retain universal relevance:

a. Apropos humankind's journey towards the eternal, he عليه السلام said, 'Be prepared for the journey but before you depart make ready that which you need to take with you, for you may be certain that while you are in pursuit of the pleasures of *Dunya*, death is in pursuit of you.'

b. Apropos the balance between this life and the hereafter, he عليه السلام said, 'Stay active in your worldly affairs as if you are to live forever, but remain continuously aware of the hereafter, as if your demise will be tomorrow.'

c. Apropos wealth, he عليه السلام said, 'Do not concern yourself with the day that has yet to come but ensure that you do not focus on the accumulation of more wealth than you need for your survival, because what you accumulate is for someone else. Know too that you will have to present a precise account of your lawful earnings, that you will be punished for what you have acquired unlawfully, and that you will be blamed for all things that are dubious.'

d. Apropos status, dignity and the respect of others, he عليه السلام said, 'If you seek dignity that is not relevant to your background, or status that is not in line with public acclaim, then refrain from disobedience to Allāh so that you are worthy of the status, dignity and respect of being obedient to him.'

e. Apropos socializing, he ﷺ said, 'If you feel the need to socialize, befriend those from whom you may gain wisdom and assistance. For such people will appreciate your good characteristics, and if they observe your behaviour to be lacking, they are in a position to provide sound advice.'[63]

Third Imām – Al-Ḥusayn ﷺ

The second of the Prophet's grandsons, Imām Ḥusayn ﷺ was born on the 3rd Shaʿbān in 4 AH. Like his brother Imām Ḥasan ﷺ, he was nurtured by his grandfather and his parents, later co-assigned the title 'Masters of the Youth of Paradise' and divinely appointed as Imām.

As the Prophet ﷺ had no surviving son, his bloodline was continued via his daughter Fatimah and his cousin Imām ʿAli ﷺ. Many authentic *āḥadīth* confirm the Prophet ﷺ to have said, 'The lineage of every Prophet has been ordained to flow from their loins, but my lineage will be passed down via ʿAli and Fatimah.'[64] Thus it is that throughout the centuries his genetic line has been continued via his grandsons Ḥasan and Ḥusayn.

It has been reported that at a crucial moment of the battle of Ṣiffin, Imām ʿAli ﷺ became concerned about the whereabouts of his two boys, 'lest the lineage of the Prophet be discontinued.'[65]

Prior to Ḥusayn's birth, Um al-Faḍl had dreamed that a piece of the sun had broken off and dropped on to her lap. As this was such an unusual dream she asked the Prophet ﷺ to interpret it for her, at which time she learned that his daughter Fatimah was pregnant with her second child and that Um al-Faḍl was to be charged to help her look after it.

Singularly, the Prophet ﷺ stated that his grandson Ḥusayn was from him and he was from Ḥusayn.[66] While the first part of this statement is clear, in its entirety it is understood to convey the reality of the

Prophet being the founder of the Faith of Islām, and Ḥusayn being the rescuer of Islām from corruption by tyrannical Muslim leaders. It will later become clear that had it not been for Imām Ḥusayn's opposition to Yazid's endeavours to turn all Islāmic values upside down, Islām could not have survived.

Indeed, the title, **Household of the Prophet,** mentioned in Qur'ān 33:33, applies specifically to Imām ʿAli, Fatimah and their two sons عليهم السلام.

His characteristics

His parents and grandfather inspired in him all the characteristics that exemplify Islāmic moral values: bravery, generosity, devotion, humility and patience.

- An example of his bravery is seen in his bidding farewell to Abu Dharr – the Prophet's honourable companion whom ʿUthman ordered to leave Madinah and reside in Rabathah – commanding that none witness his leaving. In spite of that, Imām ʿAli, with Ḥasan, Ḥusayn, ʿAqīl and Ammar ibn Yasir, went to the city's gate to see him off. While each spoke a few words of consolation and farewell, Imām Ḥusayn is recorded to have said, 'O Uncle, while these people concern themselves with the affairs of this world you concern yourself with adherence to the faith of Islām. How needless you are of what they keep you from – and how needy they are for what you caution them against. Remain patient and rely on Allāh Almighty.[67]

  Having listened to him, Abu Dharr is reported to have wept and said, 'Peace be with you, O Household of the Prophet. You remind me of Allāh's Messenger and there is no one in Madinah whom I value more.'

  All the chronicles that recorded detailed accounts of the battle at Karbala proclaim Imām Ḥusayn a most courageous warrior who, even on losing most of his family, maintained composure.

- His generosity is illustrated by his concealing his identity in nightly carrying on his shoulders provisions to sustain the poor of Madinah, especially its widows and orphans. This was discovered when he passed away, by his shoulders being found to be callused and that the service no longer continued.

A man once knocked at his door to beg assistance. When Imām Ḥusayn ﷺ observed him to be destitute he asked his servant to bring all the money in the house. On being told that only 200 dirham remained for the upkeep of the house, the Imām said, 'Someone with greater entitlement to it has just arrived.' In giving it, he apologized for it being such a trifling amount.

- A model of how to communicate with Allāh Almighty is to be found in Imām Ḥusayn's supplication on the Day of ʿArafah:

O He whose compassion pardons the greatest sin
O He whose generosity provides abundance
O He who sustains me in adversity
O He who is present when I am on my own
O He who supports me when I am in pain
O my Lord, Lord of my forefathers
O refuge when hope is not realized
Had it not been for your protection I would have been dishonoured
Had it not been for your help I would have been overwhelmed.
O He who healed me when I called upon him;
clothed my nakedness;
satisfied my hunger;
provided water when I was thirsty;
rescued me from humiliation;
And provided funds when I was in need.
O He who frees the enchained
O He who nourishes the new-born
Bless Muḥammad and his household and grant me this day the best of all the things You grant Your servants.[68]

- He once passed a group of indigent souls sitting on the side of the road eating dried bread, who, when he greeted them, invited him to join them. He replied that, 'Had it not been given to you as alms that

I am not entitled to accept I would have loved to join you.' He instead invited them all to dine with him at his home and after the meal presented each with new clothing and ready money.[69]

- When a man from Shām, his head full of Muʿāwiyah's antagonism to the Prophet's Household, came to Madinah and set eyes upon Imām Ḥusayn he assailed him in an angry outburst of vituperation. The Imām, who remained silent while he spoke, then said, 'I assume you to be a stranger. So, if you have not yet found accommodation you are welcome to stay at my house, if you are financially straitened I am happy to assist you and if you need anything else I am always here to be of help.' His invitation was accepted and when, after three days, he left Madinah the man said, 'I entered Madinah thinking Ḥusayn to be the most hated of people and left Madinah knowing him to be the most loved by me.'[70]

Muʿāwiyah's intent to destroy Islām

That neither Muʿāwiyah nor Abu Sufyān (his father) sincerely embraced Islām is evidenced by their lifelong opposition to the Prophet Muḥammad ﷺ. At a gathering of his clan Abu Sufyān advised them, 'O children of Umayyah, pass all advantages you hold amongst yourselves as members of the same team. By the one in whose name Abu Sufyān swears, there is no life after death, paradise nor hell.'[71] Yazid (Abu Sufyān's grandson) said something similar when he addressed his courtiers and captive prisoners of war, all the while employing his cane to strike the severed head of Imām Ḥusayn عليه السلام that had been laid upon a plate before him, and recited:

> 'I wish my ancestors killed in the battle of Badr could witness how I now take our revenge on Aḥmad's progeny. They would praise my bravery. The tribe of Ḥashim dabbled in revelation but without any doubt, no news has come and nothing has been revealed.'[72]

Muʿāwiyah's stratagem to destroy Islām is evidenced by:

- His abuse of *Bayt al-Māl*'s funds to procure political allegiances
- His promotion of internecine disagreement by which he could divide and rule
- His supplanting divine Islāmic governance with his lineage of monarchical rulers
- His relentless attempt to divest the *Ahl al-Bayt* of eminence and destroy those who remained loyal to them
- His instructions that all those who lead prayer use the *qunūt* of the prayer to curse ʿAli عليه السلام and brand him an atheist.[73]

Lessons to be drawn from Imām Ḥusayn's stance

Imām Ḥusayn's reaction to Yazid's atrocities was to safeguard Islāmic principles from corruption; his success in achieving that objective is still evident today. Some of what we learn from it is discussed below.

1. *Not to resign oneself to humiliation*: Imām Ḥusayn عليه السلام told his followers that the authorities in Kufah had left him only two options: humiliation or death. He continued, 'We do not accept humiliation.' Another *ḥadīth*, reported by Imām Ṣādiq عليه السلام, records that Allāh Almighty permits believers choice in all things, other than the acceptance of humiliation.

2. *Always to be broad-minded*: This follows from independent thought, remaining just in one's judgements and not blindly following the opinions of others.

   On the Day of *ʿAshūrā*, Imām Ḥusayn عليه السلام addressed Yazid's troops, 'O followers of Abu Sufyān, if you are not following the teachings of Islām, then as freemen, remain broad-minded and independent in your judgement. Reflect on the basis for your fighting me.'

3. *To seek to comprehend the significance of death*: Few welcome death. Imām Ḥusayn عليه السلام extended our comprehension of death via the discussion of three different aspects:

Death is written for all and none can escape it. He عليه السلام is reported to have remarked that 'Death enhances the quality of life as a necklace does the appearance of a woman.'

- Death with dignity is preferable to a life lived in humiliation.
- Death for the cause of Islām is the honour of martyrdom. In his farewell to his relatives in Madinah, Imām Ḥusayn عليه السلام said, 'Those who join us will be martyred while those that remain here will forfeit that victory.'

4. *Disgrace is to be preferred to hell*: In a dialogue between Imām Ḥusayn عليه السلام and the Umayyad commander ʿUmar ibn Saʿd, two differing viewpoints were expressed. Ibn Saʿd regarded hell preferable to disgrace, Imām Ḥusayn عليه السلام preferred death to dishonour – embarrassment on this earth being of shorter span than eternity in hell.

5. *To maintain awareness:* Military courts martial and firing squads discourage troops from fleeing action. Never has a commander, before or after Imām Ḥusayn عليه السلام, given troops permission to evade the battlefield. The Imām عليه السلام is unique in ensuring that those who volunteered their service to him were aware of the consequence, and had the choice to join him or not.

6. *Always to support truth*: Imām Ḥusayn عليه السلام said, 'Do you not see that truth has been replaced by falsehood? We must sacrifice everything that is precious to support truth!' For truth, the 'essence' of Islām, underpins the values that Allāh emphasizes in the Holy Qur'ān.

   ʿAli al-Akbar asked his father Imām Ḥusayn عليه السلام, 'Are we not supporting the truth?' When he replied in the affirmative ʿAli said, 'So, we need not be concerned if death comes to us or if we approach it.'

7. *It is never too late to repent*: Ḥur Riaḥi, the first commander to prevent Imām Ḥusayn's followers from accessing the waters of the Euphrates, provides a notable example of repentance. When he later regretted his action and asked the Imām عليه السلام if his repentance would be accepted, Imām Ḥusayn عليه السلام assured him of it never being

too late to repent. Upon hearing this Ḥur joined Imām Ḥusayn's camp and was honoured by becoming one of its first martyrs.

8. *Fidelity and loyalty*: Fidelity is a characteristic admired by all. If friends meet in times of comfort and wealth but leave in times of hardship and difficulty, it is clear that their friendship has not been genuine. On the Day of *ʿAshūrā*, Imām Ḥusayn عليه السلام told John, a servant of Abu Dhar, the Prophet's loyal companion, 'You have accompanied us all this way but you may now leave.' John replied, 'It is not fair that I draw benefit from your company and hospitality in times of ease but leave you in your time of hardship.' His fortitude exemplifies fidelity and loyalty.

9. *The importance of the participation of women*: Without 'The Lady Zaynab' witnessing the events at Karbala, Imām Ḥusayn's mission would not have been fulfilled. For it is from her eloquent speeches – in the courtyard of Ibn Ziyād, governor of Kufah, and in Damascus in front of Yazid – that the necessity of the Imām's stance became known to the public, and it is from them that Yazid's labelling the Imām عليه السلام and his companions rabble-rousing rebels was proven to be unfounded. People only came to realize that they had been misled after she had exposed the facts.

10. *To aim steadfastly to please Allāh Almighty*: The intention of believers should be to please Allāh. Imām Ḥusayn عليه السلام reported that the sole objective of the Prophet's household is to please Allāh. When he witnessed his family being butchered one after the other, he uttered, 'This is only bearable because Allāh witnesses it.'

11. *To give preference to the needs of others over one's own*: In Islamic terminology this is known as *Ithār*. On the Day of *ʿAshūrā* Imām Ḥusayn's brother Abbas demonstrated what it means. Despite being parched by the heat and his exertion in accessing the waters of the Euphrates, without thought of his own need, he carried the water straight to the tents of the women and children.

12. *To remain patient in adversity*: Allāh tells us in the Qur'ān, 'Those who are patient will be rewarded without measure.' Imām Ḥusayn عليه السلام, nurtured in this view, remained, in hardship and atrocity, patient and happy with his Lord.

    Patience is neither weakness nor helplessness, but the embodiment of courage and bravery. Those who saw Imām Ḥusayn عليه السلام on the Day of *'Ashūrā* reported, 'We have never observed anyone maintain their composure to the extent that Imām Ḥusayn عليه السلام did as he witnessed his family being slaughtered before him.

13. *The significance of enjoining good and forbidding evil*: Imām Ḥusayn عليه السلام asserted, 'I have acted to emphasize the significance of enjoining good and forbidding evil – *Amr bil Ma'rūf* and *Nahy 'an al Munkar*'.

14. *The importance of only employing lawful means*: In his attempt to prevent the Umayyad army commander 'Umar ibn Sa'd from fulfilling his iniquitous objective, Imām Ḥusayn عليه السلام said, 'While you have been promised the governorship of 'Ray' (Tehran) if you kill me, you will never eat the wheat of that area.' Ibn Sa'd retorted, 'Barley will then have to suffice.' On realizing Ibn Sa'd would not change his mind, Imām Ḥusayn عليه السلام then told him, 'Those who use unlawful means will not achieve their objectives.'

15. *To protect women from having to witness the obscene*: After the tragic Day of *'Ashūrā* all the women and children, now prisoners of war, were taken from Karbala to Kufah and then on to Damascus. Tortured and taunted *en route*, they were obliged to follow behind soldiers bearing aloft the heads of Imām Ḥusayn عليه السلام and his companions on spears. When they arrived at Yazid's headquarters in Damascus, Imām 'Ali bin Ḥusayn عليه السلام asked that the women and children be spared the gaze of spectators by having the grisly heads removed from their proximity.

Fourth Imām – ʿAli ibn Al-Ḥusayn Al-Sajjad ﷺ

Imām ʿAli ibn Al-Ḥusayn ﷺ was born in Madinah in 38 AH. His father was Imām Ḥusayn ﷺ and his mother the Persian princess Shahr Banū, also known as Shah Zanān, daughter of Yazdgird, the last of the Persian kings.

He has two titles, *Zayn al-ʿAbidīn* (Pre-eminent in Worship) and *Al-Sajjād* (Incomparable in Prostration).

Many companions lauded his characteristics:

a. Jābir ibn Abdullah al-Anṣari said, 'There are none like ʿAli ibn Al-Ḥusayn to be seen in the offspring of other prophets.'[74]

b. The famous companion Abdullah ibn Abbas, in spite of being much older than ʿAli ibn Al-Ḥusayn, always expressed his respect, bowing his head and saying, 'Welcome, beloved son of the beloved'.[75]

c. The famous *faqih* of Hijaz and Shām, Al-Zuhari, is reported to have said, 'I have not met anyone who has greater knowledge of jurisprudence than he has.[76]

His characteristics

Imām ʿAli ibn Al-Ḥusayn ﷺ exemplified the Islāmic moral values of forbearance, generosity, charity and asceticism. For example:

- *Forbearance*: Once while he performed his ablutions the jug of water slipped from the maid's hands, cut his face and made it bleed. In apology she quoted from Qur'ān 3:134, 'Those who control their anger.' The Imām replied, 'I have controlled it!' The maid then went on, 'And forgive people', to which the Imām said, 'May Allāh forgive you.' Then, completing the *āyah,* she said, 'Allāh loves those who do good.' To which he ﷺ responded, 'I grant you your freedom.'[77]

  When a man hurled insults at him, he ﷺ ignored it. When the man then pointed his finger at him saying, 'I mean you!' The Imām calmly responded, 'And I am deliberately ignoring you.'[78]

- *Generosity*: Much mention has been made about the Imām's generosity: The ill son of Usāmah, Muḥammad, wept when the Imām visited him. On being asked why, he said it was because he was heavily in debt. When the Imām learned the extent of this was 15,000 dinars he عليه السلام presented him with the outstanding amount.[79]

  It is reported that 100 families in Madinah were sustained by the Imām, none being aware of their benefactor's identity until after his demise.[80]

- *Charity*: In Islām it is highly recommended that charity be offered in secret, and Imām ʿAli ibn Al-Ḥusayn عليه السلام is one of the finest exemplars of this. It was his custom to conceal his identity as he shouldered the sacks of food he delivered each night to the poor and needy. Once he heard a cousin, whom he regularly supplied while incognito, complaining of his not coming to his aid. Despite this, he did not disclose that it was he who regularly met his cousin's needs. He continued this practice until his demise, when his cousin finally discovered the identity of his benefactor and visited the grave to apologize for his tardy behaviour.[81]

- *Asceticism*: Al-Zuhari was once asked who the most ascetic person of his day was, to which he replied, 'He is ʿAli ibn Al-Ḥusayn.' [82]

Stages of his life

We investigate two distinct periods in the life of ʿAli ibn Al-Ḥusayn عليه السلام: before his appointment as Imām and during his Imāmate.

a. When Imām ʿAli ibn Al-Ḥusayn عليه السلام was 12 years old his grandfather Imām ʿAli عليه السلام was martyred and thus, for the next 20 years, the exemplars from whom he learned and drew benefit were his uncle Imām Ḥasan and his father Imām Ḥusayn عليهما السلام. During those critical years the stability of Islāmic governance was being endangered by Muʿāwiah's divisive and destructive refusal to submit to the Imām, who had been acknowledged by the consensus of the Muslim nation, and his intent to establish himself as 'Umayyad Autocrat', monarch and absolute ruler with uncontrolled authority. Academic research has revealed Muʿāwiah's strategies to supplant revealed Islāmic values with restored pre-Islāmic customs and behaviour. It began with his war against Imām ʿAli عليه السلام at Ṣiffin, followed later by the assassination of many of the Prophet's remaining companions. He expended huge *Bayt al-Mal* funds bribing narrators to falsely claim that *ayāt,* revealed in praise of Imām ʿAli عليه السلام such as Qur'ān 2:207, were really praise for his murderer Ibn Muljam, and that *ayāt* revealed to condemn hypocrites, such as 22:11, were targeted at Imām ʿAli عليه السلام.[83]

Atrocities against *Ahl al-Bayt* peaked when Muʿāwiah appointed his son Yazid to succeed him. Yazid's most heinous acts were the murder of Imām Ḥusayn عليه السلام and the persecution of his family. During the terrible incident in the year 61 AH, now referred to as *ʿAshūr*ā, he treated them as slaves and subjected Imām ʿAli ibn Al-Ḥusayn عليه السلام to callous humiliation after his father's murder.

b. After the martyrdom of Imām Ḥusayn عليه السلام, the Fourth Imām had to shoulder the responsibility of divine leadership in spite of his perilous personal circumstances. His first and foremost task was to reawaken the Muslim nation and revive the Islāmic teachings revealed to the Prophet Muḥāmmad صلى الله عليه وآله وسلم. He succeeded in doing so by exposing the chicanery that had been employed in the many attempts to destroy it.

Imām ʿAli ibn Al-Ḥusayn عليه السلام was witness to all the tragic events that led to the martyrdom of his father, brothers, cousins and companions on the Day of *ʿAshūrā,* when acute fever kept him supine in his tent and unable to support them. Had it not been for Divine Will, continuance of the chain of Divine Leadership (*Imāmah*) would have ended at Karbala. As it happened, while still ill with fever, Imām ʿAli ibn Al-Ḥusayn عليه السلام was captured with the women and children. They were bound, bundled astride saddleless dromedaries and pulled tightly upon them by ropes, passed below the animals' stomachs, tied at each end to their legs, and thus transported to Damascus, all

> the way being submitted to contemptuous abuse and ill-treatment by Yazid's troops.[84]
>
> On Imām ʿAli ibn Al-Ḥusayn's return to Madinah after *ʿAshūrā*, he had to make it known to the Muslim community there that his father's focus had never been the fomenting of trouble, as put out by Yazid's propaganda, but the restoring of the Prophet's teachings that had been neglected. That initiative led to the Madinah Rebellion, put down when Yazid authorized his troops to massacre its inhabitants and loot the city for three days. This heinous event occurred during the second year of Yazid's reign. Historians record 700 remaining *Muhājerūn* and *Anṣār* and ten thousand other inhabitants being murdered and one thousand women being raped.[85]
>
> During the third year of Yazid's reign, Abdullah son of Zubayr led a revolt in Makkah, upon which Yazid's troops attacked them and set fire to the Kaʿbah to force their surrender.[86]

Imām ʿAli ibn Al-Ḥusayn عليه السلام left us two precious texts, regarded as being the most profound spiritual guidelines of Islām. These are *Al-Ṣaḥifah al-Sajjādiyah* (The Psalms of Islām) and *Risālat al-Ḥuqūq* (Treatise on Rights).

Al-Ṣaḥifah al-Sajjādiyah

After *Nahj al-Balāghah,* the most influential authentic *Ahl al-Bayt* عليهم السلام source of Islāmic teaching is *Ṣaḥifah al-Sajjādiyah.* This is a collation of 54 humble entreaties of the Imām Zayn al-ʿAbidīnʿ, recorded in Madinah after the tragic martyrdom of his father. While entreaty, prayer and formulaic remembrance are basic spiritual exercises, *Al-Ṣaḥifah al-Sajjādiyah* provides profound insight into the theological, ethical and social aspects of the religion of Islām. Its content discloses the expansive diversity of themes covered, for example:

- behaviour towards parents and appreciation of their love
- children's rights
- disciplines of repentance and seeking of pardon

- how to behave in times of hardship
- wishing neighbours and others well
- noble moral traits
- acceptance of and contentment with one's lot in life
- natural phenomena such as new crescent moons and thunder
- supplication for when one is at Arafat

Throughout the centuries hundreds of *Ṣaḥifah al-Sajjādiyah* manuscripts have been safeguarded in the libraries of Iran, Iraq, India, Turkey and many other lands. Commentaries on it vary from one to as many as seven volumes. Supplication number 20 (dealing with noble and moral traits) exemplifies the methodology and doctrine of the school of *Ahl al-Bayt*, particularly in regard to ethical matters. In-depth study of this specific supplication is evidenced by the many scholarly commentaries upon it alone.

Treatise on Rights – Risālat al-Ḥuqūq

Other than supplications, short sayings and letters, the only work attributable to Imām Zayn al-ʿAbidīn ﷺ is *Risālat al-Ḥuqūq* (Treatise on Rights). The fact that it appeared as a written document suggests that some of his supplications may also have originally appeared in written form.

The 'Treatise on Rights', an elaboration of a well-known saying of the Prophet ﷺ, appears in a wide variety of versions, most probably because it was repeated on many different occasions. Shiʿite sources provide many relevant *āḥadīth* in regard to believers' duties towards one another. For example, the Prophet ﷺ said,

> Allāh has established that those of faith [*mu'minīn*] are bound to uphold **seven** rights due to their fellows. 'To respect their person, to harbour love for them, to share property with them, to accept that it is against the law to make unkind remarks about them, to visit them when they are ill, to escort them to their burial and to say nothing other than good about them after their death.'[87]

Imām Zayn al-ʿAbidīn's 'Treatise on Rights' appears to have been written in response to a request from one of his supporters, as in one of its two versions it is prefaced by: 'This is a treatise of ʿAli ibn al-Ḥusayn for one of his companions.' In it he عليه السلام meticulously explains what is meant by the phrase 'everyone who possesses a right' mentioned in the above *ḥadīth*. Throughout, he provides apposite quotes from the Qur'ān, Sunnah and the actions and sayings of the preceding Imāms.

While the word *haqq* is here translated as 'right', one needs to bear in mind that this word has a variety of other closely related meanings: suitableness, justice, truth, reality, correctness, properness, appropriateness, necessity, incumbency, obligation, due and duty. Scrutiny of the 'Treatise on Rights' reveals that it is not primarily focused on the rights of individuals, but on the rights of others that believers are obliged to uphold. Thus, the word 'rights' might have been more appropriately translated as 'obligations'. Nonetheless, use of the term 'rights' does make clear that Islāmic reflections on 'rights' are considerations of individual responsibilities rather than the contemporary understandings of what is meant by 'human rights'.

Islām views individuals holistically: first, their relationship with Allāh, and then, their relationship with Allāh's creatures. The primary objective of an individual's relationship with Allāh is the purification of their soul, that may be arrived at when their life becomes focused on adherence to His guidance – an emanation of His mercy to ensure their best interest. Islām is not concerned with individual perspectives motivated by worldly interest but calls attention to people's everlasting happiness, in appreciation of their inability to perceive their own ultimate good in the absence of His divine guidance. The Islāmic objective is to dispel individual ignorance by undermining egoism and self-centred desire. Thus while believers have many duties and responsibilities, they have only one undeniable right – to purify their souls.

As soon as the context for attaining this right is realized, a wide range of obligations become apparent. The Imām عليه السلام makes clear that their various organs and activities are included as it is these that determine the individual's relationship with their maker. One's organs have 'rights' because they share one's destiny, one's activities have rights because they shape one's destiny, and other human beings have rights because they are the context in which activity occurs. Human actions may only be considered correct when the rights of all aspects of Allāh's creation are observed.[88]

Fifth Imām – Muḥammad ibn ʿAli Al-Baqir عليه السلام

Born on the first of Rajab 57 AH, Imām Muḥammad al-Baqir عليه السلام inherited characteristics from both his maternal grandfather (Imām Ḥasan) and his paternal grandfather (Ḥusayn) عليهما السلام. To foretell the significant role that his descendant would play, the Prophet ﷺ told his close companion, Jābir ibn Abdullah Anṣari, that he would meet Muḥammad al-Baqir shortly before he died, and asked him to please remember then to give him his late great-grandfather's greetings. It is reported by Ibn ʿAsākir that when Imām Zayn al-ʿAbidin عليه السلام went with his young son Muḥammad to visit the venerable and now blind Jābir, he asked who had come with him. On hearing it was his son Muḥammad, Jābir hugged the boy saying, 'Your great-grandfather asked me to convey his greeting when I met you.' Weeping, he then said it was a sign that his days were coming to an end.'[89]

Islāmic coinage

Prior to, and during the lifetime of, Imām Muḥammad al-Baqir عليه السلام, all the coinage used in the Muslim world had been minted in Rome. It was only during the reign of the Umayyad Caliph Abdul Malik ibn Marwan, that it was noticed that all Egyptian imports of paper and clothing bore the symbol of 'The Trinity'. On learning this, Abdul Malik ordered his governor in Egypt to replace such symbols with the phrase, 'There is no deity other than Allāh – *La Illāha il Allāh*. The Roman emperor, angered by this effrontery, threatened to stop coins being minted for the Muslim world. Abdul Malik was so troubled when he heard this that he expressed himself to be the most ill-favoured person in Islām. In a quandary, he consulted Imām Muḥammad al-Baqir عليه السلام, recognized at the time to be the wisest person in his realm. The Imām advised him of the necessary elements to be included and how to design the coins and moulds from which to strike the Islāmic currency that constituted legal tender in the Muslim world for some time.[90]

Scholarship under Imām Baqir عليه السلام

As the result of scholars' different understanding of the Qur'ān and the *āḥadīth* of the Holy Prophet صلى الله عليه وآله وسلم, a variety of versions of theology and jurisprudence began to be circulated during the Umayyad dynasty. Fabricated *āḥadīth*, ideas concerning anthropomorphism, predestination, the possibility of being able to see Allāh and denial of the prophetic message being free of error (*ʿiṣmah*), were all widely disseminated. In addition, there were followers of the *Ahl al-Bayt* who exaggerated the status of Imām ʿAli عليه السلام.

It is the duty of every Imām to clarify truth – to extricate it from a plethora of unfounded opinion. As his father had been detained under the strict supervision and censorship of the Umayyads, he was obliged to leave it to Imām Muḥammad al-Baqir عليه السلام to fulfil this duty. To enable it to be effectively undertaken, he drew together and prepared a circle of the finest intellects of the time, to refute distortion and falsification with factual information and logical argument.

Imām Muḥammad al-Baqir عليه السلام, gifted with the ability to impart comprehension of complex concepts, expounded significant and difficult-to-explicate theological issues that challenge comprehension, for example the concept of Allāh Almighty, the incomparability of Divine Attributes, and confusion wrought by the *Jabriyah* doctrine (of all human action being predetermined).

> Al-Baqir also contributed to the theological doctrines concerning *Imān, Taqiyya, Qaḍā' wa Qadar*, The Unity of God, as well as a host of other topics that were discussed and hotly debated in his time. Thus, he emerges not only as the guide and spiritual leader of a particular group, having founded a separate school and provided a doctrinal basis for it, but also as one of the most distinguished scholars of the period, disseminating knowledge on all aspects of Muslim life.[91]

One of the topics that arose during Imām Baqir's time was the uniqueness of the words *Islām* and *Imān*. In clarification of their meaning, the Imām عليه السلام first cited Qur'ān 49:14: 'The Bedouins say, "we believe", say [O Muḥammad], You do not believe, so rather say, "We have accepted Islām. Faith has not yet entered your hearts."' Then, to illustrate the difference between *Islām* and *Imān* he عليه السلام referred to the Kaʿbah and the *Masjid al-Ḥarām* and said, 'If one sees someone within the Kaʿbah one can say with absolute certainty that they have been in the mosque. However, if one sees someone in the mosque, one cannot say with any certainty whatever that they have been within the Kaʿbah'.[92]

A Kharijite asked Imām Muḥammad al-Baqir عليه السلام if he had ever seen Allāh. The Imām responded, 'Even though eyes do not see him, with the reality of faith the heart is able to. He is not known via analogy or felt by the senses, and He cannot be likened to a human being. He is not unjust in judgement – truly there is no divinity other than He.' As he left, the questioner quoted Qur'ān 6:124, 'Allāh knows whom to place His message with.'[93]

Imām Muḥammad al-Baqir عليه السلام inherited the in-depth knowledge needed to fulfil his responsibility from his great-grandfather Imām ʿAli عليه السلام, whom the Prophet himself referred to as being 'The Gate to the City of Knowledge'.

His heritage of theology, jurisprudence, exegesis and the other branches of Islāmic teaching, transmitted via reliable chains of narrators, was continued by his son Jaʿfar al-Ṣādiq عليه السلام and constitute the teachings of the Islāmic School of *Ahl al-Bayt*.

He was the first to explicate the sources of one of the most important principles of jurisprudence: 'Islamic Law does not occasion unbearable hardship'. Despite the basis of this principle being traced to many Qur'ānic references, such as 20:78, 5:6, 2:185, 4.28 and 7:157, it was Imām Muḥammad al-Baqir عليه السلام who evinced it as a general principle of jurisprudence, to be deduced from the above sources. Indeed, another widely used tool of *Ijtihād* – the principle that 'Islamic Law does not occasion harm' – was first made clear by Imām Baqir عليه السلام when he put forward his great-grandfather's view on the 'Palm Tree of Samurah ibn Jundub' in a garden that belonged to an Anṣāri in Madinah.[94]

'Presumption of Continuity' is another principle, evinced by Imām Muḥammad al-Baqir عليه السلام when he responded to Zurārah ibn A'yun's query. Clearly, students of the Imāms and later jurists have expanded upon the principles evidenced by Imām Baqir عليه السلام.

Historians record that Imām Baqir عليه السلام trained 483 students to lecture on and disseminate his teachings. The foremost of these were: Abān ibn Taghlib, Ibrāhim ibn Azraq, Buraid ibn Mu'awiyah, Bukayr ibn A'yun, Thābit ibn Hurmuz, Thuwayr ibn Abi Fākhetah, Jabir ibn Yazid al-Ju'fi, Hasan ibn Ṣalih and Zurārah ibn A'yun. Many of these continued their studies under Imām Ṣādiq عليه السلام.

Anguish and demise

The life of Imām Muḥammad al-Baqir عليه السلام was contemporaneous with the notorious Umayyad caliph 'Abdul Malik ibn Marwān and his four sons. 'Abdul Malik's most heinous crime was his appointment of the bloodthirsty Al-Ḥajjāj ibn Yusuf al-Thaqafi to preside over the Muslim nation as its autonomous administrator. Another Umayyad caliph, 'Umar ibn 'Abdul Aziz, said, 'If every nation were to name their most corrupt citizen and we identified Al-Ḥajjāj as ours, the evidence of his deeds would overwhelm those of all rivals.'[95] Another scholar, 'Āṣim, said, 'There is not an unlawful act that Al-Ḥajjāj did not commit.'[96] When Al-Ḥajjāj died, the scholar Ibn 'Imād Ḥanbali celebrated it as being a blessed day for the Muslim community, saying, 'His greatest happiness was in spilling the blood of others.'[97]

Some historians record 120,000 innocent souls being killed by Al-Ḥajjāj, including the famous jurist of Kufah, Sa'id ibn Jubair, about whom Al-Ḥasan al-Baṣri said, 'Today, Sa'id ibn Jubair has passed away while Muslims in the East and West are in need of his knowledge.'

One can imagine the difficult life of Imām Muḥammad al-Baqir عليه السلام in the unremitting circumstances of Walīd ibn 'Abdul Malik's caliphate. It was only when Sulaymān ibn 'Abdul Malik became caliph that justice brought about the release of some 81,000 prisoners throughout the land.

After Sulaymān's death, ʿUmar ibn ʿAbdul Aziz became caliph. During his reign he banned the cursing of Imām ʿAli ﷺ in the *qunūt* of prayers, returned the lands of *Fadak* to the descendants of Fatimah al-Zahrah ﷺ and paid his official respects to Imām Muḥammad al-Baqir ﷺ. At this time the Imām advised him, 'Regard elders as fathers, minors as sons and daughters, and adults as your brothers and sisters.' That ʿUmar ibn ʿAbdul Aziz appreciated that advice is evidenced by his then saying, 'By Allāh, you have taught me how to guarantee salvation in this life and the one to come.'

Poisoned by Hisham ibn ʿAbdul Malik, Imām Muḥammad al-Baqir ﷺ was buried in the cemetery called *Baqiʿ* in Madinah on the 7th day of Dhul Hijjah in the year 114 AH.

Sixth Imām – Jaʿfar ibn Muḥammad Al-Ṣādiq ﷺ

Imām Ṣādiq ﷺ was born in Madinah on the 17th Rabiʿ al-Awwal in the year 83 AH. Trained by his father Imām Baqir ﷺ, he followed in his footsteps and, like him, is regarded as having been the font of Islāmic teaching of his time. His mother Um Farwah, was the daughter of Al-Qasim (the son of Muḥammad ibn Abu Bakr, who is recorded to have been one of the greatest jurists of Madinah). Biographical research on Imām Ṣādiq ﷺ reveals the esteem and admiration that contemporaneous and subsequent scholars accord him. For example:

1. Ibn Ḥubban (d. 354 AH) said, 'His knowledge, jurisprudence and merit establish him a most notable *Ahl al-Bayt* luminary.'[98]

2. Abu Nuʿaim (d. 430 AH) said he was 'the foremost Imām to focus on dissemination of knowledge and eschewal of worldly attraction'.[99]

3. Abu Ḥanifa (d. 150 AH) said, 'I have never met anyone more knowledgeable than Jaʿfar, son of Muḥammad. Had it not been for my two years of study under him, I would have perished.'[100]

4. Muḥammad ibn Ṭalḥah al-Shāfiʿi (d. 652 AH) said, 'It is not possible to overestimate his significance. He imparted profound knowledge

of the Qur'ān and *āḥadīth* from limitless oceans of wisdom that encompass every branch of Islāmic study.'[101]

5. Ibn al-Ṣabbāgh al-Māliki (d. 855 AH) said, 'Vis-à-vis the *ḥadīth* he narrated, no one else has been able to match the depth and insight of his wisdom'.[102]

Revolt against Umayyad rule

Many of the Prophet's progeny, disgusted by Umayyad caliphs' conspicuous transgressions, especially those of ʿAbdul Malik and his sons, felt an obligation to rise up and oppose them. With the Muslim public now informed that the Prophet's grandson and his family had been slaughtered at Karbala and their survivors enslaved, it was not difficult for Zayd, Imām Zayn al-ʿAbidin's son, to incentivize the discontented public to revolt. Sayyid Abdul Razzāq Muqarram lists supporting jurists and scholars of Zayd's mission, who had studied under Imāms Baqir and Ṣādiq عليهما السلام. Despite Zayd feeling the need to consult the Imām of the time, i.e. his nephew Imām Ṣādiq عليه السلام, he ignored his advice that it was not a propitious time to take such action. History records that Zayd's revolt failed, with him being killed and his dead body crucified in the year 121 AH.

While some in that period thought Zayd's actions had been to claim the Imāmah for himself, Imām Ṣādiq عليه السلام declared that to be unsubstantiated nonsense.

After Zayd's death, his son Yaḥyā departed Kufah for Khurasān where he and 70 of his supporters planned another civil insurrection. When his intention was discovered, the governor of Kufah commanded that Naṣr ibn Sayyar insist Yaḥyā's host surrender him. When this was declined he sent 10,000 troops to enforce it. In the year 125 AH Yaḥyā and his followers were put to death, Yaḥyā's dead body being crucified, and, like that of his father, then put on public display.

People's frustration persisted until the collapse of the Umayyad dynasty. In the period before it was replaced by the Abbasids, many urged the Imām عليه السلام to take the political initiative, but he عليه السلام felt that he could not rely on adequate support.

Imām's reaction to theological problems

During Imām Ṣādiq's lifetime, antipathy to prophetic teaching promoted confusion in relation to three theological concepts: predestination, atheism and Muʿtazilite doctrines. These needed clarification via a restatement of Islāmic beliefs.

1. *Predestination.* A belief widely encouraged during the Umayyad dynasty was that as human beings lack free will, every human action is pre-set. History records faux scholarship justifications of corruption, by those referred to as caliphs, on the basis of predestination, which asserts that every human action is an expression of Allāh Almighty's immutable will, and, furthermore, that the attribution of actions to humankind is inconsistent with true faith in Allāh. This is on the ground that human beings are but feathers to be blown by the winds. However, the propagation of such views served to confuse the public to the extent that belief in their being accountable for their own actions began to be conveniently considered not to exist.

   As discussed earlier, Imām Ṣādiq عليه السلام spared no effort in his refutation of such claims and the re-presentation of precise proof for the doctrine of free will advocated by Imāmi theologians.

2. *Atheism.* Another attempt to counter faith, disseminated during the time of Imām Ṣādiq عليه السلام, was effected by a vociferous atheist, Ibn Abi al-ʿAwjā', who elected to decry the existence of God in the mosque of the Holy Prophet صلى الله عليه وآله وسلم, and whose views were regurgitated by the equally vociferous Al-Juʿd ibn Dirham.

   Al-Juʿd apparently believed that the truth of his view was proven by the experiment he conducted – he had placed soil in a container, watered it and then shown onlookers that it contained a few earthworms and insects. As he then told his audience, 'Now you see me as a creator!' When Imām Ṣādiq عليه السلام heard about it he retorted, 'If his claim to have created them is to be accepted, let him tell us precisely how many there are, how many are male, how many female and how much each of them weighs.'

Ibn Abi al-ʿAwjā' asked the Imām what prevented God from manifesting himself so that none can doubt or dispute his existence. In reply the Imām عليه السلام asked him, 'Why do you deny His existence when your own growth and development is a manifestation of His power?'

As already mentioned, when the Imām's student Mufaḍḍal spoke to him about the confusion being spread by atheists such as Ibn Abi al-ʿAwjā', Imām Ṣādiq عليه السلام dedicated four consecutive days to providing Mufaḍḍal with teleological examples for the existence of Allāh (see p. 55).

3. *Muʿtazilite doctrine.* Contrary to many orientalist claims that Imāmi theology imitates Muʿtazilite doctrine, even a brief overview of the subject exposes their widely differing perspectives. The Muʿtazilite doctrine that drew most attention during the lifetime of Imām Ṣādiq عليه السلام relates to an absence of theological objection to the merits of Muslim community leaders being inferior to those of their subjects. This was cited to justify the positions of those who had claimed the caliphate over Imām ʿAli عليه السلام, whom the Prophet صلى الله عليه وآله وسلم himself had titled 'The Gate to the City of Knowledge'. Thus, it is no surprise to discover that the Muʿtazilite scholar Ibn abi al-Ḥadīd prefaced his commentary on *Nahj al-Balāghah* with the phrase, 'Praise be to Allāh Almighty who gave precedence to one with lesser merit, over the one with definitive merit.'

As such a claim does not resonate with, and has no basis in, Islāmic teaching, Imām Ṣādiq عليه السلام clarified the prerequisite for the Imām or Muslim leader – that they be acknowledged to have greater intellect, knowledge and impeccability of character than other claimants (in contrast to renown for self-interest, brutality and menace), so that they are unanimously recognized as being worthy of undisputed acceptance.

Another point at issue between Imāmi and Muʿtazilite doctrine concerns the Imāmah – the former consider it divinely covenanted, the latter that it is determined by electoral choice. In seeking to understand this difference of position, one of Imām Ṣādiq's young students, Ḥishām ibn al-Ḥakam, travelled to Baṣrah specifically to seek the opinion of the famous Muʿtazilite scholar ʿAmr ibn ʿUbayd. After hearing his detailed responses, Ḥisham left Baṣrah wondering, 'How could it be that Allāh Almighty provided each person with means (i.e. the central nervous system) to process and interpret sensory messages, and did not provide people means (i.e. the Imāmah) to process and interpret His divine message?

Regarding the Principle of Jurisprudence

A well-known principle of Imāmi jurisprudence is that 'Speculative Analogy is not a valid basis for *ijtihād*'. Yet in spite of Abu Ḥanifah studying under Imām Ṣādiq عليه السلام for two years and his claim never to have met anyone more knowledgeable, Abu Ḥanifah continued to rely upon analogy, regardless of it being definitive or speculative. (Analogy is considered by most Sunni scholars as a useful tool in *ijtihād* in the absence of any clear text to determine the ruling of the subject matter.) Pertinent to Abu Ḥanifah's esteem of the value of analogy, Imām Ṣādiq عليه السلام therefore asked, 'What is of greater importance, the Prayer or the Fast?' To this Abu Ḥanifah responded, 'Prayer is, of course'. The Imām then said, 'According to your analogy, women should make up for the prayers and not the days of fast that they miss during their monthly periods, in contradiction to the stipulation of Islāmic Law'.

On another occasion, Imām Ṣādiq عليه السلام asked Abu Ḥanifah, 'What is more filthy, urine or semen?' Abu Ḥanifah responded, 'Urine is more filthy than semen.' The Imām then said, 'According to your analogy, one should perform major ablution (*ghusl*) every time urine is passed, but not when semen is ejaculated, in contradiction to the stipulation of Islāmic Law.'

In conclusion, we are now well-enough informed to appreciate the importance of Imām Ṣādiq's contribution to comprehension of *shariʿah* matters. Indeed, he referred to his *āḥadīth* having been authentically transferred from the Holy Messenger of Islām when he said, 'My *ḥadīth* is from my father, my father's *ḥadīth* is from my grandfather, my grandfather's *ḥadīth* is from Imām Ḥusayn. That was narrated from Imām

Ḥasan from the Commander of the Faithful, who attributed it to the Holy Prophet – who received Allah Almighty's revelation.'[103]

Most of the scholars trained by Imām Muḥammad al-Baqir عليه السلام were fortunate enough to continue their studies under Imām Ṣādiq عليه السلام, including Abān ibn Taghlib, Buraid ibn Muʿawiyah, Bukayr ibn Aʿyun, Jabir ibn Yazid al-Juʿfi, Hasan ibn Ṣalih, Zurārah ibn Aʿyun and Jamil ibn Darrāj.

The major biographies of *ḥadīth* transmitters (*ʿIlm al-Rijāl*), such as Najashi, Kashshi, Alamah Ḥilli, Mamaqani and Khoei, verified their authority and analysed the contributions each made to the spread of Imām Ṣādiq's teachings.

Unsurprisingly, many Sunni scholars also quote from the authoritative works of the above-mentioned luminaries. Ḥasan ibn ʿAli al-Washshā' said, 'In the Kufah mosque I observed 900 study circles, in which every one of the lecturers attributed their knowledge to Imām Ṣādiq'.[104] This is the reason why the Imāmi 'School of Law' is referred to as *Jaʿfari.*

After his elaboration on the significance of the 'Principles of Islāmic Law' established by Imām Ṣādiq عليه السلام, ʿAbdul Ḥalīm al-Jundi (a famous Egyptian Juridical authority) then states, 'Despite Imām Ṣādiq's School being referred to as *Jaʿfari*, this is, in reality, nothing other than the firming up of the School of Imām ʿAli عليه السلام, which was based upon the true teaching of the Prophet ﷺ'.[105]

Despite the new Abbasid caliph Abu Jaʿfar al-Manṣūr's early assertion of support for the Household of the Prophet ﷺ, Imām Ṣādiq عليه السلام was made to suffer the consequences of the caliph's paranoia (he feared that the Imām's presence threatened his leadership), a state of affairs that was only resolved to the caliph's satisfaction in the year 148 AH, when he had the Imām poisoned and laid to rest in the Baqīʿ cemetery of Madinah.

Seventh Imām – Mūsa Al-Kāẓim عليه السلام

After the death of Imām Ṣādiq عليه السلام, a group of Shiʿites claimed his eldest son Ismāʿil to be his rightful successor, despite his having already predeceased his father. This group, who came to be known as Ismāʿilis, later fragmented into subgroups now referred to as Dawoodi Bohras and Agha Khanis. It is a matter of historical fact that Imām Ṣādiq عليه السلام used the occasion of Ismāʿil's funeral to disabuse attendees of the idea that it was possible for a deceased person to succeed him, for he asked them all to bear witness to Ismāʿil no longer being alive before he announced that his son Mūsa would succeed him.

Sulayman ibn Khālid narrates that Imām Ṣādiq عليه السلام summoned his son Mūsa, and in his presence announced that the latter was to be his successor. Fayḍ ibn al-Mukhtār narrates, 'I was honoured to meet Imām Ṣādiq عليه السلام at the time when his young son Mūsa entered. I stood up to hug him and heard the Imām say, 'You all represent the ship and this is its captain.' Many of the Imām's companions report that whenever the Imām was asked who would succeed him he would point to Mūsa.[106]

Born in the year 128 AH Imām Mūsa Al-Kāẓim عليه السلام was trained by his father. His lifetime was contemporaneous with the rule of the Abbasid caliphs Abu Jaʿfar al-Manṣūr, al-Mahdi, al-Hādi and Hārūn al-Rashid, each of whom in turn subjected him to the most atrocious contempt and mistreatment.

As an acknowledged exemplification of divine leadership, Imām Mūsa Al-Kāẓim's knowledge was unrestricted and all-encompassing, one example being his mastery of different tongues. Abu Baṣīr narrates that the Imām عليه السلام used the Farsi language to answer a Khurasani visitor's Arabic questions. When the Khurasani expressed surprise at his fluency in that tongue the Imām عليه السلام said, 'Ability to respond to those who seek guidance is a necessary characteristic of the Imām.'[107] This characteristic was further confirmed when visitors came to him from as far afield as Abyssinia and China.

Imām Mūsa Al-Kāẓim عليه السلام during the reign of Al-Mahdi

The Abbasid caliph Al-Mahdi ordered Imām Mūsa Al-Kāẓim عليه السلام to Baghdad where he was imprisoned, released and then sent back to Madinah. That Al-Mahdi was set to have him murdered is evidenced by the following incident.

Ḥamīd ibn Qaḥṭabah was summoned by Al-Mahdi in the middle of the night to be told, 'Your father was known to be a loyal subject but you do not appear to have the same reputation.' Ḥamīd responded, 'I am ready to sacrifice my soul and my property for you!' Al-Mahdi then said, 'That is what all people say.' So Ḥamīd said, 'I am ready to sacrifice my soul, my property and my children for you!' As this statement was not well received either he declared, 'I am ready to sacrifice my soul, my property, my children and my faith for you!' This seemed to pacify Al-Mahdi as he then ordered the Imām be killed before sunrise. However, when Al-Mahdi dreamed that he heard Imām ʿAli عليه السلام recite the *āyah*, 'If you hold authority you are likely to make mischief on earth and sever your ties of kinship' (Qur'ān 47:22), he was so alarmed he rose from his bed to annul his instructions.[108]

Historians have recorded Al-Mahdi's unbridled expenditure of *Bayt al-Mal* funds on ostentatious vainglories, inducements and rewards. For example, Ghiyath ibn Ibrāhim knew that, other than for stakes wagered between archery, or horse and camel race contestants, Islāmic law deems the laying of bets to be unacceptable. However, to win favour with the caliph, whose pastime was racing pigeons, he fabricated a *ḥadīth* attributed to Abu Hurairah that included betting on pigeon races being also acceptable. Although he was given a reward of 10,000 dirhams for that bit of chicanery, as he left his presence Al-Mahdi is recorded to have said, 'By Allāh, even though he has borne false witness, he only did so to please me.'[109]

Al-Mahdi encouraged poets to decry the esteem of Imām ʿAli's progeny by giving enormous gifts to those who could produce the most defamatory lines. For example, he awarded Marwān ibn Ḥafṣah 70,000 dirhams for a poem that asserted that the Prophet's cousins (the Abbasids) were more dignified and thus closer to him than his own children (Imāms Ḥasan and Ḥusayn عليهما السلام). When Imām Mūsa Al-Kāẓim عليه السلام came to know about it he عليه السلام was dismayed at *Bayt al-Mal* funds being misused on nonsensical activity and confronted the caliph over extravagances that flouted Islāmic values

The most outrageous report relates to the expense of the wedding celebrations of Al-Mahdi's son Harūn to Zubaydah – claimed to have far exceeded anything ever paid for by the emperors of Rome or Persia.

To feign friendship with the Imām, Al-Mahdi said he would give him back the ownership of the *Fadak* estate, that he imagined to be a garden in the outskirts of Madinah. However, when he asked the Imām to cite its boundaries and was told, 'One boundary is the Mountain of Uḥud, another the land of Egypt, the third boundary is the Red Sea and the fourth Syria', the astonished Al-Mahdi asked, 'All that represents *Fadak*?' When that was answered in the affirmative Al-Mahdi realized that the Imām claimed authority over all Islāmic lands, and angrily said he would need to reconsider his gift.'[110]

Like the Imāms before him, Imām Mūsa Al-Kāẓim عليه السلام concerned himself with the education of his companions and the transmission of traditions he had inherited. The major biographers of *ḥadīth* transmitters (*'Ilm al-Rijāl*), name 319 of his students, the six most outstanding being: Yunus ibn 'Abul Raḥman, Ṣafwān ibn Yahya, Muḥammad ibn abi 'Umair, Abdullāh ibn al-Mughrirah, Ḥasan ibn Maḥbūb and Aḥmad ibn Muḥammad ibn abi Naṣr al-Bazanṭi. The Imām عليه السلام inculcated in them the need for them to function as a harmonious whole – to the extent that, when he asked how helpful they found one another to be and was told, 'they are the very best', he عليه السلام asked, 'Are you so close that whoever is in need may, without any objection, help himself from his brother's pockets?' On learning that their relationships did not extend that far he عليه السلام then said, 'So you have yet to attain the desired level of cooperation.'

In a *ḥadīth* recorded by Ḥisham ibn al-Ḥakam, Imām Mūsa Al-Kāẓim عليه السلام expounds the significance of intellect and the profound contributions made by those whom the Almighty has blessed with this inestimable gift. Referring to Qur'ān 2:163–164, he highlights that it is via intellectual reasoning that it has been possible for humankind to recognize the Almighty and His messengers. He then elaborates on what we now refer to as 'The Teleological Argument for the Existence of God'.[111] He also enlarges on another aspect of this *ḥadīth:* the interrelationship between intellect and knowledge.[112]

Many are misled by the thought that 'right' rests with majorities and, conversely, that minorities are therefore always wrong. In refutation of this, the Imām ﷵ pointed Ḥisham to *ayāt* in which Allāh condemns majorities[113] and *ayāt* in which He praises minorities.[114]

He then went on to describe the characteristics of believers who maintain vigilance over the manner in which they behave and handle their affairs.[115]

Imām Mūsa Al-Kāẓim ﷵ during the reign of Mūsa al-Hādi

Al-Mahdi died in the year 169 AH after having had his son, the 26-year-old Mūsa al-Hādi appointed his successor. Despite Mūsa al-Hādi's short reign, of approximately one year, his antagonism towards the *Ahl al-Bayt* and its followers resulted in the sanction of oppressions, humiliations and mistreatments that made their lives unbearable. Imām Ḥasan's great-grandson Ḥusayn, who came to be known as 'The Warrior of Fakhkh', appealed for the support of prominent Hashemites in Madinah, such as Yahya, Sulayman, Idris and Abdullah, son of Ḥasan al-Afṭas, who then together with 300 equally provoked warriors, set off towards Makkah. When they were confronted by Abbasid troops at the village called Fakhkh, a ferocious encounter ensued in which Ḥusayn and his troops were slain, with their severed heads then being sent to Mūsa al-Hādi. After that tragic outcome, the Imām's loyal followers cautioned vigilance, as they thought he too would likely be targeted. In response, the Imām ﷵ faced the *Qibla* to offer the supplication now known as the 'Minor Armour' (*Jawshun Sagheer*). He then turned to his companions, pointed to the shrine of Allāh's Holy Prophet ﷺ and said, 'I confirm by the dignity of the one who is here buried, that the caliph Mūsa al-Hādi has today passed away in Baghdad.' After this he recited the *āyah* 'By the Lord of the heavens and the earth, it is certainly true as you speak'.[116]

A short time later Madinah received the news from Baghdad that Mūsa al-Hādi had died and that his brother Hārūn al-Rashid had been appointed his successor.[117]

Imām Mūsa Al-Kāẓim ﷺ during the reign of Hārūn al-Rashid

During the reign of Hārūn al-Rashid, Islāmic mores in Baghdad were supplanted by a culture of profligacy, decadence and debauchery. This is borne out by the poetry of Abu Nuwās, one of Hārūn al-Rashid's inner circle, who became famed for drinking songs that extolled licentiousness and the pleasures of the fruit of the vine (*Khamriyāt*). Orientalists such as Wellhausen and Goldziher describe this period as 'the Era of Hereticism'.[118]

Thus, the mission of the Imāmah in the time of Imām Mūsa Al-Kāẓim ﷺ was focused on the re-establishment of the ethos of Islāmic ethics. One initiative was educational, in that he charged his most intellectually able students, Ḥishām ibn al-Ḥakam, Ṣafwān ibn Yahya and Ḥasan ibn Muḥammad ibn Samā'ah, with the dissemination of *Ahl al-Bayt* jurisprudential teachings. This aspect of Imām Mūsa Al-Kāẓim's heritage is covered in 30 books on judicial methodologies produced by these three students alone. They cover many principles of *Ijtihād* such as Rejection of Speculative Analogy, the Principle of Permissibility, the Binding Nature of Summary Knowledge and the Presumption of Continuity – all invaluable 'tools' by which to deduce Islāmic Law from its sources.

A second initiative was to identify and encourage caliphate personnel, loyal to the *Ahl al-Bayt*, to prevent atrocities from being perpetrated. In line with the injunction, 'do not cooperate with the tyrant',[119] Imām Mūsa ﷺ always made himself available to advise on matters that might impinge on the public's welfare. One of those to consult him was Hārūn al-Rashid's vizier, 'Ali ibn Yaqṭīn, but other high-ranking Abbasid officials who also sought his ﷺ advice included Ḥafṣ ibn Ghiyath, appointed Qāḍi in Baghdad and later Kufah, Abdullāh ibn Sinān, Muḥammad ibn Isma'il ibn Bazī' and Ḥasan ibn Rāshid.

Another initiative employed to subvert official injustice was to equip his students with profound Islāmic ethical arguments by which to combat anti-Shi'ah radicalization and to expose flaws in the beliefs of Mu'tazilites and heretics. Ḥishām ibn al-Ḥakam became renowned for his effectiveness.

Imprisonment

As increasing numbers come to pay their respects to Imām Mūsa Al-Kāẓim عليه السلام, Hārūn al-Rashid grew ever more insecure and determined that the only way to safeguard his position would be to imprison the Imām. He first realized that when he visited the Prophet's grave and addressed his salaams to him, 'O Holy Messenger', only to hear the Imām address his salaams with the words, 'O grandfather'. After that, Hārūn apologized to the Prophet for his intention to imprison his grandchild, which he claimed was necessary to avoid the blood of the Muslim nation being shed. Historical records indicate that the caliph exploited ʿAli or Muḥammad, sons of the Imām's late brother Ismāʿil, to falsely accuse the Imām of rallying troops for a future uprising. (As mentioned earlier, Ismāʿil, late brother of Imām Mūsa Al-Kāẓim عليه السلام, had predeceased his father Imām Ṣādiq عليه السلام.)

While the Imām عليه السلام was still in prayer alongside the grave of Allāh's Holy Messenger, the caliph had him chained and taken to the prison in Baṣrah. Then, to be able to satisfy himself that the strictures of his highly secure incarceration were maintained, Hārūn al-Rashid had the Imām عليه السلام moved into solitary confinement in Baghdad. On one of his visits he asked the guard, 'What is that pile of cloth on the floor?' When the reply came that they were not cloths but Mūsa ibn Jaʿfar in his daily sunrise to noon prostration, he remarked, 'One of the sages of the Hashemites.' The guard took this opportunity to seek alleviation of the prisoner's conditions but Hārūn rejected any consideration.[120]

Many scholars of the period pleaded for the Imām's release. Although some of these were successful, it never took long before he was re-arrested and re-incarcerated. Eventually poisoned, he عليه السلام died on the 25th Rajab 183 AH.

With the Seventh Imām imprisoned and inaccessible, the collection of religious dues had been delegated. When on his demise it was announced that Imām Mūsa Al-Kāẓim عليه السلام had declared his son ʿAli his successor, those who did not want to lose what they saw as an opportunity to control such dues, denied that he had done so, and in so doing have come to be remembered as *Wāqifiyah* (those who hold back progress).

Eighth Imām – ʿAli ibn Mūsa Al-Riḍā عليه السلام

On the 11th Dhul Qiʿdah in the year 148 AH, ʿAli ibn Mūsa known as Al-Riḍā, was born in Madinah. His father, the Seventh Imām, Mūsa Al-Kāẓim عليه السلام, was obliged to employ a variety of means by which to declare his son's succession. During the period between the years 150 and 178 AH he was able to share it freely with his closest companions, but during his incarceration he was afforded little opportunity to speak with anyone. In relation to the first period, Dawūd ibn Ruzain narrates that when he once brought funds to the Seventh Imām, 'He عليه السلام took only a part of it, instructing me to keep the balance in trust for the one who will later claim it.' When the Imām died, his son ʿAli came to collect it and from that I learned that ʿAli ibn Mūsa had been appointed the Imām to succeed his father.[121]

In another narration, ʿAli ibn Abdullah al-Hāshemi tells us that, 'While near the grave of the holy Messenger of Allāh صلى الله عليه وآله وسلم in the company of some 60 others loyal to *Ahl al-Bayt*, we observed Imām Mūsa Al-Kāẓim عليه السلام coming towards us hand in hand with his son ʿAli. He عليه السلام asked us, "Do you recognize me?" When we responded that we did indeed recognize our master and leader, he said, "Name me and my father". We replied, "You are Mūsa, son of Jaʿfar the son of Muḥammad." He then asked, "Who is this who is with me?" We replied, "He is ʿAli, son of Mūsa, son of Jaʿfar". To which he عليه السلام then said, "Bear witness that he is my *wakīl* during my lifetime and my successor after my death."'[122]

On several different occasions, he عليه السلام made similar announcements. However, during his imprisonment (in the years 179 and 180 AH) the Seventh Imām was clearly only able to communicate ʿAli's appointment to those who were permitted to visit him.

When the Seventh Imām departed this world in the year 183 AH, Hārūn al-Rashid's officials suggested his son ʿAli ibn Mūsa al-Riḍā be arrested and held under similar constraints as his father had been. He, however, declined to do so, on the grounds that for the moment, the condition of his father's confinement was bound to have been a sufficiently salutary forewarning.

In spite of being aware that his son, Muḥammad (known as *al-Amīn*), lacked capacity to hold the position, Hārūn appointed him his successor.[123] While al-Amīn did manage to hold on to power for the five years between 193 and 198 AH, insurrection and rivalry with his brother al-Ma'mūn so occupied his attention that he did not give a thought to Imām Riḍā عليه السلام.

History records that in 194 AH the population of Ḥumṣ rebelled against al-Amīn's rule, that his army commander wiped out its influential elite, imprisoned large numbers of its population and completely demolished many parts of the city. It is also recorded that al-Amīn dispatched troops to Khurasān in 195 AH to confront those of his brother al-Ma'mūn and that they were defeated; and that in 198 AH, al-Ma'mūn's forces conquered Baghdad, killed al-Amīn and massacred thousands of its citizens.[124]

The tumultuousness of al-Amīn's reign afforded Imām Riḍā عليه السلام freedom from harassment in which to concentrate on the elucidation of theological principles and clarification of extraordinary notions that had begun to spread throughout the Muslim community. He had to refute anthropomorphism, predetermination and inveigh against fabricated and falsified *āḥadīth,* for example, those intended to validate assertions that Allāh descends to earth each and every Thursday evening, about which he عليه السلام said, 'May Allāh curse those who alter what has been said. By Allāh, Allāh's Messenger did not say that; what he said was, "An Angel is commanded by Allāh to descend during the last third of each night, and throughout the night that precedes Friday, to ask, "Is there any one who offers supplication, so that I may grant their wish? Is there anyone who repents, so that they may be pardoned?"' Imām Riḍā عليه السلام then declared, 'This is the true *ḥadīth* that I narrate from my father, from his forefathers, from the Holy Prophet صلى الله عليه وآله وسلم.'[125]

The Imām عليه السلام clearly also needed to dispel uncertainty spread by *Wāqifiyah* denial of the death of the Seventh Imām and his appointment of a successor. When Imām Riḍā عليه السلام asked, and Muḥammad ibn ʿĀṣim confirmed, that he was in contact with the *Wāqifiyah,* the Imām عليه السلام told him, 'They are misled and mislead others. Do not associate with them.' When Yunus ibn Yaʿqoūb asked Imām Riḍā عليه السلام, 'Shall I give *zakāt* to the people who claim that your father is still alive?' he عليه السلام replied, 'Do not pay anything to those who try to divide and mislead the community.'[126]

During the reign of al-Ma'mūn

After his forces had conquered Baghdad and killed al-Amīn, in anticipation of his authority being acknowledged, al-Ma'mūn declared himself caliph. Despite support from a few judges and jurists, its population that had experienced the tyranny of previous Abbasid rule and survived the atrocities perpetrated by each and every one of them, saw this as the latest attempt to grab non-legitimate power. The *Ahl al-Bayt* descendants of Imām Ḥasan and Imām Mūsa al-Kāẓim عليهما السلام, known to oppose injustice and defend the oppressed, were consequently associated with uprisings, in Aleppo, Mūṣil, Baṣrah, Yemen, Ahwāz and several other places; al-Ma'mūn's battle-hardened forces quelled these.

Between 197 and 201 AH, governance in Baghdad became ever more tenuous as the effects of years of brutality, injustice and soaring cost of living exploded into insurrection, disorder and looting.[127] In an attempt to appease the *Ahl al-Bayt,* remove opposition and cement his authority over Baghdad's citizenry, al-Ma'mūn extended an invitation to Imām ʿAli ibn Mūsa al-Riḍā عليه السلام to grace him with his presence at court in Marw (a city in the north-eastern part of Khurasān).

There, he offered Imām Riḍā عليه السلام a position he thought he could not possibly refuse, and said, 'O son of the holy Prophet, I recognize your knowledge, righteousness and merit and believe you to be more worthy of the *Khilafah* than I am.' To this the Imām عليه السلام responded, 'My distinction is only to be a good servant to Allāh Almighty, and, in avoidance of what is prohibited, to seek the reward He promises his obedient servants.'

Al-Ma'mūn went on to say, 'I have decided to abdicate the *Khilafah,* and I now offer it to you and swear my allegiance to you.' To this, the Imām عليه السلام replied, 'If the *Khilafah* was granted to you by Allāh Almighty, you do not have authority to abdicate it or to grant it to another. And if the *Khilafah* has not been granted by Allāh, it is not possible for you to grant the thing that you do not have.'

Al-Ma'mūn responded, 'O son of the holy Prophet, you must accept it!' To which the Imām عليه السلام replied, 'I will never willingly do so.' Meetings continued for several days until it was finally proposed that Imām Riḍā عليه السلام become al-Ma'mūn's vicegerent, a position the Imām عليه السلام also rejected. At that, Al-Ma'mūn's faux sincerity vanished and he threatened, 'By Allāh, if you refuse to accept to be my vicegerent I will force it upon you, and if you object I will have you beheaded.' At that point there was no other option but to accept.[128]

Shaykh Mufid narrates that al-Ma'mūn quoted ʿUmar's notice to the council of six: 'Whoever refuses to accept the outcome of your selection will be beheaded.'[129]

When the Imām عليه السلام was asked why he accepted al-Ma'mūn's vicegerency, he answered, 'For the same reasons that induced my great-grandfather Imām ʿAli عليه السلام to become a member of the council of six.'[130] Both Imāms عليهما السلام willingly sacrificed their own prerogatives in order to ward off internecine strife and fragmentation of the Muslim nation.

Nonetheless, the Imām عليه السلام was thereby afforded many opportunities by which to attain his objectives. Thus, he stipulated Islāmic conduct be maintained by the established order: ministers of state, judges, minor officials and by the public in their commercial interactions, debates and other involvements. In furtherance of harmonious relations, al-Ma'mūn banned the black Abbasid flag and replaced it with the green flag associated with the *Ahl al-Bayt*, and ordered coinage bearing the name Imām Riḍā عليه السلام to be minted.

A debate in al-Ma'mūn's court

Imām Riḍā عليه السلام, with scholars from Iraq and Khurasān, was invited to attend al-Ma'mūn's court to debate the meaning of the term *Iṣṭifā'* (divine selection), that frequently appears in the Qur'ān.[131] When Al-Ma'mūn had heard the joint opinion of the invited scholars, that it is Allāh's reference to 'the entire Muslim nation', he asked the Imām عليه السلام for his. He عليه السلام responded, 'I do not agree with what has been said for I believe the Prophet's progeny is indicated by that term.' When Al-Ma'mūn asked how so? the Imām عليه السلام cited and elaborated on 12 *ayāt* in support of his view. In this manner he عليه السلام evidenced the Prophet's last will to be clarification of the statement, 'Hold fast to both the Qur'ān and his صلى الله عليه وآله progeny', as divine revelation and the 'divine selection' of his صلى الله عليه وآله progeny, whom Allāh Almighty purified so that the pristine teachings of Islām would continue to be promulgated.

Regrettably, only three years after having accepted his 'not to be refused' official position, Al-Ma'mūn had the Imām poisoned and buried alongside Hārūn al-Rashid's grave in Ṭūs (known today as Mashhad). In prediction of that occurrence, the Imām عليه السلام informed his closest confidants of it, and once, after a recitation by the famous poet Diʿbil al-Khuzāʿi, he عليه السلام asked the poet if he would like to add two lines on the Imām's عليه السلام being buried in Ṭūs. When the poet asked why he was to be buried there, the Imām عليه السلام outlined what was to occur.[132]

Throughout the centuries, the shrine of Imām Riḍā عليه السلام and the educational institutions that have developed around it, which together constitute one of the foremost centres of Islāmic education in the world, have drawn scholars and devotees of *Ahl al-Bayt* from every corner of the world.

Ninth Imām – Muḥammad Ibn ʿAli Al-Jawād عليه السلام

Muḥammad, son of Imām Riḍā عليه السلام and his Egyptian wife Sabikah, also known as Rayhāna, born on the 10th Rajab in the year 195 AH, succeeded his father in the line of the Imāmah. His father supervised his education until his demise in 203 AH, when Imām Muḥammad al-Jawād عليه السلام was eight years old.

Imām Riḍā عليه السلام had often declared his son to be his successor, first when he confided to his closest companions, 'This is the new-born who will have no peers in terms of being a blessing to me and our Shiʿahs,' and when he said, 'Allāh has granted me a successor to continue the legacy of the family of Dawūd.' (The Qur'ān records Dawūd to have been granted both worldly and spiritual authority, and he thus symbolizes wisdom, power and divine authority. Allāh also tells us that He granted his son Sulaymān authority over the winds and all His creatures including humankind.)[133]

The famous poet Diʿbil al-Khuzāʿi narrates that when he once recited before Imām Riḍā عليه السلام he was told, 'The Imām to follow me will be Muḥammad, then his son ʿAli followed by ʿAli's son Ḥasan who will be followed by the awaited Proof of Allāh.'[134] In response to doubts raised about the authority of such a young Imām being accepted, Imām Riḍā عليه السلام said, "ʿIsā occupied his position from birth and Yaḥyā was granted divine authorization while still in his childhood.'[135]

To entice support from the followers of *Ahl al-Bayt*, Al-Ma'mūn proposed that his daughter Um al-Faḍl marry Muḥammad al-Jawād. Abbasid objections to this were apparently based on his being of tender years as they suggested that the discipline of study should first be allowed to develop his character and maturity. Al-Ma'mūn responded, 'You have to understand that this is a household of inspired individuals imbued with divine knowledge. Muḥammad al-Jawād, like his ancestors before him, has profound knowledge of all religious disciplines and social etiquette. If you need this to be confirmed, examine him.' Satisfied by that answer, they offered the great Mufti of the time, Yahyā ibn Aktham, a not-insubstantial encouragement to expose the youth's ignorance. A date was set, spacious accommodation hired and at the tender age of nine years and three months, Imām Muḥammad al-Jawād عليه السلام was publicly pitted against the most notable Mufti in the land.

In response to the question, 'What ruling is to be applied to a pilgrim in the state of *iḥrām* who hunted and killed prey?' the young Imām عليه السلام sought clarification on the following points prior to giving his ruling, 'Did this take place within the boundaries of the *Ḥaram* or outside of it? Was it done knowingly or in ignorance? Was it a deliberate act or one committed in error? Is this pilgrim a free man or a slave? Is he a minor or an adult? Is this the first incident of this type that he has committed or a subsequent one? Was his prey a fowl or not? Was the prey mature or not? Did he regret his action or is he eager to repeat it? Did it occur at night or during the day? Was he in the state of *iḥrām* for *'Umrah* or for *Ḥajj*?'

The audience observed Mufti Yahyā ibn Aktham's surprise, visible embarrassment and seeming unawareness of the significance of those different circumstances. During this lull in proceedings, Al-Ma'mūn announced that he would like the wedding of his daughter and the Imām to be formalized that very day.

As the majority of the crowd began to disperse, Al-Ma'mūn requested that his future son-in-law detail the rulings for those different circumstances and also pose a question for the Mufti. Thus he asked, 'What ruling applies to a man that is considered to have looked inappropriately at a woman in the early hours of the day, who three hours later becomes lawful to him; that is then considered to have looked inappropriately at that woman at noon, who in the afternoon becomes lawful to him; who at sunset becomes unlawful for him to look inappropriately at but at dusk becomes lawful to him; and who at midnight becomes unlawful for him to look inappropriately at but who at dawn becomes lawful to him?'

The Mufti responded, 'By Allāh, I have no idea whatever of how such circumstances might arise with regard to *Shari'ah* rulings. Do clarify them!'

Imām Muḥammad al-Jawād عليه السلام then explained, 'It was unlawful for that man to lust after a slave woman owned by someone else. However, three hours later, after he had bought her from her owner, it became lawful for him to look at her appropriately or inappropriately. At noon, after he had set her free, this man's inappropriate looks again became unlawful. In the afternoon, on their marriage, she became his lawful wife. At sunset, when he declared *Ẓihār*, it again became unlawful for him to look at her inappropriately. [*Ẓihār* is a pre-Islāmic type of divorce declaration prohibited by Islām – for those who continued the practice, it led to the separation of husband and wife. However, if a return to normal matrimonial relationship was later sought, the husband was required to pay a penalty.][136] At dusk, after the man had paid the imposed penalty, they were again free to continue legal marital relations. At midnight, he granted her a revocable divorce but at dawn was reconciled with her.'[137]

At that, al-Ma'mūn turned to his relatives to ask, 'Are any of you able to explain the details of *Sharīʿah* law with such clarity? All had to admit their inability to do so. Al-Ma'mūn continued, 'Age is not material to perfection. Do you not know that when the Prophet ﷺ began to deliver his message the first person to hear it was the ten-year-old ʿAli, whose Islām was accepted by the prophet. Both Ḥasan and Ḥusayn عليهما السلام pledged allegiance to the Prophet when they were still under six years old.'

During al-Muʿtaṣim's reign

When al-Ma'mūn died in the year 218 AH his brother al-Muʿtaṣim succeeded him. In contrast to al-Ma'mūn, who had acknowledged Imām Muḥammad al-Jawād's status, al-Muʿtaṣim felt threatened by the Imām's pre-eminent knowledge and wisdom. Thus, in the year 220 AH, in response to his being summoned, Imām Muḥammad al-Jawād عليه السلام left Madinah to settle in Baghdad towards the end of the month of Muḥarram; there his doings could be more easily monitored. When the caliph called for a debate over the application of *Ḥadd* punishment for theft, the Mufti of the time Ibn Abi Du'ād, declared that thieves' hands must be amputated at the wrist. When asked the basis of that ruling the Mufti referred to the *āyah* that deals with *tayamum* (dry ablution), which requires the palms of both hands to be placed upon the earth. Other jurists present claimed amputation should occur at the elbow, based upon the *āyah* that deals with *wuḍu'* (ablution). However, Imām Muḥammad al-Jawād عليه السلام objected to both assertions saying that only four fingers should be amputated, so that during the prostration of prayers the seven specified parts of the body, that include the two palms, be available to support the body.[138] Everyone was astonished by this not having been considered, but the Mufti, enraged at the rejection of his opinion, said, 'I wish I had died 20 years before being obliged to suffer today's embarrassment.'

Three days later the Mufti met al-Muʿtaṣim to warn of consequences that would likely follow that incident. He said, 'It is my duty to provide your eminence with the best of advice. You gathered all the prominent jurists together to discuss a *Sharīʿah* ruling but rejected their juridical opinions in favour of that of a person from *Ahl al-Bayt*, who is regarded by many to have greater entitlement to hold the position of supreme authority than you yourself. This will surely encourage his followers to rebellion.'

Al-Muʿtaṣim thanked him for drawing his attention to that risk and determined to silence the Imām. Historians report that he succeeded in this when his niece Um al-Faḍl laced the Imām's food with fatal poison. Thus, at 25 years of age he is the youngest Imām to have passed away.

Maxims of Imām Jawād

A font of wisdom and knowledge like the Imāms before him, Imām Muḥammad al-Jawād عليه السلام evinced inexhaustible profundity in his expositions on faith, ethics and social behaviour.

1. Trust in Allāh is the price of the most valuable commodity and the ladder by which to attain the most elevated status.

2. Do not feign public devotion to Allāh while being indifferent to Him in private.

3. Health, wealth, knowledge and divine assistance are four fundamentals necessary for the achievement of one's objectives.

4. Action taken in ignorance is likely to be detrimental rather than beneficial.

5. Communication with Allāh Almighty via one's heart is of greater efficacy than that attempted via exertions of the body.

6. Do not feel enmity towards anyone before you examine their relationship with their Lord. If you think the intent of their actions is to

please Allāh, be assured that they will not be without His support. However, if you think their actions not to be acceptable to Allāh, then leave Him to deal with them.

7. A bounty that is not appreciated is the equivalent of a sin that is not forgiven.

8. The dignity of a believer lies in not looking to others for anything.

9. Those who pursue gratification of desire aid their enemy [*Iblis*] in their destruction.

10. A pure heart, fairness and kindly behaviour are all fundamental to the establishment of harmony and love.

Tenth Imām – ʿAli ibn Muḥammad Al-Hādi ﷺ

Born in a small village called Ṣeria three miles from Madinah on the 5th Rajab in the year 212 AH, he was tutored by his father Imām Muḥammad al-Jawād ﷺ until he was eight years old. His life was contemporaneous with the six Abbasid caliphs: Al-Muʿtaṣim, Al-Wāthiq, Al-Mutawakkil, Al-Muntaṣir, Al-Mustaʿīn and Al-Muʿtazz.

On several occasions, Imām Muḥammad al-Jawād ﷺ told companions that his son ʿAli would succeed him as Imām.

1. When he ﷺ was first summoned to Baghdad, Ismāʿil ibn Mahrān reported that he asked the Imām, 'If something should happen to you, who is to succeed you?' To this he responded, 'There is no need to think about succession right now.' But when Al-Muʿtaṣim summoned him there a second time and he repeated the question, the Imām answered, 'My son ʿAli is to succeed me.'

2. Umayyah ibn ʿAli al-Qaysi reports that when he asked Imām Muḥammad al-Jawād ﷺ who was to succeed him he had replied, 'My son ʿAli.'

3. Muḥammad ibn Ismāʿil ibn Baziʿ reported from Umayyah ibn ʿAli, that when he had asked the Ninth Imām the same question he was

told, 'When the three names: Muḥammad, then ʿAli, then Ḥasan appear in succession, they will be followed by a fourth who will be *Al-Mahdi*.'[139]

During the reign of Al-Mutawakkil

Contrary to al-Ma'mūn and al-Muʿtaṣim, who favoured Muʿtazilite doctrine based upon rational argument over the interpretation of traditions, al-Mutawakkil prohibited administrative application of Muʿtazilite rationality and demanded that his officialdom adhere to Ashʿarite doctrine. He also affirmed enmity to Imām ʿAli عليه السلام and his followers. In the year 236 AH he ordered the destruction of Imām Ḥusayn's shrine in Karbala and all houses that surrounded it. Deeming that to be insufficient, he then also ordered all who subsequently visited the area to have both hands cut off. Thus, believers were submitted to amputation of their hands.[140]

When al-Mutawakkil asked Yaʿqūb ibn al-Sikkīt, the teacher of his two sons al-Muʿtazz and al-Mu'ayyad, if they were dearer to him than Ḥasan and Ḥusayn he replied, 'Imām ʿAli's servant Qanber had greater nobility than both of your sons.' On hearing it, al-Mutawakkil ordered Yaʿqūb's tongue be ripped out prior to having his head cut off.[141]

In the year 234 AH, al-Mutawakkil sent Yahya ibn Harthama to Madinah to summon Imām ʿAli al-Hādi to Sāmarrā, his new Abbasid capital. Yahya narrates that when the people of Madinah learned of the summons they rioted to express their disapproval. However, he said, 'I did manage to assure them that I had no instructions to harm him. When I searched his accommodation I found nothing other than copies of the Qur'ān and manuscripts on Jurisprudence, and I must confess to being greatly impressed by the scholarly distinction and noble stature of this personage.'[142] What we may deduce from the above is that:

1. Imām ʿAli al-Hādi's personality, which embodied the qualities of his forefathers', drew forth the expressions of love and dedication of the people of Madinah.

2. The Abbasid fear of the Imām gaining ever more widespread support motivated al-Mutawakkil to have him عليه السلام removed from Madinah, the seat of Islāmic study, to a remote location where he عليه السلام could more easily be monitored and controlled.

3. The military officer Yahya ibn Harthama was not party to al-Mutawakkil's plan, but later understood that the alleged intent of the Imām to overthrow the caliph had been fabricated.

4. As the new Abbasid capital of Sāmarrā was the military base for external Turkish troops, unfamiliar with and thus indifferent to the internecine nature of Islāmic cultural history, there were no grounds for them to question the harsh treatment of the Imām.

When the Imām عليه السلام arrived in Sāmarrā, al-Mutawakkil ordered him to be quartered at the *Khān al-Ṣaʿālīk,* insalubrious accommodation in a deprived area that housed the destitute, disreputable and depraved elements of society.[143] He later repented that harshness and had him moved to better accommodation within the garrison. On the many occasions that the caliph and his scholarly advisors found the determination of *Shariʿah* rulings difficult, they had little option but to consult the Imām.

Historians record that al-Mutawakkil indulged himself in fine wines. While in an inebriated state, he once summoned the Imām to his palace and offered some to him. The Imām declined, saying, 'By Allāh, neither my flesh or blood has ever been in contact with that substance.' When al-Mutawakkil then said that his pleasure would be greatly enhanced if the Imām عليه السلام recited some poetry for him, the latter's response was, 'I do not remember much poetry.' But when al-Mutawakkil insisted, the Imām recited the following lines to rouse him from his stupor.

> Even though on summits protected by troops – all was in vain,
>
> For they were humbled on being lowered six feet under their domain.
> After their burial a caller called, "Where is their throne, their jewels and crown?

> What happened to the face screened from pests, that awed all who gazed upon their renown?"
> The grave responded, 'Worms have dined upon the faces that they called their own'.[144]

While the company present feared al-Mutawakkil's reaction, to their great amazement and surprise they observed tears in al-Mutawakkil's eyes as he ordered the wine removed and apologized to the Imām.

In Sāmarrā, Imām ʿAli al-Hādi عليه السلام had to undergo frequent bouts of imprisonment and searches while under house arrest; these only ended when the plot to assassinate him was hatched.

Al-Mutawakkil's secretary Faḍl ibn Aḥmad narrates that when he once went with al-Muʿtazz to meet the latter's father, they found his vizier al-Fatḥ ibn Khāqān struggling to calm him down. They heard him say that reports concerning this man (i.e. Imām ʿAli al-Hādi) might not be true and needed to be verified. However, beside himself with rage, al-Mutawakkil would hear nothing of the sort and insisted the Imām be eliminated. He ordered his vizier to position assassins equipped with swords ready to cut the Imām to shreds when he next entered court. However, the secretary Faḍl ibn Aḥmad further narrates that the moment the apparently talking Imām entered, the positioned and armed assassins fell in prostrated submission at his feet. When asked why, they said it was because they saw themselves confronted by the raised swords of a hundred bodyguards set to defend him. It is reported that this was attributed to the Imām's 'Supplication of the Suppressed against their Oppressors', as three days later Al-Muntaṣir's Turkish guard assassinated his inebriated father, al-Mutawakkil.[145]

The appointment of deputies

To prepare followers of *Ahl al-Bayt* for the coming occultation, during which they would have no direct access to the Imām, Imām ʿAli al-Hādi عليه السلام appointed reliable and trustworthy delegates to communicate and exercise the authority of the Imām when that would happen. While deputies had been appointed to represent previous Imāms when they were to be temporarily unavailable, the time of the Tenth Imām called for wider representation. Thus their duties extended not only to the collection of religious dues such as *Khums* and *Zakāt* but also to *Shariʿah* rulings and pronouncements on all issues of public interest.

These deputies were to be supervised by the three more senior incumbents, Abu ʿAli ibn Rāshid, charged with overseeing all matters related to Iraq, ʿAli ibn Mahzeyār, charged to head the deputies in Ahwāz, and Ibrahīm ibn Muḥammad, for Hamadān and its surroundings.[146]

The Imām's students

Imām ʿAli al-Hādi's focus on the education of his community gave rise to a plethora of erudite scholars able competently to disseminate the bona fide teachings of the error-free Imāms. The most notable of these were:

1. Ibrāhīm ibn ʿAbdah al-Naisābūrī
2. Ibrāhīm ibn Muḥammad al-Hamadāni
3. Ibrāhīm ibn Mahzeyār
4. Aḥmad ibn Isḥāq al-Qummi
5. Aḥmad ibn Muḥammad ibn ʿIsā al-Ashʿari
6. Ayūb ibn Nūḥ ibn Darrāj
7. Al-Ḥasan ibn Rāshid
8. Al-Ḥasan ibn ʿAli (the great-grandfather of Sayyid al-Raḍī)
9. Al-Ḥasan ibn ʿAli al-Washshā
10. Dāwūd ibn al-Qasim al-Jaʿfari
11. ʿAbdul ʿAẓim al-Ḥasani
12. Al-Rayyān ibn al-Ṣalt
13. ʿUthmān ibn Saʿid al-ʿAmri (who became the first deputy of the Twelfth Imām during the minor occultation)
14. Al-Faḍl ibn Shādhān al-Naisābūrī (author of *Al-Īḍāḥ fi al-Imāmah*)

His demise

Although the 19-year-old al-Muʿtazz became *de facto* caliph after al-Mustaʿīn, he reigned only as the puppet of Turkish troops who found it expedient to maintain him as their nominal leader. His mistreatment of the Tenth Imām mimicked that of his predecessors until the Imām عليه السلام was dispatched by poison on the 3rd Rajab 254 AH. A multitude of loyal Shiʿahs arrived in Sāmarrā to attend their Imām's funeral and interment in his own house, where his shrine, that remains to this day, was erected.

Eleventh Imām – Al-Ḥasan al-ʿAskari عليه السلام

On 8th Rabiʿ al-Thāni in the year 232 AH the Tenth Imām ʿAli al-Hādi عليه السلام and his household in Madinah, overjoyed by the birth of his first son, named him Ḥasan in honour of Imām ʿAli's first son. His integrity, sagacity and natural ability were inherited from his forefathers, whom Allāh Almighty cleansed of impurity, to ensure that error-free teaching of His revealed faith would continue to guide the Muslim nation.[147]

Evidence that the Imāms, including Al-Ḥasan al-ʿAskari عليهم السلام, had inherited the legacy of their ancestor Imām ʿAli عليه السلام, 'Gate to the City of Knowledge', is that in all periods, scholars not able to clarify complex issues in the fields of theology, jurisprudence, exegesis and the other branches of Islāmic teaching, referred it to the error-free Imāms عليهم السلام for clarification.

> [This lamp is lit] in houses that Allāh Almighty has exalted, and His name is remembered therein. He is glorified therein in the morning and in the evening, by men whom neither trade nor profit divert from their remembrance of Allāh, the constancy of their prayer or giving in charity to the poor. They fear the day when hearts and eyes shall shudder in terror.[148]

It was in such a house that Imām Al-Ḥasan al-ʿAskari عليه السلام was born and raised. His father, the Tenth Imām, praised him for his trustworthiness and elegibility to succeed him in the line of divine leadership.[149] He migrated with his father from Madinah to Sāmarrā and was witness to the Abbasid caliphs' mistreatment of his father.

In their biographical notes, Muḥammad ibn Ṭalḥah al-Shāfiʿi,[150] ibn al-Jawzi,[151] Shiblinji,[152] and ibn al-Ṣabbāgh[153] laud the Eleventh Imām as being one of the most honourable and knowledgeable men of his time.

Imām ʿAskari's challenge to Al-Kindi

An Iraqi philosopher and contemporary of the Eleventh Imām, Abu Yūsuf ibn Isḥāq of the Kinda tribe in Kufah, was given the honorific title, 'Philosopher of the Arabs'. Despite being closely associated with the Muʿtazilites, he was not one of them. When in Baghdad, triggered by the translation of Greek texts into Arabic, he became involved in a scientific movement. It is recorded that to stir up the Muslim community, this philosopher gathered a few *ayāt* from the holy Qur'ān that appeared to him to be controversial and derided them in his lectures.

In recognition of the danger of such activity, Imām Al-Ḥasan al-ʿAskari asked one of al-Kindi's students, 'Are you going to challenge his attempt to destroy belief in the Qur'ān?' He responded that, being al-Kindi's student, he dare not. The Imām then asked if he would be prepared to convey to his teacher what the Imām said? On his agreement, the Imām told him, 'Visit him to emphasize your interest in his subject and your desire to be of assistance to him in any way you can. When your relationship with him has been established, ask him to clarify the question, "Is it possible that the One who brought the Qur'ān to you might have meant something other than what you have concluded?" As an intellectual he will have to agree to that being a possibility. Then, ask him if his controversial statements regarding the Qur'ān might possibly also be wrong.' When, having followed all the Imām's directions, the student sought al-Kindi's clarification of the above question he was asked to repeat it. After some reflection, the philosopher then agreed that this was both a lexical and a logical possibility. Al-Kindi then asked his student what had induced him to ask that question, and was told that it had merely popped into his mind. Not convinced, al-Kindi insisted on his right to be informed of its background. When he finally discovered it was Imām Al-Ḥasan al-ʿAskari عليه السلام who had raised it, he asserted that such inspiration could not have emanated from a source other than that distinguished family, and he duly destroyed his controversial writings on the Qur'ān.[154]

Juridical authority

During their lifetimes, ultimate authority rested with the error-free Imāms عليهم السلام, either directly or via an appointed deputy. As the time for occultation drew near it became important to make the community aware that in the future authorized deputies would represent the 'Imām of the Time' as their source of guidance in all matters of religion.

Indeed, Imām Ṣādiq عليه السلام had previously indicated this when he said, 'Search for scholars well acquainted with our *āḥadīth* who specialize in our jurisprudence, so that you may safely accept their verdicts in all disputes. I have appointed such people to be "referees". Those who submit to their judgements have submitted to us and those who have rejected their verdicts have rejected us.'[155]

While the error-free Imāms عليهم السلام had occasionally appointed a deputy to deal, in their absence, with specific matters, the Tenth Imām عليه السلام had, as already mentioned, outlined the essential administrative structure to oversee the deputyship of pious and reliable jurists who would deal with the public interests of the community. As he had expressed it, 'If there had been no learned advocates of religious teaching to protect the community from deception, the entire essence of faith would have disappeared. In the eyes of Allāh, the best of people, without doubt, are those who pilot the community to the safe waters of His guidance.'[156]

The marriage of the Eleventh Imām عليه السلام

Shaykh Ṣadūq narrates, on the authority of Bishr ibn Sulaymān, that the Tenth Imām had sent him to Baghdad to undertake a specific task. From the bank of the river Tigris he was to await the arrival of a shipment of captives from a recent battle with the Eastern Roman Empire and then attend the sale of its human cargo. The Imām عليه السلام said he would easily identify the young woman he was interested in by the resentment she would express at being exposed before the public. He was to buy her with the purse of gold coins that he had been provided with and immediately grant her her freedom. When this was done, he was to courteously invite her to accompany him to Sāmarrā. En-route he observed her to have been of noble birth. She was captured in the fort of a defeated Roman battalion. Her marriage to Imām Al-Ḥasan al-ʿAskari عليه السلام took place after Ḥakima Khātūn, the Tenth Imām's sister, had familiarized her with Islāmic practices and etiquette and she had taken the Muslim name Narjis.[157]

The Twelfth Imām was born from this blessed marriage on the 15th Shaʿbān in the year 255 AH.

The deputies of the Eleventh Imām

During the six years of Al-Ḥasan al-ʿAskari's divine leadership, he appointed several deputies to take charge of the followers of *Ahl al-Bayt* عليهم السلام. Two of these were to serve the community during the minor occultation of the Twelfth Imām عليه السلام.

1. Ibrāhīm ibn ʿAbdah Naisabūri
2. Ayyūb ibn Nūh al-Nakhaʿī
3. Ayyūb ibn al-Nāb
4. Aḥmad ibn Isḥāq al-Qummi
5. Jaʿfar ibn-Suhail al-Ṣayqal
6. ʿUthmān ibn Saʿīd al-ʿAmrī
7. Al-Qasim ibn ʿalā' al-Hamadani
8. Muḥammad ibn Ṣaliḥ al-Hamadani
9. Muḥammad ibn ʿUthmān ibn Saʿīd al-ʿAmrī
10. ʿUrwah ibn Yaḥyā al-Bagdadi

The Imām's demise

The Eleventh Imām's trusted confidential assistant Abul Adyān narrates that while the Imām عليه السلام was ill prior to his demise, he ordered him to deliver letters to the town of Al-Madā'in, previously known as Tisfūn, and told him, 'In fifteen days' time when you return to Sāmarrā you will find my household in mourning.' When Abul Adyān asked the Imām عليه السلام to whom he should thereafter transfer his loyalty, he was told that the three following events would make that clear. 'It will be the one who leads my *Janāzah* prayer, the one who will request the replies to my letters and the one who is able to tell you the precise amount of religious dues (*Khums*), in each of the various bags that are to be delivered.'

Abul Adyān further narrates that when he returned home precisely fifteen days later, he did find the Imām's household to be in mourning and his body being readied for interment. He saw many people offer condolences to the Imām's brother Jaʿfar, with congratulations being given by those who imagined he would succeed. However, Abul Adyān reports that he had felt uneasy because Jaʿfar was not acknowledged by all to be a person of any great merit. 'When the deceased was brought to the service and Jaʿfar stood up to lead the prayer, a five-year-old boy firmly gripped his uncle's cloak and said, "I have a greater entitlement to lead my father's *Janāzah* prayer than you have." Jaʿfar had no option but to give way to him. When, after the prayer and burial, the boy asked me for the replies to his father's letters I said to myself, "Praise Allāh, I have now witnessed two of the confirmatory events".'

While those who asked Jaʿfar who the boy was were being told that he did not know, a group from Qumm with bags full of *Khums* dues arrived and asked to see the Imām. On learning that he had already been buried, they asked to whom they should address their condolences. Referred to Jaʿfar, they told him that they had brought *Khums* and letters and, as was their custom, asked him to identify who the communications were from and to verify the precise amount in each of their collection bags. At this Jaʿfar snorted his incredulity and said, 'These people now demand I see the unseen (*ghayb*)'.

At the behest of the boy who had led the *Janāzah* prayer, the late Imām's trusted assistant was able to tell them the names of those who had replied to his father's correspondence and the precise amounts contained in each of the various bags. Abul Adyān was gladdened to have now also witnessed the third foretold event that would identify the Eleventh Imām's lawful successor.[158]

As we will later see, the five-year-old boy was none other than the Twelfth Imām, Muḥammad son of Imām Al-Ḥasan al-ʿAskari عليه السلام, known as *Al-Mahdi* – may Allāh hasten his reappearance.

Twelfth Imām – Al-Mahdi عليه السلام

His birth/witnesses who reported seeing him

Many authentic *āḥadīth* from the holy Prophet ﷺ state that if only one day remains for life on this earth, Allāh Almighty will maintain it for one of his progeny to materialize and replace the injustice, tyranny and corruption that permeates the earth with justice and truth. The Prophet ﷺ referred to that person as *Al-Mahdi* – the one who is guided to guide.[159]

The Prophet ﷺ further clarified Al-Mahdi to be his descendant via his grandson Ḥusayn عليه السلام.[160] Nonetheless, throughout the ensuing centuries there have been many who have claimed to be Al-Mahdi. The Prophet ﷺ clarified to his companions that as Al-Mahdi is to be screened by occultation not all believers will be convinced of his existence. Indeed, when the companions were told about the length of the occultation, Jābir ibn Abdullah Anṣari asked, 'How then will people benefit from a hidden Imām?' His response was, 'In the same manner that people draw benefit from the sun when it is obscured by cloud.'[161]

The Prophet ﷺ said that another sign of al-Mahdi is that his reappearance will coincide with that of the prophet ʿIsā عليه السلام.[162]

In order to remove all ambiguity, the Eleventh Imām stated on several occasions that his son Muḥammad is the twelfth appointed Imām.

1. Qundūzi Ḥanafi reports that Abu Ghānim, the Eleventh Imām's servant, corroborated that when Imām Ḥasan al-ʿAskari عليه السلام introduced his son Muḥammad to his close companions three days after his birth, he told them, 'This is the Imām who is to succeed me. He is the one who will arise (*Qā'im*), the one future generations will long for when the earth is oppressed by tyranny and injustice.'[163]

2. ʿUmar al-Ahwāzi said that the Eleventh Imām introduced him to his son saying, 'This is the Imām who is to succeed me.'[164]

3. Muḥyidin Ibn ʿArabī (d. 638 AH) confirmed al-Mahdi as being the son of Imām Ḥasan al-ʿAskari.[165]

4. Ibn al-Ṣabbāgh al-Māliki (d. 855 AH) traces the family tree of al-Mahdi from his father back to Imām ʿAli عليهم السلام.[166]

5. Ibn Ṭalḥah al-Shāfiʿi (d. 652 AH) traces the birth and family tree of the Twelfth Imām and adds six lines of poetry in his praise.[167]

6. Al-Khazzāz reports that Abu Hashim al-Jaʿfari said, 'I heard Imām ʿAli al-Hādī عليه السلام say, "My son Ḥasan will be my successor but his successor will be faced with difficulty." When I asked what that difficulty would be, he said it would result from his not being accessible to everyone.'

7. Al-Khazzāz reports that Mūsā ibn Jaʿfar al-Bagdadi heard Imām Ḥasan al-ʿAskari عليه السلام say, 'Confusion will arise about my successor. Those who recognize all the Imāms after the holy Messenger but do not recognize him are like those who recognize all the prophets but do not recognize Muḥammad صلى الله عليه وآله. Some will be confused by his being screened by occultation.'

8. Al-Khazzāz reports that Muḥammad ibn ʿUthmān al-ʿAmrī said, 'While I was present, my father asked the Eleventh Imām about the *ḥadīth* transmitted from his forefathers عليهم السلام that states, "Whoever dies without having recognized the Imām of his time will be thought of in the same light as those who died in the *Jāhiliyah*." He said,

"One can be as certain about that as one is about daylight". When he was then asked who was to be the Imām after him, he responded, "My son Muḥammad will succeed me as Imām and proof of Allāh. Whoever dies without having recognized him will be thought of in the same light as those who died in the *Jāhiliyah*."[168]

His longevity

Ithnā 'Asheri Shi'ah belief is that the Twelfth Imām of the Prophet's progeny, namely al-Mahdi, who was born on 15th Sha'bān in the year 255 AH, remains alive and will continue to, until his final appearance – a longevity questioned by many.

To put this into perspective, we need to bear in mind that all Muslims believe that 'Isā عليه السلام has remained alive for a far longer period. According to Qur'ān 4:157–158, Allāh elevated him to a celestial sphere in which his life continues. According to Ṭabarī, both *al-Khiḍr* (the one from whom Mūsā عليه السلام sought wisdom and knowledge) and *Iliās* are still alive, despite both having predated 'Isā عليه السلام. Indeed Nūh عليه السلام is reported in Qur'ān 29:14 to have lived 950 years before the flood. As his life did not end then, it must have continued for some time thereafter.

After quoting the longevity of 'Isā, al-Khiḍr and Iliās, Al-Kanji al-Shāfi'i (d. 658 AH) said, 'Thus the longevity of al-Mahdi should not surprise Muslims.' He then quotes Qur'ān 61:9 and the commentary on it, in which the famous companion Sa'id ibn Jubair confirms that it refers to al-Mahdi being a descendant of the Prophet's daughter Fatimāh عليها السلام. He concludes that according to many authentic *āḥadīth,* three persons are to experience longevity towards the end of time: al-Mahdi, 'Isā عليه السلام, who will pray behind him, and the *Dajjāl* (Antichrist).[169]

How do people benefit from the Hidden Imām?

In an eloquent sermon Imām 'Ali عليه السلام emphasized the necessity of divine guidance being delegated to *Al-Ḥujjah* (the proof of Allāh), if he is apparent or screened by occultation.[170] This sermon refers to occultation having been previously predicted, as was earlier cited when Jābir ibn Abdullah Anṣari asked the Prophet صلى الله عليه وآله, 'How will people benefit from a hidden Imām?' His response was, 'In the same manner that people draw benefit from the sun when it is obscured by cloud.'[171]

Similarly, Ḥamawayni reports, on the authority of Sulaymān ibn Mahrān al-Aʿmash, that when Imām Ṣādiq عليه السلام explained the necessity of *Al-Ḥujjah,* saying that it does not matter if he is apparent or hidden, he asked the Imām the same question and the Imām responded, 'In the same manner that people draw benefit from the sun when it is obscured by cloud.'[172]

Allamah Majlisi comments on the similarity of these responses and gives eight different elaborations on it.[173]

Throughout the centuries Shiʿah scholars have laid great emphasis on the central aspect of the concept of divinely guided leadership, *Al-Ḥ*ujjah, made clear by the following three essential Islāmic precepts – what occured at al-Ghadīr, *Ḥadīth al-Thaqalain*, and al-Mahdi being the twelfth successor of the Prophet ﷺ. (See pages 239, 243 and 248 for details of the above.)

In the same manner as the earth's unfailing gravitational field is necessary for us to remain anchored to its surface, *Al-Ḥujjah* is the necessary constant that enables humankind to remain anchored to spiritual guidance.[174]

As history shows, at al-Ghadīr the Prophet ﷺ clearly delegated his unquestioned authority over the Muslim nation to the first Imām/*Ḥujjah*; in *Ḥadīth al-Thaqalain* he confirmed that Allāh's holy book and his progeny will remain absolutely inseparable until they arrive at 'The Pool' on the 'Day of Judgement'; and the *ḥadīth* in which he attests to his successors being limited to twelve. It is the logical conclusion from the above that it is not possible for anyone other than al-Mahdi to be *Al-Ḥujjah* of the time.

Deputies invested with authority

After Imām Ḥasan al-ʿAskari عليه السلام died in the year 260 AH and the Abbasid caliph al-Muʿtamid learned that a five-year-old had claimed entitlement to lead his father's *Janāzah* prayer, awareness dawned on him of the threat that a child prodigy with that quality and ability might pose to his position. If he was obeyed at such a tender age, as he grew older and his reputation spread he would no doubt attract an ever-increasing following that al-Muʿtamid felt should rightly be his. Determined to capture the last person who could continue the line of the Imāmah he immediately ordered troops to enter the house of the Eleventh Imām and seize him. Despite searching every nook and cranny from basement to rooftop, no boy was to be seen there. By Allāh's will the last *Ḥujjah* had been cut off from view. Somewhat oddly, those who deny the existence of the Twelfth Imām habitually claim that Shiʿah Muslims believe the Imām's occultation occurred in the basement of this house (*Sardāb*).

There are two separate periods of Al-Mahdi's occultation: the minor, that began in 260 AH and ended in 329 AH and the major, that commenced in 329 AH and continues today.

His minor occultation corresponds with the consecutive lifespan of the four deputies who were appointed to mediate between him and the public:

1. *ʿUthmān ibn Saʿīd al-ʿAmrī:* His dependability was so highly valued while he worked under the authority of the Tenth Imām that the latter عليه السلام characterized him as 'Trustworthy' and 'Reliable' and counselled followers of *Ahl al-Bayt* to accept his reports as accurate representations of the Imām's own views.[175] After the Tenth Imām died in the year 254 AH ʿUthmān ibn Saʿīd, who earned his living as a ghee merchant, was appointed deputy to the Eleventh Imām عليه السلام and presided over his communiqués. The Imām repeatedly praised his effectiveness and trustworthiness and, in confirmation of his entrusted status, appointed him to deal with the needs and religious dues of delegates from Yemen who had come to see the Imām.[176]

   As the result of his long-standing confidential relationship with the Imām, he was called upon to participate in his funeral preparations. When ʿUthmān ibn Saʿīd died, the Twelfth Imām expressed his condolence to his son (Muḥammad) with the statement, 'Your father strove in the path of the Imāms to please Allāh Almighty – may He shower him with His mercy.'

He was the first deputy of Al-Mahdi and served in that capacity for five years.

2. *Muḥammad ibn ʿUthmān ibn Saʿīd al-ʿAmrī:* The second deputy, appointed by the Twelfth Imām after the death of his father, served for 40 years until his death in the year 305 AH. Most of the correspondence between the public and the Imām (later referred to as *Tawqīʿāt*) was filtered through him. He exercised authority in conjunction with many highly respected members of the Shiʿah community such as Abu ʿAli ibn Humām, Abu ʿAbdillāh al-Katib and Ḥusayn ibn Rūḥ.

3. *Ḥusayn ibn Rūḥ al-Nawbakhtī:* During the lifetime of the second deputy, a group of Shiʿahs who had brought 400 dinars to him were instructed to hand it into the care of Ḥusayn ibn Rūḥ. As he had not been appointed the Imām's deputy they appeared slow to act until Muḥammad ibn ʿUthmān confirmed that that request had come directly from Imām Al-Mahdi عليه السلام. While on his deathbed, the second deputy announced to those present that the person to continue the deputyship was to be Ḥusayn ibn Rūḥ.

   When ʿAli ibn Bābawayh (Shaykh Ṣadūq's father) met Ḥusayn ibn Rūḥ in Iraq, he asked him several questions before he handed him a letter addressed to the Twelfth Imām in which he solicited his prayer for him to be granted a son. Ḥusayn ibn Rūḥ later conveyed the Imām's response, 'We have prayed to Allāh on your behalf and you will indeed be granted two goodly sons.' History records two sons being born: Muḥammad (who later became known as Shaykh Ṣadūq) and Ḥusayn. It is reported from the younger of the two that Muḥammad was so proud of the circumstances that lay behind his birth that he would often tell others, 'I was born as the result of Al-Mahdi's prayers.'[177]

   Ḥusayn ibn Rūḥ served as deputy for 21 years until his death in the year 326 AH.

4. *ʿAli ibn Muḥammad al-Ṣaymurī:* He served as the Imām's deputy after Ḥusayn ibn Rūḥ and continued in that position for approximately three years until he died in the year 329 AH. During his relatively brief deputyship the *Tawqīʿāt* (the communicatory record between Al-Mahdi and the public) is less extensive than that produced during deputyships of longer span. The last communication he received from the Twelfth Imām was, 'O ʿAli ibn Muḥammad al-Ṣaymurī, may Allāh reward your fellow Shiʿahs on the occasion of your demise. You will die in six days' time, so do not appoint anyone to your position because the major occultation is soon to begin. There will be many false claims regarding meetings with me but be assured that none will be true until the appearance of *Sufyānī* and *Ṣayḥah* – the outcry related to a portentous occurrence.

Tawqīʿāt

While the contemporary usage of the word *Tawqīʿ* refers to a name, initial or distinctive mark signed at the end of a letter or document, the theological application of the word *Tawqīʿāt* refers to the documentation of communications between the Twelfth Imām and the public via his deputies. This corroborates that each deputy in turn was able to authenticate communications from the Imām – from the distinctive signature and hand in which they were written, prior to acceptance of their content. *Tawqīʿ* were either in response to requests or to convey advice and instruction directly from the Imām. An example of the latter is the instruction to his fourth deputy not to appoint a further deputy.

There are reports of *Tawqīʿ* in response to questions being received within two or three days, as well as reports of petitioners being given verbal responses. There is, too, a report of an application being ignored, that on investigation turned out to have been from a *Qirmiṭi* (a member of a group of Ismāʿilis who attacked pilgrims in Makkah, tore off the Kaʿbah covering, removed the black stone from its lodging and took it to the Yemen).

There are many well-known *Tawqīʿāt* from the Twelfth Imām to Shaykh al-Mufīd, who was born in the year 336 AH. His title, *al-Mufīd* (the one who affords immense benefit) was applied to him by his peers. Ibn Ḥajar ʿAsqalāni wrote that 80,000 people embraced Shiʿah belief because of him. During his 30 years as the most prominent leader of the Shiʿah community, he received 30 *Tawqīʿāt* from Imām Mahdi عليه السلام, always prefaced by the words, 'Dear devoted brother pure in faith'.

In one such *Tawqīʿāt*, Imām Mahdi writes, 'In the name of Allāh, the Beneficent, the Merciful, Dear devoted brother pure in faith, peace be with you . . . We inform you of our being directed to communicate our instruction to you to fulfil all our obligations, may Allāh support and approve your actions . . . We are well aware of your situation as nothing about you is hidden from us . . . Without our supervision and prayers for your protection the enemy would destroy you but Allāh Almighty will not permit His light to be extinguished despite that being the desire of others.'[178]

His role in the spread of justice and truth

As stated earlier, the Prophet صلى الله عليه وآله وسلم disclosed that al-Mahdi is to reappear at the same time as the prophet ʿIsā عليه السلام descends. This points towards the belief in a promised restorer of faith being shared by all divine religions, including Christianity. In other words, the spread of justice and truth at the end of time will be brought about by the person known in Islām as Al-Mahdi and in Christian and Jewish understandings as the Messiah.

Bukhari narrates from the holy Prophet صلى الله عليه وآله وسلم that he asked his companions, 'How would you feel if you knew that the son of Maryam has descended, while the one who will lead is from amongst you?'[179]

Muttaqi Hindi refers to Abu Saʿīd's report that the Prophet صلى الله عليه وآله وسلم said, 'The one who ʿIsā will pray behind is one of my progeny'.[180]

Abu Nuʿaim reports on the authority of Jābir that the Prophet صلى الله عليه وآله وسلم said, 'When ʿIsā son of Maryam descends, Al-Mahdi will invite him to lead the prayer, but he will desist and assert Al-Mahdi's right to lead it.'[181]

When Kanji Shafiʿi (d. 658 AH) reflected on how it could be possible for an Imām to lead a prophet in prayer, he presented a detailed consideration that supported it with the aforementioned authentic *ḥadīth*.[182]

To conclude, the reappearance of Al-Mahdi will occur at the same time as the prophet ʿIsā ﷷ descends, after which the world will witness their cooperation. As stated in Qur'ān 4:159, thereafter all the followers of divine scriptures will surrender to ʿIsā before his death.

The Prophet ﷺ predicted the reappearance of Al-Mahdi and his role in spreading peace and justice, while Imām ʿAli ﷷ described that event when he said, 'He makes whims and desires follow the Path of Guidance after guidance has been made to follow whims and desires. He will refer all opinion to be judged by the Qur'ān, after the Qur'ān has been judged by people's opinions.'[183]

Those who have distanced themselves from the Path of Guidance, specified by the Holy Prophet ﷺ as being nothing other than *Ahl al-Bayt* ﷷ, will only realize how very far they have strayed from it after the reappearance of Al-Mahdi.

Signs that presage 'the end of time'

Many Muslim scholars confuse portents of the Day of Judgement (*Ashrāṭ al-Sāʿah*) with portents of 'the end of time', which will be clearly revealed prior to the reappearance of Al-Mahdi ﷷ.[184]

Some signs refer to specific events while others are symbolic expressions. Over the centuries attempts have been made to apply them to historical events. However, events to occur prior to the end of time are:

1. *Wars, destruction and societal disorder*: Muslim reports on the authority of Abu Hurairah that the Prophet ﷺ said, 'Towards the end of time two major powers will involve themselves in the conflicts of others in which huge numbers of people will perish.'[185]

   Muttaqi Hindi narrates on the authority of Nuʿaim ibn Ḥammād from Imām ʿAli ﷷ that wars prior to the appearance of Al-Mahdi will lead to a third of the world's population being killed, another third dying of natural causes, leaving only one-third remaining.[186]

Shaykh Mufid reports from Imām ʿAli عليه السلام that he said, ‘Before the one who will arise (*al-qā’im*), there will be red death and white death; there will be locusts at their usual time and at their unusual time like the colours of blood. As for red death, it is (from) the sword, while white death is (from) a plague [a contagious disease spreading rapidly over a wide area with great mortality].’[187]

2. *The emergence of the Antichrist/Dajjāl*: Bukhari reports on the authority of Anas ibn Mālik that the Prophet ﷺ said, ‘The *Dajjāl* will appear in the outskirts of Madinah where he will be joined by every disbeliever and hypocrite.’[188]

   When Imām ʿAli عليه السلام urged his Kufah congregation to raise issues they were unclear about, Ṣaʿṣaʿah ibn Ṣawḥān asked him about *Dajjāl* and the time of his emergence. In his response, the Imām عليه السلام talked about the end of time; by then long-established traditional values will have been debased and people emboldened to pursue unfettered self-indulgence. This indicates that *Dajjāl* is not necessarily an identifiable individual, but rather a condition or state of affairs.[189]

   The word *Dajjāl* is also applied to anyone who brainwashes and manipulates others, with claims that he is guiding them on the right path while actually steering them away from it.

3. *The emergence of Sufyānī*: This title has been frequently used to indicate a likely descendant of Abu Sufyān, who will direct his troops to attack various Muslim countries. According to some reports, these attacks will begin around Damascus, where women will be disembowelled and the lives of children destroyed.

   Al-Ḥakim al-Nishabūri acknowledges the above *ḥadīth* to be authentic on the ground that it meets all the criteria laid down by both Bukhāri and Muslim.[190] According to other reports, *Sufyānī* will send 30,000 troops to Makkah, where a sinkhole (*khasf*) will swallow up all but two of them. However, the gap between *Sufyānī* and the appearance of Al-Mahdi will be no longer than one year.

Al-Faḍl ibn Shādhān reported on the authority of Abu Ḥamza al-Thumālī that he had asked Imām Baqir ﷷ, 'Is the revolt of the *Sufyānī* one of the things that must happen?' To which the Imām responded that it was indeed.[191]

Nuʿmāni refers to 18 traditions from the error-free Imāms in his discussion regarding the emergence of *Sufyānī* prior to the re-appearance of Al-Mahdi.

4. *The approach of black flags from the East*: Ibn Mājah narrates from the holy Prophet ﷺ that he said, 'My progeny will suffer horrendous atrocities and torture until a man from the East appears leading troops with black flags, who will be granted victory over the unjust until they submit to the leadership of an Imām of my progeny, who will fill the world with justice and peace. Those that have the opportunity to witness this occurrence must rush to join them even if it requires them to crawl over snow.'[192]

   The Abbasid caliphs misconstrued what was meant by 'black flags' in their presumption that it referred to the black standards carried by their troops, particularly those of Abu Muslim al-Khurasāni. This clearly was not the case as all such standards disappeared many centuries ago without the appearance of Al-Mahdi.

   Interestingly, M. Sharon linked contemporary Middle Eastern political disputes with the aforementioned sign of the end of time.[193]

5. *The frequent occurrence of sinkholes/khasf*: Suyūṭi (d. 911 AH) reports from Um Salamah that the Prophet ﷺ said, '313 people near the Kaʿbah will pay allegiance to a person whom Iraqi troops and pious Syrians will join. An army sent to confront them will be swallowed up by a sinkhole that will open up beneath them.'

   On another occasion he reported from Abdullah ibn ʿUmar that when such holes swallow people up it is a sign of the coming of Al-Mahdi.[194]

   Muttaqi Hindi reports from Ibn Masʿūd, 'Before the end of time sinkholes will frequently occur.'[195]

6. *Murder of the purified soul/al-Nafs al-Zakiyah*: Jamāl al-Din Maqdisi Shafiʿi (d. 685 AH) reports on the authority of ʿAmmār ibn Yasir that he said, 'When the purified soul is murdered, a call from the heavens will announce, "The appearance of your *Amīr Al-Mahdi* is imminent. He will fill the earth with justice and peace."'[196]

   Nuʿmāni reports from Imām Ṣādiq عليه السلام that three signs will presage the appearance of Al-Mahdi: a call from the heavens, the murder of the purified soul and the emergence of *Sufyānī*.[197]

   The purified soul is a reference to an exceptionally spiritually developed pious man who will be murdered shortly before Al-Mahdi appears. In the past, a descendant of Imām Ḥasan عليه السلام, namely Muḥammad son of Abdullah, who rebelled against the Abbasid caliph al-Manṣūr in 145 AH, and was consequently beheaded, was referred to by this title.[198] However, we know that as this occurred without being immediately followed by Al-Mahdi's appearance, this sign did not apply to him.

7. *A call from the Heavens/Ṣayḥah*: Jamāl al-Din Maqdisi Shafiʿi reports on the authority of Imām Ḥusayn عليه السلام that, 'A call from the heavens, audible to everyone in the East and the West, will announce the appearance of Al-Mahdi. Those asleep will be aroused by it and those seated will stand up. May Allāh have mercy upon those who respond to that call because it is the voice of the archangel Jibrā'il.'[199]

   Kanji Shafiʿi reports from Abdullah ibn ʿUmar that the Prophet ﷺ said, 'When Al-Mahdi appears, an angel from above will call out, "This is Al-Mahdi, come and join him."'[200]

   Nuʿmāni reports from Imām Baqir عليه السلام, 'When the one who will arise (*al-qā'im*) emerges, there will be a call from the heavens that will be audible to those in the East and the West, even to those who are asleep.'[201]

8. *The dissipation of established moral conventions*: Many reports from the Holy Prophet ﷺ and error-free Imāms عليهم السلام predicted the spread of corruption, decadence, degradation of long-established social mores and depressingly low ethical standards in public life

> that will exist towards the end of time. For example, neglect of daily prayer, blatant and unrestricted pursuit of lusts, desires, power and wealth, marriage failure, acceptance of usury, bribery and mindless violence; unprincipled people in power who believe themselves entitled to illicit expenditure and extracurricular income; malfeasance and manipulation of entrusted responsibilities, misappropriation of charitable funds, accord on same-gender couplings, etc.
>
> Misinterpretation of the Qur'ān, disregard of the advice of pious jurists, praise for those who sin, censure of those with merit and other perversities – these will have established a milieu in which people regard bona fide Islāmic norms as irrelevant, risible, backward and positively dangerous.[202]

To conclude, we need to be absolutely clear that no approval has ever been given for people to link the above signs with specific events. Indeed, many reports counsel followers of *Ahl al-Bayt* not to try to predict the likely reappearance of the Twelfth Imām from specific events, and rebuke those who attempt it as being liars.

Notes to Part Four

1 For the definition by Shi'ah scholars, refer to:
Allāmah Ḥilli in *Al-Bāb al-Ḥadi 'Ashr,* p. 62.
Naṣir al-Dīn Ṭūsi in *Tajrīd al-I'tiqād,* p. 86.
Al-Sayyid al-Murtaḍā in *Al-Shāfī,* Vol. 2, p. 18.
For Sunni references see:
Ghazāli in *Al Iqtiṣād fi al-I'tiqād,* p. 234.
Āmidi in *Ghāyat al-Marām fi 'Ilm al-Kalām,* p. 363.
IJī in *Al-Mawāqif,* p. 395.
Taftāzāni in *Sharḥ al-Maqāṣid,* Vol. 2, p. 271.

2 Shahrestāni in his famous work: *Al-Milal wal Niḥal,* Vol. 1, p. 24.

3 Qur'ān 16:44.

4 Qur'ān 2:124.

5 Qur'ān 14:39.

6 Qur'ān 15:51–55.

7 Qur'ān 26:214.

8 The following sources confirm the content of this report:
Ṭabari in his *History,* Vol. 2, p. 216.
Ibn al-Athīr in *al-Kāmil fi al-Tārikh,* Vol 2, p. 62.
Tha'labi in his *Commentary* on Qur'ān 26:214.
Kanji Shafi'i in *Kefayat al-Ṭalib,* p. 89.
Ahmad ibn Ḥanbal in his *Musnad,* Vol. 1, p. 159.
Muttaqi Hindi in *Kanz al-'Ummāl,* Vol. 6, p. 391.
Al-Ḥalabi in *al-Sirah al-Nabawiyah,* Vol. 1, p. 311.

Ibn abi al-Ḥadid in *Sharḥ Nahj al-Balāghah,* Vol. 13, p. 210.

Abu al-Fidā' in *al-Tārikh,* Vol. 1, p. 116.

Ḥamawini Shafi'i in *Farā'id al-Simṭain,* Vol 2, p. 86.

Zarandi Ḥanafi in *Naẓm Durar al-Simtain,* p. 83.

9 Qur'ān 5:67.

10 Qur'ān 5:3.

11 *Musnad Aḥmad ibn Ḥanbal,* Vol. 1, p. 119.

12 Scholars who recorded the phrase that 'Umar used include:

1. Al Fakhr al-Rāzi in his *Tafseer,* Vol. 12, p. 49;
2. Aḥmad ibn Ḥanbal in his *Musnad,* Vol. 4, p.281;
3. Al-Ṭabari in his *Tafseer;*
4. all references to it are documented by 'Alamah Amini in *Al-Ghadīr,* Vol. 1, p. 270.

13 See Al-Amini, p. 344, for detailed references.

14 See for example:

Ṣaḥiḥ Muslim, Vol. 7, p. 122.

Sunan al-Tirmidhi, Vol. 2, p. 307.

Musnad Aḥmad ibn Ḥanbal, Vol. 3, p. 17; Vol. 4, p. 366; and Vol. 5, p. 182.

15 Further references that cite *Ḥadīth al-Thaqalain:*

Al Mustadrak 'alal-Ṣaḥiḥain, by Nishabūri, Vol. 3, p. 109.

Al-Durr al-Manthūr, by Suyūṭi, Vol. 6, p. 306.

Jāmi' al-Usūl, by Ibn al-Athīr, Vol. 1, p. 187.

Usd al-Ghābah fi ma'rifat al-ṣaḥābah, by Ibn al-Athīr, Vol. 2, p. 12.

Al-Ṭabaqāt al-Kubrā, by Ibn Sa'd, Vol. 2, p. 194.

Farā'id al-Simṭain, by Ḥamawini Shafi'I, Vol. 2, p. 143.

Majma' al-Zawāid, by Haythami, Vol. 9, p. 166.

Al-Mu'jam al-Kabir, by al-Ṭabarāni, p. 137.

Iḥyā' al-mayt, by Suyūṭi, pp. 30–32.

Naẓm Durar al-Simtain, by Zarandi Ḥanafi, p. 232.

16 Qur'ān 3:61.

17 *Al-Durr al-Manthūr,* Vol. 5, p. 199.

18 Qur'ān 5:55.

19 *Al-Durr al-Manthūr,* Vol. 3, p. 105.

20 *Tafsīr al-Ṭabari,* Vol. 4, p. 272.

21 *Tafsīr al-Rāzi*, Vol. 4, p. 1162.

22 *Almuʿjam Al-Awṣaṭ*, Vol. 7, p. 130.

23 *Aḥkām al-Qur'ān*, Vol. 2, p. 446.

24 *Asbāb al-Nuzūl*, p. 133.

25 *Tārikh Madinat Dimashq*, Vol. 12, p. 305.

26 *Al-Riāḍ al-Naḍirah*, Vol. 3, p. 182.

27 *Jāmiʿ al-Uṣūl*, Vol. 9, p. 478.

28 *Tafsīr Al-Bayḍāwi*, Vol. 1, p. 272.

29 *Al-Ghadīr*, Vol. 3, pp. 220–230.

30 *Minhāj al-Sunnah*, Vol. 2, p. 30; and in its *Būlāq* edition, Vol. 1, p. 155.

31 Qur'ān 3:173.

32 Qur'ān 5:11.

33 Qur'ān 16:120.

34 Qur'ān 20:50.

35 Qur'ān 33:6.

36 Qur'ān 9:36.

37 Qur'ān 7:160.

38 Qur'ān 5:12.

39 *King James Bible*, Genesis 25: 12–16.

40 *Ṣaḥiḥ Bukhāri*, Vol. 9, p. 729, *ḥadīth* no. 2034.

41 *Ṣaḥiḥ Muslim*, Vol. 3, p. 1452, *ḥadīth* no. 1821.

42 *Ṣaḥiḥ Tirmithi*, Vol. 4, p. 501, *ḥadīth* no. 2223.

43 *Musnad Aḥmad ibn Ḥanbal*, Vol. 1, p. 398.

44 *Al Mustadrak ʿalal-Ṣaḥiḥain*, Vol. 3, p. 618.

45 *Kanz al-ʿUmmal*, Vol. 6, p. 201.

46 *The Right Path*, p. 285.

47 *Nahj al-Balāghah*, Sermon 192.

48 All of the above have been transmitted in dozens of sources, including *Ṣaḥiḥ Bukhāri*, *Ṣaḥiḥ Muslim*, *Musnad of Aḥmad ibn Hanbal*, *Al-Mustadrak ala al-Ṣaḥiḥain*.

49 For historical details of his life refer to:
Tārikh al-Ṭabari, Vols. 2 and 3.
Al-Kamil fi al-Tārikh, Vol. 3.
Murūj al-Thahab, Vol. 2.

Al-Ṭabaqāt al-Kubrā, Vol. 3.

50 *Musnad of Imām ʿAli* عليه السلام.

51 *Ghurar al-Ḥikam wa Durar al-Kalim,* by Āmidī.

52 *Maṭlūb kul Ṭālib min Kalām ʿAli ibn Abi Ṭālib.*

53 *Nahj al-Balāghah,* translated into English as *The Path of Eloquence.*

54 *Maṣādir Nahj al-Balāghah wa Asāniduhu,* Beirut, 1395 AH.

55 Qur'ān 3:59–61.

56 *Ṣulḥ al-Imām al-Ḥasan,* by Shaykh Rāḍi Āl Yāsin, p. 259.

57 Ibn abi al-Ḥadid, in *Sharḥ Nahj al-Balāghah,* Vol. 16, p. 15.

58 Abul Faraj al-Isphahāni, *Maqātil al-Ṭālibyīn,* p. 46.

59 *Nahj al-Balāghah,* Sermon 97.

60 *Nahj al-Balāghah,* Sermon 25.

61 *The Book of Sulaym ibn Qays,* p. 458.

62 Ibn Shahrāshūb, in *Al Manāqib,* Vol. 3, p. 176.

63 *Biḥār al-Anwār,* Vol. 44, p. 138.

64 *Tārikh Baghdad,* Vol. 1, p. 316.
Mizān al Iʿtidāl, Vol. 2, p. 116.
Kanz al-ʿUmmāl, Vol. 6, p. 152.

65 *Nahj al-Balāghah,* Sermon 207.

66 *Musnad ibn Ḥanbal,* Vol. 4, p. 172.
Sunan al-Tirmithi, Vol. 5, p. 658.

67 *Murūj al-Thahab,* Vol. 2, p. 350.

68 *Zād al-Maʿād,* by Majlisī, p. 146; and *Al-Balad al-Amīn,* by Kafʿamī, p. 251.

69 *Tafsīr al-Burhān,* Vol. 2, p. 363.
Aʿyān al Shiʿah, Vol 1, p. 580.

70 The same story is also reported vis-à-vis Imām Ḥasan. See *Biḥār al-Anwar,* Vol. 43, p. 344.

71 *Murūj al-Thahab,* Vol. 2, p. 350.

72 *Hussaini Encyclopaedia,* Vol. 2, p. 131.

73 *Sharḥ Nahj al-Balāghah,* by Ibn Abi al-Ḥadīd, Vol. 4, p. 54.

74 *Al-Amāli,* by Shaykh Ṭusi, p. 637.

75 *History of the City of Damascus,* Vol. 36, p. 147.
Al-Bidāyah wal Nihāyah, Vol. 9, p. 124.

76 *Shatharāt al-Thahab,* Vol. 1, p. 105.

77 *Siyar aʿlām al Nubalā',* Vol. 4, p. 397.
Al-Irshād, by Shaykh Mufid, Vol. 2, p. 146.

78 *Al-Bidāyah wal Nihāyah,* Vol. 9, p. 105.

79 *Siyar aʿlām al Nubalā',* Vol. 4, p. 239.

80 *Kashf al-Ghummah,* Vol. 2, p. 289.

81 *Biḥār al-Anwar,* Vol. 46, p. 100.

82 *Biḥār al-Anwar,* Vol. 42, p. 75.

83 For details of the above *ayāt*, refer to Thaʿlabi, Ghazāli and others.

84 *Maqtal al-Ḥusayn,* Vol. 2, p. 54.
Muthīr al-Aḥzān, p. 93.

85 *Al-Bidāyah wal Nihāyah,* Vol. 8, p. 220.

86 *Tārikh al-Ṭabari,* Vol. 5, p. 498.

87 *Wasā'il al-Shīʿah,* Vol. 12, p. 208.

88 This Treatise has been transmitted in two versions, one by Shaykh al-Ṣadūq (d. 581/991) that appears in two of his titles, *Al-Khisāl* and his *Al-Amāli*, and the other in *Tuḥaf al-ʿuqūl*, by his contemporary, Ibn Shuʿbah.

89 *Tārikh Ibn ʿAsākir,* Vol. 54, p. 276.

90 *Al-Bidāyah wal Nihāyah,* Vol. 9, p. 122.
Ḥayāt al-Ḥaywān, Vol. 1, p. 91.

91 Arzina R. Lalani, *Early Shiʿi Thought,* p. 13.

92 *Al-Kāfi,* Vol. 2, p. 27.

93 *Al-Kāfi,* Vol. 1, p. 97.

94 For details see *Thirty Principles of Islāmic Jurisprudence,* pp. 39–49.

95 *Tahdhīb al-Tahdhīb,* Vol. 2, p. 185.

96 *Tārikh ibn Kathir,* Vol. 9, p. 157.

97 *Shatharāt al-Thahab,* Vol. 1, p. 106.

98 *Al-Thuqāt,* Vol. 6, p. 131.

99 *Ḥelyat al-Awliyā',* Vol. 1, p. 72.

100 Khawarazmi's biographical notes regarding Abu Ḥanifa, Vol. 1, p. 172.

101 *Maṭālib al-Sa'ūl,* Vol. 2, p. 56.

102 *Al-Fuṣūl al-Muhimmah,* p. 222.

103 *Al-Irshād*, by Al-Mufīd, p. 257.

104 *Rijāl al-Najāshi,* p. 39.
Safinatul Biḥār, Vol. 4, p. 677.

105 *Al-Imām Ja'far al-Ṣadiq*, p. 187.

106 *Uṣūl al-Kāfi,* Vol. 1, p. 309.
Al-Irshād, Vol. 2, p. 218.

107 *Biḥār al-Anwār,* Vol. 25, p. 133.
Ithbāt al-Hudāt, Vol. 5, p. 535.

108 *Tārikh Baghdad,* Vol. 13, p. 30; *Wafayāt al-A'yān*, Vol. 5, p. 308.

109 *Tārikh Baghdad,* Vol. 2, p. 193.

110 *Biḥār al-Anwār,* Vol. 48, p. 156.
Uṣūl al-Kāfi, Vol. 1, p. 543.

111 In doing so he عليه السلام cited the Qur'ānic *ayāt* 16:12, 40:67, 45:5, 57:17, 13:4, 30:24 and 6:152.

112 For which he عليه السلام cited the Qur'ānic *ayāt* 29:43, 2:170, 2:171, 10:42, 25:44, 59:14 and 2:44.

113 Qur'ān 6:116, 31:25 and 29:63.

114 Qur'ān 34:13, 38:24, 30:28, 11:40, 7:31, 5:103 and 10:60.

115 *Al-Kāfī, the Book of Reason and Ignorance*, *ḥadīth* No. 12.

116 Qur'ān 51:23.

117 *Biḥār al-Anwār,* Vol. 48, p. 217.

118 For further information regarding the above, refer to *Muslim Studies,* Vol. 2, pp. 64, 74 and 325; and Ignaz Goldziher in *Introduction to Islāmic Theology and Law,* pp. 59–60.

119 Qur'ān 11:113.

120 *Biḥār al-Anwār,* Vol. 48, p. 220.

121 *Al-Kāfī,* Vol. 1, p. 313.
Al-Irshād, Vol. 2, p. 251.

122 *'Uyūn Akhbār al-Riḍā,* Vol. 1, p. 36.
Biḥār al-Anwār, Vol. 49, p. 15.

123 *Tarikh al-Islām,* by Thahabi, p. 232.

124 *Ṭabari*, Vol. 6, p. 544 and Vol. 7, p. 49.
Ibn al-Athīr, Vol. 6, p. 222.

125 *Al-Tawḥīd,* by Shaykh Ṣadūq, p. 176.
Al-Iḥtijāj, Vol. 2, p. 192.

126 *Rijāl al-Kashshi,* Vol. 2, p. 756.
Biḥār al-Anwār, Vol. 48, p. 263.

127 *Ṭabari*, Vol. 7, p. 51.

128 ʿUyūn akhbār *al-Riḍā,* Vol. 2, p. 151.
Al-Amālī, by Shaykh Sadūq, pp. 125–127.

129 *Al-Irshād,* Vol. 2, p. 259.

130 *Biḥār al-Anwār,* Vol. 49, p. 140.

131 For example, Qur'ān 35:32.

132 For confirmation of his being poisoned see:
Al-Ṣafadi in *Al-Wāfi bil Wafayāt,* Vol. 22, p. 156.
Ibn Ḥibbān in *Al-Thiqāt*, Vol. 8, p. 456.
Al-Yaʿqūbi in *Al-Tārikh,* Vol. 2, p. 453.

133 Qur'ān 38:35–37.

134 For references regarding this refer to: *Al-Kāfi*, Vol. 1, p. 320.
Al-Irshād, Vol. 2, p. 280.
Biḥār al-Anwār, Vol. 50, p. 18.

135 Qur'ān 19:12.

136 Qur'ān 58.2–4.

137 *Al-Irshād,* Vol. 2, p. 281; and *Iʿlām al-Warā bi Aʿlām al Hudā*, Vol. 2, p. 101.

138 *Biḥār al-Anwār,* Vol. 50, pp. 5–7 and Qur'ān 72:18, that detail the parts of the body needed during prostration and thus not to be amputated.

139 Refer to:
Kamāl al-Din wa tamām al-Niʿmah, Vol. 2, p. 334;
Kifāyat al-Athar, p. 284.
Biḥār al-Anwār, Vol. 50, p. 123.

140 *Tarikh al-Khulafā',* by Suyūṭi, p. 347.

141 *Ibid.*, p. 348.

142 *Tathkirat al-Khawāṣ,* by Ibn al-Jawzī, p. 203.

143 *Al-Kāfi*, Vol. 1, p. 498.

144 *Wafayāt al Aʿyān,* Vol. 3, p. 273.

145 This supplication that first appeared in its entirety in *Muhaj al-Daʿawāt* by Sayyid ibn Ṭāwūs (d. 664 AH), also appears in *Biḥār al-Anwar,* Vol. 50, p. 209.

146 *Kitāb al-Rijāl,* by Al-Kashshī, the earliest biographical resource of Shiʿah narrators.
Aʿlām al-Hidāyah, Vol. 12, p. 202.

147 Qur'ān 33:33.

148 Qur'ān 24:36–37.

149 *Al-Kāfi*, Vol. 1, p. 327.
Al-Irshād, Vol. 2, p. 319.

150 *Maṭālib al-Sa'ūl*, by Muḥammad ibn Ṭalḥah al-Shāfiʿi.

151 *Tadhkirat al-Khawāṣ*, by ibn al-Jawzi.

152 *Nūr al-Abṣār*, by Shiblinji.

153 *al-Fuṣūl al-Muhimmah*, by ibn al-Ṣabbāgh al-Māliki.

154 *Al-Manāqib*, by Ibn Shahrashūb, Vol. 3, p. 526 (Vol. 4, p. 424 in another edition).
Biḥār al-Anwār, Vol. 50, p. 311.

155 *Al-Ghaybah*, by Sheikh Ṭūsi, p. 394.

156 *Al-Iḥtijāj*, by Ṭabrisi, Vol. 2, p. 260.

157 For details of the aforementioned battle, refer to Ibn al-Athīr in *Al-Kāmil fi al-Tārikh*, Vol. 7, p. 162; and for the full report of Shaykh Ṣadūq, refer to *Kamāl al-Dīn wa Tamām al-Niʿmah*, p. 418.

158 *Kamāl al-Dīn wa Tamām al-Niʿmah*, by Shaykh Ṣadūq, Vol. 2, p. 475.

159 *ʿIqd al-Durar fi Akhbār Al-Mahdi al-Muntaẓar*, Ch. 1, *Ḥadīth* no. 25.

160 Refer to:
Al-Bukhāri in *Al-Tārikh al-Kabīr*, Vol. 2, part 1, p. 316.
Abu Dawūd in *Al-Sunan*, Vol. 4, p. 151.
Al-Ḥākim al-Naishāburi in *Al-Mustadrak ʿala Ṣaḥiḥain*, Vol. 4, p. 557.
Al-Ḥāfiḍ al-Thahabi in *Mizān al-Iʿtidāl*, Vol. 1, p. 355.

161 *Yanābīʿ al-Mawaddah*, by Qundūzi Ḥanafi, p. 494.

162 *Ṣaḥiḥ al-Bukhāri*, Chapter on The Descent of ʿIsā, Vol. 4, p. 205.
Al-Burhān fi ʿAlāmāt Mahdi Ākhir al-Zamān, by Muttaqi Hindi, p. 160.

163 *Yanābīʿ al-Mawaddah*, p. 494.

164 *Al-Kāfi*, Vol. 1, p. 328; and *Al-Ghaybah* by Shaykh Ṭūsi, p. 234.

165 *Al-Futūḥāt al-Makkiyah*, Vol. 3. ch. 366.

166 *Al-Fuṣūl al-Muhimmah*, p. 292.

167 *Maṭālib al-Sa'ūl*.

168 *Kifayat al-Athar*, pp. 260, 285 and 291.

169 *Al-Bayān fi Akhbār Ṣahib al-Zamān*, pp. 102–10.

170 *Nahj al-Balāghah*, Maxim 147.

171 *Yanābīʿ al-Mawaddah,* p. 494.

172 *Farā'id al-Simṭain,* Vol. 1, p. 46.

173 *Biḥār al-Anwār,* Vol. 52, p. 93.

174 *Al-Kāfi, The Book of Divine Proof,* Ch. 5, Wofis, Tehrān 1981 CE.

175 *Al-Ghaybah,* by Shaykh Ṭūsi, p. 215.

176 *Ibid.*, p. 216.

177 *A Shīʿite Creed*, translated by Asaf A. A. Fyzee, Introduction, p. 9.
The Shīʿite Religion, by Donaldson, p. 285.

178 *Al-Iḥtijāj,* by Shaykh Ṭabrisi, Vol. 2, p. 497, Beirut 1401 AH.

179 *Ṣaḥiḥ al-Bukhāri*, Chapter on the Descent of ʿIsā, Vol. 4, p. 205.
Ṣaḥiḥ Muslim, Chapter on the Descent of ʿIsā, Vol. 1, p. 136.

180 *Al-Burhān fi ʿAlāmāt Ākhir al-Zamān,* p. 160.

181 *Ibid.*, p. 158.

182 *Al-Bayān fi Akhbar Ṣahib al-Zamān*, p. 77.

183 *Nahj al-Balāghah,* Sermon 138.

184 Shaykh Mufid in *Al-Irshād.*
Nuʿmāni in *Al-Ghaibah.*
Shaykh Ṭūsi in *Al-Ghaibah.*
Muttaqi Hindi (d. 975 AH) in *Al-Burhān fi ʿAlāmāt Mahdi Ākhir al-Zamān.*
Others also provide information on such signs based upon traditions related from the holy Prophet ﷺ and error-free Imāms عليهم السلام.

185 *Ṣaḥiḥ Muslim*, Vol. 4, p. 2214.

186 *Kanz al-ʿUmmāl,* Vol. 14, p. 587.

187 *Kitāb Al-Irshād,* translated by I. K. A. Howard, p. 544.

188 *Ṣaḥiḥ Bukhari*, Vol. 9, p. 74.

189 *Kamāl al-Din wa Tamām al-Niʿmah,* Vol. 2, p. 526.

190 *Al-Mustadrak ʿala Ṣaḥiḥain,* Vol. 4, p. 520.

191 *Kitāb Al-Irshād,* p. 543.

192 *Sunan Ibn Mājah,* Vol. 2, p. 1366.

193 *Black Banners from the East*, Jerusalem 1983.

194 *Al-ʿUrf al-Wardī fi Akhbār al-Mahdi,* Vol. 2, pp. 129, 136.

195 *Kanz al-ʿUmmāl,* Vol. 14, p. 276.

196 *Iʿd al-Durar fi Akhbār al-Mahdi al-Muntaẓar,* Ch. 4.

197 *Al-Ghaybah,* p. 252.

198 *Tarikh al-Ṭabari*, Vol. 7, p. 595.

199 *I'd al-Durar fi Akhbār al-Mahdi al-Muntaẓar*, Ch. 4.

200 *Al-Bayān fi Akhbar Ṣahib al-Zamān*, p. 93.

201 *Al-Ghaybah*, p. 257.

202 *Al-Kāfi*, Vol. 8, p. 38.

Al-Burhān fi 'Alāmāt Mahdi Ākhir al-Zamān, p. 136.

Al-Ghaybah, p. 572.

PART FIVE

Resurrection

In order to deliver his message, the Prophet Muḥammad had to focus on dispelling pre-Islāmic polytheism. It took him ﷺ three years to establish belief in there being **no deity other than Allāh**. During the following ten years of his stay in Makkah, the focus of his teaching extended to physical life being but a step towards the eternal life that is to follow. Examination of the last *Juz'* (thirtieth section of the Qur'ān) illustrates the depth of detail, the signs of resurrection and the accountability of people on the **'final day'**.

Just as every academic establishment requires students to sit examinations at the end of their course of study, humankind are also to be examined at the end of their life's course.

The Arab population appeared to find this a very difficult message to accept. 'If you tell them you will indeed be raised up after death, the faithless will surely say that that would be nothing other than a magic trick'.[1] They confronted his ideas with the disrespect that they thought these deserved. 'They considered it odious that a warner, from among themselves, would tell them such things and said, "What! When we are dead and have become dust [we shall be raised again?] is a far-fetched idea."'[2]

13 The Necessity of Resurrection

In the Holy Qur'ān Allāh provides a variety of reasons to support resurrection:

1. Deprived of resurrection, creation would not have purpose.
2. Divine justice demands resurrection.
3. The examples of earlier events: the 'Companions of the Cave', the 'Cow and the Children of Isrā'il' and Ibrāhim عليه السلام and 'The Four Birds'.
4. Resurrection is the fulfilment of all Divine Promises.
5. Completion of the journey to human perfection depends upon resurrection.

1 Deprived of Resurrection, Creation Has No Purpose

Life after death is considered to be the purpose of our existence, as our stay in this world is only temporary. Materialists' visions of life are limited to the short period of existence that begins at birth and ends at death. They do not accept, and thus do not contemplate, or have aspiration or objectives for, the time after death. In contrast, the Prophet of Islām صلى الله عليه وآله وسلم emphasized that all of humanity is continuously and inexorably being driven towards eternity. Believers thus seek perfection – by the elimination of shortcomings and negative thoughts – in order to pursue the elements of salvation and spiritual advancement.

Many *ayāt* in the Qur'ān point to the inevitability of humanity ultimately meeting their Lord:

> Truly, we are Allāh's and to Him we shall return.[3]
>
> Your final destination is with your Lord . . . [on the Day of Resurrection].[4]
>
> You will be driven to your Lord on that day [Day of Resurrection].[5]
>
> And your Lord is your final destination.[6]

In Qur'ānic terminology, 'The Lord' is the Absolute, Perfect, Limitless and Eternal Existent, and thus it is to this that the whole of humanity is being directed. Imām 'Ali عليه السلام described this temporary life as the bridge that spans the gap between 'what is limited and what is unlimited'. He عليه السلام explained the role of this analogy in the establishment of Islamic personality:

> This world is a thoroughfare but the next world is a permanent abode. So, garner in this thoroughfare all that you will need for your final abode . . . take your hearts away from this world prior to your bodies being taken from it, because here you are 'on trial', but your final destination is the everlasting hereafter. When a person dies people ask what property they have left, but the Angels ask what good actions they have sent forward. May Allāh bless you – send forward something that will benefit you and do not leave anything behind that will be burdensome to you there.[7]

In some *ayāt* of the Qur'ān, those who do not strive for advancement in their spiritual life are described as being losers, and in others, as animals. Vis-à-vis temporal and eternal life, Allāh tells us in the Qur'ān:

> You prefer the life of this world, even though the hereafter is everlasting and superior. Indeed, this is mentioned in previous scriptures, the scriptures of Ibrāhīm and Mūsa.[8]

The strongest Qur'ānic statement in regard to the purposefulness of our creation is: 'Do you suppose that We created you aimlessly, and that you will not be brought back to us?'[9] In this *āyah* Allāh condemns those who imagine that there is no purpose to existence and that the whole of creation is pointless. To elaborate on the purposefulness of creation, we need to explain three premises:

a. Everything that exists in the universe is in its proper place, with not a thing being superfluous, disordered or in the wrong location – any change to this orderliness would be likely to have consequences that are beyond our understanding.

b. In the Holy Qur'ān humankind is referred to as Allāh's vicegerent upon earth: 'When your lord said to the angels, "I am going to appoint a vicegerent upon earth."'[10] Such vicegerency serves two purposes: first, to examine humankind, 'He, who created death and life that He may test you [to see] which of you have the best conduct,'[11] and, second, to 'know' Allāh and worship Him. 'I did not create Jinn and human beings other than to worship me.'[12]

c. Allāh created humankind's journey for them to attain perfection via worship and test. To this end, humankind is subjected to trials and tribulations. The following *ayāt* emphasize purpose in the creation of the universe and humanity:

> We did not create sky and land and all that lies between them in vain. That is a conjecture of the faithless.[13]
>
> Do those who perpetrate evil imagine that We will treat them in the same manner as We treat those who have faith and undertake good deeds? That their lives and deaths will be the same? Such thought is tantamount to evil.[14]
>
> Do you imagine that We aimlessly created you and that you will not be brought back to us?[15]

2 Divine Justice Demands Resurrection

> Everything in the world has been carefully gauged to rest upon the foundation of divine justice. 'We certainly sent Our messengers with manifest proofs, and We sent down with them the Book and the Balance so that humankind may maintain justice . . . [16]

The legislative aspect of justice governs society's observation of rights and duties. This is achieved via a careful balance of the Principles of Justice in which every individual finds their rights protected and their boundaries and limits clarified – so that none violates the rights of others in the enjoyment of their own freedom.

The following *ayāt* emphasize the accountability of every individual in determining their reward or penalty:

> Today, [the Day of Resurrection] every soul will receive the reward for what it has earned. There will be no injustice on this day.[17]

> To Allāh belongs all that is in the heavens and all that is on earth: and so He will reward those who do evil in accordance with their deeds and will reward those who do good with ultimate good.[18]

> Truly Allāh does not wrong people in the least, it is people who wrong themselves.[19]

> Those who behave righteously benefit their souls while those who commit evil deeds do so to the detriment of their souls. Your Lord does not behave tyrannically to His servants.[20]

The principle of accountability in the above *ayāt* leads to the logical conclusion that as the reward for our good actions and bad actions are not levied in this life, **there must be further life** in which they will be.

3 Examples of Earlier Events

Some of these earlier events are the 'Companions of the Cave', the 'Cow and the Children of Isrā'il', and Ibrāhim عليه السلام and 'The Four Birds'.

There is an immense difference between theory and practice. Despite the faithful believing what Allāh has imparted about the necessity of resurrection, there are several degrees of certainty. For example, in relation to the following statements:

- Someone hears the word 'fire' in a foreign language and consults a dictionary.
- Someone observes smoke rise from behind a building.
- Someone comes face to face with flame under a kettle.
- Someone is accidentally touched by flames and is burnt.

Is it reasonable to expect the degree of comprehension of fire in the above examples to be the same? Without doubt, direct contact with flames maximizes understanding of the characteristics of fire. In the same way, when Allāh Almighty tells us of incidents that happened to people in the past, for example that they observed the dead being revived, the level of a believer's understanding is heightened. Here are two such examples from the Qur'ān:

- *The Prophet Ibrāhim* عليه السلام *and 'The Four Birds'*: Exegetes report that the Prophet Ibrāhim عليه السلام saw wild beasts tear at the carcass of a dead animal and said to Allāh Almighty, 'I discovered how You disseminate dead flesh but want to see how You bring it to life again.' Allāh replied, 'Do you not believe?' Ibrāhim said, 'I do, but my heart seeks a deeper level of certainty.' Allāh said, 'Train four birds to follow you, then kill them, cut them in pieces, leave a part on every mountain, and then call them – they will come flying to you . . . '[21]

  Exegetes report the birds to have been a rooster, a wood pigeon, a crow and a peacock. Ibrāhim cut them into pieces, retained their beaks and mixed the feathers and blood of all the birds together before placing a portion of this mixture on each of the ten nearby mountains. Then, holding the beak of each bird he called it to return to him. When he had observed all the birds fly to him, his certainty of how Allāh revives the dead was increased in intensity.

- *The story of ʿUzayr* (*Ezra*): 'Or the like of he who passed a ruined village and exclaimed, "How shall Allāh give it life after its death?" So Allāh caused the man to die for 100 years and thereafter raised him back to life. He then asked the man, "How long have you remained here?" He responded, "Perhaps a day or a part of a day." He then told him, "You have lain here for 100 years, look at your food and drink! It is still fresh. Now look at your donkey. Truly We will make you a sign to humankind. Observe how its bones are being reassembled and clothed by its flesh." When he had witnessed this he exclaimed, "I now understand that Allāh has power over all things."'[22]
  - Reviving a group of the Children of Isrā'il.[23]
  - Reviving a murdered man of the Children of Isrā'il.[24]
  - Reviving 70 of Prophet Mūsa's companions.[25]
  - Prophet ʿIsā عليه السلام reviving the dead.[26]
  - Companions of the Cave.[27]

4 Resurrection Is the Fulfilment of All Divine Promises

According to Qur'ānic teaching, justice is the bedrock of Allāh's creation and legislation. He alludes to justice vis-à-vis creation in, 'The sun and the moon follow [precisely determined] courses, and herbage, stars and trees prostrate in submission [before Him]. He raised the heavens and set the balance.'[28] This establishes that He founded the heavens and the earth upon His perfect order and absolute justice. This order and harmony in the workings of the universe was revealed at a time when conjecture and superstition still reigned. Thus, our ability to use the same methodology to determine and disclose that everything He created, including far-off galaxies, functions with the order and harmony established by the same set of laws, is referred to by theologians as 'the justice of creation'.

As for the justice in legislation, Allāh has commanded humankind, 'Maintain what you weigh with justice and do not shorten your measure.'[29] He also tells us, 'We certainly sent our messengers with manifest proof, and we sent down with them the Book and the Balance, so that humankind is equipped to maintain justice.'[30]

For the rights and duties that regulate and maintain society to be observed, they need to be based upon carefully balanced justice. The Lawmaker has set boundaries and limits of actions so that none may assume freedom to disregard or transgress them. Despite this, history records an unlimited number of iniquities that led to bloodshed. Dictators ignored what is today referred to as human rights, and trampled over the justice of others in order to gratify their own whims and desires. If there were not a time allocated for divine justice to hold them to account, the whole concept of justice could not exist. To emphasize this Allāh asks us, 'Shall We treat those of faith and righteous behaviour in the same manner as we treat those who spread corruption on earth?'[31] In another *āyah* He says, 'On that day each soul is to be recompensed for what it has earned. There will be no injustice on that day. Indeed Allāh is swift in reckoning.'[32]

The concept of being held accountable for one's deeds is repeated in many, many Qur'ānic *ayāt*. Most importantly, our rewards or chastisements are reflections of our actions during our temporary stay in this world. 'Indeed, Allāh does not wrong people in the least; rather, it is people who wrong themselves.'[33] 'Those who behave in a righteous manner benefit their own souls and those who behave in an evil manner disadvantage their own souls. Your Lord is not tyrannical to his servants!'[34]

As our time on this earth is limited, we are afforded a lifespan to draw maximum benefit from it, with our recompense being meted out thereafter.

5 Human Perfection Depends upon Resurrection

The universe, from its smallest particles to its greatest aspects, was not created without purpose. Rather, it came into being as an intentional and continuous progression towards perfection. Everything in the cosmos, infinitesimally small or infinitely large, and every type of living thing is on a journey towards its own perfection. For example, consider human physical progression from oocyte, ovum and sperm, zygote, blastocyst, embryo, fetus, parturition, babyhood, infancy, adolescence, adulthood, old age and death. Such journeys are unceasing and it is inevitable that all will one day arrive at their final destination. Such non-voluntary movement is governed by causal predestination (*al-Jabr al-ʿIllī wal Maʿlūlī*). Allāh's will – as both *irādah* and *mashī'ah* (decree) – is fashioned within this precisely structured cause and effect. Therefore, everything other than Allāh will fade away on its journey towards the highest goal of perfection – that is, Allāh Almighty Himself.

Al-Fayḍ al-Kāshānī (d. 1091 AH/1680 CE) says, 'Man has an essential and innate movement (as opposed to a voluntary one) from his point of origin to his resurrection when he will meet with his Lord in his afterlife. Allāh alludes to this when He says, "O man, you truly strive to move towards your Lord and thus you will meet Him" (Qur'ān 84:6). That continual striving refers to humankind's final destination.'[35]

By causal predestination, philosophers refer to the fact that when the essential elements of a **cause** are complete, the existence of their **effect** becomes necessary. For example, the elements needed for this to occur in regard to wood-burning are the strength and proximity of fire and the absence of fire protection. Once all these requirements are present the wood **must** burn. Philosophers consider it illogical and impossible to postulate doubt over the above-mentioned statement.

To elaborate further, all of humankind automatically moves, willingly or not, towards a specified destination. The sole choice each one has is: to move towards perfection and virtue, that enables them to attain the highest rank they are equipped to achieve, or to move towards deficiency and vice, that leads them each day closer to the brink of the abyss.

14 Portents of the Day of Judgement

A portent of the Day of Judgement (*Ashrāṭ al-Sāʿah*) is referred to in the Qur'ān, 'Do they wait for anything other than the hour that may all of a sudden overtake them? Its signs have [already] appeared'.[36] Many portents are mentioned in Qur'ānic *ayāt* and elaborated upon in many *āḥadīth*.

1 Portents Referred to in the Qur'ān

The collapse of the dam and emergence of Gog and Magog

Dhul Qarnayn is requested to erect a 'dam' to protect a population from incursion and pillage by Gog and Magog (*Ya'jūj and Ma'jūj*).[37]

Dhul Qarnayn, who had the necessary skills and abilities to undertake this task, organized the population to carry out the labour. The barrier was constructed of iron blocks cemented together with a molten alloy. On completion he said, 'This is a mercy from my Lord but when the promise of my Lord comes to pass, He will raze it to the ground, and the promise of my Lord is true. We will let them move to and fro [in anarchy and confusion], to surge upon each other **until the trumpet is blown and We gather them all together.**'[38]

The last *āyah* refers to the levelling of that barrier, followed by a proliferation of anarchy, disorder and confusion; these characterize 'Portents of the Day', that are also mentioned in the Qur'ān.[39]

The Descent of ʿIsā ﷺ

Allāh tell us, 'When [the nature of] the son of Maryam is set forth as an example, behold your people raise an outcry [to ridicule it]. They said, "Are our deities better, or is he?" It is only in the spirit of dispute that they present this comparison. Yes, they are contentious people. He was merely [Our] servant. Upon whom We bestowed Our favours and made an example for the Children of Isrā'il. Had We so willed, We would have made you angels to succeed yourselves on earth. And behold, this [divine writ] is indeed the portent of the hour [of reckoning]. Have no doubt whatever about it – so follow Me on the right Path.'[40]

The above *ayāt* link the descent of ʿIsā ﷺ with the portents of the Day of Judgement. We will see later that towards the end of time both ʿIsā and Imām Mahdi ﷺ will join to fill the earth with justice and truth immediately prior to the Day of Judgement.

A live created being

An illustration of what is to occur at the end of time is to be found in *ayāt* 81–87 of Surah 27. Allāh Almighty begins His clarification with the bringing forth of 'a live created being' (*Dābbah*),[41] and continues with 'resurrection' and 'the trumpet being blown'.

To expound on the above *ayāt* and clarify what is meant by 'a live created being', we need methodically to examine the following:

1. What is meant by 'When the **word** is raised concerning them'?
2. What is meant by the 'live created being'?
3. What is the 'live created being' to speak about?
4. Does the phrase 'that people did not believe Our Signs' refer to what the 'live created being' is to say, or to the point raised in question 1 above?

5. What is the purpose of 'bringing forth the live created being'?

6. When is this to occur?

The variety of exegetical opinion regarding the above leads us to conclude that no other *āyah* in the Qur'ān is surrounded by as much ambiguity. We thus need to deal with all of the above questions.

- To answer question 1, we need to be aware first that 'word', here employed, does not refer to one that is voiced, but is being utilized to denote an action. Refer to Qur'ān 39:19, in which Allāh Almighty describes chastisement as the 'word of chastisement'. In brief, Allāh Almighty refers to humankind being accountable for their deeds, and liable to chastisements for injustices they have perpetrated.

- To answer question 2, we need to refer to lexicographers. The term 'live created being' (*Dābbah*) appears frequently in the Qur'ān, such as in 11:6, 'There is not **a creature that moves on this earth** that is not sustained by Allāh Almighty.' However, it is not indicated anywhere whether it is a human being or an animal. Indeed, some other Qur'ānic references, for example 35:28, refer to both human beings and beasts. For the latter, Allāh employs the word *Dawābb,* the plural of *Dābbah*.

- To answer question 3 we refer to *āyah* 82, 'That people did not believe in Our Signs'.

- To answer question 4, both possibilities may be postulated.

- In dealing with question 5, the purpose is to announce that the Day of Reckoning is soon to occur.

- As for question 6, the time for such an event is in itself a Portent of the Day.

We conclude, from examination of all of the above, that Allāh Almighty has referred to three events: two as being Portents of the Day of Judgement (emergence of the live created being and the resurrection of a group that represents all nations) and the third, itself a reference to The Day (the final blast of the trumpet).[42]

Smoke permeating the Heavens[43]

'Wait then for the Day when [heavy] smoke permeates the heavens [a prelude to the approach of the last hour], that will envelop all of humanity in painful torment, [Then people that did not believe in Our Signs will say] O our Lord, please remove this torment for we [now] truly believe [in You].

[But] how can such an awakening avail them [in the Last Hour], for when the Messenger was sent to them to clearly expound the truth, they turned their backs upon him saying, 'He is a lunatic [instructed] by those [who have bad intentions].

[Still,] behold, We shall remove the torment for a little while [but] you shall surely revert [to your evil ways]. [Then] on the Day We seize [those who have transgressed] We shall exact Our retribution [on you as well].'

The above *ayāt* emphasize two distinct occurrences:

- Smoke permeating the heavens; and
- The Lord extracting His retribution.

The second is a clear reference to the 'Day of Judgement' during which Allāh Almighty is to hold all those who have transgressed and spread injustice accountable for their deeds. Thus, the first is acknowledged a portent of that day.

2 Portents Referred to in the *Aḥādīth*

a. Ḥuthayfah ibn Usaid al-Ghifari reports that when the Prophet ﷺ saw his companions in an earnest deliberation, he asked what their subject was. Their response, 'The Day of Judgement'. He ﷺ then said, 'This will only occur after ten signs have been observed: The Smoke; The Charlatan [the Antichrist]; The Live Created Being; The Sun rising in the West; The Descent of ʿIsā son of Maryam; Gog and Magog (*Ya'jūj and Ma'jūj*); three major incidences of the earth subsiding (*khasf*), one in the East, one in the West and one in the Arabian peninsula; and, lastly, the fire that pushes all humanity towards resurrection.'[44]

Note: *Khasf* occurs when the earth's 'crust' is not able to withstand dynamic forces that are natural results of corrosion, seismic discontinuity and volcanic activity.

b. Abdullah ibn Abbas reports, 'When we accompanied the Prophet ﷺ on his farewell pilgrimage he ﷺ, whilst holding on to the door of the Kaʿbah, turned to us and asked, 'At this point, would you like to know more about the Portents of the Day of Judgement?' The one of us closest to him at that moment, Salmān, begged him to continue. The Prophet ﷺ then said, 'They are: neglecting to pray; focusing on one's own desires; being party to misinforming the community; showing servile deference to those perceived to have wealth, when predilections for the things of this world take precedence over faith (when these occur, believers will suffer the result of no longer having opportunity to change) . . .'[45]

While the first *ḥadīth* deals with geological portents, the focus of the second is the social aspects of those portents. In other words, the first indicates physical suffering, and the second, both moral and spiritual suffering. There are hundreds of reported *āḥadīth* from the Holy Prophet ﷺ and error-free Imāms عليهم السلام regarding these aspects.

15 Witnesses on the Day of Judgement

On the Day of Judgement, the dead are to be resurrected and assembled in the Court of Divine Justice, 'where records of deeds will be opened'.[46] Each is to be presented with comprehensive evidence of their deeds – large and small. Some will receive theirs in their right hand, others in their left: 'Those whose record is given in their right hand . . . shall be blissful in an exalted garden . . . however, those given it in their left hand will say, "I wish I had not received it . . . my wealth is no longer of any avail and my power and position are dissipated."'[47]

In another *āyah* we learn that some are to be given their record from behind: 'The reckoning of those who receive their records in their right hand will be easily balanced and they will joyfully return to their own people, but those who receive their record from behind, will lament as they enter the flames.'[48]

As in every court of justice, the evidence presented by witnesses is essential to the establishment of the facts of each case. Allāh tells us in the Qur'ān that various witnesses are to have a role in the final judgement. They are:

1. *The Almighty Himself*: An essential aspect of Islāmic belief is Allāh being both Omnipresent and Omniscient. It follows that He is witness to all that occurs here and in the hereafter. He is aware of the manifest and the unseen, His knowledge extends from what is whispered to what is proclaimed and not a thing is hidden from Him.

'Allāh will judge them on the Day of Resurrection, truly Allāh is witness of all things.'[49] In another *āyah*: 'O people of the Book, why do you disbelieve Allāh's signs, when Allāh witnesses all that you do?'[50]

2. *A prophet for each nation*: Allāh tells us that 'on the Day We raise people there will be a witness from amongst themselves – and We will bring you [O Muḥammad] to be witness over them.'[51] This *āyah* indicates that the prophets Allāh appointed to guide different nations will bear witness in the Court of Divine Justice. This establishes that:

    a. Every prophet will bear witness as to how each person in their community responded to the message they delivered.

    b. The trustworthiness and immunity from error of these prophets ensures that only unbiased, accurate and reliable evidence is provided to that court. The *āyah* continues to declare that the Holy Messenger of Islām will bear witness to the evidence given by the other witnesses.

    Being a witness for a whole nation demands all-encompassing knowledge of both the manifest and the unseen, i.e. continued prophetic access to the external and inner secrets of 'all the people of their nation'.

3. *The Muslim nation*: 'Strive in the way of Allāh, who has chosen you and has not laid any religious hardship upon you; this is the faith of your father Ibrāhīm who named you Muslim. The Messenger shall bear witness to the truth before you, so that you may bear witness to it before humankind.'[52] The reason behind such a privileged role for the Muslim nation is explained in Allāh Almighty's words: 'Thus We have made you a justly balanced group [neither materialistic nor ascetic] so that you may be a role model for humankind.'[53] It is clear that that honour is only extended to worthy exemplars of the Muslim community.

4. *Limbs and organs*: Having cited the outside witnesses, Allāh Almighty introduces constituent witnesses, i.e. the limbs and organs. In one *āyah:* 'On the Day when their tongues, hands and feet bear witness against them'.[54] In another: 'On that Day We will seal their mouths for their hands to communicate with Us and their feet to bear witness to all that they have done'.[55] Regardless of the absence of any scientific explanation as to how limbs bear witness, we believe Allāh Almighty to be Omnipotent.

5. *Epidermis*: The Almighty also tells us, 'When Allāh's enemies are driven to The Fire . . . their ears, eyes and skin will bear witness against them. They shall ask their skin, "Why did you testify against me?" And it shall respond, "Allāh, who orders all things, made us speak."'[56]

6. *Angels*: Allāh Almighty appoints two angels to accompany each person, from the time they attain maturity until they breathe their last breath. Their function is to maintain a record of each person's deeds, both good and evil. 'There is no [thought or] word that these solemn recorders do not include [in their Record of Deeds].'[57] And on the 'Final Day', an angel is to propel each one to the Divine Court of Justice, accompanied by another angel who is to be witness for and against them.[58]

7. *The Earth*: Allāh Almighty tells us of the tumultuous earthquake that is to precede the Day of Judgement. 'On that day, [the earth] will yield up all the events that your Lord has revealed to it.'[59] On Allāh Almighty's command, the earth will testify to all the events that ever occurred on it. And, as with fingerprint evidence that identifies those present at crime scenes, the earth will reveal all those who were present when each event occurred. Nowadays, archaeologists regularly inform us about early cultures' societal habits and artefacts, while palaeontologists uncover wildlife that lived and flourished and the reasons for their becoming extinct in different prehistoric periods.

It has been reported that the Prophet ﷺ did not move away from any piece of land without first offering two *rakʿāt* upon it. When asked why this was so, he replied, 'In order for the earth to be able to bear witness for me.'[60] Further, Shaykh Ṭūsi narrates via a reliable chain, on the authority of Abu Darr, that the Prophet ﷺ said, 'O Abu Darr, no person prostrates on any part of the earth without it bearing witness, on the Day of Judgement, that they did so.'[61]

8. *Physical embodiment of deeds*: According to Islāmic teaching, every action that humans make has two distinct aspects: one that corresponds with their materialistic life in this world, the other with everlasting life in the hereafter. Thus, when a believer glorifies Allāh Almighty, one aspect of the words they utter is in the form of the energy utilized in that articulation, the other in the form of materials to be used to construct dwellings in paradise. Similarly, one aspect of wrongdoing is in the form of its physical action, the other is described in *āḥadīth* as 'the darkness of the Day of Judgement'.

Those who accumulate wealth but never contributed to the welfare of others are to be tortured by the very same treasure that they hoarded. 'Those who hoard gold and silver but do not spend any of it in Allāh's way, announce the news of painful chastisement. On the day when it shall be heated in the fire of hell, their foreheads, flanks and backs will be branded with it [while it is said to them]: This is what you hoarded for yourselves, now taste what it was that you hoarded.'[62] It is clear from the above that it is the same treasure that has been hoarded that will turn to flames and inflict punishment. This leads us to an understanding of what is meant by 'the physical embodiment of deeds'. Allāh tells us, 'Those who perform [even] an atom's weight of good shall see it, and those who perform [even] an atom's weight of evil, shall see it.'[63]

16 The Balance

Balance refers literally to equipment used to weigh and value things, from heavy industrial equipment to feather-light items. However, in Qur'ānic terminology, the word 'balance' is used to differentiate between **what is true and what is false** in regard to bodies, words, actions or doctrine. 'He raised the heavens, and set the balance.'[64] Thus, balance here refers to justice. Universal balance in the behaviour of humankind is only to be found in the actions of the error-free entities that exemplify ideal human behaviour.

After all the witnesses called to the Court of Divine Justice have testified, it is by the balance that their every deed is to be measured. 'We shall set up the balances of justice on the Day of Judgement, so that not a soul shall be treated unjustly. Even if there is the weight of a grain of mustard seed, We shall bring it to account and We are sufficient as Reckoner.'[65]

Of course, people's scales will be differently weighed. 'Those with heavy scales [full of good deeds] will be successful and those with light scales [with few good deeds] unsuccessful.'[66]

However, this 'Day's Measurements' must not be imagined to be restricted to beam balance scales, for they will encompass every measurement imaginable, plus some that are far beyond our comprehension. For example, how many of us truly understand the complexity of the scientific and philosophical discourse that attempts to evaluate and measure the importance of each and every minuscule particle and/or aspect of such study? Indeed, do non-specialists have any comprehension whatever of the real meaning of the vocabulary utilized in such endeavours? And this must also apply to everything that has not yet even been exposed to human investigation. Yet Allāh Almighty, the Creator of all things, is fully aware of every aspect of the knowledge that humankind gropes towards. For example, the principle of least action; the laws of motion; universal gravity theory; wave theory; thermodynamics; electromagnetism; and the theory of relativity, **which all relate to the macrocosm**. Atomic theory; quantum mechanics; the uncertainty principle; quantum field theory; quantum entanglement and unification, **that all relate to the microcosm.** Natural selection; sociobiology; and the origin of language **vis-à-vis human evolution.** Psychoanalysis; behaviourism; cognitive psychology; genetic medicine, and the effect of placebos, **that relate to our minds and bodies**. Solar nebula theory; continental drift; global warming and the rare earth hypothesis, **that relate to the planet earth.** The big bang theory; dark matter; dark energy; inflation; the anthropic principle; cosmic topology; parallel worlds; the fate of the universe; the Ekpyrotic universe theory, **that relate to the universe**. And **vis-à-vis knowledge**: information theory; Moore's law; memetics; game theory; chaos theory, etc. etc. etc.

Thus, as the contribution of all manner of assessment, measurement and valuation are comprehended, understood and readily available for use by our Final Arbiter, why would He restrict Himself to the use of beam balance scales?

17 Material Bodies or Immaterial Souls?

Muslim theologians have debated over the centuries whether Allāh Almighty revives us bodily on the 'Day of Resurrection' or if it is only our souls that He resurrects? There is, of course, the third possibility that both are to be resurrected. Despite some philosophers' disdain for the possibility of bodily resurrection, many Qur'ānic *ayāt* – endorsed by interpretations of the Prophet ﷺ – support this opinion. When the *ayāt* 77–79 of Surah 36 were revealed, it is narrated that Ubayy ibn Kaʿb, while crumbling a decayed bone between his fingers, contemptuously demanded of the Prophet ﷺ, 'Do you think that Allāh will revive this bone after it has been reduced to dust?' The Prophet's response was, 'Yes, and He will raise you and send you to hell.' This clarifies Islāmic understanding that both body and soul are to be resurrected.

1 Immateriality of the Soul

In order to obtain a clearer picture of the Islāmic concept of the soul, we need to be aware that Muslim scholars understand human beings to have three dimensions: the body, the spirit and the soul.

All animals have a **body** that has similar functions and characteristics: these are the subjects of scientific research (biology, physiology, medicine, surgery, etc.). The **spirit** is that element that maintains the life of each body. Muslim scholars deem that in the fourth/fifth month of gestation, this spirit is 'breathed' into the fetus – a body that it only departs at its final breath. Although animals are also live, sentient creatures, Allāh Almighty refers specifically to the spirit of humankind 'being breathed into them from His own spirit.'[67] The first two Qur'ānic references are to this spirit being 'breathed into' Adam عليه السلام while the third is a general reference to this spirit being breathed into all of humankind. Vis-à-vis Maryam عليها السلام, Allāh tells us in the Qur'ān, 'We breathed into her from Our spirit.' This is in reference to her conception of the prophet ʿĪsā عليه السلام.[68]

It follows that had Allāh Almighty 'not breathed His spirit into humankind', human beings would not be characteristically different from other animals.

The **soul** is defined as the principle of thought and action in a person, regarded as an entity distinct from the body: a person's spiritual, as opposed to corporeal, nature. It is the centre of consciousness and awareness.

Qur'ānic references talk of the soul having three characteristics:

1. *Ammārah*: that commands satisfaction of physical appetites and ill desires, and encourages them to commit evil deeds.[69] This is the aspect of the soul that is referred to in the English language as the 'ego'.

2. *Lawwāmah*: that censures and reproaches.[70] This is the aspect of the soul that is referred to in the English language as 'conscience'.

3. *Muṭma'innah*: that has been purified and consequently elevated to the state of ultimate tranquillity and, as described by Allāh, 'content with their Lord who is also content with them'.[71]

In order to obtain a clearer picture of the non-materiality of the soul, we need to examine the difference between the corporeal and the non-material, namely:

a. The body/matter: everything corporeal has three dimensions: length, breadth and depth, by which everything that is not material is unable to be measured.

b. The material/corporeal is necessarily governed by space and time, while everything that is immaterial is not confined within those boundaries.

c. The materialistic/corporeal is divisible, but it is not possible to reduce anything that is immaterial into smaller units.

With the above understood, we become conscious that our bodies fulfil all the requirements of the corporeal and materialistic, and that our souls transcend all such limitations. Good examples of this may be found in dreams. All three dimensions of human beings who dream remain constrained by time and space, while their souls are able to travel long distances free of all limitations of time and space. It is souls that convey news from the future, beyond the boundaries of time, that alert the 'dreamer' to matters completely hidden within the 'unseen'. Of course, information made available in such a manner may or may not have clarity. In the latter case, they appear in symbolic forms that are the province of interpreters of dreams. For example, when Yusuf عليه السلام dreamed that the sun, moon and eleven stars prostrated before him, his father cautioned him not to disclose that to his brothers. Many years later, it became clear that that dream had referred to his father and brothers humbling themselves before him, after he had attained high status and authority in the Land of Egypt.

At the time of death both spirit and soul, freed from the immaterial sphere, depart the body. In contrast, during sleep both body and spirit remain restricted and confined by their span of life, while the soul is able to manoeuvre freely. This is mentioned in the following *āyah*:

> It is Allāh who takes souls at the time of death, and in the sleep of those who are still alive. He then withholds those upon whom He has decreed death, and returns the others [to their bodies] for an appointed term. Truly there are signs in this for those who reflect.[72]

2 Qur'ānic References Regarding Physical Resurrection

There are several *ayāt* that make clear that the body of each and every person that has ever lived is to be resurrected. We may examine and categorize these *ayāt* as follows:

a. Qur'ānic references to resurrection as people emerging from their graves. 'The Day when they shall hasten from their graves as if to rush toward a direction indicator.'[73] 'They shall emerge from their graves like a swarm of locusts with eyes downcast.'[74] 'When the Trumpet is blown, they shall hasten to their Lord from their graves.'[75]
   It is clear from all the above that physical bodies will emerge from their graves.

b. Qur'ānic references that confirm people's organs will testify against them. '. . . their hands shall speak to us and their feet shall bear witness to all their doings.'[76] 'Until they arrive [at the gates of hell] their ears, eyes and skin will testify against what they used to do.'[77] '. . . as their skins become charred We shall furnish them with fresh skin . . .'[78]

c. Qur'ānic references about humankind having all been fashioned from the earth to which they are to return. 'We brought you forth [from earth] and We will return you into it – and We will then bring you forth from it a second time.'[79]

3 Qur'ānic References Regarding Spiritual Joy/ Suffering

In addition to bodily resurrection, many *ayāt* refer to psychological elation and depression. For example:

a. *Grief and unhappiness on the 'Day of Judgement'*: Allāh Almighty tells us in the Qur'ān that when those who have earned it face the fires of hell, yet see the bliss of others enjoying the Lord's bounty, they will undergo the most severe grief and depression at having squandered their opportunities during their sojourn on earth. 'When those who were followed see the chastisement and renounce their followers, all ties between them will be severed. Indeed, followers shall claim, "Had there been a return for us, we would have renounced them in the same manner that they renounced us". Thus, Allāh will show their deeds to be [the source of] **intense regret**.'[80]

Intense regret is clearly psychological and not physical.

b. *Meeting the Lord*: On the Day of Judgement, one of the pleasures of the righteous will be the possibility of meeting their Lord. '. . . whoever desires to meet their Lord, let them do good deeds, and not associate others with their Lord during their worship.'[81]

As it is illogical to imagine meeting the Lord to be a physical possibility, some exegetes interpret the above *āyah* as: coming face to face with the Lord's reward or chastisement. However, a more profound interpretation of this *āyah* relates to the enjoyment/joy beyond description that is promised to the righteous. Being transferred from the mundane to the celestial, from darkness to unadulterated light, from misery to elation, is an almost unbearably joyous occurrence that is tantamount to being with the Lord.

c. *The joy of being a pleasure to one's Lord*: 'Allāh has promised believing men and believing women gardens in which rivers flow where they will remain for eternity, with excellent mansions in these gardens of perpetual bliss. But Allāh's goodwill is the supreme achievement – the greatest joy of all.'[82]

Based upon the above we may conclude that resurrection deals with both the material and immaterial aspects of our being.

18 Intercession/Shafā'ah

The concept of intercession has created some confusion in the minds of so-called 'intellectual' Muslims, to the extent that some even establish similitude between intercession and 'cheating in exams'. In order to analyse this concept and its relation to accountability, we need to undertake the following:

a. To classify the Qur'ānic references with regard to intercession.

b. To clarify what precisely is meant by the word 'intercession'.

c. Is there a need for intercession?

d. Conditions before intercession is granted.

e. To respond to confusions regarding intercession.

1 Qur'ānic References with Regard to Intercession

Many Qur'ānic *ayāt* refer to intercession. However, one is only able to comprehend, and arrive at clear conclusions about their precise meanings, after they have been classified into appropriate sections.

Qur'ānic references that reject intercession

Allāh Almighty tells us in the Qur'ān, 'O you who believe, spend from what We have provided you, before the day comes when there shall be no bargaining, no friendship and no intercession – it is those who disbelieve who are the unjust.'[83] Some of the less well-educated only refer to this *āyah* in order to claim that Islām rejects intercession completely. However, another Qur'ānic *āyah* sheds light on those referred to in the one above. In the following *āyah* Allāh excludes 'groups of friends' from chastisement, 'On that day former friends will feel enmity towards one another – other than those who are pious.'[84]

As Muslim scholars unanimously agree, any Qur'ānic reference employed to make a **general** statement may be rendered more **specific** by another *āyah*.

A Qur'ānic reference that refutes a misconception regarding intercession

In addressing the Jews of the Arab peninsula, Allāh Almighty tells them, 'Safeguard yourselves with full awareness of divine laws against the day when no soul will be able to make up for another, no intercession be accepted on its behalf, no ransom be taken from it, nor help be provided it.'[85] This *āyah* was revealed to refute the Children of Isrā'il's claim that they were immune from chastisement on the grounds that 'they are the offspring of the prophets', and thus free to spread mischief and corruption. However, in the above *āyah* Allāh Almighty made clear that that view was false.

Qur'ānic references clarifying that 'idols' cannot intercede

In pre-Islāmic times Arabs worshipped idols, asking them to intercede with the Almighty on their behalf. To reject this practice, Allāh Almighty tells us, in many *ayāt*: 'We do not see you accompanied by the intercessors that you imagined were associated with Us.'[86]

Qur'ānic references clarifying that it is Allāh who intercedes

Allāh Almighty tells us in many *ayāt* that the whole matter of intercession rests with Him. For example, 'Warn those who fear they will be gathered before their Lord without any guardian or intercessor besides Him.'[87] It is an essential Islāmic belief that authority over creation, sustenance and all bounties, in this life and the one to follow, rests with Allāh Almighty Himself. However, there are *ayāt* in which He declares that He has granted specific authority to some of His servants; thus, seeking such assistance from His deputized servants can in no way be interpreted 'as seeking assistance from anyone other than Him'. 'On that day, no intercession shall be possible other than via those to whom *Al-Raḥmān* has granted permission – whose words have been approved by Him.'[88] Necessity for permission to intercede is clearly stated in Qur'ān 2:255, 10:3, 19:87, 34:23 and 43:86.

Indeed, it is clear that Allāh commanded His Final Messenger,[89] 'And forsake sleep for [part] of the night in order to offer additional prayers, for your Lord may well raise you to an honourable position.' All exegetes concur that the Prophet's honourable position is nothing other than his having been granted the authority to intercede.

To conclude, analysis of all the Qur'ānic references that refer to intercession leads to understanding of there being two categories in which intercession is mentioned: acceptable intercession offered by Allāh Almighty and His deputized servants; and hoped-for intercession via idols or belief in the specialness of one's position – that are not valid.

2 What Is Meant by the Word 'Intercession'?

Intercession corresponds to the Arabic word *Shafāʿah,* which is derived from the three-lettered root *sh/f/ʿ*. In Arabic, this refers to someone or something that is accompanied or assisted by another/being part of a pair/or an even number. All the above meanings gather around one aspect, namely joining together to achieve an effective result. Such effectiveness may be observed both in nature and in legislative systems.

Effectiveness in nature is evidenced by the link between natural causes and their effect. In spite of all natural causes maintaining the order of the universe, they only do this with the support of the Omnipotent. Interestingly, Allāh Almighty uses the term *Shafī‘* (intercessor) in referring to natural causes. 'Your Lord is Allāh who created the heavens and the earth in six days and is firmly established on the throne. He regulates everything, no intercessor exists without His permission.'[90] In the following Qur'ānic quotations it is clearly observed that natural causes only function within the authority granted by Allāh:

a. In Qur'ān 26:80, both cure and remedy are recognized to be the work of Allāh, while in 16:61 honey is named as a remedy.

b. In Qur'ān 39:42, taking souls at the time of death is an act by Allāh; however, in 32:11 this task is undertaken by the Angel of Death.

c. In Qur'ān 56:64, in spite of farming and cultivation being recognized as the action of human beings, Allāh clearly states that He has caused all vegetation to flourish.

The effectiveness of legislative systems is evidenced in the *āyah* that considers pardons granted by Allāh to be possible only when seeking His forgiveness, alongside the Holy Messenger ﷺ seeking forgiveness on their behalf. 'When they [people] who had been unjust to themselves come to you to seek Allāh's forgiveness, the Messenger [also] asks for them to be pardoned; they will frequently find Allāh to be forgiving and merciful.'[91]

The above *āyah* clarifies that Allāh's mercy, forgiveness and bounty reach His servants via those whom He has chosen. It is thus no wonder that 'His chosen ones' are granted permission to intercede on the Day of Judgement.

3 Is There Need for Intercession?

It may be imagined that as long as believers observe all their religious duties and commit themselves to do good and refrain from evil actions, they will attain the salvation and prosperity of the Day of Judgement. In the light of this, is there any need for intercession?

In clarification, we need to learn that in spite of salvation being dependent on one's own actions, these also need to 'Encompass Allāh's Mercy' in order for us to achieve comprehensive guidance and salvation. In this context, many believers with spiritual comprehension would beseech Allāh to treat them with **His Mercy rather than by His justice**. This is affirmed in Allāh's statement, 'If Allāh were to seize people on the grounds of what they have done, there would not be a single living soul left on the surface [of the earth].[92]

Furthermore, belief in intercession provides tranquillity and justified hope for His true servants, in similar manner to the tranquillity that repentance provides. For those who have sinned and firmly determine to forgo their old habits and turn their lives around, the promise of being pardoned and the hope for intercession provide important motivations in their decision-making. Of course, reliance upon intercession without positive action is not effective.

4 Conditions before Intercession Is Granted

Within the corpus of *aḥādīth* of the Prophet ﷺ and error-free Imāms عليهم السلام there are many references that lay down the conditions to be met before entitlement to intercession is granted. These include:

a. not to associate anyone with Allāh

b. to have sincerely declared the *Shahādatain*

c. to have avoided all types of deceit

d. not to have harboured enmity towards *Ahul Bait*

e. not to neglect daily prayer

f. not to deny that the Prophet ﷺ was granted the right of intercession

5 Confusion Regarding Intercession

a. Muḥammad Rashid Riḍa, a well-known *Azhari* scholar, stated that no clear Qur'ānic text exists to indicate that intercession has ever occurred, only that there is the merest possibility of it.[93]

Response: In the Qur'ān, Allāh clearly states that He is pleased with the intercession of those He has chosen.[94] This confirms that He has already granted His permission for them to intercede. In the Qur'ān[95] Allāh Almighty guarantees the intercession offered by those who bear witness to truth after they have discovered it. What could possibly be clearer?

b. Muḥammad Farid Wajdi, the author of the Arabic-language *Encyclopaedia of the 20th Century*, claims that 'intercession encourages sinners to feel free to commit whatever crimes they wish, in expectation of their evil actions being erased via intercession'.[96]

Response: Such an argument would surely also apply to 'repentance' – emphasized in many Qur'ānic *ayāt*. If the above argument invalidates the need for intercession, it would also negate the validity of repentance. However, Allāh tells us, 'He does not forgive those who associate any with Him, but that He pardons everything other than that.'

Conditions apply prior to intercession being granted – explained above – that make it clear that entitlement to *Shafāʿah* is not unconditional. For example, just before his death, Imām Ṣādiq (ع) told his gathered relatives, 'Our *Shafāʿah* does not cover those who have abandoned regular daily prayer'.[97]

c. Muḥammad Rashid Riḍa claimed, 'References regarding *Shafāʿah* are ambiguous and as such do not provide access to its reality. We must thus believe that Allāh is far from the ordinary person's understanding of the concept of *Shafāʿah*.'[98]

Response: With an abundance of Qur'ānic references concerning intercession and a detailed methodology for its classification, it is astounding for someone to make claim of there being any 'ambiguity' concerning this subject!

It is important to comprehend that seeking intercession from the Prophet ﷺ or error-free Imāms عليهم السلام has nothing whatever to do with '*shirk*', as has been incorrectly stated by some. Rather, it falls within the criteria of 'reliance upon Allāh's permission', granted to those who have been chosen and approved by Him to intercede on our behalf.

> When they [people] who had been unjust to themselves come to you to seek Allāh's forgiveness, the Messenger [also] asks for them to be pardoned, and they will frequently find Allāh to be forgiving and merciful.[99]

19 Paradise and Hell

There are approximately 135 Qur'ānic *ayāt* regarding Paradise (*Jannah*) being a reward for those who believe and undertake good deeds. Vis-à-vis Hell (*Jahannam*) being a consequence of evil deeds being committed, there are approximately 77 *ayāt*, plus a further 136 *ayāt* that specifically refer to 'The Fire' (*Nār*).

'Reward' is accompanied by profoundly described detail of 'bliss' and 'joy', with similar detail being provided for 'suffering'. Some question if both Paradise and Hell already exist or if they are to be created later.

1 Arguments that Support the Existence of Both Paradise and Hell

This is the position held by both the Imāmiyah and the Ashʿarites, based upon the many Qur'ānic *ayāt* that refer to Paradise as an abode that has been prepared for those who become eligible:

> Vie one with another in hastening [to obtain] your Lord's forgiveness and Paradise – as wide as are the heavens and the earth – prepared for those who are pious'.[100]

> Vie in hastening towards your Lord's forgiveness and a garden of expanse as wide as that of the heavens and the earth, that

has been prepared for those who believe in Allāh and His messengers.[101]

The garden shall be brought near for the pious.[102]

The use of the word 'prepared' indicates that Paradise already exists. Allāh tells us that during the Prophet Muḥammad's Night Journey he saw the Eternal Abode referred to as Paradise, with the Lote-tree at its utmost boundary.[103]

It must be noted that the word 'prepared' is also used in the Qur'ān to refer to 'The Fire' that has been prepared for those who disbelieve.[104]

2 Arguments Used to Negate the Existence of Paradise and Hell

This is the position held by the Zaidis and the Muʿtazilites (with the exception of Abu Hashim), who base their views on the following:

a. It might be said that there is no point in the existence of Paradise and Hell as both are consequences that only become viable after the Day of Judgement.

   Response: such argument is nullified by the above Qur'ānic references.

b. Some claim that every created entity is to perish in time. Had Paradise and Hell already been created, it would follow that they too will one day perish. Their everlasting nature would not leave room for that conclusion.

   Response: In Allāh Almighty's statement, 'Every created entity is to perish', He refers to the materialistic nature of creation that has nothing whatever to do with the characteristics of the 'Hereafter' – Paradise, Hell and everything related to the 'World to Come' are eternal and without limit.

c. Others claim that were Paradise and Hell to exist, they would occupy space that this physical universe cannot accommodate.

Response: Do these also claim to have surveyed the ever-expanding universes to have arrived at certainty about the totality of space? Those who believe in Allāh 'The Omnipotent' whose power is not curtailed by restrictions, logically conclude that, within His 'Ultimate Authority', the availability of space poses little problem.

3 Characteristics that Distinguish Paradise from Hell

Throughout the Holy Qur'ān, bounty and bliss are promised to those who are to be sent to Paradise, and severe punishment is promised to those who are to be sent to Hell. A few examples for each of these groups:

a. *Regarding the manner in which Angels are said to treat each group*: For those destined to be sent to Hell (*Jahannam)*: 'You shall see, when Angels draw out the souls of those who have disbelieved and smite them on their faces and backs [saying] taste the torments of the fire – sent forth by your own hands – and Allāh does not wrong His servants.'[105]

For those destined to be sent to Paradise (*Jannah*), 'They will enter gardens of eternity beneath which rivers flow and in which they shall have all that they desire. In such manner Allāh rewards the pious, from whom His Angels will gently draw souls saying, "Peace be upon you as reward for your good deeds, please now enter the garden."'[106]

b. *Regarding the manner in which each group is to arrive at its final destination*: Those destined to be sent to Hell: 'Hordes of disbelievers will be herded to the gates of Hell that will open on their arrival. Those in charge will ask, "Did not Messengers from among you recite your Lord's messages that warn of the coming of this day?" To which their response will be, "Yes." Just sentences have been levied against disbelievers, who will be told, "Enter the gates of Hell and dwell within them for ever."'[107]

Those destined for Paradise, who safeguarded themselves from evil in full awareness of the Lord's command, shall be led towards the garden whose gates will be open to them. Those in charge will welcome them saying, "Peace be with you, be happy to enter this abode and remain forever."'[108]

c. *Regarding the joys of Paradise*: 'Those of the right hand [whose right hands receive the record of their deeds] will enjoy Lote trees that have no thorns, acacia fruits in orderly bunches, abundant shade, ever-flowing water, and fruits that neither diminish nor are forbidden [as they relax] upon exalted thrones.'[109]

d. *Regarding the suffering in Hell*: 'They will have nothing to eat other than pus [viscid yellowish-white or greenish liquid produced in infected tissue].[110] 'They shall be made to drink from a boiling spring and have nothing to eat other than bitter-thorns that neither satisfy nor nourish.'[111]

4 Evil Actions that Lead to Eternal Chastisement

Even though all who commit evil deeds are to be held accountable on the Day of Judgement, only a few of the acts that lead to eternal chastisement are mentioned in the Qur'ān, such as:

a. The killing of a believer: 'The requital of those who intentionally kill a believer shall be to remain in Hell to face Allāh's wrath and curse.'[112]

b. 'Those whose lives are encompassed by sin, and commit evil deeds for which they do not repent, will inhabit the fire for eternity.'[113]

Similar chastisements for wrongdoing keep Muslims' focus on their Lord's commands and prohibitions and removed from sin. May Allāh enable us to behave always in a manner that pleases Him.

Notes to Part Five

1 Qur'ān 11:7.
2 Qur'ān 50:2–3.
3 Qur'ān 2:156.
4 Qur'ān 75:12.
5 Qur'ān 75:30.
6 Qur'ān 53:42.
7 *Nahj al-Balāghah*, Sermon 203.
8 Qur'ān 87:16–19.
9 Qur'ān 23:115.
10 Qur'ān 2:30.
11 Qur'ān 67:2.
12 Qur'ān 51:56.
13 Qur'ān 38:27.
14 Qur'ān 45:21.
15 Qur'ān 23:115.
16 Qur'ān 57:25.
17 Qur'ān 40:17.
18 Qur'ān 53:31.
19 Qur'ān 10:44.
20 Qur'ān 41:46.
21 Qur'ān 2:260.
22 Qur'ān 2:159.
23 Qur'ān 2:243.

24 Qur'ān 2:67–73.
25 Qur'ān 2:55–56 and 7:155.
26 Qur'ān 3:49 and 5:110.
27 Qur'ān 18:10–12.
28 Qur'ān 55:5–7.
29 Qur'ān 55:9.
30 Qur'ān 57:25.
31 Qur'ān 38:28.
32 Qur'ān 40:17.
33 Qur'ān 10:44.
34 Qur'ān 41:46.
35 *'Ayn al-Yaqīn,* by Allāmah Majlisi, p. 422.
36 Qur'ān 47:18.
37 Qur'ān 18:94–97. The word 'dam' is here used in the sense of it being a construction or barrier to effectively seal a mountain gorge – to hold back and stop incursions of pillage and plunder by barbarian tribes who dwelt on one side of a mountain range – in order to protect the populations that dwelt on the other side, thought to be the peaceful, industrious inhabitants of Armenia and Azerbaijan. Ezekiel used these names for a mysterious, probably symbolic enemy of Isrā'il, against whom God 'will summon every kind of terror'. The Book of Revelation mentions Gog and Magog as 'the nations which are at the four corners of the earth whom Satan deceives and leads to battle'. See: Ezekiel 38:2, 18 and Revelation 20:8.
38 Qur'ān 18:98–99.
39 Qur'ān 21:96–97.
40 Qur'ān 43:57–61.
41 Qur'ān 27:82–87
42 For deeper discussion with regard to the above, please refer to:
Tafsīr al-Ṭabari, Vol. 20, pp. 10–12;
Al Durr al-Manthūr, Vol. 5, p. 116;
Tafsīr al-Burhān, Vol. 3, pp. 209–211;
Tafsīr al-Mizān, Vol. 15, pp. 395–397.
43 Qur'ān 44:10–16.
44 *Jāmi' al Usūl,* by Tirmithi, Vol. 11, p. 87;

Biḥār al-Anwār, Vol. 6, p. 303.

45 *Ibid.*, Vol. 6, pp. 305–9.

46 Qur'ān 81:10.

47 Qur'ān 69:19–29.

48 Qur'ān 84:7–12.

49 Qur'ān 22:17.

50 Qur'ān 3:98.

51 Qur'ān 16:89.

52 Qur'ān 22:78.

53 Qur'ān 2:143.

54 Qur'ān 24:24.

55 Qur'ān 36:65.

56 Qur'ān 41:19–21.

57 Qur'ān 50:18.

58 Qur'ān 50:21.

59 Qur'ān 99:4–5.

60 *Al-Mizān*, Vol. 6, p. 337.

61 *Wasā'il al-Shī'ah*, Vol. 4, p. 474.

62 Qur'ān 9:34–35.

63 Qur'ān 90:7–8.

64 Qur'ān 55:7.

65 Qur'ān 21:47.

66 Qur'ān 7:8–9.

67 Qur'ān 15:29, 38:72 and 32:9.

68 Qur'ān 21:91 and 66:13.

69 Qur'ān 12:53.

70 Qur'ān 75:2.

71 Qur'ān 89:27.

72 Qur'ān 39:42.

73 Qur'ān 70:43.

74 Qur'ān 54:7.

75 Qur'ān 36:51.

76 Qur'ān 36:65.

77 Qur'ān 41:20.

78 Qur'ān 4:56.

79 Qur'ān 20:55.

80 Qur'ān 2:166–167.

81 Qur'ān 18:110.

82 Qur'ān 9:72.

83 Qur'ān 2:254.

84 Qur'ān 43:67.

85 Qur'ān 2:48.

86 Qur'ān 6:94, 10:18, 30:13 and 39:43.

87 Qur'ān 6:51, 6:7, 32:4 and 39:44.

88 Qur'ān 20:109.

89 Qur'ān 17:79.

90 Qur'ān 10:3.

91 Qur'ān 4:64.

92 Qur'ān 35:45.

93 *Tafsīr Al-Manār*, Vol. 7, p. 370.

94 Qur'ān 21:28.

95 Qur'ān 43:86.

96 *Encyclopaedia of the 20th Century*, Vol. 5, p. 402.

97 *Al-Kāfi*, Vol. 3, p. 270.

98 *Tafsīr Al-Manār*, Vol. 1, p. 308.

99 Qur'ān 4:64.

100 Qur'ān 3:133.

101 Qur'ān 57:21.

102 Qur'ān 26:90.

103 Qur'ān 53:14–15.

104 Qur'ān 3:131.

105 Qur'ān 8:50–51.

106 Qur'ān 16:32–33.

107 Qur'ān 39:71–72.

108 Qur'ān 39:73.

109 Qur'ān 56:28–34.

110 Qur'ān 69:36.

111 Qur'ān 88:5–7.

112 Qur'ān 4:93.

113 Qur'ān 2:81.

Glossary of Islāmic Theological Terms

Note: The article Al-, meaning 'the', is an essential part of all the Divine Names in this Glossary. As for all other terms, the article Al- appears in brackets at the end of the term in the headword.

Abadiyyah eternity, without end.
'Adam nothingness/non-existence.
Aḥad unique.
Aḥādīth See **ḥadīth.**
Ahl al-Bayt the household/progeny of the Prophet Muḥammad ﷺ.
Ahlul Sunnah Sunni Muslims.
Aḥwāl levels of attainment of a spiritual journey or of spiritual states.
'Ajz inability, impotence.
Al-'Adl The Just.
Al-'Afūw The Pardoner.
Al-Ākhir The Last.
Al-'Alīm The Omniscient.
Al-'Aliyy The Most High.
Al-Awwal The First.
Al-'Aẓīm The Supremely Glorious.
Al-'Azīz The Eminent (The Almighty).
Al-Bāqī The Everlasting.
Al-Bārī The Originator.
Al-Barr The Source of All Goodness.

Al-Baṣīr The All-Seeing.

Al-Ghafūr The All-Forgiving.

Al-Hādī The Guide.

Al-Ḥāfiẓ The Best Preserver.

Al-Ḥaqq The Ultimate Truth.

Al-Ḥayy The Ever-Living.

Al-Jalāl Majesty.

Al-Jalīl The Majestic.

Al-Karīm The Generous, The Noble.

Al-Khabīr The Most Aware.

Al-Malik The King (Sovereign).

Al-Muṣawwir The Fashioner.

Al-Nūr The Light.

Al-Qayyūm The Self-Subsisting.

Al-Raḥīm The Most Merciful.

Al-Raḥmān The Beneficent.

Al-Razzāq The Provider.

Al-Ṣamad The One Able to Satisfy All Needs.

Al-Wājib an abbreviation for **Wājib al-Wujūd** – Necessary Existent.

Ammārah psyche that encourages evil actions.

Amr bayn al-Amrayn (Al-) the doctrine of negation of both predestination and total delegation.

Anṣār helpers: those inhabitants of Madinah who supported migrants from Makkah.

ʻAqidah tenets of faith.

ʻAql human intellect.

ʻAraḍ accident, as opposed to substance.

ʻArsh The Throne.

Ashʻarites followers of Abul Ḥasan al-Ashʻari, who was born in Baṣrah in the year 260 AH. His School of Theology was based upon textual sources rather than intellectual reasoning.

Ashrāṭ al-Sāʻah portents of the Day of Judgement.

ʻAshūrā tenth day of the first month of the Islāmic calendar, refers to the martyrdom of Imām Ḥusayn عليه السلام and his companions.

Āthār (pl. of **athar**) trace, effect.
Āyah (pl. **ayāt**) lit. a sign. As a Qur'ānic term, a verse.
Āyat al-Kursī the Throne Āyah, Qur'ān 2:255.
Āyat al-Wilayah *Āyah* 55 of Surah 5 in the Qur'ān.
Azaliyyah with no beginning.
Baṣar sight, seeing.
Baṣāṭah maḥḍah absolute simplicity.
Bayt al-Māl Muslim treasury.
Bid'ah innovation.
Burhān al-Tamānu' theological argument to prove the 'Oneness' of God.
Buṭlān falsehood/invalidity.
Dābbah (pl. **dawābb**) any living entity that moves, normally used to refer to cattle.
Dajjāl Antichrist.
Dhikr remembrance, communication with our Lord.
Dhul-Jalāl wal-ikrām The One Full of Majesty, Bounty and Honour.
Du'a supplication/prayer.
Fāliq al-ḥabb wa al-nawā The One who splits seeds and grain to permit growth to emerge and further develop.
Fiṭrah (lit. 'primordial nature') innate instinct.
Furū' branches.
Ghaḍab wrath/anger.
Ghayb hidden/unseen.
Ḥādith contingent.
Ḥadīth (pl. **aḥādīth**) a saying of the Prophet صلى الله عليه وآله or error-free Imāms عليهم السلام.
Ḥadīth Qudsi the content of a *ḥadīth* attributed to Allāh Almighty by the Prophet صلى الله عليه وآله without it being a part of the Qur'ān.
Ḥājah need.
Ḥāl an intermediate state between existence and non-existence.
Ḥaqīqiyyah dhāt iḍāfah essential with relational aspects.
Ḥaqīqiyyah maḥḍah absolutely essential.
Ḥarakah al-jawharriyyah (Al-) substantial motion.
Ḥashawiyah anthropomorphists.
Ḥawzāt (pl. of **ḥawzah**) traditional Shi'ah theological colleges.

Ḥayāt life.
Ḥijāb curtain/barrier.
Ḥikmah wisdom.
Ḥujjah (Al-) the proof of Allāh.
Iḍāfiyyah maḥḍah absolutely relational.
Idrāk perception.
Iḍṭirār dependency.
Iḥsān doing good, kindness.
Iḥyā' life-giving.
Ijmā' consensus.
'Ilm knowledge.
'Ilm Ḥuḍūri knowledge by presence (rather than by reflection).
'Ilm Ḥuṣūli reflective knowledge based upon the five senses, acquired knowledge.
'Ilm 'Ijmāli summarized knowledge.
'Ilm 'Inā'i foreknowledge.
'Ilm Tafṣili detailed knowledge.
Imāmah Divine Leadership.
Imāmi/Imāmiyah Muslims who rely upon Islāmic teachings transmitted via the error-free Imāms of the Prophet's household.
Imāms twelve divine leaders appointed by the Prophet to lead the Muslim community.
Imātah to cause to die.
Imkān possibility.
Imtinā' impossibility.
Intiqām retaliation, vengefulness.
'Iqāb chastisement/punishment, retribution.
Irādah wanting, will.
Irādah Takwiniyah creative will.
Irādah Tashri'iyah legislative will.
Irzāq to provide; grant substance.
'Iṣmah immunity from error.
Iṭlāq absoluteness; in Islāmic jurisprudence, it may refer to an unconditional concept.

Ittiḥād unity between two or more entities.
'Izzah glory, might, high ranking, preciousness.
Jabr predestination.
Jabr al-'Illī wal Ma'lūlī (Al-) causal necessity that brings into existence an effect once the requirements of the cause have been met.
Jahannam hell.
Jāhiliyah pre-Islāmic era.
Jahl ignorance.
Jalāl majesty.
Jamāl magnificence.
Janāzah a dead human body.
Jannah paradise.
Jawhar substance as opposed to accident.
'Jihad striving.
Jism body/physical entity.
Juz'iyyāt specific concepts, particulars.
Kalām speech; as a technical term it refers to Islāmic theology.
Kalām al-Nafsi (Al-) internal speech.
Kalām Ṭayyib logical and beneficial advice.
Karāhiyyah dislike, antipathy.
Karāmiyah anthropomorphists headed by Muḥammad ibn Kirām, who believed that God has a body and limits.
Kasb acquisition.
Khabīth foul/filthy.
Khair good, goodness.
Khalq creation.
Khasf sinkhole.
Khayr Ḥaqiqi real goodness.
Khilāfah succession to the Prophet.
Kulliyāt universal concepts.
Kursi seat/chair; as a technical term in theology, it refers to Allāh's status.
Lā ilaha illa Lāh there is no divinity other than Allāh.
Lawwāmah the conscience that brings awareness after committing a wrong deed.

Laylat al-Qadr the night of destiny and measure.

Laysa nāqiṣan without any shortcoming or imperfection.

Lā yurā not seen.

Luṭf grace.

Luṭfiyyah (*ṣifah*) a graceful attribute.

Maʿanī ideas.

Mafhūm concept.

Maghfirah being pardoned, forgiveness.

Maḥall li al-ḥawādith being a centre for contingencies.

Māhiyyah quiddity.

Māhiyyāt mumkinah possible or contingent quiddities.

Malak angel.

Malik king.

Mālik owner.

Maʿlūliyyah having being caused.

Manzilah bayn al-Manzilatayn (Al-) the intermediate position, a Muʿtazilite principle.

Mashī'ah or **Mashiyyah** willing, a decree.

Mashshā'ūn peripatetic philosophers.

Masīḥ a reference to the prophet ʿIsa عليه السلام/messiah.

Maṣlaḥah interest/benefit.

Mawlā guardian, being in charge, master, as in 'ʿAli عليه السلام is mawlā'. In Arabic lexicons it has 22 different homonyms. However, it needs to be defined by the context.

Melk property.

Miṣdāq substantiation of a concept.

Mishkāt niche.

Muʿallaqāt in the pre-Islāmic era, celebrated poetry hung on the walls of the Kaʿbah.

Muʿattilites agnostics.

Mufawwiḍah delegationists.

Muhājerūn/Muhājerīn Muslims who migrated from Makkah to join the Prophet صلى الله عليه وآله وسلم in Madinah.

Muḥkam resolute, firm.

Muḥtāj in need.

Mujabbirah determinists, a title for those who believe that because Allāh is the Creator He also creates our actions.

Mūjid The One who brings something into existence.

Mu'jiz miracle.

Mukāshafah inspiration; disclosure.

Mukhtār free agent.

Mulk see **Melk**.

Mumkin al-wujūd possible existent.

Mumkināt possible existents.

Muqayyad qualified statement or concept.

Murakkab composite.

Mushrik one who associates others with Allāh (see **Shirk**).

Mutakallimūn Muslim theologians.

Mutashābihāt equivocal *ayāt* of the Qur'ān.

Mu'tazilites a school of Sunni theologians who are known as 'defenders of reason' rather than defenders of textual sources. Al-Naẓẓām is the most outstanding scholar of this school.

Muṭlaq unconditional or unrestricted concept.

Muṭma'innah psyche immersed in tranquillity.

Mutqan perfect.

Nafs self/soul.

Nafs al-Zakiyah (Al-) the purified soul.

Nār fire.

Naṣṣ text/unequivocal text.

Nidiyyah similarity.

Nubuwwah Prophethood.

Nudrah rarity.

Qadar fate.

Qādir omnipotent.

Qahriyyah (*ṣifah*) forceful attribute.

Qā'im (Al-) the one who will arise, a title for the Twelfth Imām عليه السلام.

Qaṣd intent.

Qidam dhātī without beginning and without end.

Qudrah power.

Qudūsiyyah holiness.

Rabb al-'Alamīn The Lord of the Worlds.

Rāfiḍah an abusive term directed at Shi'ah.

Raḥmah mercy.

Ṣadaqah a voluntary payment or good action for a charitable purpose.

Ṣalāh/Ṣalāt the canonical form of Islāmic daily prayer.

Sam' hearing.

Sardāb basement or cellar, a reference to the Eleventh Imām's house, from which it was assumed the Twelfth Imām disappeared.

Satr a veil.

Ṣayḥah a loud call being heard before the appearance of Al-Mahdi عليه السلام.

Shadīd al'iqāb severe in punishment.

Shafā'ah intercession.

Shafī' intercessor.

Shahādatain declaration of the two tenets of faith: belief in Allāh Almighty and the Prophet Muḥammad صلى الله عليه وآله وسلم as His final messenger.

Shari'ah Islāmic Law.

Sharīk partner.

Shirk associating partners or ascribing divine qualities to other than Allāh.

Ṣidq veracity.

Ṣifah (pl. **ṣifāt**) attribute.

Ṣifah idāfiyyah relational attribute.

Ṣifah kamāliyyah attribute that reflects perfection.

Ṣifāt al-dhāt attributes of essence.

Ṣifāt al-Dhātiyyah al-Thubūtiyyah (Al-) positive attributes that are aspects of Divine Essence.

Ṣifāt al-Fi'l attributes of action.

Ṣifāt al-Kamāl perfective attributes.

Ṣifāt al-Khabariah (Al-) attributes referred to Allāh in the Qur'ān and *ḥadīth*.

Ṣifāt al-Naqṣ attributes that might indicate imperfection.

Ṣifāt al-Nisbiyyah (Al-) relative attributes.

Ṣifāt al-Salbiyyah (Al-) privative attributes.
Ṣifāt thubūtiyyah affirmative attributes.
Subḥan Allāh glory be to Allāh.
Subḥanahu Immaculate is He.
Ṣūfī Ṭuruq orders of mysticism.
Sufyānī a trouble-maker who, it is predicted, will cause tremendous bloodshed shortly before the end of time.
Ṣunʿ fashioning.
Sūrah a division of the Qur'ān.
Taʿalā high above (in reference to Allāh Almighty).
Tābiʿūn the generation that followed after the companions.
Ṭafrah a disconnect in the chain of causes.
Tafsīr critical explanation, commentary or exegesis of the Qur'ān.
Tafwīḍ delegation.
Tahlīl the utterance of *Lā ilaha illa Lāh.*
Tajarrud immateriality.
Takallum speech.
Tanzīhiyyah (*ṣifah*) transcendent attribute.
Tasalsul infinite regress.
Tasbiḥāt the utterance of *Subḥan Allāh.*
Tashbihiyyah attributes that may suggest similitude between divine and human attributes.
Tashbīh making a similitude between two things, anthropomorphism.
Tawḥīd belief in the Divine Unity of Allāh, Oneness.
Tawqīʿ (pl. **Tawqīʿāt**) lit. signature; in reference to the minor occultation of the Twelfth Imām, it indicates his signed correspondence.
Tawqīfiyyah (*ṣifah*) suprarational attribute.
Ṭayyib wholesome.
Ummi the unlettered one.
Urafā' mystics.
Uṣūl al-Din the roots or tenets of the faith.
Wāḥid the numeral 1.
Waḥy revelation.
Waḥy kāmil complete revelation.

Waḥy takwīnī creative revelation.

Waliyy guardian, either biological or authoritative.

Waṣiy the executor of a will/vicegerent.

Wujūb necessity; in jurisprudence, it means something that is obligatory.

Wujūd al-khāriji (Al-) external/physical existence.

Zabūr Psalms of Dāwūd عليه السلام.

Ẓāhir that which is manifest.

Ẓāhiriyyah (Al-) the literalist school of Islāmic Law.

Zaidis followers of Zaid ibn ʿAli ibn Ḥusayn, who believed that he, rather than his brother Muḥammad al-Baqir عليه السلام, was eligible for the Imāmah.

Zakāh/Zakāt an Islamic religious annual welfare tax due on specific commodities.

Bibliography

Aḥmad ibn Ḥanbal: *Al-Musnad*. Cairo: Maymaniyah, 1313 AH.

Amin Razavi, M.: *Suhrawardi and the School of Illumination*. London: Curzon, 1995.

Aminī, Abdul Ḥusayn: *Al-Ghadīr* (11 volumes). Beirut: Dar al-Kitab al-Arabi, 1386 AH.

Ash'arī (Al-), Abul Ḥasan: *Al-Ibānah 'an Uṣūl al-Diyānah*. Damascus: Dar al-Bayān, 1981.

——*Maqālāt al-Islāmiyīn*. Istanbul, 1939.

Averroes: *On the Harmony of Religions and Philosophy*. tr. George Hourani. London: Luzac, 1967.

Avicenna: *Kitab al-Shifā*, ed. M. Y. Mūsā and S. Zāyid, Introduction by Madkūr. Cairo, 1960.

——*Al-Ishārāt wal-Tanbīhāt*. Cairo, 1957.

Ayer, A. J.: *The Problem of Knowledge*. London: Penguin, 1990.

Badawi, Abdul Raḥmān: *Al-Mu'tazilah wal Ashā'irah*. Beirut, 1971.

Balkhi (Al-), Abul Qasim: *Faḍl al-I'tizāl wa Ṭabāqāt al-Mu'tazilah*. Al Dar al-Tunisiyah, 1974.

Brown, David: *Trinity*, in *A Companion to the Philosophy of Religion*, ed. Philip L. Quinn and Charles Taliaferro. Oxford: Blackwell, 1997.

Corbin, H.: *History of Islamic Philosophy*, tr. L. Sherrard. London: Kegan Paul International, 1993.

Davies, Brian: *An Introduction to the Philosophy of Religion*. Oxford: Oxford University Press, 1982.

Dhanani, A.: *Muslim Philosophy and the Sciences*, in *The Muslim Almanac* ed. Azim A. Nanji. Detroit: Gale Research, 1996.

Fakhri, M.: *A History of Islamic Philosophy*. New York: Columbia University Press, 1983.

—— *Islamic Philosophy, Theology and Mysticism*. Oxford: Oneworld, 1997.

Ghazāli (Al-), Abu Ḥāmid: *Iḥyā' 'Ulūm al-Din*. Cairo, 1348 AH.

Greene, Brian: *The Fabric of the Cosmos: Space, Time and the Texture of Reality*. New York: Columbia University Press, 2004.

Gutas, D.: *Avicenna and the Aristotelian Tradition*. Leiden: E. J. Brill, 1988.

Hāiri Yazdi, M.: *The Principles of Epistemology in Islamic Philosophy*. Tehran, 1982.

Haldane, E. S. and Ross, G. R. T. (tr.): *The Philosophical Works of Descartes*. New York: Dover, 1955.

Ḥamawini Shafi'i: *Farā'id al-Simṭain*, ed. Muḥammad Baqir Maḥmūdi. Beirut, 1398 AH.

Ḥāmid Ḥusayn: *'Abaqāt al-Anwār fi Ithbāt Imāmat al-A'immah al-Aṭhār*, tr. Sayyid 'Ali Milani as *Nafaḥāt al-Azhār* (20 volumes). Qum: Mehr, 1414 AH.

Hartshorne, C.: *Anselm's Discovery*. Lasalle: Open Court, 1965.

Haythami (Al-): *Majma' al-Zawā'id*. Cairo, 1328 AH.

Hick, John: *Philosophy of Religion*. Birmingham: University of Birmingham Press, 1973.

Ḥilli (Al-), Al-Hasan ibn Yusuf: *Al-Babul Ḥadi 'Ashar*, tr. W. M. Miller as *A Treatise on the Principles of Shi'ite Theology*. London: Royal Asiatic Society, 1928.

——*Kashf al-Murād fi Sharḥ Tajrīd al-I'tiqād*. Beirut: Mu'assast al-A'lami, 1408 AH.

Holy Bible, The, New Revised Standard Version, Minster Text Edition. Cambridge: Cambridge University Press, 1992.

Ḥosaini, Abdul Zahra: *Maṣādir Nahj al-Balāghah wa Asāniduhu*. Beirut, 1395 AH.

Hourani, G.: 'Ibn Sinā on Necessary and Possible Existence', *Philosophical Forum* 4, 1972.

Ibn Abi al-Ḥadīd, ʿIzzuldin: *Sharḥ Nahj al-Balāghah*. Cairo: Al-Bābi al-Ḥalibi, 1385 AH.

Ibn al-Athīr, Majd al-Din: *Jāmiʿ al-Uṣūl*. Cairo: Al-Sunnah al-Muḥammadiyah Press, 1368 AH.

Ibn al-Athīr, ʿAli ibn Muḥammad: *Usd al-Ghābah fi Maʿrifat al-Ṣaḥābah*. Cairo, 1285 AH.

Ibn Bābawayh, ʿAli ibn al-Ḥusayn al Qummi: *Al-Imāmah wal Tabṣirah min al-Ḥairah*. Beirut: Mu'assast Āl-al Bayt, 1407 AH.

Ibn Ḥazm: *Al Feṣal fi al-Milal wal-Niḥal*. Cairo, 1317 AH.

Ibn al-Ṣabbāgh al-Māliki: *Al-Fuṣūl al-Muhimmah*. Dar al-Hadith, 1422 AH.

Ibn Saʿd: *Al-Ṭabaqāt al-Kubrā*. Beirut: Dar al-Fikr, 1405 AH.

Ibn Shahrāshūb: *Al-Manāqib*. Najaf, n.d.

Ibn Taymiah, Taqi al-Din: *Minhāj al-Sunnah* (9 volumes). Jeddah: Muhammad bin Saʿud University, 1406 AH.

Ījī, ʿAḍud al-Din: *Al Mawāqif fi ʿIlm al-Kalām*. Beirut: ʿĀlam al-Kutub. n.d.

Kadhim, Abbas: *Politics and Theology of Imami Shiʿa in Baghdad in the 5th/11th century*. Ann Arbor: University of Michigan Press, 2007.

Kanji Shafiʿi: *Al-Bayān fi Akhbār Ṣāḥib al-Zamān*. Najaf: Al-Nuʿmān Press, 1380 AH.

Kashif al-Ghiṭā', Muḥammad Ḥusayn: *Aṣl al-Shiʿa wa Uṣūluhā*. Qum: Imām ʿAli Foundation, 1415 AH.

Khazzāz (Al-), ʿAli ibn Muḥammad: *Kifāyat al-Athar fi al-Naṣṣ ʿala al-A'immah al-Ithnay ʿAshar*. Qum: Khayyam Press, 1402 AH.

Khoei, Abul Qasim: *Al-Bayān fi Tafsīr al-Qur'ān*, tr. A. A. Sachedina as *The Prolegomena to the Qur'ān*. Oxford: Oxford University Press, 1998.

Kulaynī (Al-), Muḥammad ibn Yaʿqūb: *Uṣūl al-Kāfi*. Tehran: WOFIS, 1982.

Lalani, Arzina R.: *Early Shiʿi Thought*. London and New York: I B Tauris, 2000.

Macdonald, Duncan B.: *Development of Muslim Theology, Jurisprudence and Constitutional Theory*. New York: Scribner's, 1993.

Mahdi, M.: *Al Farabi's Philosophy of Plato and Aristotle* (tr. with an Introduction of Al-Farabi's *Tahsil al-Sa'ada*). Ithaca: Cornell University Press, 1969.

Majlisi, Muḥammad Baqir: *Biḥār al-Anwār* (110 volumes). Beirut: Mu'assasat al-Wafā', 1403 AH. [Please note the different numbering of the volumes in the two different editions, after volume 50.]

Maqdisi Shafi'i, Yusuf: *'Iqd al-Durar fi Akhbār al-Mahdi al-Muntaẓar.* Jordan: Maktabat al-Manār, 1410 AH.

McGilchrist, Iain: *The Master and his Emissary:The Divided Brain and the Making of the Western World.* New Haven: Yale University Press, 2012.

Mohagheg, M. and Izutsu, Toshihico: *The Metaphysics of Sabzawari.* Tehran: Iran University Press, 1993.

Morewedge, Parviz: *The Metaphysics of Ṭusi.* New York: Society for the Study of Islamic Philosophy and Science, 1992.

Mu'adhdhin, Muḥammad 'Ali: *Tuhfa yi-'Abbasi*, tr. Dr Faghfoory. Lanham, MD: University Press of America, 2008.

Mufīd (Al-), Muḥammad ibn Nu'mān: *Al-Irshād.* Qum: Mu'assasat Āl-Bayt, 1416 AH.

Mulla Ṣadrā: *Wisdom of the Throne*, tr. J. W. Morris. Princeton: Princeton University Press, 1981.

——*Al-Asfār al-Arba'ah.* Tehran, 1865.

Murtaḍā (Al-), 'Ali ibn al-Ḥusayn: *Al-Shāfī fi al-Imāmah.* Beirut: Mu'assast Ahlul Bayt, 1407 AH.

Muṭahhari, M.: *The Theory of Knowledge: An Islamic Perspective*, tr. Mansoor Limba. Qum: Ahlul Bayt University, 2011.

Muttaqi Hindi: *Al-Burhān fi 'Alāmāt Mahdi Ākhir al-Zamān.* Cairo: n.d.

Nasr, S. H., Three Muslim Sages: Avicenna, Suhrawardi and Ibn Arabi. Cambridge: Harvard University Press, 1964.

Nasr, S. H. and Leaman. O. (eds): *The Routledge History of Islamic Philosophy.* London: Routledge, 1996.

Netton, I. R.: *Allah Transcendent: Studies in the Structure and Semiotics of Islamic Philosophy, Theology and Cosmology.* London: Routledge, 1989.

Nishābūri (Al-Ḥākim): *Al-Mustadrak 'alal Ṣaḥiḥain.* Hyderabad, 1324 AH.

Sabzawāri, Mulla Hadi: *Asrār al-Ḥikam.* Tehran: Dar al-Kutub al-Islamiyah, n.d.

Ṣadūq (Al-), Muḥammad ibn Bābawayh: *A Shi'ite Creed*, tr. Asaf A. A. Fyzee. Tehran: WOFIS, 1982.

——*The Book of Monotheism* (*Tawḥid*). Qum, 1375 AH.

——*Kamāl al-Din wa Tamām al-Ni'mah*. Qum, 1405 AH.

Ṣāfi (Al-), Luṭfullah: *Muntakhab al-Athar fi Al-Imām al-Thāni 'Ashar*. Qum, 1378 AH.

Schmidtke, Sabine: *The Theology of Allamah Ḥilli*. Berlin: Klaus Schway Verlag, 1991.

Sharaf al-Din, Abdul Ḥusayn: *The Right Path*, tr. Muḥammad Amir Haider Khan. Qum, n.d.

Shubbar, Abdullah: *Maṣābīḥ al-Anwār fi Ḥall Mushkilāt al-Akhbār*. Beirut: Mu'assast al-A'lami, 1987.

Subḥāni, Ja'far: *Al-Ilāhiyat*, lectures by Ayatollah Subḥāni compiled by Ḥasan Makki 'Āmili. Qum: Mu'assasat al-Imām al-Ṣadiq, 1417 AH.

Ṣubḥi, Aḥmad Maḥmūd: *Fi 'Ilm al-Kalām*. Beirut: Dar al-Nahḍah al-Arabiyah, 1985.

Suyūṭi, Jalāl al-Din: *Al-'Urf al-Wardī fi Akhbār al-Mahdi*. Cairo: Al-Sa'ādah Press, 1378 AH.

——*Iḥyā' al-mayt*. Beirut: Mu'assast al-Wafā', 1982.

——*Al-Durr al-Manthūr*. Cairo: Maymaniyah Press, 1314 AH.

Ṭabarāni (Al-): *Al-Mu'jam al-Kabir* (25 volumes). Beirut: Dar Ihyā' al-Turath al-Arabi, 1405 AH.

Ṭabāṭabā'ī, S. M. H.: *The Elements of Islamic Metaphysics*, tr. S. A. Qara'i. London: ICAS Press, 2003.

——*Uṣūle Falsafah wa Raweshe Realism*. Tehran: Sadrā, 1985.

—— *Al-Mizān fi Tafsīr al-Qur'ān* (20 volumes). Beirut: Mu'assast al-A'lami, 1393 AH.

Taftāzāni, Mas'ūd: *Sharḥ al-Maqāsid*. Beirut: 'Ālam al-Kutub, 1409 AH.

Thompson, M.: *Philosophy of Religion*. London: Teach Yourself, 1997.

Walker, P.: *Early Philosophical Shi'ism*. Cambridge: Cambridge University Press, 1993.

Watt, W.: *Free Will and Predestination in Early Islam*. London: Luzac, 1948.

—— *Islāmic Philosophy and Theology*. Edinburgh: Edinburgh University Press, 1962.

Yazdi, Mohammad Taqi: *Philosophical Instructions*, tr. Mohammad Legenhausen. Tehran, 1999.

—— *Theological Instructions.* London: Islamic Centre of England, 2009.

Zarandi Ḥanafi: *Naẓm Durar al-Simtain*. Najaf: Al-Qaḍā' Press, 1377 AH.

Index

Islamic Family Law

Ayatollah Sayyid Fadhel Hosseini Milani

Islāmic Law (also known as *Sharī'ah*) contains four categories: Acts of Devotion, Commercial Law, Family Law and Criminal Law. For Muslims in non-Muslim countries, Acts of Devotion are secured for all regardless of race or the religion of the country. In relation to Commercial Law, Muslims are free to formulate terms and conditions so that the contracts they enter into comply with Islām. As for Family Law, there is little contradiction/controversy between Islāmic Law and the Law of the Land. The only category where there are marked differences is the penal code; this has prompted much heated debate in European countries, particularly in the United Kingdom.

This book focuses solely upon Family Law. The other categories of Islāmic Law are to be the subject of forthcoming works.

Published by Isl≈m in English Press 2012
ISBN 978–0–9541585–5–2

The Source of Islamic Spirituality

Commentary on Surah 17 The Night Journey – Surah Israa'

Ayatollah Sayyid Fadhel Hosseini Milani

As the Holy Qur'ān is 'The Book of Guidance' for all of humanity here lay readers are presented with the analysis, critical interpretation and explanation of an 'exegete' whose contribution renders Islām's profound philosophy and significant teaching accessible.

This work, specially presented for an English readership, sets out to establish an awareness and understanding that the message of Islām is about 'Purification of the Soul' — not earthly reward, obsession with politics, or attacks on His innocent creatures.

His 'Most Beautiful Names' are fully explained, as is 'The Night Journey', while an extensive glossary summarises the most important aspects of the text.

Published by Islām in English Press 2004

ISBN 0–9541585–1–2

THE CORE OF ISLAM

Ayatollah Sayyid Fadhel Hosseini Milani

This introduction is addressed to those who seek information about the faith of Islām and its different aspects.

For an unbiased and clear picture of any faith one needs to refer to its original sources to discover its essential core. Every effort has been taken to ensure that a rounded and accurate picture is provided of the personality of the Messenger ﷺ, and the structure of the message, both in regard to faith and practice and the interactions between Muslims and those of other faiths or none.

Since daily prayers constitute 'the pillar of the faith' in Muslim life, a full chapter is devoted to the spiritual and social benefits of acts of devotion and observance, to assist both young Muslims and those new to Islām.

Published by Islām in English Press 2011

ISBN 978–0–9541585–3–8

ISLAM IN ENGLISH PRESS
for accessible guidance to Islamic knowledge